Nick Krauser

GIRL JUNKIE

"The skirt won't chase itself"

NICK KRAUSER
VOLUME V
MEMOIR

GIRL JUNKIE
THE SKIRT WON'T CHASE ITSELF

NICK KRAUSER

Girl Junkie, Volume 5 of the Nick Krauser memoir, First Edition.

© Copyright: Nick Krauser 2019.

The right of Nick Krauser to be identied as author of this Work has been asserted by him in accordance with sections 77 and 78 of the Copyright, Designs and Patents Act 1988.

All rights reserved. No part of this publication may be reproduced, stored in retrieval system, copied in any form or by any means, electronic, mechanical, photocopying, recording or otherwise transmitted without written permission from the author. You must not circulate this book in any format.

www.krauserpua.com

CONTENTS

Acknowledgements 4
Introduction 6
1 — Pay To Win 10
2 — Scandalo 22
3 — Marbella Fellas 38
4 — Cosy Nostra 52
5 — Bolshevik Broadcasting Corporation 66
6 — Beginner Daygame 84
7 — Cool Running 97
8 — Putting It In Crazy 106
9 — Bones 120
10 — Balkanised 128
11 — Nemesis 142
12 — Blackest Book 152
13 — Final Solution 162
14 — Rollercoaster Ride 176
15 — Warsaw Uprising 200
16 — Warsaw Downshifting 212
17 — Ashen One 232
18 — Normality 248
19 — Wanton and Getting 256
20 — Attraction on Riga Streets . . .272
21 — Teenybopper 280
22 — Radical Honesty 292
23 — Scatterbrained 302
24 — The Russof Muse 312
25 — Freedom Porn 320
26 — Miserable Belgrade 328
27 — Promising Belgrade 340
28 — Fantastic Belgrade 358
29 — Rumination 368
30 — The Krakow Question 380
31 — Warsaw Warrior 394
32 — Masquerade 408
33 — Eastern Front 418
34 — Hog Wild 430
35 — Shout It Out 440
36 — Mopping Up 456
37 — Chisinau 474
38 — Vampish 486
39 — Closing The Show 500
40 — Outlaws 518

ACKNOWLEDGEMENTS

Though my memoir project has clearly spiralled out of control, the team of men helping me prepare it for publication has remained remarkably stable. Once more Davorin returns with his excellent cover and interior art design, as does Cristian with his charming caricature sketches of the girls I rattled (to keep readers on their toes, I include art of a few girls I ultimately struck out with, so as not to be too predictable). Alexey provides another clean page layout.

This is the first of my memoir volumes where I did not use a hired writer at any stage of the process, either in constructing the first draft or in editing it. It is also the first volume to be written significantly after the events to which it relates yet with few contemporaneous blog posts to refer back to. Recalling the events and reconstructing their chronological order was not, after all, particularly difficult. It would seem men have an exceptional memory for the highlights of their shagging careers and of their petty squabbles with friends — two principle themes of this volume. Additionally, I was able to use my saved booking histories with the websites Airbnb and Booking.com, and my Instagram account, to precisely nail down exactly where I was on which dates throughout 2015. The photos in particular were excellent *aides memoir*. "Ah, I shagged such-and-such in that room!" I'd cry.

So, *Girl Junkie* can safely be taken as a factually-correct record of events. Obviously, I have dramatised certain conversations to make the book an interesting read, but whereas occasionally some events are not entirely factually correct they are at least true in spirit. Rest assured that *all* events described here involving me with women are absolutely correct in *both* fact and spirit. Naturally, concerning my squabbles with friends, I can only relate my direct experience of them and I try to make clear those elements that are merely hearsay. Each party has his own side to the story which I'd encourage you to research before reaching a conclusion. Eddie from *Street Attraction* helped out as a test reader and fact-checker for *Girl Junkie*, so at least we agree on the bits involving his team.

INTRODUCTION

"It is by going down into the abyss that we recover the treasures of life. Where you stumble, lies the treasure."

So says Joseph Campbell, writer of *The Hero with a Thousand Faces* (1949), and populariser of the concept of The Hero's Journey. According to Campbell, most mythic narratives are variations of a single great story, what he calls the *monomyth*. A hero leaves his mundane day-to-day existence to answer the call of adventure. He crosses a threshold — both literally and figuratively — to embark upon a journey of self discovery, personal change, and spiritual fulfilment.

And in my case, lots of shagging.

I answered the call of adventure in 2009 by diving balls deep into the underground world of pick-up artistry. It had been a long and rocky ride but by the time we reach the events of this volume, *Girl Junkie*, I'd been travelling the world chasing skirt for six years and having a bloody good time of it. My struggles had paid off and I was living the life most can only dream of. As Campbell himself puts it, "We must be willing to get rid of the life we've planned, so as to have the life that is waiting for us. The privilege of a lifetime is being who you are."

Only...... it didn't quite feel this way.

I had ventured down into the abyss seeking treasure only to find that perhaps the madcap syphilitic philosopher Friedrich Nietzsche understood the secret world better than Campbell did. Whoever shags hot birds should see to it that in the process he does not become a monster. "And if you gaze long enough into an abyss," wrote Nietzsche, "the abyss will gaze back into you."

Addiction had taken hold of me.

A journey powered first by desperation ("can I ever find a pretty girlfriend?") was now careening off course like a junkie jacked up on PCP. I was having tremendous success and thoroughly enjoyed the travel, freedom, public notoriety, and of course large amounts of casual sex with very pretty young women. Without any direction left to my journey, I was merely chasing thrills. It was addictive behaviour.

So it is within this context we reach the fifth volume of my memoir. I'd recovered from my divorce, learned how to seduce women, quit my office job, quit my country, and grown an entirely new social circle of friends. What does a man do when he has the means, motive, and opportunity to swim up to the fabled shores of Pussy Paradise?

Hopefully the book you now hold in your hands will provide some sort of an answer. Though themes of addiction, anomie, and assholery rub shoulders with heady tales of wine, women, and song don't for a moment think I've written *Girl Junkie* as a cautionary tale.

It's not. I'm but a simple seducer, a humble corrupter of youth.

I enjoyed my time in the abyss and treasure the memories of my adventures down there. Every. Single. Notch.

I remain forever grateful to long-time readers who have followed my adventures since the beginning of this memoir series. It is better to write for yourself and not find an audience, than to write for the audience and lose yourself. I'm lucky to write for myself, about myself, and fill my books with pictures of myself. Thanks for enduring it.

It is probably worth noting that I have quite deliberately eschewed the opportunity to tone down my writing style here, particularly in regards to my attitudes towards women and foreigners. There are two reasons for this. First, I am an equal-opportunities racist, sexist, homophobe. I'm equally dismissive and insulting towards anyone who is not a straight white male from Newcastle. Slants, wops, niggers, scousers, fags and slags will all be equally offended in due course. Second, a key literary goal in writing *Girl Junkie* was to capture what I was like in 2015: my passions, my foibles, my political convictions, and the various online controversies I so cheerfully provoked. It is impossible to understand the addictive influence of successful skirt-chasing on my mind without knowing its causes and sometimes deleterious effects.

So, brace yourselves!

I hope you enjoy the story that unfolds in the next few hundred pages. If you don't, send your death threats to the usual place.

Nick Kramer

Warsaw, June 2019.

Chapter 1
PAY TO WIN

I'd hoped to close out 2014 in Newcastle with a peaceful daily routine of reading, editing my new in-field product *Daygame Overkill*, and playing video games. I'd endured a long, tough year criss-crossing Europe with my friends as we all chased skirt. A year that began in London had taken me to Belarus, Serbia, Czech Republic, and Croatia. A steady accumulation of jet travel, alcohol, endlessly walking the streets, and of course my usual unfairly-large share of sex had finally burned me out.

It was an amazing year and I was done with it. I'd earned my Player Card. No-one doubted my bona fides as a talented womanizer. That comforted me. It was precisely the reputation I wanted and had struggled for six years to achieve, the end of a journey begun in 2009 as a bored, lonely, socially-awkward office worker.

Done.

Now I'd dug in for winter at my parent's house in cold, wet, Newcastle in order to edit the series of in-field videos filmed in Zagreb, Croatia, of me picking up hot university girls. Only a few weeks earlier I'd hosted a seminar in London in which I gave a play-by-play analysis of my pick-up technique and a presentation on the theory underlying it. Hours of video footage sat on the hard-drive of my brand-new laptop. I set myself a projected release date of Christmas Eve by which time it needed to be edited together and uploaded onto a video-streaming teaching platform. I was now halfway through the work, the project was on schedule, and I felt very good about myself.

I projected an easy, predictable glide into the New Year. Each morning I'd relax over coffee, sitting in my favourite easy chair by the radiator in my parent's house. In the afternoon I'd chip away with editing work at the dining room table. Then in the evening I'd stretch out on top of my duvet and take a well-earned reward of video gaming in my bedroom.

So peaceful. So tranquil.

Until, that is, I happened to browse a website called *SlutHate*.

That's a catchy domain name, is it not? I don't hate sluts any more than the next man. In fact probably less, seeing as I've banged my fair share of them. So long as you aren't naïve enough to invest emotions into your dealings with them, sluts are a lot of fun. They can be amongst the most honest and direct girls you ever meet; so long as you're the casual sex guy and not a potential husband. The website — or rather, the forum — *SlutHate* has, ironically, very little to do with hating on sluts. It was actually the new name for an old forum called *PUAhate*. I am a PUA and they hated me, which is how I first stumbled upon the website in 2011. Let's get a little background on that.

PUA means Pick Up Artist and it's shorthand for a man who has chosen the *lifestyle* of seducing many girls, and employs the *skill-set* of Game with which to achieve it. It's useful to keep those two concepts separate as they don't always correlate. There are wannabe-players whose lifestyle aim is to get laid but who are, nevertheless, hapless clowns utterly unable to succeed at it. For the first six months of my 'player's journey' I was one such clown, as is documented in *Balls Deep*. Additionally, there are players who get laid using means unrelated to game. Think of the strapping athletic captain of the football team, or the semi-popular indie guitarist, or the wine'n'dine sugar daddy. Each man has his own system to secure sexual access to women. Though their methods differ, they are 'players' because they seek sexual novelty and refuse to commit to monogamous relationships.

Players. Like me.

Rather less common, there are men who are experts in the skill-set of attracting and seducing women but nevertheless choose not to take advantage. Perhaps this man was once a player and has decided to settle down with a single woman. Could you claim he no longer has Game simply because he chooses not to play the field any longer? Some men are extremely charismatic but don't enjoy casual sex, or find promiscuity contravenes their personal moral code. Usually you find them in long term relationships with exceptionally attractive women. Good luck to them. You won't hear me criticise them.

It keeps them out of the competition. I'd rather not have to compete against such men.

Pick Up Artists are a special breed. We strive to develop our skills with women and then self-consciously, and with full malice-of-forethought, attempt to seduce a bundle of them. Some men fail while others succeed. Whichever it is, if you acquire even the slightest public notoriety in the matter you'll come to the attention of *PUAhate* (now *SlutHate*).

In 2011 they came after me.

Perhaps you assumed *PUAhate*'s membership was composed of feminist-leaning defenders of women's rights. If so, their rebranding as *SlutHate* ought to shatter that illusion. They weren't motivated by any moral code, nor a yearning for traditional gender roles. Rather, *SlutHate* was almost entirely composed of the men who'd tried Game, failed miserably, and now projected their self-loathing externally. They weren't angry so much as they were envious and ashamed. Their egos couldn't handle the fact that Game works but they, as individuals, couldn't hack it. The clinically obese sometimes blame their nutritionists rather than their own lack of willpower in following a diet. *SlutHate* blames PUAs for their sexual failures.

SlutHate really enjoyed doxxing; that is, to discover the real personal information of a dating coach and then publish it on the internet in the hope of ruining his life. In an era in which Social Justice Warriors regularly mobbed individual men and got them fired or socially excluded, doxxing was a legitimate threat. In practice, nobody cared what *SlutHate* said. It was just a cesspool of whiny losers bitching on the internet. Nonetheless, after they first tried (and failed) to dox me, I'd began reading the forum. One thing had surprised me.

SlutHate was often hilarious.

I don't mean hilarious in the way Jackie Chan fight scenes are skilfully choreographed and performed in order to be intentionally hilarious. Nor how a Bill Burr stand-up comedy show is hilarious. Rather, I mean the way smartphone videos of fat people falling down stairs is hilarious. Or how watching two soyboys try to fist-fight is hilarious. I'd gotten hooked and checked the *SlutHate* board every week to see what new nonsense was going on.

Usually, I knew of the PUAs they discussed. It's a small world. The powerhouse dating company *Real Social Dynamics* (RSD) drew most of their ire, which was hardly surprising. Not only did RSD have the largest public profile and the most in-your-face direct marketing but they also fashioned themselves like a cult. Many students were fleeced of eye-watering tuition fees and then cast aside when the RSD circus moved on to the next town. Such callous profiteering can build resentment. Additionally, RSD coaches tend to have exceedingly punchable faces. The company is owned by two men. Papa is a soft-eyed Asian chump with no ability with women at all. RSD wisely kept him out of the public eye. Their public face is a man called Tyler Durden, named after the main character in *Fight Club*, a thinly-disguised allegorical novel about the underground gay sodomy scene. I didn't hold his choice of *nom de plume* against him, as the Hollywood adaptation of *Fight Club* was my favourite movie for years: until I found out it had nothing to do with fighting and was actually an ode to bum-banditry. Tyler's real name is Owen Cook. Before you accusing *me* of doxxing, bear in mind he has openly announced his real name in his own products.

Tyler is a very smart deconstructivist, and thus contributed many valuable insights to Game theory. His flagship product *The Blueprint Decoded* is fantastic and I recommend it wholeheartedly even now. Sadly, Tyler is also a shameless bullshitter and wannabe lifestyle guru. He has an exceptionally punchable face. To balance my contradictory emotions towards Tyler, I reached a personal compromise: If he and I ever meet face-to-face, I will gladly buy him drinks all night in gratitude for his many theoretical contributions to the Game, but I'll have to sit on my hands the whole time so I don't succumb to the momentary fetish of punching him in the face.

I've somewhat digressed, haven't I? Okay, let's return to the relevance of *SlutHate* in the early days of December, 2014.

Nothing would better raise the status of a *SlutHate* loser in the eyes of his peers than to expose a famous dating coach as a charlatan. A few noble truthhounds had already succeeded. The PUA industry is rife with fakers, frauds, and scammers but they are often a slippery bunch. Pinning them down with documentary proof of deception is difficult. Seduction is, by nature, a mostly private activity. How do you catch a dating coach in the act of lying? It's like trying to prove a negative. Few coaches are dumb enough to be caught holding a figurative smoking gun. Thus only one of my eyebrows was raised when I skimmed the main *SlutHate* board and saw my friend Tom Torero's name. There was a thread called something like 'Tom Torero Hires Actress. Fakes Kiss Close'.

Interesting.

I'd known Tom since 2011 and, despite a few fallings-out, we'd spent a lot of time together. We were co-creators of the *London Daygame Model* and many bright-eyed new players considered us to be a team, like Laurel and Hardy, or the Mamas and the Papas. Quite reasonably so. We'd travelled together for much of 2013 and 2014, recorded videos together, and sometimes coached together. Doubtless some of my readers assumed we bummed each other too.

"There's a new *SlutHate* thread on you," I messaged Tom, chuckling. "They are claiming you hire actresses."

It sounded comical to me because I'd been in-field with Tom dozens upon dozens of hours. I'd witnessed him approach girls, take their numbers, meet them on dates, and sometimes bang them in the bedroom next door to mine. I'd seen it with my own eyes. I'd heard the rattling of bedposts against the wall with my own ears. The idea of Tom hiring actresses to secure what a sufficient number of willing young women already volunteered for free was ridiculous. Most PUAs are a little untrustworthy but Tom and I had built our reputations upon a foundation of unfakeable in-field reality. We videoed ourselves on the street and on dates. While coaching, we'd happily demonstrate our skills in front of the students, often on girls the students had picked out from the crowd for us. We had regular wings who could verify most of our victory stories. Indeed, we were often seen on the streets daygaming on our own account. I'd often talk to a girl and then, as I walked away, a stranger would approach me and say, "Are you Nick Krauser? I like your blog, man."

It was the London way. We were all like this.

So, Tom and I had no fear of 'exposure' because weren't fake. To us, *SlutHate* were little ankle-biting Yorkshire terriers trying to scare the postman. *Tom will get a kick out of this thread,* I thought. It was flattering really, having an army of autistic nerds desperate to take you down.

Or so I thought.

I clicked the thread and browsed the posted comments. As I did so the amused smile dropped from my face, replaced by a thin-lipped frown of consternation. *Oh fuck, Tom's gone and done me,* I thought. The original *SlutHate* poster claimed Tom had hired a French girl in 2012 to act a part in a fake street-approach video that ended with Tom kissing her. Street 'kiss close' videos were a big deal back then, as they seemed the most compelling evidence proving the magic of daygame. Sadly, most such famous videos turned out to be fakes. Some provably so, others simply too suspicious for any experienced daygamer to take at face value. I only had one recorded kiss close, filmed by my friend Mick in Camden Market, London. Sadly, the fat Aussie had actually turned his smartphone camera away from me at the crucial moment of kissing, thus totally ruining the video's demonstrative value. My other street kiss-closes weren't recorded, as most of the time we chased skirt without cameras rolling.

Reading down the thread it became clear the original *SlutHate* poster had caught Tom holding a smoking gun. Allow me to summarise the evidence of the ensuing online investigations.

Back in 2012, Tom worked for Andy Yosha as the head coach and public face of Daygame.com, a London-based dating company that was then world-leader in its niche. I'd fallen out with Tom in late-2011 when he tried to have sex with two of my girlfriends behind my back (they rejected him and told me about it). Andy offered me a coaching role at his company but I explained I wouldn't work the same events as Tom, due to personal animosity. Andy quite naturally, and justifiably, stuck with Tom and rescinded his offer to me. I didn't see much of Tom in 2012, though I followed his material on Daygame.com's YouTube channel as he often had good insights that helped me develop my own craft.

In the summer of 2012 Tom had determined that he needed a kiss-close video of his own but was unable to film one legitimately (it's rather difficult) so he messaged a French girl he'd number-closed a few months earlier and flat-out offered her £75 to appear in a fake video. He then contrived to 'approach' her outside Selfridge's department store on Oxford Street, bantered, and then after five minutes he awkwardly lunged in and kissed her. I remember watching the video in 2012, when he proudly posted it onto YouTube. It had looked awkward as hell, but it never crossed my mind it was fake. I just assumed she'd liked him a little bit and took the path of least resistance until she'd been excused from his company.

The plot thickened in 2014, when Tom and Andy's business relationship became increasingly strained, something I witnessed in real time Tom and I had made up and begun hanging out again. I only heard Tom's side of the story, when he left Daygame.com and set up independently. He leaned quite heavily on me at first, doing cross promotions with my popular blog. Tom was a friend so I was happy to help him get the word out about his new website and YouTube channel. I don't wish to exaggerate my importance, mind, because Tom was already a big name from having been the face of Daygame.com. He'd have done well without my help too.

The aforementioned French girl had, by 2014, begun a career as a minor actress and thus posted her resume onto an internet casting database. It listed two entries for the role of 'girl picked up' working for a producer called Tom (under his real name). Google indexed her resume and a *SlutHate* sleuth came across it, inspiring the thread I was now reading. The screencaps and hyperlinks contained damning evidence. Her resume photo showed clearly she was the same girl from Tom's video. She'd even dated the resume entry at 2012.

"Just typical *SlutHate* bullshit," Tom replied to my text message. "I'm getting back from Hong Kong, I'll have a look at it later."

The plot thickened further.

Andy had an axe to grind against Tom, and he was indignant that the fake video had been hosted on his own Daygame.com channel, thus dragging his name through the mud too. I'd never been friends with Andy but he'd struck me as a fundamentally honest man. I highly doubted he'd have approved Tom's chicanery at the time. Andy reached out to the French girl and swapped text messages where, in answer to Andy's specific questions, she explicitly confirmed Tom had hired her to fake the video. Andy then persuaded her to appear on Skype with permission to video and share the conversation. In glorious video, she told the story that dug Tom's grave ever deeper. Andy posted the video online and *SlutHate* linked to it.

This entire drama unrolled over one afternoon, on the 10th of December. I'd woken up that morning ready to meander through a paperback detective story and a few coffees. Instead, I'd been drawn into a squalid tale. My name was inextricably linked to Tom's.

Laurel and Hardy. Milli and Vanilli.

So far I'd sunk six weeks of full-time work into filming and editing my own flagship in-field product. It was almost ready to launch, my big release. The new fucking-hell-look-how-cool-this-is showcase I'd grown excited about. My reputation was beyond reproach, fortified by six years of hard work and hyper-documentation of my journey. Yet now Tom had been busted faking an in-field. I couldn't help but wonder what whispers would begin concerning my legitimacy.

Have you heard Nick and Tom got caught faking a video?

Yeah, a French actress admitted to it on Skype. They are frauds.

I asked Tom for an explanation and he didn't reply to my messages. He went dark for twenty-four hours, probably suffering a nervous breakdown. He owed me both an apology and an explanation. He couldn't but know the bind he'd placed me in.

Nothing.

What a coward! I raged. *He cheats and manipulates behind the scenes and then when he's caught out, he runs and hides. Leaves his friends behind.*

My phone buzzed off the hook with my fellow daygame buddies asking what on earth was going on. The comments section of my blog filled up, both regulars and first-timers asking my opinion. Confusion reigned. Had they been wrong about me? Was I crooked too? Fortunately, the overwhelming majority of my readers knew well enough to trust me. Years of honest conduct and dozens of vouchsafes from my peers meant my reputation within the serious daygame community wasn't at all affected. Several friends suggested I'd be better off rid of Tom, that he was a bad apple constantly getting me into trouble. I was mostly concerned about the beginners — the lads who hadn't been around long enough to know I wasn't one of the frauds. They didn't know up from down so could easily tar me with the faker brush Tom had handed them.

Furious though I felt, I was in a quandary. A dilemma. There were only two options I could see, and each one broke a rule of my moral code.

Option one was to join the pile-on and throw Tom under a bus. He deserved it. He'd maliciously and premeditatedly sought to cheat the daygame community by faking a video. Trust is absolutely paramount in the seduction community precisely because it's so difficult to establish a man's bona fides. Tom had recklessly and selfishly abused that trust in order to grandstand. He'd betrayed me personally. Again. I was sorely tempted, as denouncing him was the honest thing to do. I should stand up for integrity and for the self-policing of the PUA community.

The problem was this first option broke a very important rule of mine: don't abandon your friends in their hour of need.

What kind of man runs from the mob, leaving their friends behind? The whole point of being a friend is that you have each other's back. Without that you aren't worthy of the name 'friend'. Tom had done something wrong in 2012 and now a thoroughly despicable group of internet haters were mobbing him, trying to ruin his life. He was very likely plunged deep into depression at that moment (Tom has posted publicly about being clinically diagnosed as depressive). Disgusted though I was by his behaviour, I did not intend going through life as a man who can't be depended upon by his friends.

Finally, Tom replied to me. It was a short text admitting his fault and apologising to me personally. He also posted a short *mea culpa* on his blog.

That sounded like repentance, so I defended him.

I wrote a post — still on my blog — called *Tom Torero Fakes An Infield Kiss Close* in which I gave my opinion on the controversy. The gist of which was that I aware of the fraud until *SlutHate* exposed it, that Tom's was a dishonest and reprehensible act, but that I could personally vouch for Tom's daygame skills and thus though readers would be entirely justified in dumping Tom as a now-discredited dating coach they'd risk missing out on a treasure trove of his accumulated daygame knowledge.

I felt dirty. There was no good option. Either lean towards integrity, or lean towards loyalty. I chose the latter and resented Tom for forcing me into it. It was a horrible way to end a great year. For the next few months I'd have ankle-biters popping up on my blog accusing me of fraud and I felt constrained in any discussion of the topic.

Beavering away on my Magnum Opus

And drinking with John and my brother

Chapter 2
SCANDALO

My 2015 began with me standing patiently at the Arrivals terminal in Malaga airport in the beautifully sunny climes of southern Spain. A line of furtive-eyed taxi drivers stood with their backs against the windows, their faces stony as they scanned each arriving traveller as a potential fare. One such man, a stringy Arab with face leathered like my own dark-brown rucksack, shuffled up alongside me and whispered out the corner of his mouth.

"Hashish?"

I did a double-take. Surely I hadn't already been offered illegal drugs just ten minutes after touching down in the *Costa Del Crime*, as we English describe Marbella due to its storied history as a non-extraditable bolt hole popular with East London gangsters on the lam. The street Arab's eyes darted left and right, though whether due to a guilty conscience or a hereditary deformity from first-cousin in-breeding I didn't dare ask.

"Taxi?" he repeated.

Ah, it was just his accent. I was not in fact being offered an early opportunity to break Spanish law. I shooed him away and looked around. Ten metres above my head, the air conditioning succeeded marvellously in pushing a cool refreshing air down into the wide hall. Every few seconds the automatic sliding doors to the roadside whooshed open and a warm breeze whooshed in as an excitable tourist whooshed out. It was my turn to scan the room, looking for my driver.

I was looking for a heavy-set burly skin-head with a Soft Scottish accent. His name was Jonathan and he'd invited me to stay in his holiday home by the beach, along with my old friend Steve Jabba who'd already been there a month. I saw no such Scotsmen, so I wheeled my little suitcase across the lobby and sat down heavily on a wooden chair at an espresso bar. I whipped out my phone.

It rang and the call was picked up in two rings. I heard car engine noises, rushing wind, and a faint suggestion of AC/DC music through my phone's speaker. And then a clatter like something had been dropped, a scrabble, and finally a human voice.

"Fuck. Bastard. Hang on a sec." More scrabbling. "Right, you cunt. Got you. Nick!"

"Jonathan, buddy. I'm here."

"Literally in a minute…. Look outside."

I heard brakes, a car door shut, and a familiar whoosh. Jonathan strode into the lobby waving over at me as he weaved between a quartet of female flight attendants striding off to their next shift. He wore faded blue jeans, sneakers, and a sports shirt with a pair of expensive Ray Bans tucked into the open collar. He also had sun-kissed skin, in stark contrast to my own pasty white face from having spent early winter in Newcastle.

"Let me take that," he said, wresting the suitcase from my hands and turning towards the door. He was smiling. "I'm parked on double yellows. Let's go."

I followed him out into the blazing sunshine. The sky was clear blue, as if spray-painted specially for my arrival and without a cloud in sight. The cluster of airport buildings gave way to a long high mountain range.

"Fucking hell, this is nice," I opined.

"Lovely place, mate. Chuck your rucksack in the boot here, and we'll get on home."

Jonathan popped the trunk to his blue open-topped BMV, threw in the suitcase and then revved up the engine as I came round to the passenger side. Barely had I parked my arse down before he gunned the engine and shot out into traffic.

"You like AC/DC?" he asked, reaching for the stereo controls. "Ace driving music."

The long straight motorway flashed by as we ate up the miles. I gawped out of the windows in amazement at the serene summer beauty of nature. All around me were green trees, brown foothills, and azure sky. It felt like a time-warp, like old movies of Audrey Hepburn and Carey Grant driving through the French Riviera. It had been snowing when I'd boarded my flight in Newcastle. Presently, Jonathan turned off into a residential district that hugged the foothills. We snaked through small steep back roads lined on both sides by expensive gated houses. Every car was flash and the only pedestrians were slim middle-aged women either walking dogs or sweating out a jog in lycra.

"They'd never let me into a place like this if I wasn't with you." I said.

"That's more true than you think. It's a small world here. Very insular." We pulled to a halt halfway up the hill, behind a big Range Rover SUV. "That's my errands wagon. Come on, let's see if Steve's gotten out of bed."

Jonathan led me into a spacious two-storey villa in Spanish style, tossed his keys onto a large mahogany table, and walked into a big lounge. I was shocked at the opulence of it, having become accustomed to grotty little apartments on all my Eastern European holidays. A plush sofa that could seat a dozen guests stretched around three sides, facing a massive wall-mounted television at the open end of the horseshoe. There was a modest swimming pool in the back garden, and a balcony looking out over vineyards, scrubland, and a mountain range.

The view was sensational. I estimated it at two miles, with no obstructions to the line of sight. Armed with a good rifle, you could keep out a Muslim horde for weeks with such a field of fire.

"Your room is upstairs. Come on, I'll show you around."

I was to be quartered in a bedroom with an en suite bathroom and small balcony facing the street. It was as new and tidy as a holiday hotel room and better than I'd expected. We poked our heads into Steve's room, where he was sprawled in bed fast asleep. Jonathan's room was even better again, reminding me of a Turkish emir's seraglio.

"Wait till you see the basement," he said, eagerly.

We traipsed down the stairs and into a single low room that spanned the entire floor-plan. There was a smooth marble floor, more sofas, and a massive projector screen set up with home cinema speakers dotted around. There was a small home gym against one wall and a big workstation against the far wall with PC towers, multiple monitors, and piles of technical books.

"The nerve centre. Headquarters. The hub of my axis of evil."

Do you know those spy movies where shadowy hacker groups set up hi-tech rigs with which to penetrate the security of US weapons systems? The kind that get stormed by special forces in the final act, with silenced SMGs and grenades blasting. It looked like that. I wondered if it had a self-destruct mechanism.

"What on earth do you do in here?" I asked. I was dimly aware than Jonathan was a 'black hat', meaning he earned money outside of normal taxable channels.

"I can't tell you unless Steve agrees. It's tech stuff."

He clicked a few keys on a wireless keyboard, squinted at a screen, and then reached under the desk to flick a switch. Had he armed the bomb? I waited to hear a warning klaxon and an evacuation countdown. Jonathan turned around, beaming with pleasure. "There, that'll do it."

"Do what?"

Welcome indeed

Before there was time to wonder, there was an explosion of noise. Fortunately, it was the rock band AC/DC and not gelignite. *Highway To Hell* blasted out of every corner, the surround sound speakers very convincingly surrounding me, and the basement walls shook. A minute later Steve came tumbling down the stairs dressed only in boxer shorts and a gym vest. His hair was mussed up and there were bags under his eyes.

"Fucking hell, mate! Can't you let a man sleep off a hangover?" He noticed me. "Ah, Nick! Welcome to Marbella!"

The plan was to enjoy winter sun for three weeks. Steve and Jonathan were working hard every day on a new online business that I only dimly comprehended. Essentially it involved buying internet traffic — which I didn't even know the buying of was a thing — from a small cartel of approved vendors, cleaning and rationalising said traffic, and then reselling it at a profit to other businesses. If pressed to envision such a business model I'd have assumed it involved phone calls with sales agents, occasional sit-down meetings in cafes and restaurants, and haggling over contracts.

"No Nick, you're well behind the times," said Steve. "This is all tech now. Look, let me show you something. Jonathan, is it okay to show him The Army?"

We were sitting on big leather swivel chairs at the Nerve Centre. A half dozen screens were scrolling and updating by the second. The big Scotsman nodded approvingly, sitting comfortably with a large mug of steaming coffee and a small blunt of dope dangling from his other hand.

"I focus on the content editing and Jonathan here does all the programming. This business is all about margin. We have to calculate the best sources of traffic in real time based on feeding in click-through rates from that same traffic sold through the back-end. Then we fine-tune our bids on the front-end so we are pouring quality in, which is easier to sell through."

"Okay."

"Well, this is where The Army comes in. Jonathan has written dozens of AI bots and each one handles a separate account or suite of accounts. So, let's say were are bidding on slices of traffic from Source 1 here," he said, pointing to a rapidly-updating line of incomprehensible numbers which seemed to switch from red, to white, to green. "You can see it's got a sell-through at 0.02 which is very slightly above acceptable. Now, any time it gets to 0.03 we up this percentage here," and his finger stabbed at a different incomprehensible number, "so that our ratio is upped by three points."

I was just about following it and would finally wrap my head around the system within a couple of weeks. I'd write it here more clearly, but it's not my place to give away this dastardly duo's business secrets.

"But what's The Army?"

"The bots! The bots!" he grinned. "They are crawling all over the internet for us doing our bidding. Jonathan's a genius, you should see what some of them can do. We give them names. We just finished the Gymcel bot, so named because all it does is the same five calculations every day and doesn't interact with the other bots."

Girl Junkie

Such conversations went on most days, sprinkled amongst tokes on joints, kung fu movies on the big screen, and trips out to restaurants. Steve and I also trained together in the home gym. Just before the first gym session, I had a quiet word with Jonathan.

"Is Steve still insecure about his neck?" I asked. Steve is an extremely muscular man, missing only the leopard fur underpants to turn him into Tarzan. His chest, shoulders, arms, and legs all considerably out-sized mine yet curiously his neck was the same size. Perhaps it was due to an oddity of genetics, or perhaps because my years of fight training emphasised neck development — wrestling is essentially a game of "let's twist the other guy's neck so he moves where we want him to go" — but that fact had stuck in Steve's craw. I was determined to twist the knife.

"Yeah, I think so."

"Right. Let's bait Steve into demanding we measure each other, and you'll do the measuring. You can give him his wins on everything but the neck. Measure me first, because he'll be looking, and then when you measure him he can't see the tape. So, whatever my neck is, call his a quarter inch less."

"Lol. Definitely. It'll take him weeks to cotton on to the scam."

Ten minutes later Steve came downstairs in his gym gear, his biceps rippling. "Ready there, Nickie-boy? Ready for the Beast to smash all strength records?" I agreed I was and we began training. As Steve curled a heavy dumbbell, I commented favourably on his biceps development. He grunted, his energy rapidly draining from manhandling such a heavy weight. As he approached his final reps, at failure, I dropped the bait.

"It's funny. Your arms look big but I'm sure your neck got smaller."

Jonathan sniggered out of sight. Steve spluttered and almost dropped the dumbbell, one rep short of target. He affected unconcern. "Nah, man. I've been smashing it. I'm up to sixty head raises per side."

He was referring to a neck exercise popular in boxing and wrestling. The athlete lies on his back, crosses his arms, and then raises his chin to his chest and relaxes it down almost-but-not-quite touching the mat. It's very easy the first few repetitions but as the number of lifts rises, the weight of your head provides formidable resistance. Twenty lifts a side — front, left, right — for sixty raises in all is a decent neck workout. Steve had already built himself up to treble that toll in his quest to out-neck me. I was determined to push him into yet harder toil.

Jonathan chipped in. "I think Nick's right, Steve. At first I thought it was an optical illusion because your arms are a bit bigger. But no, now I think about it, your neck looks a bit thinner. Or maybe your head and ears have grown."

"An adult man's head doesn't grow, you plonker!" Steve remonstrated. "I'm telling you, my neck hasn't shrunk."

"It has," I piped in. "You're forty now. It's totally normal for old men to build down. Yours has just started to shrink a few years ahead of schedule. A year from now it'll be two inches less. You'll end up looking like the singer of REM."

Steve dropped the dumbbell on the cushioned mat and strode purposefully to the desk, rifling the drawers until he emerged triumphantly with a measuring tape. Jonathan and I caught eye contact and flashed each other a look of amusement.

"Right then, dickheads. We'll prove this objectively. My neck has not shrunk."

Feigning reluctance, I shrugged. "Okay, if you insist. Jonathan, you do the honours."

Steve handed over the tape and stood tapping his foot impatiently as Jonathan made a big production of unfurling the tape, correcting my posture ("so you don't cheat by bringing in your delts"), and wrapping it around my neck sufficiently tight to remove the slack without digging into my skin. His fingers held the tape where the ends met, and invited Steve to confirm.

"Fifteen and a half inches, no?" he asked.

"Yes, yes. Get on with it," said Steve and stood still with his chin up and shoulders squared. "Now do me."

Jonathan once again stalled, hummed, and ha'd before finally settling the tape on Steve's neck to his satisfaction. He waved me over. "Nick, what do you make it?" I screwed up my eyes, set my head at a number of different viewing angles, and finally shook my head as if in surprised disbelief.

"Are you sure you aren't pulling it tight? Steve, how does it feel? Are you getting light-headed from restricted blood flow to the brain?"

"Fine, mate. Get on with it."

"And this is the same tape measure?" I asked Jonathan, who nodded in reply. "Well, it is what it is. That's fifteen and a quarter inches." That made it a quarter inch less than mine, according to our fake reading.

"Yep, that's what I read but I didn't want to prejudice you," agreed the Scotsman. "It was fifteen and a half a few months ago. Steve, your neck is shrinking."

"I don't get it. It can't be. I'm doing more head raises than before. It's just not right. What should I do?"

"It might be genetic," I added, helpfully. "You might just have a little gay neck."

With great effort we remained straight-faced until the end of the gym session, then as soon as Steve went for a shower, we burst out laughing. We kept up the charade for a week, by which time Steve was doing one hundred head raises per side, before he finally rumbled our game.

Once I'd acclimatised to the reality of daily sunshine in January, I found Marbella greatly relaxing. My bed was comfortable and I'd be awoken gently each morning by birds singing and dogs barking. Best of all, I'd released my big video product — *Daygame Overkill* — just a week earlier so I'd come on holiday at the peak of its launch sales window. I remember vividly one particular morning: I woke up around ten am to see light shafts stream through the wooden window slats and onto my light duvet. Rubbing my eyes, I reached out to find my phone on the bedside cabinet to switch it on, then stumbled into the en suite bathroom to relieve myself and clean my teeth as it booted up. Returning to check my messages, I found two emails with the best possible mail headers:

Notification: Item No.5 (sale — PayPal)

That is an email from PayPal's auto-checkout notifying me of a *Daygame Overkill* sale. Each and every time I get that message, my PayPal account gets $191 fatter. Unlike books, with their unit printing and shipping costs, video products have a flat monthly hosting rate with the platform (Kajabi inc.) and everything above that is pure profit. I'd made $382 on *Daygame Overkill* while sleeping. It reminded me of a famous quote from the legendary investor Warren Buffet, "if you don't find a way to make money while you sleep, you will work until you die."

Feeling very upbeat and financially independent, I sat down on the toilet for my morning shit. The phone beeped again and I checked my gmail.

Notification: Item No.5 (sale — PayPal)

I was another $191 dollars richer, just five minutes after mentally logging the overnight sales. I then showered in a modern walk-in unit with floor-to-ceiling frosted glass and a high-power head fitted into the tiled ceiling. It was glorious. I kept thinking, "bloody hell, I'm making money while I shit. Can Warren Buffet do that?"

With that thought uppermost in my mind, I dressed and joined the lads downstairs. Steve was chomping at the bit to show me a local Mexican restaurant so Jonathan drove us out. It was all surreal to me, adapting so quickly to Mediterranean life. We were driving everywhere, either in Jonathan's big

SUV or in his flash sports car. I was used to walking hours on end, sometimes with a heavy rucksack over my shoulders. The restaurant was indeed excellent. We drank red wine, ate nachos and burritos, and the waitresses fawned over Steve. After we settled the tab Jonathan needed to go home. "Got to finish my work before the missus comes around," he explained.

"You got a bird here?" I asked.

"Yeah, ball and chain. She's alright though." He'd trade her in for a superior Eastern European at a later date.

"What about you?" I said, turning to Steve.

"*Seeking Arrangement*, mate. There's no normal birds in town during the off-season. So I've been tapping up lasses online. There's a Spanish slag the next town over who is keen to see me. Also, a bird has promised to fly in from London next week."

"How'd you manage that?"

Steve shrugged, guzzling the last of his red wine. "I just send 'em dick pics. Anyway, enough of this clowning. Let's have a walk down to the seaside. I need to go to the mall there."

The walk was along a series of back lanes and winding paths down a gentle incline. Within five minutes a path opened suddenly onto the beach-front promenade that stretched miles in each direction. I was struck by the cleanliness and opulence of Marbella. This was not a tatty walkway with chipped concrete and spray-painted graffiti, but rather an immaculately-swept path with frequent runs of intricately tiled floor patterns. Expensive yachts were moored in a harbour and cars costing more than my parent's house were parked nose to tail outside boutiques selling diamonds and designer clothes. Yet, for all this splendour, it was a ghost town. In ten minutes walking along the promenade toward the town centre, we saw three other people.

The centre was more lively — only just — and Steve took us into the mall to buy some socks. There was a small Starbucks concession near the womenswear department and while we ordered coffee I noticed a pair of women join the queue behind us. They weren't very hot and I placed them as Brazilian MILFs, but they were the only women I'd seen out of doors who might still own functioning ovaries. I opened one.

"You look Brazilian."

She liked that, explaining she was in fact from the south of that awful country, and then introduced her sister. We swapped numbers but neither I nor Steve wished to pursue it further. We then explored the central area.

Girl Junkie

I noticed the book shop had a special bookcase filled entirely with paperbacks of the English 'guvnor' genre. For non-English readers, allow me to explain. A mythos has built up around the archetypical East-End of London petty gangsters of the 1960s. Principle among these vermin are the criminal twins Ronald and Reggie Kray who ruled protection rackets in London for several years (as rivals to the Richardson brothers) before both getting sentenced to life imprisonment for very public and utterly pointless murders. Everyone associated with these gangs has either written a memoir or been written about, such as their enforcer Mad Frankie Fraser. Over time, interest in such gangsters mushroomed with television shows on low-rent cable channels with titles such as *Britain's Hardest Men* and *Underground London*, and even a sub-genre of films starring luminaries such as soon-to-be James Bond Daniel Craig (*Layer Cake*), Ray Winston, and former boy-band singer Luke Goss. A couple of the movies are even good — particularly Guy Ritchie's movies *Snatch* and *Lock, Stock And Two Smoking Barrels*. The literary craze seems to have begun with the autobiography of London enforcer and former bare-knuckle boxing champ Lenny McClean whose *The Guv'nor* (tag-line: "I am what I look: a right hard bastard") was briefly a UK bestseller.

The reason Marbella dedicated a bookshelf to these petty criminals is because that's where they all fled from the law. So, for example, celebrity gangster Dave Courtney lived in Marbella and had several self-aggrandising books on these shelves. Squalid stuff. It was my first intimation of what would soon develop into a pervasive distaste of the town. It was vulgar.

That evening the lads were keen to show me a good night out, in welcome to the city. I'd arrived midweek so when Saturday came they were bristling with excitement. We began sampling the Scotsman's whiskey collection, with some dope to help it along. Then we took a taxi into the main bar strip in the centre of Puerto Banus — the even more opulent end of Marbella popular with footballers and Essex reality television celebrities. Sadly, it was empty.

"This bar is usually alright," said Jonathan, pushing open the doors of a US Western-themed joint with swinging saloon doors and faux-log walls. It was a single long room that could easily hold a peak-season crowd of a couple hundred punters. At the moment we walked in, I counted nine people besides ourselves: a bouncer, two bar men, and six Romanian hookers.

I mean that literally and I'm not embellishing for dramatic effect. The only girls in the bar were actual prostitutes. I'm guessing on the Romanian bit, because we didn't speak to them. They looked Romanian, and in 2013 after visiting their country I'd concluded that the reason there are no hot girls remaining in Bucharest is because they all went overseas to work in the sex industry. Jonathan assured me that during regular season the bar had 'proper' girls too. We had a drink and soon left.

"Let's dispense with the preliminaries, mate," declared Steve, "and go to a proper knocking shop."

"I know a great one. Nick, you'll like this one. *Scandalo*."

"Scan-da-lo," repeated Steve, rolling the syllables around his mouth like gobstopper sweets. "Good call, pal. You in, Nick?"

"Sure, you two know the city."

We jumped into another taxi and soon sped along the main dual carriageway that bisects the town. The Spaniards are devious buggers, Jonathan explained. They fly all the tourists into Malaga airport then segregate them according to social class. The vest-wearing chumps on a cheap package holiday get stationed close to the airport. As you drive further east along the coast, however, the towns gradually rise in niceness along with the airs and graces of the people inhabiting them. Marbella is at the posh end of this chain and its where the likes of Dolph Lungren and Alan Sugar can be spotted wandering around the pretty streets in Gucci loafers.

The taxi took us outside city limits to what appeared to be an out-of-town retail park. Large buildings loomed around the big car park, with recognisable big box stores selling electronics, furniture, and toys. The whorehouse was tucked away one street over and from the outside looked like a normal strip club. Inside, it was composed of two main rooms. One was a bar area not unlike the side-rooms in a regular night club. The second room, further in from the main entrance, was like a strip club with a podium, a pole dancer on it, and numerous discreet booths. A staircase wound around the outer wall leading to what I assumed to be private rooms upstairs. I noted a scantily-clad woman lead a goofy grinning man up there a few minutes later.

It was seedy, suspect, and squalid. In my whiskey-soaked dope-fogged haze I was sanguine.

We bought beer and posted up at a high table.

"These birds are better than the last lot," I commented approvingly. A bleached-blonde was gyrating around the pole with only her panties and heels remaining from her original costume. She bent over to inspect her toes, giving me quite an eyeful from the rear. "Those Romanian slags were just sitting around doing nothing. This lot are hustling."

Girl Junkie

"Told you, mate. This is the best whorehouse in Marbella," said Jonathan.

Naturally, these hookers-of-the-more-earnest-type didn't long leave us to our men-only chat. A trio sidled up to open the bidding. The lady draping herself over my shoulder was of the caramel brown skin colour that is sexy on women but signifies a-rape-looking-for-its-victim on a man. She had reasonable curves but looked a bit ragged, like Lance Armstrong mid-way through an uphill Tour De France stage. I made polite conversation, as I don't dislike hookers while they are drumming up business, but telegraphed my lack of interest. Any time I talk to whores I always feel the urge to explain to them that I usually bang much hotter women for free. The couple of times I tried that route, it ended badly, so I've learned to hold my tongue.

I noticed Steve seemed exceptionally sincere with the brunette who was hustling him. "But you see, you seem like a lovely girl. Shouldn't you consider going to college and learning an employable skill? This club work can only go so long," he advised. She answered appropriately and Steve continued suggesting alternate career paths for her until she gracefully slipped away and never came back. My girl had finally shut down, upon realising I wasn't buying. Alone among us, Jonathan was having a fun lively conversation with his hooker.

"Are you gonna bang her?" I whispered into his ear.

"Nah, mate. But girls are girls. Might as well have a little crack on while they are here. No point being a miserable cunt, is there?"

The girls left us alone for ten minutes so we returned to the bar area for another round of drinks, then back into the dance area to see the next girl in the floor show. It was another blonde, this time with oversized fake breasts and a tattoo of a stalking tiger wrapping from her liver down to upper thigh. She had that grotty sexualised vibe of a girl you'd rape out of lust, but then murder in disgust. Her gyrations had inspired movement in my trousers. I was getting horny.

After two more beers I lost all sense of judgement.

"How much are the hookers here?" I asked.

"Half a note," said Jonathan, meaning fifty euros.

"I can get three hookers for each *Overkill* sale. Right, if my phone goes off with an Item No.5 notification while we are here, I'm going to bang her," I said, pointing out a thin dark-haired girl who could've been born anywhere along the edge of the old Ottoman Empire. Being drunk, I wasn't too circumspect in my actions. She saw me point, blinked in surprise, then walked over and said hello. I swiftly decided a baller does not wait upon his emails. I confirmed her price and she took me upstairs.

Let me interject here that I've always found going behind the curtain in strip clubs and whorehouses to be a very odd experience. Sitting on a stool underneath a podium while a painted-up tart pushes her arse into my face doesn't strike me as at all unusual. I can sip my drink, appreciate the arse, and continue discussing football, politics, and literature with my friends. However, the thick velvet curtain that separates public from private feels like the curtain separating the sacred from the profane. When you cross over the threshold it's no longer fun and games. You've made a decision to pay for sex, and thus enter into a seedy underworld. The world of the guv'nor.

Sigmund Freud would likely tell me I'm sublimating repressed desire. Carl Jung may blame my shadow self and Friedrich Nietzsche may chide me on my will to power and acting out of an Ubermensch fantasy. In this case, I blamed Steve and Jonathan for getting me drunk. I followed the girl upstairs and admired her ass, paid off some old woman in a cubicle behind the curtain who handed us a room key, and walked along a narrow red-lit hallway to a private room.

Being drunk, I don't remember details — only impressions that flash in my mind, loosely connected. I remember a double bed with dark blue sheets and the brunette reclining back on it. I remember quite enjoying shagging her at first, as she went through the motions of pretending to enjoy my rutting. I also remember the wheels coming off the track mid-way through. She was riding on top, bouncing up and down with a fair show of feigned enthusiasm. It was about fifteen minutes in and my head was clearing unexpectedly fast, no doubt the alcohol sweating out through my pores.

"Take your bra off," I said.

The girl, who turned out to be Romanian after all, obeyed and reached behind to unhook herself. I wish she hadn't. As she threw the white bra across the room to a chair, her small-ish breasts flopped loose and they were... ghastly. They looked like a balloon you find under a chair the morning after a party, with half the air leaked out. The skin around her nipples was wrinkled up like Angelina Jolie's neck, the creases streaking away for several inches. I doubt the girl was older than in her mid-twenties, but she had tits like an old woman. She looked like a corpse halfway through having its blood drained by a vampire.

"I can't do this," I said to myself. My fun little romp had suddenly turned gross. I pushed her off, rolled her into missionary position, closed my eyes and tried to come. I couldn't. *Shit!* I thought it would be unforgivably rude to simply dismount and leave, especially as this whore had been very pleasant and was giving it the royal college try. I needed to make myself come.

I began visualising Valeria, my 24-year old Belarusian girlfriend whom I was due to meet in Palermo for a holiday after Marbella. That visualisation exercise was working, until I was struck by a new fear: that by mentally associating Valeria with the Romanian hooker, I might tarnish future sex with the Belarusian. The last thing I wanted when fucking the beautiful Valeria was to have images of this whore's scraggly tits come to mind.

So, I began to visualise Tatiana, a Russian fuck buddy, as she was hot but I never expected to see her again. No, that wouldn't do either. I liked Tatiana and didn't want to sully the purity of our past with the stink of sulphur. Finally, I visualised my favourite porn actresses, selecting one who most facially resembled the Romanian hooker. I still couldn't cum, so I faked it, rushed to the en suite bathroom and pretended to clean off. With the door closed, what I really did was rinse my crotch under the shower head to scrub off any potential STDs. If the whore was any the wiser, she didn't show it.

I said goodbye and rejoined Jonathan in the bar area. My mood had soured.

"I'm knackered. I'm ready to leave any time you are. Where's Steve?"

"Over there, being creepy with the whores."

I looked towards a high table against the wall, ten yards from our own. Steve was towering over a tiny woman in a bright green bikini. He was stroking her hair, whispering into her ear, then leaning back to cast her an earnest look. She seemed to be shivering, though it wasn't cold.

"What on earth is he doing?" I asked.

"He's saving them. While you were upstairs he was trying to persuade a girl to quit the business and work in the Starbucks at the mall. She stormed off. Now he's telling that bikini bird to learn computer programming."

"She looks creeped out. Like, she fancies the fuck out of him because he looks so good, but she feels queasy at his white knighting."

"Exactly. Notice the security have their eye on him. If he doesn't stop, we'll get chucked out. I don't want to get barred from the best whorehouse in Marbella. That would be scandalous."

"Scandalo, indeed," I agreed.

Fortunately Steve let us drag him away and we took a taxi home.

Chapter 3
MARBELLA FELLAS

After the extravagant drinking and tomfoolery of the first week, the villa soon settled into a sedate routine. Steve and Jonathan busied themselves in building, deploying and — occasionally — rescuing their bespoke Army of artificial intelligence bots as it raided the internet for profit margins. I found a delightful cafe overlooking the beach, with big bay windows and comfortable sofa chairs. Each morning I woke up feeling refreshed, took a steaming hot shower, then walked leisurely to my favourite cafe. Typically I'd spend four hours alternating between reading and gazing across the ocean, my mind lost in reverie. Every other day Steve would join me for lunch, as turtling in the basement bunker all day could grow oppressive and he appreciated the break. It was nice, sipping LaVazza coffee from dainty cups and listening to the waves crash against the rocks.

Our conversation often turned towards business.

"How do you keep coming up with all this new content?" he asked. "I know game, but I'm fucked if I can keep talking about it for the YouTube monkeys."

"You've done fine so far. There was *Primal Seduction* and then *The Secret Society*," I replied, referencing Steve's textbook and video products respectively. "Those are hardly lightweight products. Even before we did the second edition *Primal Seduction* you had seventy thousand words for it. Most PUA clowns do shitty little 20k e-books."

"Yeah but…. look, I've got the marketing down. They sell and I know how to write sales pages and place Google ads. But those products emptied the tank, in terms of theory. Getting laid all comes down to not being a faggot. How much can I write about that?"

Just a week earlier Steve had released a video for his YouTube channel with the title of *Just Stop Being Such A Faggot*. It had received a mixed reception. The real reason he couldn't generate new content is because he didn't want to. He resented being in the pick-up business. All players have a run of high enthusiasm, when every day presents limitless opportunities to chase skirt and then talk about it. Steve had his run from around 2006 to 2009. By the time I met him in 2011 he'd already burned out and wasn't even particularly interested in chasing skirt, much less writing about it. He'd started up his *Authentic PUA* online business mostly because he needed the money, and also as an attempt to rekindle his desire for the game. It had worked, but in fits and starts.

I tried to explain why I felt like I had an unlimited store of fresh content to draw upon.

"Steve, part of the difference is our personality types. I like to withdraw into contemplation and allow ideas to percolate. I take pleasure in constructing elaborate systems and fitting every piece into its place. At heart, I'm a craftsman. If I wasn't chasing skirt I'd be creating custom watches or designing indie video games. You're a do-er and any time you're sitting on your arse is time you're not out there," I waved towards the pedestrian promenade, "doing stuff. So, you have far less patience for the ruminations from whence content emerges."

"And? Get to the point."

"I will. I look at content as an expert system. To me, game is an interlocking web of systems and sub-systems that can be elucidated. In that sense it's like chess, with its gambits, pins, skewers, and splits at the tactical level and then there's a whole other deep strategic level. If you're Garry Kasparov you can talk about chess forever. It's as simple as pausing a match and analysing the pattern of the board. That's how game is for me. I can take an idea and immediately multiple directions spring up, directions I can take the ideas."

"I'm not sure I get you," he wondered aloud. Steve is a smart man with a sharp mind, but his brain strives to reduce the space between thought and action, not increase it. Already he seemed impatient for my conclusion.

"Well, take the example of DHVs. It's one of many individual concepts in pick-up, in this case demonstrating high value to a woman." He looked at me with increasing impatience as I was now telling him what he already knew. "So, the first way to create content is to simply explain it to beginners. But there's no need to stop there. You can immediately look vertically, upwards.

How can you refine and build on the idea for use by increasingly adept players? Mystery explained DHVs to noobs, but intermediate and advanced players can do better DHVs, so talk about that. There's no need to stop there, either. You can look vertically downwards too. How about a deep dive into the theoretical underpinnings of DHVs, the principles of game or human nature that the concept rests upon? Pull the DHV apart into its constituent elements and understand every piece. That's more content."

"More mind-wank," he joked, ordering another coffee. The waitress favoured him with a smile.

"Then there's lateral movement. Think about the cross-disciplinary equivalents to the DHV. What other concepts are there in social psychology that fit with it, or theories in other expert systems that carry the same shape, or serve the same purpose as the DHV? I'll grant, that angle is more mind-wank than it is practical but some people — myself included — enjoy thinking in these directions. It's a mental workout on a topic we like. Lastly, you can create content by example. Take real DHVs you've used, or other people's, or hypothesis them, or find naturally-occuring DHVs in literature and movies, and then break them down. Show the reader how they relate to the theory." I was on a roll now. "Look, I could write an entire book just on how to tell a good DHV, based entirely on this little outline."

"Nah," Steve was shaking his head, gazing vacantly across the sea. "Nah, I just can't do that. I've got no patience for it. My mind is in the practicalities. I can focus for hours on graphs and stats, and sift theories with Jonathan, so long as I see the dollar signs at the end of it. This game theory you talk about is too far away from the cash. Not enough in it for me."

We knocked our heads together long enough to come up with a concept that would help Steve generate content with the minimum of effort. I suggested he canvas his readership for technical and theoretical questions and then sit in front of a video camera to answer them. That type of reactive thought-generation feels much less like hard work. We then walked around the harbour shooting video of Steve posing around yachts and sports cars in order to do a parody montage of the 'high value playboy lifestyle'. He sent the files off to the video editor of my *Daygame Overkill* credit sequence with instructions to copy the Tony Ferrino TV special, a parody of Julio Iglesias by British comedian Steve Coogan. We called it *The Steve Jabba Show*. Sadly, most of his viewers never got the rather obvious joke. They commented that he'd sold out and that getting rich to score women wasn't real game.

As with most game-related projects that Steve starts, he abandoned it within a couple of weeks.

The most memorable book I read during my Marbella trip was an old novel by Garet Garrett called *The Driver*. I'd stumbled upon it entirely by accident but found it fascinating. A key moment in my intellectual life had been reading Ayn Rand's seminal novel *Atlas Shrugged* in 2008 during a business trip to Santiago, Chile. I still rate it as my all-time second favourite novel, behind Alexandre Dumas' *The Count Of Monte Cristo*. This was at a time when the global economic crisis had hit and I'd completed my two-year hobby project of studying finance to try to figure out why the crisis had happened. It red-pilled me on economics and showed me that modern finance is spectacularly corrupt, though not in the way commonly thought: the reality was less *The Wolf Of Wall Street* and more *They Live*. That sucked because I'd previously considered my work in a large investment bank to be at least morally neutral.

Atlas Shrugged is a ponderous book with predictable plot twists. Its one-dimensional characters are mere mannequins, existing only to dress up philosophical archetypes in human form. It's also extremely long. Despite this, it fascinated me and finally closing it after the finale felt like concluding an epic, satisfying journey. The plot is simple, and timely for a book written in the 1950s at the peak of Soviet power globally: Communism has overrun the world except for the USA. That last bastion of capitalism and freedom is coming under increased pressure from communists within and, as they worm their way into cultural and administrative power, the USA starts to collapse. That collapse is used to justify an ever-tighter communist stranglehold. Exacerbating matters, there is a shadowy figure visiting each of the last great capitalist entrepreneurs and captains of industry, persuading them to destroy their businesses and then disappear. I won't spoilt the ending. If you can stomach the length, give it a read.

Rand was inspired to write the book due to her personal experience living through the economic collapse of Russia in 1920-21 following the Bolshevik coup d'etat and the closing out of civil wars (e.g. against the Mahknovist anarchists in the south). Food supply lines had completely broken down when Soviet commissars took over businesses and ineptly ran them into the ground. Suddenly, rolling stock was idling in the wrong stations, gasoline was scarce, and the year's harvest rotted in the fields with no-one to transport it to the starving cities. Thus Ayn Rand made her protagonist Dagny Taggart, the acting chief of the USA's Transcontinental Railroad company as she desperately fights to prevent the same famine striking America.

Atlas Shrugged was published in 1957 and inspired by the events of 1920-21. So, imagine my surprise when I realised there was a book published in 1922 about an economic collapse in the USA brought about by socialism, with the central protagonist a railroad executive who struggles to keep the country together. Reading Garrett's *The Driver* was freakishly similar to *Atlas Shrugged*, like seeing old childhood photos of your best friend for the first time. Even weirder, that protagonist is called Henry M. Galt, and the ultimate hero of *Atlas Shrugged* is called John Galt.

I looked into that, and sure enough there had been discussion on whether Rand had plagiarised Garrett. Writer Bruce Ramsey observed, "Both *The Driver* and *Atlas Shrugged* have to do with running railroads during an economic depression, and both suggest pro-capitalist ways in which the country might get out of the depression. But in plot, character, tone, and theme they are very different."

I disagreed.

Nonetheless, I was having a great time reading. I couldn't imagine anything more satisfying than sitting in a sea-front cafe in a rich Spanish city, sipping coffee, and hanging out with mates. It was quite the palate cleanser after a hard year chasing women across Europe in 2014.

One morning, the BBC emailed me. The producer of a reality TV show called *Tyger Takes On* wanted to feature me on a show about daygame. I hadn't yet come to believe the media are the enemy of the people, so I replied to ask what they had in mind. The producer Skyped me and explained. There was a teenage D-list celebrity called Tyger Drew-Honey (literally the gayest name I've ever heard) who had a show based on Jack Osbourne's famous challenge show. Each episode, Tyger entered a 'manly' subculture and was coached in the key elements before testing himself in the relevant competition. In season one there'd been three episodes: on porn, bodybuilding, and online dating. The production company was shooting season two for BBC Three television and wanted to tape a pick-up seminar then have me coach Tyger in-field.

"Are you gonna do it?" asked Steve. "There could be sales in it."

"I dunno. I don't want to be on television. It's bad enough having my face in public as is."

"It's worse for the poor bastards who will have to look at it," chuckled Steve.

"Yes, well. I already have haters. I shouldn't have any issues going back to real finance work because it's skill-based and I'm good at it. But why push my luck? You saw what happened with Roosh last year. The last thing I want is to be rolling up in Zagreb to chase skirt and having myself recognised as an evil pick-up artist. Why put a target on my back?"

Jonathan was used to working in the shadows so he knew all about keeping a low profile. Many of his friends and associates in his early days of 'black hat' internet profiteering had simply disappeared. "One day the Secret Service knocks on their door and they aren't heard from ever again," he'd said. So, he understood why I didn't like to push my luck. The normie world is generally hostile towards players, and moreover in early 2015 we were suffering peak Leftism. Every week a man was run out of his job by a social media lynch mob of Leftists because of a single injudicious comment. Football commentators, car enthusiast television presenters, and even literal rocket scientists had all by mobbed by blue-haired mentally-ill Leftist inquisitors. I'd rather avoid their Sauron-like eye.

"How bad can it be?" said Steve. "It's on BBC Three so no-one will watch it anyway."

"I suppose I could use them to give me a free seminar and product. If they are hiring the venue, paying my train ticket and hotel, and providing the impetus to get off my arse... well, it could be a good thing. So long as I'm allowed to film it with my own camera-man, I don't even care if their show ever broadcasts. I can stand in front of a crowd, chunter on with new content, then release it on video."

Remember, *Daygame Overkill* was selling extremely well at this juncture, just three weeks after launch. Every ker-ching sound of dollars dropping into my swag-bag gladdened my heart. I quite liked the idea of reproducing the feat at low-effort, even if it wasn't so profitable. I messaged the producer again and obtained her explicit consent that I could record everything and release whatever I wanted (except where Tyger was on-screen) commercially. That was enough, I agreed. We settled on shooting over a weekend in mid-February.

"They'll fuck you over, mind," warned Steve. "So be careful."

I didn't care. It gave me something to do in February.

I had something else to do in early February. My relationship with Valeria had entered a familiar stage, of waxing and waning. We'd enjoyed the first bloom of lust and excitement in spring of 2013 with my two trips to Minsk (see *Younger Hotter Tighter*). After meeting there in April, I'd returned in June to take her virginity. Later that year I twice brought her to London and even up to Newcastle to meet my family. By 2014 she'd begun to tire of being my long-distance non-exclusive girlfriend and by the time I returned to Minsk in April 2014 she'd been reluctant to sleep with me, having recently gotten a new boyfriend. She then entered the familiar territory of liking me too much to cut me off but wishing to turn her attention towards finding a real boyfriend. We'd hooked up again in Prague in the summer of 2014 and remained in WhatsApp contact since (see *Adventure Sex*).

I still liked Valeria a lot, and very much enjoyed fucking her. Dare I say it, I enjoyed her company even when I wasn't fucking her. She told me she'd quit her old job and found a sweet deal with a friend whereby she was technically employed (work is compulsory in Belarus) but didn't actually have to do any work. So, we both had a clear schedule in early February.

"Would you like to come on holiday with me?" I asked her one January evening.

"YES!!" she replied.

We tossed around ideas, mulling over where would be warm in February but not oppressively expensive to fly to (seeing as I would be paying both for myself from Newcastle and Valeria from Minsk). Palermo, Sicily was the clear winner so we booked a week together and I found a delightful old apartment built into fortifications on the sea front.

"Great, I know when I'll next have sex with a girl who isn't a hooker," I enthused to Steve.

"Didn't Valeria tell you she felt like a whore when having sex with you, because of cheating on her boyfriend?" retorted Steve. "And, technically, you are paying for her flights and board. How about that, eh? No different to visiting Scandalo."

During my third and final week in Marbella, Jonathan made plans to go skiing in the nearby mountains. I was shocked, noting the difference between the balmy t-shirt weather by the sea with what I presumed must be snowy freezing cold weather necessary for skiing. He assured me there was a real ski resort with real snow. "You'll see, mate," he said.

He tapped his social circle and invited another three lads, one Norwegian, one Dutch, and the last a German who claimed to be English, to fill the spare seats in his big Range Rover. He already had a chalet rental up at the resort so one fine afternoon we piled into the car and Jonathan drove us two hours north, into the mountains. We passed Granada, home of one of the few Muslim castles that wasn't razed in the Reconquista. From there, I watched in awe as the weather changed with the increasing elevation to three kilometres above sea level, the highest road in Europe. Falling snow eventually forcing us to creep carefully around tight corners on icy roads. The temperature had dropped from twenty degrees at the beach to slightly below zero at the resort, Sierra Nevada. I made good use of the journey, arguing with the Norwegian guy about politics. Heated as it got, we dropped the topic upon arrival and were pally again as the first beer cans were opened.

Jonathan hadn't oversold us. It was a real ski resort.

A real ski resort, yesterday

There was a central strip with a boardwalk, cafes, bars, and equipment stores. At the edges of the commercial zone were many apartment buildings and chalets, which is where we stayed. Jonathan's chalet had a lounge, kitchen, and two bedrooms. He fired up the stove and packed it with logs while the rest of us sprawled out and dug into the beers. The room soon warmed up nicely. Large windows gave us a corner view across the resort, though visibility was sharply reduced by falling snow. What a change of scenery!

"Can you ski, Nick?" asked the German. I don't remember his name. Probably Fritz, or Adolf.

"Nope. I once went on a kid's dry slope when I was ten. That's it. I'm gonna pass. I'll only hurt myself."

"You'll be fine. It just takes a few hours to get set."

"Nope. I saw what happened to Michael Schumacher. Twenty years racing at 300kph around deadly corners without a scratch, and then a single tree stump on the ski slope makes him a vegetable. I'll pass."

I love sausage trees

A debate ensued as everyone but Steve tried to persuade me to conquer my fear of skiing. I tried explaining that an adverse risk-assessment is not the same thing as fear. I have a long-standing rule that I won't try any leisure activity that carries with it single-mistake-catastrophic-risk. Kickboxing is fine, though consistently painful, because the injuries are superficial and scaleable. It's impossible to be seriously injured in kickboxing except under very specific and easily-avoidable circumstances. In contrast, I'd never go snowboarding, motorcycling, parachuting, or surfing. All four activities can ruin your life with a single error: torn ACL ligaments on a bad turn, hitting a car, a faulty chute, getting swept under a wave's backwash....

no thank you. I place a higher value upon my own skin than to engage in such tomfoolery.

Nobody was convinced. They all thought I was a faggot.

While the lads were out skiing, Steve and I drank beer in the main resort bar overlooking the slopes. Before long the others called in, padding around in ludicrously puffy clothes and dropping snow everywhere. All had cold-reddened faces and beaming smiles. My risk-management system did curtail my fun a bit, it would seem. They went back to change then joined us in the bar. Most of the evening passed in a drunken haze. I do remember we visited a sausage bar, where we drank beer while chains of massive linked sausages were hung from hooks above us.

Back at the apartment everyone slipped into sleep, except Jonathan and myself. We sat in front of the roaring stove while he rolled a joint, handing it to me to light. We'd first met in Budapest the prior summer but he'd then only been in town for a few days. We'd now spent nearly three weeks together and were finally getting to know each other. The beer, dope, and whirling snow fostered an atmosphere of self-revelation. I needn't outline my own revelations, as all of it can be found in previous volumes of this memoir. Jonathan filled in many of the blanks of his own background, resolving several of my unspoken questions.

"How did all this black hat stuff start? You don't strike me as a rogue, but what you describe about your past is basically the equivalent of being a highwayman."

"I had a normal job and normal life once," he explained. "But then my brother got sick and died. It was freakishly bad luck, something that's not supposed to happen so young. He was a good man and we were close, then I watched him just die. Something snapped. The world didn't seem fair any more, didn't operate according to rules. It turned me, and I had a *fuck the world* attitude. I decided I'd get what I wanted and that's that. No rules."

I could relate to that, having had a less extreme equivalent experience with my divorce. I understood how it felt to be robbed by fate and rationalise it, feeling unfettered by moral constraint. So, I probed.

"Steve explained your shared business and it's not even illegal. Shifty, yes. But I don't see a single law being broken. It's not really black hat, you both just talk like it is."

"You're right, compared to my old businesses it's tame. This last year or so, I feel like I'm fitting in again, back in the real world. The old years were dark. I can't even tell you some of what I did, but I'm not joking about the Secret Service. Nobody ever believes it, but they are the force that the US assigns to cyber crime, or at least did then. For a year I was in fear, all these guys — we'd never physically met but we knew each other on the dark web forums and I worked with some of them — they'd literally disappear. Not in the military junta sense, but, they'd be posting in forums, on encrypted emails, and then one day suddenly everything goes quiet. It's like they never even existed. A couple of times I know law enforcement got them, and it was unreported. They went into black sites and never came back. It was scary."

It made my PUA adventures look anaemic.

"So, what now?" I asked. "You are going straight with Steve?"

"More or less, yes. I have all these skills I learned, staying one step ahead of the law, and jostling with all the other black hats. It's dog-eat-dog and everyone is ripping everyone off. Even now, in the legit business, we attract all kinds of parasites. We get people writing bots to steal our information in order to backward engineer our business and steal our lunch money."

"Fucking hell. That, at least, sounds like my PUA world. So many plagiarists."

We worked our way through two more joints and finally fell asleep by the fire. The next morning we took the Range Rover back into town. Soon after that, I flew back to Newcastle. It had been a thoroughly enjoyable break to my winter routine.

Seaside reading
in Marbella

Trying to be cultural
in Sicily

Palermo hillside

Chapter 4
COSY NOSTRA

I've always considered Sicily to be a joke island. Not a real place with real people. Given that Italy is shaped like a boot and Sicily is the football being punted, I didn't expect much of the place. Sure, I'd seen the awful third *The Godfather* movie with old-time gangster scenes set in the little Mediterranean island. I was also dimly aware Sicily had been kicked around like a football between the Greeks, Romans, Spanish, Normans, Prussians and various Muslim hordes throughout its long history. As of 2015, Sicily was the primary port-of-invasion for slimy African rapefugees streaming out of Libya.

Naturally, I hoped to avoid those darkies. If anyone was going to rape Valeria, it would be me.

Valeria flew in from Minsk via a short layover in Rome, meeting an Italian friend for coffee there inside the airport. I landed in Palermo only an hour ahead of her, which was surprisingly fortuitous considering the logistical barriers in synchronising our arrivals. The airport was a clean modern building with shiny grey and black marble floors, wide open spaces, and long rows of red chairs. I plonked myself down at a cafe facing Arrivals and waited.

I was excited yet slightly anxious. Valeria and I hadn't met since July the previous year, when she'd visited me in Prague for a week. We'd had a good time but I knew that she could drop out of my life at any moment, as soon as she found a boyfriend with whom she could envision a future. Her agreeing to the Palermo trip had surprised me. So, questions rolled around inside my empty skull. *Is she still hot? Did she put on weight? Will she cause a fuss before putting out? Will she still swallow my cum?* That last question was uppermost in my mind when the automatic sliding doors hissed open and passengers from the Rome flight disgorged.

Valeria spotted me immediately and strode across the lobby in her long black leather boots, black tights, and short woollen skirt. Perhaps she was putting on a show, amusing herself, because she seemed to hold an exaggerated poise, like a catwalk model. My heart leapt briefly. I'd forgotten how hot she was.

"Hello Nick."

"Hello Valeria."

The air was thick with tension, with the mutual knowledge that this was a week-long booty call between former lovers who were now fuck buddies. She was clearly happy, but I felt an intangible barrier between us. Was I imagining things? Valeria always was mischievous with me, enjoying every opportunity I gave her to indulge her primal urges. Perhaps she was just easing into the role after having spent a few hours playing a different role with her friend in Rome.

"You take," she said, handing me her wheel-case. It didn't sound rude. Then we walked outside and found the coach into Palermo town. It was dark. We sat on the back seats and made small talk while whizzing along the motorway. An hour later we disembarked at the town centre bus terminal and followed my printed map to our apartment.

It was cold. Bitterly cold.

Our apartment was on the second floor of a square brick building that had been part of the shore fortifications centuries ago. It bore no ornamentation, nor balconies. The windows were small and the roof completely flat and surrounded by low ramparts. I dare say soldiers were quartered here in olden days. The entrance was on the landward side, a large tarmac car park in front. The seaward side looked over the main East-West coastal road, sandwiched between us and the beach. It was nice, and a radical departure from my norm.

The landlady was a young local woman who met us on the stone steps outside then led us through a heavy battered oak door, through a winding damp corridor, and up a winding staircase which I expected to see defended by valiant knights. Our apartment was rather medieval. There was a lobby, a kitchen, a small dining room, and a large bedroom. All the walls were unburnished sandstone and hung with old paintings, coats of arms, and even a tapestry. It was beautiful. The landlady threw some logs into a stove and explained its use, then waved goodbye. Valeria and I stood in the middle of the bedroom looking up at the ceiling, which was painted like a Roman bathhouse.

"It's beautiful," said the Belarusian.

"It's really cold," said me.

The apartment never did heat up the whole week we were there. It had been built long before the invention of radiators and the poor stove simply couldn't project enough heat to cover what was lost from the ill-fitting single-glazed windows and the uninsulated walls. On the positive side, the bed was also a medieval affair strewn with a dozen blankets, furs, and draperies. If only it hadn't been so cold, it would have been delightful.

More imperial than my usual fare

Best start shagging, I thought.

Valeria stood room centre, twirling slowly to take in the wall paintings, a smile on her face. I watched her slim legs, flat stomach, and her sizeable breasts pushing out through her sweater. I was very much looking forward to fucking her. So I stood up, walked to her, and we kissed. Then I picked her up over my shoulder and dumped her onto the bed.

It was very good sex, after six months of waiting. She was immediately into it, as eagerly as myself. I stripped her naked and banged away as normal, enjoying her familiar reactions and then turned her over to smash her from behind. Then I flipped her on her back and dragged her across the bed until her head was hanging over the side. That's a common move of mine, as it

Girl Junkie

lets me face-fuck a girl while she's upside down, folding her arms across her breasts and reaching over to finger her. Valeria rather liked that. Then she took top position and did yet another of her little idiosyncrasies, a dozen of which still linger in my mind. This one was cute. As she straddled me and settled herself onto my dick, she stretched both her arms into the air theatrically as if celebrating a victory and said, "yeah!".

It was so cute. She was telling me she felt like a winner for getting the chance to sit on my dick.

After letting her have the run of play — and thoroughly enjoying watching her lithe body bounce up and down — I dragged her to her knees in front of the stove and came in her mouth. She swallowed, and now I felt like a winner too. Then we fell asleep with Valeria curled into me with her head on my stomach.

Sadly, that was the high point of the trip.

The next few days were also good but Palermo itself was a let down. I'd nurtured unrealistic expectations of quaint harbour villages, trattoria restaurants, local wines, and ornamental churches. Sicily does indeed have these things but it's also the poorest province in Italy and very cold in February. It took half an hour to see the town's best attractions — which I'll grant were very nice — but I wasn't in the mood for tranquil pleasures. Little did I realise at the time, but my brain chemistry had set itself to a shorter wavelength and I now needed faster stimulation than Palermo was designed to provide. We tried some cafes, parks, a museum, and a walk along the sea front. It was pleasant but boring.

Valeria and I continued to have sex every day and it was always good. When not degrading each other before the eyes of God, we curled under the blankets and shivered. How to optimise the stove's output of heat was a constant topic of discussion. More than anything else the pervasive chill robbed our beautiful apartment of its comfort. I'd have loved to lounge there every afternoon with Valeria, switching back and forth between eating, shagging, reading, resting, and more shagging. We tried but couldn't shake the mild discomfort of the cold. So, we'd always need to go out and find a warm cafe.

By the third day I was uneasy and distracted. Valeria hadn't lost her appeal to me but the slow pace of Palermo grated. We took a bus up into the mountains to visit a famous chapel carved into rock. It was like Santa's grotto, if you replaced all the elves with statues of the Virgin Mary, and walking inside made me feel like a small child. After five minutes I was bored. Valeria inspected every nook and cranny, wide-eyed. I suppose they don't have religion in the godless communist hellhole of Belarus. I grew impatient but, knowing it was unreasonable to hurry her, I remained quiet.

Found this lovely watch
at a flea market

"What's wrong with me?" I thought. "Everyone else who comes here will adore the sculptures, examine the paintings, and wile away an hour or more lost in the beauty. I'm done in five minutes and want to play *Zelda*."

"Are you okay?" asked Valeria, walking back clutching a souvenir key chain she'd bought at a kiosk. "Can you take some photos of me?"

We took some pictures then walked outside to admire the city view from the mountainside. Palermo stretched below us as a sea of yellow lights, as the sun had set. The last bus back to town was turning in the car park and the driver indicated to us and a couple of stragglers that we'd best not miss it. Valeria and I sat on the back seats, looking out the windows as the bus wobbled slowly along the winding mountain roads.

"Are you sure you're okay?"

"Yeah, fine." I replied, mechanically. I wasn't fine at all. If I wasn't receiving fresh stimulus in five minute intervals, I became agitated. I looked down and realised my phone was in my hand with the Twitter app open. *Did I do that?* I asked myself. I had no memory of taking it out of my pocket.

Girl Junkie

We ate at a pizza restaurant and drank red wine. Valeria explained she had a new boyfriend in Minsk but they'd only recently started dating and she hadn't yet slept with him. She asked about my plans for the year so I kept it vague, talking of travel and friends. She knew all about my Nick Krauser alter-ego — even spectating one of Tom Torero's London boot camps with me in 2013 — but it didn't feel right to explain I intended to bang a load of hot girls in 2015. Valeria took on a wistful melancholy expression at times, as if wondering how we could have created something so special together and yet I was completely unable to simply choose her and move things forwards.

I wondered that myself. There wasn't a single thing I'd change about her — she was perfect for me in every way — and yet I knew with one hundred percent certainty that I didn't want to marry her. Not in 2015, at least. Not until after I'd performed indecent acts on at least a few dozen more young ladies. It wasn't even as if I particularly *wanted* to bang a lot more women. I just knew I had to. I wouldn't be at peace until I'd bled that wound.

Sex that night was good. Ten minutes after we finished, Valeria started tugging on my dick and rubbing her arse into me. It was out of character: it's my habit to only bang a girl once a session, and she knew that.

"What are you doing, you crazy girl?" I asked, in good humour. She wrapped her hands around my dick and kept tugging. I'd gotten hard.

"I want sex!" she demanded.

"Okay. Suck me off."

She dived under the blankets and gave me a hungry blow job, then turned into spoon position and backed up onto my dick. I hadn't moved at all during the whole episode. I may as well have been a mannequin. Now, I did actually want to hold her down and smash her, but seeing Valeria so wanton amused me so we tacitly made a game of it — her doing all the work and forcing me into sex while I pretended I wanted to sleep.

For the next ten minutes Valeria lay on her side in spoon position and ground herself back and forth on my dick. It was the only time we'd ever had sex where she wasn't making the slightest effort to please me — again, I think she was making a game of getting herself off selfishly. She rode, and rode, her eyes shut and lips softly parted. There was no kissing and no talking. I simply rested my hand on her rounded hip and let her go. Finally I sensed her breath quicken. She rode harder then suddenly tensed, gasped, and let go.

Her orgasm subsided and she seemed to collapse deeper into the mattress.

"Are you okay?" I asked.

She turned and gave me a sweet smile. In a sing-song voice she replied, "Yes, I am okay. I am the happiest girl in the world."

It was so sweet. I rose up to my knees and came on her face.

"I'm happy too," I said. She gave me a playful slap and ran off to the bathroom. It was the last time we'd ever have sex.

My PUA business was still going strong. *Daygame Overkill* sales were slowing down, and I'd come to learn that video products follow a life cycle more like Hollywood movies than printed books. That is to say, a movie will typically make half of its total worldwide gross within the opening two weeks of release. Then it gets pushed out of its cinema screen allocation by the next crop of movies, relegated to smaller screens and off-peak showings, and eventually dumped onto Blu-Ray and cable at considerably lower revenue per audience viewing. That's why studios pump up the marketing so hard on the opening weekend and fight for a strong early gross: it'll persuade cinema owners to keep the movie on more screens the following weekend. Upon eventually checking my statistics at the end of 2015 I'd find *Daygame Overkill* too made almost half of its total gross in the first six weeks. Checking my phone in Palermo each morning, I could already see sales slow.

Earning $191 per shit, into perpetuity, had been too good to be true. An impossible dream.

It was raining heavily and our poor old stove now barely heated the air directly in front of the grate. We wrapped up with scarves and gloves, I opened an umbrella, and Valeria clung onto my arm as we walked to a fancy hotel in the centre. It had a sleek modern lobby with sofa chairs and fast Wi-Fi. She took a paperback novel out of her bag and settled in with a Martini. I booted up my laptop and spent the next five hours copy-pasting the text of *Balls Deep* into a series of blog posts, then scheduled one to post every three days. Tedious work, but it gave me a couple of months of automated content to help up-sell the book. I also swapped emails with the BBC to confirm details of the upcoming shoot.

I'd long heard that TV people are the worst scum in the world, and I was starting to believe it. The production company I dealt with where total clowns. BBC's junior channels operated on a "production company" model, meaning shows weren't made my BBC's own teams. Rather, small fly-by-night media firms would pitch concepts to the network and get the green light to produce. Then the BBC would either pick up the show or not, externalising risk onto the media firms should a production run into trouble. This arrangement encourages a world of bullshit, glibness, and back-stabbing as firms fight over scraps. BBC bureaucrats play them off against each other, and low-paid low-IQ interns get exploited in producing shows that never turn a profit or pay a salary. I was now dealing with such morons.

It quickly became apparent that the production company were chancing it, trying to spin numerous plates without committing themselves to any financial outlay. They wouldn't tell me which venue they'd booked (because they didn't have one yet, because the venue proprietors would demand a deposit, depleting the firm's tiny cash float), nor send my train tickets or hotel reservation. They seemed determined to hold out until the very last minute. Upon realising this, I decided to play by their rules: I'd be ready to welsh on any deal if it ever turned unfavourable. Worse, there was only one competent white person at the production company, a middle-aged senior producer. She was the only person able to answer my questions directly and to make decisions. Most of the time I was corresponding with some Indian or Pakistani with a stupid name and low IQ as they tried to blow smoke up my arse with the most unconvincing patter.

Most of the shoot's details were easily agreed, once I got the senior producer face-to-face on Skype video chat. Filming would take place on the second weekend in February, on a Friday, in the West End. I'd take a train from Newcastle the prior afternoon and stay overnight in a hotel. They agreed to cover me for three nights and a return ticket home on Sunday. We also agreed I'd present a 'beginner daygame' seminar on Friday morning pitched at total noobs — so that the television audience could understand the clips — and then have a two-hour infield session with Tyger mic'd up. They'd interview me in the afternoon and I'd give Tyger personal feedback. There were no restrictions on what I could teach.

"We want to be like flies on the wall. Do your usual thing. We'll just film," she said. That much was easy.

The big points of contention were as follows. First, they wanted me to find six total beginners to fill out the seminar in order to give it a real boot-camp feel. I had just ten days to do so. Not only that, but the attendees must be available all day on Friday, when normal people have jobs to go to.

"Let's do it on Saturday, it'll be miles easier. Everyone is free," I suggested.

"No, it has to be Friday." They didn't give a reason.

"That'll be difficult. Also, most students want to remain anonymous because it's a controversial topic. They can get in trouble at work if word gets out. You'll have to film the backs of their heads or blur their faces."

"Yeah, that's fine. This show is all about Tyger. The other students are basically extras."

I posted a casting call on my blog and waited to see if there was enough interest for six noobs to sign up at short notice for a Friday morning free daygame seminar. I messaged some friends who might enjoy helping out as approach-coaches, so I wouldn't carry the whole in-field burden, and also engaged the camera-man who'd shot the *Daygame Overkill* seminar.

Valeria thought it was all rather exciting, what with the BBC being involved. "Are you going to be on television?"

"Something like that. I doubt anyone will watch it but it'll pay for a new product." I explained the schedule to her and she nodded along.

"If you're filming everything on Friday, why are they paying your hotel until Sunday?"

"Because I want a weekend in London. I haven't lived there in nearly a year but still have friends around. So, I negotiated a longer trip. For all I know this shoot will be a total abortion so I don't want to travel all that way just for one day."

"Is it much work?"

"No. It'll take a few hours to prepare the slides and I'll have my graphic designer in Serbia make them pretty. That's what I'll work on tomorrow. It's beginner's material, so I don't need to think very hard. The speaking is easy, as I can go off the slides. The only thing I'm wary of is them trying to backstab me during the infield. Every time the media covers PUA it tries to make us look like idiots. I know they want to film me approaching girls specifically so they can cherry-pick a few blowouts and pretend that's all I ever get."

"Oh!" she said, as if encountering media dishonesty for the first time. Coming from Belarus, she was used to propaganda being overt and obvious. Underhand manipulation was new to her. "So what did you say?"

"I told the senior producer explicitly that's what I expected her to try, and therefore to spike her guns I would not do any demonstration sets. I sent them a copy of *Daygame Overkill* and told them they could reach a conclusion on my bona fides from that. She conceded and agreed it was enough to record the little faggot lad doing the sets."

"It sounds so.... hostile," she said. "Why deal with these people at all if you don't trust them?"

"They are paying for my weekend in London. My ticket, hotel, and event room hire together are worth about £600. It's a chance to film a product for free."

"Then why don't you do two?"

"What do you mean?"

"You are free on Saturday and Sunday. So, hire a second room and talk about a second topic."

Thus was my *Womanizers Bible* product born. It was a great idea. I could talk about whatever the hell I liked, I was already in London, and I wouldn't have all those multi-cultural spivs buzzing around me like gay mosquitoes.

Valeria and I didn't have sex that evening simply because we'd overdone it a little in the first four days. The next morning we'd planned a bus ride across to the eastern shore to climb up the famous Mount Etna. There was a motorway clinging to the northern seaboard along to Catania, the eastern capital, and from there a little minibus drove to the foot of the mountain proper and cable cars would carry us up. We pottered around a flea market set up in the car park by our apartment in the morning then took a lunchtime bus to Catania.

I'd made a mess of the planning. All the mountains I've previously climbed have either been in England — where nobody controls them and you simply walk up them at your leisure — or in Japan where a sophisticated tourist industry maps it out for you with excellent customer services. Naively, I assumed the lazy wops of Sicily would adopt one or the other systems. How silly I was! Tourists were only allowed to Mount Etna on a single specially-licensed minibus that made a single journey, at 8:15am from Catania bus station.

Incredible! No wonder Sicily is the poorest province in Italy. They can't even run a proper bus service to their greatest tourist attraction. We didn't, however, find this out until arriving in Catania. We stepped off into the open-air bus terminal full of high hopes at around 2pm. Everywhere was closed. A few drivers sat in a dingy waiting room chain-smoking cigarettes and a cafe next to them had a half dozen limp sandwiches wrapped in cling film on display. Everyone looked older than Don Corleone in the final scene of *The Godfather III* where he falls over and dies of old age. I felt the creeping touch of death just by looking at them. Nobody wanted to answer our questions and when they did tell us the only bus had already departed, and thus our trip was wasted, we needed to hear it three times before we'd believe it.

"Not even Belarus is this stupid," said Valeria. That's quite a damning indictment of Sicily.

"Well, we're fucked. We might as well have a look around Catania."

It was a normal city and nice in its own grimy poverty-stricken way. We walked uphill from the bus-station into the town centre. We noticed several groups of teenagers hanging around looking extremely suspicious, following us with sullen eyes but not so obviously that I'd have known had I not already been assessing them for their threat-level. Our road gave out onto the edge of the commercial district and we saw our first bank branches, shoe shops, and grocery stores. Where the pavement made space for it, we saw a handful of makeshift tents with a homeless person in each. Occasionally, we walked past an illicit street vendor sitting on a mat with his wares lined up at his feet. Stolen mobile phones, mostly.

The surly youths, homeless squatters, and fences of stolen property all had something in common, I noticed. Valeria noticed too.

"What are these people?" she asked, clinging nervously to my arm. It felt dangerous.

"Niggers."

She stifled a laugh. "No! Obviously I see their colour. I mean why are they here? Why are they on the streets? Why are criminals doing this so openly?"

Valeria had experienced her first taste of the Soros-funded African invasion, the globalist attempt to destroy the nations of Europe with the willing connivance of Angela Merkel and her European Union cronies.

"This could not happen in Belarus," she said. "People selling stolen phones in the street! They'd be arrested immediately."

"Do you have black people? I never saw any in Minsk."

"God no! Sometimes I see an American tourist who is black, but nobody like that lives in Belarus. We get Turkish and Chinese. They have special business deals with us."

"The Turks fuck you for money and then the Chinese massage out the muscle pain?"

She hit me and we carried on walking.

It quickly became apparent Catania had nothing for the tourist we hadn't seen already in Palermo. There were little restaurants, wine bars, and souvenir shops so we pottered around a little but both of us were tired and irritable. Finally, we sat down for dinner in a pleasant trattoria and ordered pizza. Out conversation started to falter and we didn't speak much over the food. When the bill came I paid it, as usual.

"You can leave the tip," I said. Valeria didn't make any move to do so.

"Really, you should leave ten percent. The service was fairly good."

"No, I don't like to tip now. You pay." She was firm. It was quite unlike her. Clearly she had the hump about something but, this time, so did I. I'd paid for the entire trip and all of the food. She hadn't even made the gesture of buying coffee when in cafes. Her sole outlay on me had been a specially-engraved pen with my name on that she'd brought from Minsk. Admittedly, that was a nice gesture. However, I'd be surprised if it cost more than twenty pounds. I was down about £650 so far, all things considered. If she'd just made the occasional gesture, a £2 coffee one day, a £2 tip the next, I'd have let it lie. Instead, it rankled me.

"I don't like to be treated like a wallet."

"I don't treat you like that."

"You have this week. You expect me to pay for everything."

"You invited me! You're the man! You are English, and older, and a professional. I'm Belarusian, and a young woman. This is normal."

She was right, to a degree, and I never resent spending money on a girl who has already fucked me for free, as Valeria had. If an internationally-travelling middle-aged man is picking up broke university students in shitbox countries then it's rather unfair to split the bill, in my opinion. Pulling a career woman in London is a different story — they have money, and they are all feminists — but you can't split the bill with a Belarusian student when her side of it costs her five hour's salary and the same amount on your side is only 1/10th of a *Daygame Overkill* sale (or half of the first turd to drop into the bowl).

No, it wasn't that. We were arguing about something else: what would happen to our relationship when we said goodbye at Palermo airport? Both of us were anxious and handling it badly. We had a tight-lipped and sharp-tongued exchange. She called me a psychopath. I may, perhaps, have called her a whore. We took the two-hour bus back to Palermo in silence. I sat at the back and Valeria at the front.

We didn't talk much that night and in the morning Valeria caught her early flight home. She paid for her own bus ticket to the airport. We weren't nearly so frosty by then, and exchanged a hug and pleasant farewells. An hour later she sent me a long rebuke by WhatsApp, telling me she didn't want to date a man who called her a whore.

"Ok" I replied, and left it at that.

BOLSHEVIK BROADCASTING CORPORATION

CHAPTER 5

LONDON

Chapter 5
BOLSHEVIK BROADCASTING CORPORATION

"Julieta, you there?"

I was typing into Facebook messenger two days before my train ride to London. I hoped Julieta could solve a little last-minute planning issue that had been thrown up.

The slides for my upcoming presentation, now titled *Black Book*, lay open on my laptop. They covered the basics of daygame and I was satisfied I'd avoided the usual teaching trap, of giving beginners a list of canned lines to repeat. Nobody really learns that way. I wanted students to engage their critical faculties in order to create their own personalised patter for girls. To this end, I'd set out a series of exercises that walked students through the process of first observing girls, then putting a fun label onto them (e.g. "Russian sniper", or "lost tourist", or "scary Amazonian") and from those seeds of creativity building a series of compliments and teases. I hoped this would enable students to capture the uniquely playful experience of each set while still giving them a chain of stepping stones across troubled conversational waters.

The BBC had written an hour earlier to inform me they'd be packing up their cameras after the lunchtime infield session of the event and wouldn't even bother attending the afternoon seminar. So, I was now freed to devote

Girl Junkie

that later portion to dating technique. I'd already written about dating abstractly, and in no little detail, in *Daygame Mastery* but the students would really benefit from physical demonstrations, like the street phase of pick-up had received in *Daygame Overkill*'s infield footage. Emails between the BBC producers and myself had gotten a bit testy. Here's the final email I sent them, after I'd grown tired of them sticking their oar in to mess with my scheduled seminar plan. Their attempts to assert control annoyed me:

"I'm happy to do the date bit after you leave, but it has to be at a reasonable time. Remember I'm coming down from Newcastle to do a special one-off seminar for you that I had to organise in a hurry, with narrow specifications on the attendees, on a difficult day, and I'm not getting paid beyond minimum expenses. So, I'm insistent that I get to do it my way, within reason. Remember I'm not on your payroll and I answer only to myself."

I was ready to walk away and they knew it. At this point my complimentary train ticket had only just arrived, that morning, and I still hadn't received details of my hotel reservation. I was convinced they still didn't even have a venue booked. A producer replied to my message. They'd folded and promised not to interfere any more.

To do dating technique justice within the seminar entwo vironment, I needed a live female to demonstrate on. There were only girls I was still close to in London who also knew about my PUA persona: the large-chested Suriname fashion designer Demi, and the equally large-chested Argentine clown Julieta. I don't mean 'clown' as an insult to Julieta's mental health, by the way. She used to work in the circus and was sometimes hired as a clown for children's parties. We hadn't spoken since August the prior year, when I'd shagged her in the arse in an upstairs corner of *Instant* ruin bar in Budapest. That had been the outcome of the unusual coincidence of us both passing through the same town at the same time without any prior coordination.

Julieta had come online now and seen my message, so I decided to ask her first.

"Hi Nick! How are you?" she replied.

Great, not only was she still talking to me but she'd replied fast. We hadn't fallen out but girls do have a way of dropping off if you aren't paying them sufficient attention.

"I'm coming to London the day after tomorrow!"

"Oh, great!"

We caught up on the chit chat and then I made my pitch. Would she be interested in appearing on camera in a seminar, which would air on the BBC? I'd demonstrate body language on the first date, for a room of seven students.

"I don't know. What sort of body language?"

"Nothing sleazy. Just how to sit, touching arms, holding hands. Not even kissing. You'll keep all your clothes on."

"That's alright then. Yes, I'll do it."

"There's no money, though. I'll buy you dinner afterwards."

I'd have dated Julieta much longer than I did if not for logistical barriers. We'd met in February exactly a year earlier, 2014, and a month after that I'd received notice to leave my London house. That had been the catalyst to embark upon the European tour recorded in *Adventure Sex*. Around the same time, Julieta had received an offer to join an Italian circus for summer season. Thus we were pulled apart at a time when our relationship was going great. She was now twenty-three years old, had luscious long black hair, and giganormous firm tits. I'd taken her virginity in spring and that summer she dated a young knife-thrower she met in the Italian circus. In Budapest in August she claimed the knife-thrower and myself constituted her entire carnal experience of men.

"You're the only one who did my ass," she'd assured me.

Julieta having agreed to be my model, I spent the next hour drafting additional slides and then sent them off to my Serbian graphic designer. Two new mails landed in my inbox, the senders two students from the *Black Book* course. Reading through, I was aghast.

"Fucking BBC commie traitors," I muttered under my breath. "Fucking media scum."

Both students explained that the production company had emailed them that morning demanding they sign a 'model release form', a wavier that gave the BBC permission to broadcast footage of them on-air and the exclusive right to royalties and artistic control. Such waivers are completely routine in reality TV, but the producer had specifically promised — at my explicit insistence — that the students would *not* have their faces broadcast on television. The lying Leftist pieces of shit had gone behind my back, bullying the students and claiming they wouldn't be allowed into the seminar otherwise.

I was livid. I'd have deported those interns back to the third world immediately, if I could.

I sent out a group message, and cc'd in the producers, with words to the effect that I would not accept a change of key terms only two days before the event, after everyone had already arranged time off work (and two were flying in from overseas). If the BBC continued to pressure my students, I would simply walk out of the seminar and hold it elsewhere. To my surprise, the students all agreed that being on camera wasn't such a big deal after all so what seemed like an impasse quickly dissolved. Things were getting stressful. I wondered why I'd let myself get talked into dealing with the media. Finally, all outstanding issues were settled and an intern sent on my hotel reservation details. The Covent Garden branch of Travel Lodge would be blessed with my patronage.

Clowns.

The train ride south was pleasant and I checked into the hotel. Zaria, the Uzbek-Russian catwalk model I'd dated way back in 2011, still lived in London so I pinged her. She agreed to meet for coffee.

An hour later I stood waiting outside Covent Garden underground station. The Thursday rush hour throng buzzed past. *I used to work this patch*, I reminisced. My first few hundred daygame sets had been in and around this part of town, from the market square up to Neal Street. It was where Johnny, Fernando and I had run our *Rock Solid Game* boot-camps on Saturday afternoons. London is so much busier than my favourite European cities. It was positively alive with energy. Pedestrains seemed to walk twenty percent faster than normal, like an old B/W cinema reel sped up.

Zaria arrived, immaculately dressed and strutting in her well-drilled catwalk manner. She'd tied up her black hair and blue eye shadow looked great on her coffee-coloured skin. She didn't look a day older than when we'd first met nearly five years earlier though she was now pushing thirty-four. We sat down at a Caffe Nero and chatted. I felt the urge to fuck her again, for old time's sake. She always was good in bed.

"I'm in a hotel just down that street," I said. "Want to see?"

"Not really."

"It's nice. I don't usually live the high life. Come on!"

"We won't have sex. I promise you."

When a drunken girl says that as she stumbles to your apartment on a first date, it means — of course — quite the opposite. However, every time stone cold sober Zaria had said that to me in the past, it had been the literal truth. Slightly crestfallen, I walked her in and up to my suite. She sat on the edge of the bed while I sprawled out like a dissipated old beggar in an Elizabethan gin house.

"You look disgusting like that," she said, turning her nose upwards. "I never understood you. I see the potential for a great man but you run around drinking with your stupid friends and chasing sex. You waste yourself."

"I like it."

"I was thinking about this recently, Nick. I had a good idea. Listen to me. It is a solution to a problem of mine, and it means you do not waste your life."

I was all ears. "Go on."

"I want you to make me pregnant. Stop! Listen!" She'd seen me go white with fear. "I do not want you to be a father. I will raise the child and I do not ask you to take any responsibility or give me any money. I can get by comfortably. My problem is I have dated men after you and I don't find any suitable for marriage. I know I am getting older and I am happy to be alone, but I want a child. You have excellent DNA and I want it. I will carry your baby. I am happy, and you can continue your worthless ways knowing you have a legacy."

Her pitch had stunned me into silence. I reached over and pawed her thighs and tried to pull her down onto the bed. She swatted my hands aside and shuffled a few inches further away.

"No! I will have sex with you only if you agree to make me pregnant."

"You don't *want* to have sex with me?"

"Definitely not! I'm sure it will be very pleasurable for me, but you disgust me. No, we can have sex for babies only."

I'll admit I was tempted. Zaria was offering a free lunch. She'd do all the work of bearing and raising a child while I'd get some jollies now and the satisfaction of knowing that even if I got beheaded by a jihadi on Oxford Street the next afternoon my genetic line would nonetheless continue. It was 6pm and I wasn't due to meet my London daygame friends until 7pm. That left an hour free to drop a load in Zaria, shower, and go on the lash. Unfortunately, I had to refuse her kind offer. I couldn't believe the words as they came out of my mouth but it was all true, and all sincere.

"I can't, Zaria, sorry. Believe me I want to. You're a beautiful, intelligent woman and I can't think of a better mother for my children. If it was as simple as that I'd agree right now. But I can't. Let me explain. First, there's the legal issue. You say you wouldn't demand anything from me but the government of the UK thinks otherwise. At any time in the next eighteen years you could change your mind and clean me out financially. So, while I absolutely believe you are sincere now, I can't rely on your word when you would hold the means of my financial ruin. Second, I can't deliberately sire a fatherless child. Fatherlessness is a blight on society. It must be awful growing up without a dad, especially if your dad willingly abandoned you. I can't do that to my own child. And lastly, it would be easy for me to hand off all responsibility towards my son or daughter now, but what happens when he's born? Many fathers say that when their child is born a switch flips inside and life changes forever. What happens if that switch flips in me? Either you would make me honour our initial deal and I'd never see my son, or else suddenly we'd enter into a complicated arrangement, or a forced marriage."

I was genuinely touched by Zaria's offer but I meant every word. I'd have loved to father a child with the beautiful Uzbek if not for these problems. She argued the toss a bit but, deep down, she agreed with me.

"I understand. I really want a child now and you are my preferred option. My only acceptable option."

"Zaria, you're hot as fuck. You'll find a good man."

I pawed at her again and she slapped my hands away again. We chatted a while longer then I walked her to the station and went to meet my friends in Soho. It was the last time I'd ever see her.

Three local daygame lads were waiting at the boozer. Dark Rob is a tall half-Spaniard who'd been on the streets a couple of years. We'd finally had a real one-to-one conversation at the drinks session following *Daygame Overkill* filming in November. He was good friends with Tom Torero's wing Ramy, a Syrian-born man who'd been around daygame since 2010 and I'd already met a handful of times. We were also joined by Onder, a London-born Turk I'd hung out with in Prague for a week the previous summer. He'd agreed to approach coach to help me out at the *Black Book* infield session.

Considering my racial epithets earlier this chapter, perhaps it surprises you that I went drinking with an Arab, a Turk and a half-Wop. The micro is not the macro. While I fervently hoped Europe would initiate mass deportations of non-whites (that is to say, non-Europeans) and ethnically cleanse itself, I believe that until that happens there's no reason to be rude to the law-abiding, tax-paying, non-Europeans who live here. They may be very nice people but I wish them to be so very nice in their own lands, thank you very much. Having a policy goal aiming for a mostly-white Europe is not in contradiction with liking and being friends with non-whites on an individual basis.

I liked these lads. I promised to hide them in my basement when the lynch mob comes knocking. Perhaps it also surprises you they'd chosen to remain friends with me.

As my dissatisfaction with Europe's darkening trend continued, I'd taken to voicing my thoughts on Twitter. Remember the era. This was a time of peak-ISIS when every week those dirty Muslim goat-fuckers would video a new atrocity, such as mass-beheadings of defenceless civilians, and burning prisoners in cages. It was when Muslim immigrants drove trucks down French streets to mass murder children. When Muslim rape gangs forced white children into prostitution. When communist agitators encouraged parents to force gender-twisting hormones into young children in the name of transexualism. Anyone wishing to censure me for using terms like "nigger" and "paki" can go fuck off right now.

My country was, and remains to this day, under siege by the enemy.

Rob, Ramy and Onder, however, were not the enemy. We had a good old drink. Sometime after the second pint we found outselves in *The Duke Of Argyll*, an old man's pub on Brewer Street behind the neon-decked Piccadilly Circus. It is of a type found everywhere in London: Victorian era furnishings, dark polished mahogany tables, brass bannisters, and a line of guest ales on the pumps. We sat at a high table discussing the upcoming seminar when my phone rang.

"Hello?"

"Is this Nick? Nick Krauser?" It was a man's voice. Around thirty years old, and strained.

"Yes."

"I am to understand we are supposed to be filming with you tomorrow." Ah! It's one of the muppets from the production crew, I realised. They still hadn't given me venue details. When we'd spoken that morning they'd said something about still being in Cardiff wrapping up a shoot. The students were nervous, wondering where they should go in the morning.

"Yes", I replied.

"I'm the executive produce for Blah Blah Faggot Productions. Well, we are cancelling you. Ok?"

Girl Junkie

I paused to process this. I'd expected the event to fall through, from incompetence if nothing else. By now I didn't much care because I'd lost all interest in being on television, on account of being neither a woman nor a homosexual. I had my train tickets and my hotel. That was good enough.

"Ok," the producer repeated, and then paused expectantly. He sounded outraged, like he was gee'd up for a big confrontation only to be disappointed I wasn't playing along. Finally, he spoke again. "We read your Twitter."

"Ok," I replied, finally.

That afternoon I'd tweeted something about wanting to burn down every mosque in the UK, or that I wanted to sink the NGO boats carrying African invaders from Libya to Sicily. I forget exactly. Something like that. The pause lengthened. I knew the cuck on the other end of the line was waiting for me to justify myself, or perhaps beg his forgiveness. I'm pretty sure he thought himself to occupy the moral high ground.

I waited. He blinked first.

"We don't want to be associated with people like you."

"Ok."

Again, my calm acknowledgement surprised him. Did he expect his approval was important to me? I'd already mentally marked his card. When the Day Of The Rope came, I'd cut his balls off personally. Well, that might be difficult because I hadn't caught his name. Perhaps he'd escape my wrath. I was drunk.

"Yes. So. We're cancelling you."

I'm sure when he'd rehearsed this riposte it had thudded home with all the power of an Alan Shearer penalty kick. Now it sounded limp and weak, like my dick had been after Zaria finally wriggled from my grasp two hours earlier.

"Ok."

"And we are going to cancel your hotel too."

"Good luck," I said, and hung up.

Rob, Ramy and Onder looked expectantly. They'd only heard a non-committal series of okays and yesses. I related the conversation.

"What a bunch of cunts," said Rob. "Nine o'clock on a cold February evening and they try to get you thrown out of your hotel."

Tried and failed, as it happened. The hotel told them to fuck off, to my relief, because I'd already checked in and this guaranteed the stay. There was the minor matter of tomorrow's venue. I couldn't cancel the event, not when

I'd given my word to six students and roped in a few friends to help out. I was rattled, because my reputation was on the line.

I emptied my pint in one long gulp. Time to put out this sudden conflagration.

"I have to go. I have maybe an hour or two remaining to walk around the local pubs and find one with a free function room tomorrow morning."

They wished me well. It would be tight.

To my surprise, it took just an hour before I got lucky with a bar near Goodge Street station, a traditional English pub with an upstairs function room. At first, the manager was taken aback but upon my explaining it was a "self development" course and I'd willingly put money behind the bar, he soon warmed to the idea. I fired out an email informing the students and my cameraman of the venue change. The more I mulled it over, the more I came to doubt the production company's story about getting delayed in Cardiff. Probably, they used my Twitter account as a pretext to escape their obligations in London. They'd known about me since early January and claimed to have read my blog, watched my YouTube, and studied *Daygame Overkill*. It simply wasn't plausible they'd only now discovered my Twitter account, at 9pm the night before filming.

Then again, maybe they really were that amateurish.

Clowns.

Steady hands

With the steady hand of Nick Krauser back at the helm, filming of *Black Book* went smoothly. If you're interested in the material I presented there, feel free to head over to the sales pages and buy yourself a copy in glorious high definition video. The audience had a tangible noob vibe. In contrast,

Girl Junkie

you can always spot an experienced, competent daygamer: they have been forged in the furnace of the streets, their excessive psychological fat melted away by adversity. What remains is a hawk-eyed predatory male who is intimately aware of his own body language and vibe, smooth and controlled in his movements, and exuding the confidence of having faced and passed a series of stiff tests. It's like how my time around the fight game made it easy for me to pick fighters from a line-up of equally fit and muscular gym guys. Game recognises game. Noobs have their own tangible vibe: a timid earnestness, and a disorganisation in manner as they flip-flop between their initial ingrained chumpiness and the more charismatic poise they are endeavouring to learn.

Sometimes their chumpiness was comical.

I'd begun the aforementioned creativity exercise in which I displayed an image of a girl — I'd found a dozen by browsing through Google Image search results for the terms "street fashion female" — and then invited the audience to put a label onto her, as the first step towards building an opener and stack.

"How would you label this girl?" I said, pointing at a slim blonde Slav cast onto the large projector screen. She had high cheekbones and was photographed striding down a shopping street. A hand went up in the audience and the French lad at the front offered a cold-read on her.

"Leggy blonde."

"Yes, that's the idea. Try to make it a little more fantastical. Less literal."

He chewed that over but was momentarily stumped. Another hand was thrown up, a cheerful Colombian sitting in the second row.

"Those skinny legs are like a bird. She's a blonde flamingo."

Right! They'd understood the concept. That's exactly what I was hoping for. My thoughts briefly drifted back to when Tom Torero had tried to engage the audience in building openers for his *The Girlfriend Sequence* taping two years earlier. It had been disastrous. Having witnessed his audience clam up I'd learned from his pain and this carefully structured my exercise to build out with smaller leaps of creativity, supported by photos. Make it easy for them.

"What would you say?" an intent Pakistani in the front row asked me.

"Lost model, maybe. She's got the catwalk look, so I'd probably accuse her of being a runway model who has gotten lost and can't find her catwalk. That puts a tease in with the label."

I brought up the next photo. It was a brunette in winter clothes lighting a cigarette. "What do you see here?"

"She looks miserable," offered one of the audience.

"Right, good spot. I agree, she's somewhat bitch-faced. How would you work that into a label and a stack?"

The Pakistani's hand shot up and I looked closer at him. He had wild wavy black hair and wore thick glasses. I imagined he was probably a jihadi sent by Saudi Arabia on a scholarship to that nest of terrorist training, the School Of Asian Studies in London.

"She's on her way to a funeral. Her dad just died," he said.

There was an awkward hush. Errors in social calibration tend to create tense silences. I winced.

"Um, Salman. It is Salman, isn't it? You've expanded the theme correctly but it's a bit.... dark. Daygame has to be lighter than that."

The students gave it a good try but over a sufficiently long time frame, their chumpiness was always going to come out. It was especially noticeable from my position standing at the front of the room looking across the audience because right behind the noobs lounged a handful of my experienced friends, such as Ash and Onder. Black was contrasted to white, starkly. Herein lay the challenge: it was my job to nudge these lads further along in their project of self-development until the Salmans of this world became more like Ash or Onder.

We wrapped up the "how to daygame" presentation at lunchtime and plates of complimentary food were brought up from the pub kitchen. The students milled around getting to know each other while I decompressed my brain with small-talk amongst friends. The cameraman showed me some playback from the morning session on his viewfinder screen, and it looked good. I was getting decent material in the can. Before long it was time for the street infield session. We all paired up with students, one approach coach for each.

I got Salman.

"I'm not Pakistani," he insisted as we walked down the pub stairwell and onto the quiet street. "My dad is Indian and my mum Irish. I'm half white."

I spotted a viable girl walking towards us on the opposite side of the road carrying a white Pret A Manger paper bag stuffed with takeaway food. Her hair was dyed red in a modest natural hue and she wore a wool cardigan over a t-shirt. Probably an intern from one of the advertising agencies on her way back to the office to eat lunch at her desk, I surmised. My guts churned, because I needed to push Salman into a set but this girl looked out of his league. He was focused and intense beside me, talking quickly.

"I'm a maths PhD," he was saying. "I work in tech." Oh god. A Pakistani maths nerd with *Big Bang Theory* hair and fashion. "Oh, there's a set. I'll do her," he continued. He ran across the road while I stood still, bracing myself like a condemned man who hears the captain of the firing squad order them to take aim.

I may have closed my eyes.

So imagine my surprise when Salman completed a textbook-perfect run-around to get in front of this lucky lady, at correct distance, and then confidently told her to stop. From the opposite side of the road, the distance was too great to hear the chatter but that didn't matter yet, as getting an assessment of his non-verbals was more important at this stage. The girl smiled, stopped, and gave him a few minutes. She seemed to enjoy it. Jesus, *he* seemed to be enjoying it. I'd expected him to be terrified, dragging himself into set like he was about to eat a pork sandwich in front of an Imam. *He's doing the Daygame Overkill style*, I realised. All the subtle giveaways were there: the gently rocking hips, the schoolboy-like bashful kick of the heel, the step forwards. It was like watching myself in an alternate universe, if I'd been born an awkward Pakistani maths nerd.

What an eye-opener.

The redhead eventually gave some excuse about having a boyfriend and went on her way. Salman came back with a satisfied expression, though whether that satisfaction came from the set itself or his having demonstrated competence to me in daygame, I didn't know.

"Good set. Very textbook," I said. "I want to see another one or two before I give any specific feedback."

Off we went towards Regent Street and Salman opened every viable set, putting in a solid workmanlike performance each time. I quickly realised he was an odd mix of two incongruent opposites. His vibe was awful. It was dark, intense, and mechanical — like the black-clad ISIS executioners robotically sawing through the necks of captured journalists. That's the opposite of the light carefree happy vibe a daygamer needs. However, Salman wasn't one of the typical Pakistani no-hopers that clutter London's busy streets. His technical application of the London Daygame Model was outstanding. All the high intelligence and diligence he'd once applied to excel in mathematics was now channelled into daygame. There was potential here.

"How many sets have you done?" I asked.

"About a thousand."

"Right, that explains it. You have absolutely no issues with the model. You're doing it right. Your weaknesses are all in the subtleties, mostly vibe. That's what we need to work on."

There's only so much you can do in an hour but I gave him some pointers on loosening up his body as he jogged up to catch a girl, to visualise a secret joke before opening in order to get the right type of smile, and other little tricks. He did exactly as I told him and was a pleasure to teach, showing visible improvement immediately. When first leaving the pub I'd thought I'd drawn the short straw but it turned out to be a fun session. He was a more interesting character than I'd expected. Time was up and we walked back to the pub. I gave him a short summary.

"Salman, I think you can — for the next six months at least — de-prioritise your further technical learning. You are doing everything in the model to a competent standard. Body language, opening, stacking, running attraction and all that stuff is fine. Not perfect, but good enough. First thing is to work on your personal presentation, so you look cooler. Second, and this is a bigger project, is you need to soften your vibe. Lighten it up. If you can improve your vibe, all that technical stuff will start hitting the sweet spot and your results will shoot up."

"Thanks, I'll do that."

He deserved recognition for the level of skill he'd already attained. I thought through how best to pay him a compliment.

"I must admit, I'm surprised. I really thought you were going to be difficult. You've got the best daygame I've ever seen in a Pakistani."

"I'm Indian. Half-Irish."

"Oh, right."

Julieta arrived. I briefed her on the planned demonstration exercises and she enthusiastically played her part. By the time we wrapped three hours later, I was exhausted. The camera-man and I decamped to a nearby cafe so he could upload the video footage from his memory cards to my laptop's hard drive. Julieta hung around reading a book until we finished, which took forever because I had only USB 2.0 ports and the files were massive. Nothing would divert me from getting the footage, though, because it was the entire purpose of being in London.

Finally, two hours later, I took Julieta to dinner in a Pizza Express near Goodge Street. We caught up on the past six months apart. She'd found

Girl Junkie

a job in London and wasn't in any hurry to leave, though she had a short trip home to Buenos Aires lined up, her first time back since arriving in London.

"I don't know what to expect," she said. "I'm a completely different person now. All my friends are doing the same things as when I left. I love them dearly, but their conversation can be so boring."

"Will you tell them everything about your year in Europe?"

"Just the clean things. The cathedrals and museums, the Argentine cultural festival in London, the language study and so on. I won't say much about you, just that I had an English boyfriend for a while." She was smiling mischievously, enjoying the idea of having her own secrets while living thousands of miles from home.

I'd have liked to take her to my apartment to fuck her but she claimed to be exhausted and had work the next morning. That was probably true. I was disappointed, but Julieta had already done me one big favour that afternoon. It seemed too much to also expect her to let me do her in the ass.

Saturday was a rest day, which I passed meeting more friends. Sunday was devoted to my second seminar, *Womanizer's Bible*, which was a considerably less painful scheduling process. I'd become friendly with a professional writer around my age who lived in Camden with his Lithuanian girlfriend, and mother of his child, though she allowed him a measure of sexual adventure on his frequent world trips. Ryan was very much interested in the deeper theoretical musings of game and offered to help find a venue for the seminar and gave feedback on my first draft of the slides.

"I need a quiet function room, a door that closes, and an HDTV. Because of the subject matter it would be ideal to get somewhere a little gentlemanly — leather sofas, nice fittings, the kind of place you'd enjoy a cigar and a whiskey," I wrote in my email to Ryan. "We want to be a sophisticated bunch."

He came through, and booked the upstairs function room of *The Library* pub, in Highbury & Islington. It was a perfect venue, being a long open-plan room furnished like a Victorian-era pub. My cameraman was hired again, and I filled the ten audience seats by invitation-only. I wanted only intermediate daygamers there so that I could focus on higher-level topics and field more educated questions. It was to be held on Sunday, 8th of February.

I loved the idea of it being underground, of addressing a secret society of rascals who shared forbidden knowledge. My goal was to present my recent ideas on the meta-level of Game, and to avoid the on-the-street practicalities entirely. I discussed sexual market value, the mindsets of a successful player, and made the kind of sociological connections between Game and society of the kind so brilliantly popularised by the blogger Chateau Heartiste. Part of my presentation used a diagram of sexual market value created by the blogger Rollo Tomassi so I emailed him and he gave me permission to include it in the final product (and in return I gave him a few free logins to give away in one of his podcasts).

even steadier hands

The *Womanizer's Bible* atmosphere was completely different to the *Black Book*. At the latter, I felt like a hybrid motivational speaker and personal trainer, giving listeners a structured path to improvement and then jostling them along it. Even now, years later, I find coaching game can be quite stressful. Daygame is all about facing the real world naked, putting yourself in front of girls (not literally naked, yet) and trying to seduce them. Every day the daygamer is buffeted by the harsh gales of randomness and rejection. It's a breath of the wild and we come to envision ourselves as adventurers, like Hercules seeking out the Hydra in its lair. The *Womanizer's Bible* content, by contrast, was so high in its ivory tower that the grime of London's streets weren't figuratively visible below. I felt like an academic presenting a paper to his peer reviewers. There was a self-imposed pressure to deliver good material but no sense that the audience might reject it.

The presentation took around five hours and I was mentally exhausted. We had a long lunch-break with pub food funded by pooling the admittance fees behind the bar. On the cigarette breaks I drank pints of beer and chatted with the lads in the ground floor saloon. There was only one lad there I didn't remember meeting previously, a tall blonde Englishman called Rob, or "White Rob" as he was called to distinguish himself from "Dark Rob", another London daygamer at the event. White Rob looked, then, like a normal London young professional so it came as a surprise meeting him a few years later by which time hard gym work had turned him into The Hulk.

There hadn't been much time to draw breath all weekend but when I finally boarded the train home for Newcastle I felt a warm glow of accomplishment. I stretched my feet out and plonked my Uppercrust hog roast sandwich and Pret cafe latte on the table. There was an elderly woman on the seat across from me who looked like Miss Marple with her thick tweed coat and wool hat. Little did she suspect but stored on my hard drive on the laptop under her very eyes, was ten hours of high-definition video footage that would become two new products. Well, would eventually become products.

I did nothing at all with them for the next six months.

BEGINNER DAYGAME

CHAPTER 6
PRAGUE

Chapter 6
BEGINNER DAYGAME

Tom Torero was on the blower.

"Nick, remember that idea we had to do a beginner's daygame book, back in Minsk?" He was referring to an afternoon in April the prior year, in Belarus, when we'd sat at a table in Guru Cafe on Karl Marksa street dictating into an audio recorder. It was the same Guru Cafe wherein Richard La Ruina, Minsk-based owner of *PUA Training* and star of a truly execrable Playstation 4 'seduction' video game, finally caught up to Tom a few days later and punched him in the ear. I was sitting across from Tom that day too.

"Yes, I remember." My memory was rather vivid in this case, it preceding the fisticuffs so closely.

"I was thinking we should do a book and video tie-in. Shoot some infield and edit it into a how-to video for free on YouTube, and up-sell to a £10 PDF book. Up-sell that book into our proper products."

Good idea. In my existing books, I'd been strongly biased towards high-falutin' theory because that's what intellectually satisfied me. I more-or-less ignored the lucrative beginner's market. Tom had seen the runaway success of my *Daygame Mastery*. He'd glimpsed the possibilities of an independent income through his own *Badass Buddha* seminar product, an offering he'd pitched at a similar level as my upcoming *Black Book* that he'd filmed the previous autumn. By now Tom had now completely split from his former employer Andy Yosha at Daygame.com. The lifeless corpse of the once-thriving company was now owned by Yad. Given that in Minsk it had been Yad who had egged on Richard, saying, "Go on hit him! You promised you were going to hit him!" it was fair to say Tom wasn't on good terms with

Girl Junkie

the new owner either. Thus Tom was hard at work building up his YouTube channel. We'd already done some videos together for it.

"I like the idea, mate. Let's talk specifics," I replied.

"Here it is. We go to Prague for a weekend. I'll handle the camera-man. We'll crank out some sets on video and then I'll edit it all. You do the book. It's win-win. I like video editing and you like book production."

This was all true and I agreed. Thus I found myself in Vaclav Havel airport outside Prague early on Friday 6th March as a chill wind whipped through my flimsy leather jacket. I zipped the collar tight, donned my hat and gloves, and took the 119 bus into the city. My apartment was next to Mustek station, at the west-most end of the daygame hotspot. I had a little walkabout but was in no mood for daygame.

That evening I met Klara for dinner, a Russian post-graduate student I'd banged the previous November. We ate goulash in a traditional restaurant a few streets from Wencelas Square, had a drink, then I took her back to apartment and banged her out. That consolidated her as a regular, something I'd been uncertain of given the passage of time since we'd last met. The next morning I met Tom for an early coffee under a crisp bright blue sky, to discuss plans.

He was waiting outside the iconic New Yorker apparel shop on the square, a popular meeting point. The weather had gotten out nice so the streets already buzzed with tourists. A long-haired street performer dipped long poles into a bucket of soapy water and waved them through the air, creating a cloud of large transparent bubbles. Little kids whooped and hollered as they jumped around chasing and popping them. A few Segueway riders rattled past on their motorised scooter contraptions. At night the square would fill up with African strip club touts dressed in matching long red wool jackets but it was as yet too early for them to make an appearance. I noticed a shifty Turk milling around by New Yorker, of military draft age with a thick-set body and wavy hair to his ears. Behind him, I saw Tom waiting.

"Hey boss!" I called, and strode over. "Was the flight alright?"

"Yeah, no bother. Here, I'll introduce you. Samir, Nick. Nick, Samir."

I found myself shaking hands with the shifty Turk. He didn't seem as shifty up close, though his eyes held an odd intensity. Tom had offered him free coaching in exchange for coming over to serve as camera-man. We adjourned to a Costa cafe on the corner behind New Yorker and ran through final logistics. It was all rather simple. We'd take turns wearing Tom's big obvious wireless microphone, with its big blue flashing light, clipped to our chest. Samir would follow at a discreet distance and any time we wanted to open, we'd signal him to start recording. The technical aspect of recording street infields is extremely easy. It always amazes me how people can mess it up. The tough part of recording yourself is the psychological effect of knowing the tape is rolling. I find such pressure can upset my vibe.

We'd agreed our sets would follow the model closely: Open, Stack, Vibe, Invest, Close. There'd be no messing around or freestyling. Our purpose was not to impress viewers with a highlight reel but rather to give a clear demonstration of the sequential model. It felt limiting, but was the obvious best strategy for our mooted product.

After a couple of hours walking up and down Wencelas square and the shopping street leading to Palladium mall, Na Prikope, we'd gotten a few infields each. Tom struggled to find his vibe so his sets were flat and strained. It didn't worry me because we all have off days and I was confident he'd find his form the following day.

I got lucky with a visiting Russian tourist called Yana. She strode along Na Prikope, the cobbled pedestrian shopping thoroughfare, in rickety black heels, black tights, and a short skirt. She was so obviously Russian that both Tom and I turned to look at each other and laughed. Nobody but a Russian — or perhaps Ukrainian — girl would be dolled up as if for a nightclub at two in the afternoon on a fresh spring day. I had the microphone, so it was my set. Samir started the camera and I got ahead of her. The whole set is on my YouTube channel and also the bonus features section I added to *Daygame Overkill*.

It felt good immediately. Yana couldn't speak much English so I mostly fluff-talked very slowly and got in close to her. Eye contact was exceptionally strong and I felt the familiar thrill of sexual tension. *I've got a good set on video*, I thought. You could walk around with a camera on you for days and not find such a simmering sexual hook point, yet I'd already gotten one. I blabbed on to fill the silence but none of that mattered as Yana was sizing me up non-verbally. She liked me. She was from Tajikistan, a country whose female representatives were not yet acquainted with my DNA. I'd have liked to invite Yana for coffee immediately but we were filming and needed more sets. We exchanged numbers and a promise to meet in the evening after her sightseeing concluded.

The rest of the day's filming was so-so, both of cranking out mediocre sets. Tom had brief success with a tall MILF in the queue to a fruit juice bar and their flirting looked great at a distance, so it came as a surprise when she wouldn't give up her telephone number.

"You seemed a lot bolder than usual there. More touching, more excitable vibe. Looked great," I said.

We soon tired and called it a session. Yana had agreed to meet for a drink but Tom, Samir and I had a few hours spare until then. We filled it by shooting theory footage, explaining daygame technique to the camera. The top floor of Palladium mall has an expansive food court so we sat at a quiet cafe and took turns talking into the camera. Our agreement was to rigorously adhere to a fifty-fifty split of screen time so that neither one of us came across as the senior partner in the project. Soon, we'd logged an hour of quality material to bolster the infields. Time was now pressing so I begged off home, showered, and changed. Next up, some magic with the Tajik.

Would I get a same day lay with a hot communist on my first day of 2015 daygame? Perhaps that was too much to count on. I fancied her a lot so I was optimistic. Tom commandeered the video camera and came with me, hoping to at least obtain footage proving the number close had led to a real date. Yana wanted to meet in the lobby of her hotel, a little east of the Old Town, in Florenc.

So, at eight o'clock I found myself waiting in a stiff leather sofa chair in the lobby of Hotel Merkur. Tom sat at another table a discreet distance away, maintaining a clear line of sight. The elevator pinged and Yana stepped out. She walked across the lobby to me still wearing the same fancy get-up as earlier.

"I like a drink" she said.

I walked her outside and into a nearby traditional Czech bar located around a corner a few doors down from the hotel. I glanced over my shoulder to check on Tom following behind with the camera. A minute later he texted me, "I recorded a bit but had to go in case she got suspicious."

Yana explained she was flying home to Moscow early the next morning. She was on a business trip and had ditched her boss because he'd been hitting on her too insistently.

"He think he pay hotel he sleep me," she said. "I not that girl. I Tajiki."

I made a fast calculation of those elements of Yana's situation that were most relevant: hot, young, poor English-speaker, Moscow resident, and almost out of vacation time. The obvious conclusion hammered itself home: I must pull hard and try to bang her that night. There wasn't any time to piss about and her poor English would make the long route way too tedious anyway.

Bad Boy Krauser figuratively rolled up his shirt sleeves, coughed politely, and stepped into the fray. Almost immediately, I began touching her, playing with her hair and squeezing her thighs.

"What you do? You animal!" she screeched, not without a hint of admiration.

"Don't tell my mum."

By the time we reached the bottom of our first beers, Yana had well and truly gotten the message. The date was mostly non-verbal. We used Google Translate on the more complex sentences. Crunch time approached. Yana knew what I wanted and, should she disapprove, with the first drink finished she had a perfect excuse to claim fatigue and return to her hotel. She instead chose to join me for a second drink at another bar further around the corner. I aimed to bar hop on a route ending at my apartment.

We were kissing, sitting together on hard wooden bench seats in the corner of a pub basement bar. My hand roamed her arse and she reached up to cup my face between her hands. She moaned deep in her throat each time we kissed. By now, my hands had wandered up her shirt but she pulled back and re-arranged her clothes.

"No! You animal!" she admonished, unconvincingly.

"I like these," I said, pointing to her legs. "And I like these," my finger now poking her breasts. "And all of this," I indicated her jet black hair, "and this" as I held her chin between my thumb and forefinger. "I like you and I want to do bad things to you."

She blushed bright red and let me maul her some more. Prudence reasserted itself and Yana began bleating about her early flight. "I must go hotel," she said.

"Yes. Later."

"Now."

"Boring. I will show you my apartment."

"No. I go hotel."

I'd pushed all my chips into the table on achieving a fast pull, heating her up in the hope her sense of adventure eventually overwhelmed her chastity. Perhaps a finessed approach was preferable, but the language barrier made that impossible. I offered what comfort I could, talking about hobbies, family, and common interests, but conversation remained as stilted as porno dialogue. Lacking verbal options, I judged the smoothest route to be through physical escalation and a reliance upon our mutual lust.

"Another drink?"

"No. I go now." She stood up.

"Yes, let's go."

My chances were rapidly dwindling. *What is holding her back?* I asked myself. Attraction was certain. So much so I'd bet my life savings that her panties were going straight into the trash can that night, as no laundry detergent exists that can clean out the amount of wetness she'd been doubtless producing. So, what was missing? Comfort? If so, there was nothing I could do about that. There was one more possibility: perhaps she needed plausible deniability, for me to lead her until sex "just happened".

It was the only path to victory that seemed at all likely, so I turned my min towards leading her astray.

First, I tried walking her in the wrong direction — towards my apartment — but Yana remembered her route home as reliably as Theseus unspooling a thread before heading into the labyrinth to face the Minotaur. Adjusting to this, I followed her back to Hotel Merkur while spouting nonsense as if there was nothing in the world I'd like more than a nightcap in her hotel bar.

"I go room," she announced, from the lobby.

"No. Let's get one last drink."

Luckily for me she wavered by the escalator and let me lead her to the bar. I ordered whiskey, sat in a heavily padded sofa chair, and pulled her onto my lap. This was a major step forward in intimacy.

She welcomed it, settling in.

The waiter scowled as he set down my glass of Johnnie Walker Black on the low table while we both smooched on. Yana was writhing in excitement and I wormed my fingers between her legs to rub her ragged. She let it happen and for a moment I thought I'd tipped her over the edge and successfully impeded her decision-making.

"Ooooooh," she moaned.

I gave her a good rub for five minutes until my wrist ached from holding it at an odd angle. Yana looked sold. "Let's go up," I suggested.

"No, I can't. I not that girl."

"I'm that man."

"No!"

Her shutters came down. She stood up, pecked my cheek, then rushed off to the elevator, waving goodbye over her shoulder. There was no question about it. It wasn't an invitation to chase. She was breaking up our party.

I'd see Yana a year later in Moscow and we'd make out some more but by then she'd put on seven or eight kilos and I didn't even want to fuck her.

"No luck," I texted Tom then walked along the dark empty streets by Florenc and on to my apartment. Despite the ultimate disappointment, I was exhilarated. That afternoon, I'd only just started my first daygaming of 2015 and I'd already had a near miss with a very pretty Russian tourist. Coming off a very strong run of increasingly good results over the past years, I began to sense big things for the coming year.

Didn't go anywhere with the Yank

This went very well

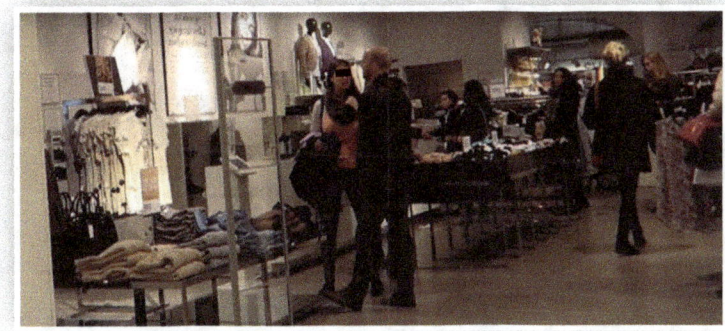
Later I was accused of hiring this girl

Chapter 7
COOL RUNNING

The next morning Tom wanted to meet one-on-one for a couple of minutes before Samir arrived. I found him standing outside New Yorker again and we walked across the road to Baguette Boulevard for late breakfast.

"What's up?"

"It's Samir. Don't take this the wrong way."

"Has he read my Twitter? Does he know I hate Turks? That's not true you know. Kenan is a mate, and so is Onder. I only hate Turks in the abstract because they keep invading Europe."

"No, no, no. Nothing to do with that. He just thinks you stole twenty pounds out of his wallet."

What?

Tom continued hurriedly, "obviously you didn't, but Samir is funny like that. He lives in a council house on benefit and gets depressed often. He makes stuff up. I'm just letting you know in case he seems a bit weird with you today."

I thanked Tom for the heads-up and we went back to New Yorker, by which time the quarrelsome Turk was waiting for us. He gave me an aloof nod by way of a welcome then we began the process of preparing our recording equipment.

"By the way," said Tom, offhand. "I banged Julia."

What?

He was referring to a Russian girl I'd banged in 2012 and with whom I'd continued an on-off relationship over the following two years. Long after we'd stopped dating, Tom had booked his first trip to Moscow, the previous winter. I'd suggest he meet her. I owed him a lay from 2011, when he'd set me up with his Romanian nymphomaniac fuck buddy, and this was the first good chance I'd had to pay off my debt. Julia had already met Tom when I'd brought her to a *Daygame.com* bootcamp in 2013 and said he seemed quite interesting. I continued to talk him up to her, pushing his image as a nomadic womaniser. When Julia moved to Moscow from Kaliningrad I'd floated the idea of her showing Tom around, to which she agreed.

A week before Tom's trip I'd explicitly told them both that if they liked each other, they should fuck. After that, I hadn't heard a whisper from either of them until now, in March, three months later.

"We had a karaoke date first, with Julia and her friend," Tom explained. Samir was still fiddling with the camera. "It was hard work. I thought that was all there was, but then a few days later she messaged me fishing for a date. I took her out, we got drunk, I popped a Cialis and banged her all night."

"Nice one," I said, relieved I'd finally settled my debt to him. Then we turned the conversation towards our immediate task, of filming in-field footage. It struck me as odd that neither of them had said anything in the three months since the sex I'd helped facilitate. I resolved to ask Julia about it.

"I want to get some indoors footage today. Girls sitting in cafes, or browsing shops. The ambush sets. It'll help the students realise it's not all about street stops." Tom was a natural teacher so he always had an eye on how to convey concepts. I was more of the ivory tower intellectual type. I just wanted to explore the concepts and build an accurate model. I didn't much care if anyone understood it.

We walked to a Starbucks by Mustek, in a tiny shopping mall that overlooked a large mechanised sculpture of Franz Kafka's head. A hatchet-faced blonde girl sat at a table plowing through a coffee-flavoured milkshake. Tom gave Samir the 'go' signal and waded in. The set went well. The blonde was surprised and possibly a little irritated, like a hippo interrupted in feeding, but Tom charmed her and she soon smiled and gave up her telephone number.

"Thank fuck for that," he said, checking the footage a minute later on the camera viewing screen. "Finally got a decent set taped."

I knew that Tom could really turn on quality daygame given sufficient time to hit his vibe, but time was against us. This was our final day. Tom kept the wireless microphone most of the next hour so he could get a few more good infields. I'd been lucky the previous day, including a great chatty set with a tall blonde American model. She'd given up her number and replied to my messages, but was leaving town. We'd tentatively arranged a date for later that same night, after Yana, but when the Russian had come on so well I'd postponed the American. There's a chance I backed the wrong horse, and the American would've been more willing, but I doubted it. The set hadn't felt very sexual either on the street or in our follow-up messages.

Finally, Tom hit some form and declared himself satisfied with his in-field haul.

"Let's eat at the food court again," he said and I agreed. Upon arriving at Palladium mall I suggested foregoing the direct upward escalator from the entrance hall to the food court, arguing we could instead take the long way floor-by-floor to get a last chance at finding sets in the mall. "I'm finished, mate," said Tom, "you take the microphone."

I wired up and almost immediately saw a pretty brunette walk into H&M. I indicated to Samir and followed her in. Tom had his indoor sets so I wanted one of my own. It went well, a giggly enthusiastic girl called Veronica. I'd have liked to idate her but we were hungry so I took a number. Upon re-watching the footage later I regretted having bailed on her because there was a real spark — not exactly a can't-miss SDL but a good solid idate prospect worth pursuing. Hilariously, in the foreground of the video, midway through the set, a small child takes a tumble right in front of the camera. That too is on my YouTube.

We ate. Tom suggested we go bobsleigh riding the next day, before his flight home. There was a dry slope up in the hills outside the city. I agreed. Our last work-related task was to shoot 'filler' footage for use in video montages. We walked around malls and streets with a camera following, then back at Tom's apartment we recorded ourselves getting suited and booted for daygame, inspired by a similar scene from Arnold Schwarzenegger's eighties action flick, *Commando*. Coincidently, that's the same movie Jon Matrix used to supply himself with his PUA pseudonym.

My little Ukrainian blonde Oksana came over that evening and I banged her. It was fun for the hedonistic thrills but I was losing interest in banging girls more than once. There just wasn't any achievement in it. Whereas having a rotation of regular girls had once satisfied my ego, to brag about a "harem", nowadays it felt like work. Like having to mow the lawn or clean the car. It puzzled me that having a lithe twenty-year old hottie in my bed could be so unsatisfying.

Tom's YouTube channel was growing and he worked hard to release regular content. He was still finding his way and honing his editing skills. What was originally a platform to show infields — to demonstrate his bona fides and show off to the crowd — had now begotten a series of podcasts, theory videos, and, increasingly, lifestyle vignettes.

"I'm doing the flowmad thing," he explained, over coffee at the bobsleigh reception building up in the mountains. It was a large cabin of logs. We hadn't yet been down the slope. Frankly, it looked dangerous.

"That's the flow — and the nomad, yes?"

"Correct. There's a digital nomad revolution going on, inspired by Tim Ferris' *Four Hour Work Week*." I remembered seeing that book on a table in Waterstones bookshop in Blackfriars, while I worked at the investment bank. Tom continued, "I was thinking, *isn't that what we do?* This euro-jaunting PUA coach lifestyle is precisely what Ferris talks about, only our version is better. Those chumps all sit in Starbucks tapping on their Macbooks then go home and watch porn. We actually do something in the foreign cities we visit. We have daygame."

Yes, indeed. I'd come to describe the Ferris-inspired material as 'freedom porn'. It was tailored to a customer base of frustrated cubicle jockeys who were locked into office work and had little control of their lives. Ferris was selling escapism. There are some digital nomads who live the dream — I'm friends with some of them — of beach huts in Acapulco, or yoga retreats in Thailand, and safaris in Kenya with the missus. Most of them, however, merely tap away on Macbooks in Starbucks like nerdy autists. We were different. We went out and engaged with the locals, or at least the female locals under thirty who rated a six or better. We answered the call of the wild.

Tom continued, "Kajabi's video hosting gives me three product slots on my subscription and, after *Badass Buddha* and *Conversation Ninja*, I've still got one spare. So I'm doing a *Flowmad* video product. It's nearly done. Already filmed. I'll coin it in and it won't cost me fuck all."

"What's it about?"

"There's a theory piece. I have a white board in my Soho room so I stood in front of that and talked to the camera. Then I recorded the good daygame streets and date venues in Prague. Edit all that together with some old videos of me snogging birds and I've got a product. $99, I reckon."

"People will buy that?"

"I reckon. I like doing the lifestyle stuff. My favourite YouTubers have a million subscribers and they travel the world hang-gliding, scuba-diving, lighting candles in temples and stuff. People eat it up and I think I'll enjoy making the content."

It sounded awful to me, but then again I'm set in my ways. Tom always had liked travel. That winter he'd been in Finland riding a husky sleigh through the snow to see the Northern Lights whereas I'd been in Marbella wisecracking with Romanian prostitutes. I'd watched his sleigh-ride video. For five minutes I'd thought, *that's awesome! Why don't I ever do that?* By the ten minute mark I was bored and thinking how I'd survive in a freezing cold cabin without video games. The only reason I'd accepted Tom's invitation to go dry-slope bobsleighing was as an awkward compromise — to tell myself I did sometimes act a little adventurous, but without straying too far from Starbucks and McDonald's.

I finally got to know Samir. He seemed to have concluded I hadn't in fact stolen his money so now he was friendly. His passion was music and he showed me a few tunes he'd written and recorded. They were good. Not my type of music, but clearly he had some ability. Then it was time to go bobsleighing. The staffer stood us next to a sleigh and explained how it worked. It was like the toboggans seen in the Winter Olympics but rather than traversing a winding tube hollowed out from snow, the experience was recreated by sheet metal, rivets, and supporting poles. It was somewhat akin to a roller-coaster, but downhill and at ground level. Just like a roller-coaster, it looked really dangerous. I noted we were far from the nearest hospital and I didn't rate my chances of an ambulance getting up that hill fast enough to rescue a serious casualty.

"I'll go first. Let's do it!" said Tom. He jumped in and flew down the bank as a cacophony of clanking and screeching metal echoed up the hill like a subway train braking in a tunnel. He wasn't wearing a helmet. I looked around. There weren't any. How cavalier.

Samir went next. Then it was my turn.

There was only one way to control the sleigh, a handbrake at the base of the seat, between my legs. It was a fail-safe mechanism in that I needed to push down against the spring to release the brake, and leaving go would release the pressure and thus rapidly apply the brake. So far, so good.

"Are there safety helmets?" I asked.

"No," said the surly Czech staffer as he put his foot against the back of my sleigh and gave it a push forward.

I picked up speed at an alarming rate so I relaxed my pressure on the handle and slowed to a comfortable speed. It was Sunday afternoon, after all, so not a time for racing around like a maniac. Really, I should've been in church. The ride took in five or so banked corners before giving out onto a long flat braking area and then a chain-ride back up the hill much like a grounded cable car.

I'd enjoyed my flirtation with catastrophe.

Tom bombed down again, a confirmed daredevil compared to me. His cheeks flushed and he was high on the adrenalin. "Awesome!" he enthused. Samir was equally enamoured. I didn't really see what the fuss was about. Perhaps I should go faster?

"Let's take turns videoing for the channel," said Tom, whipping out his GoPro camera on a selfie stick. Then he bombed down again, gurning and shouting into the camera lens he held out in front of him. I took it down the next turn, emboldened to go a little faster than my first run. The speed loosened me up and I dare say there was some whopping and hollering of my own production.

We'd noted a speed camera near the end of the slope, just before the final corner. Tom wanted a race.

"What is this, *Need For Speed*?" I remonstrated.

He went first and seemed to be zipping along. *Fuck this*, I resolved. *I'm beating that*. I never did like Tom beating me at stuff. I leant back almost horizontal like I'd seen tobogganists do on television and released the brake. The sleigh rumbled a little and on the first dip suddenly picked up speed, alarmingly so.

Someone had hit the afterburners. What had been a calm balanced ride at half-speed was suddenly a rattling deathtrap and I felt like I was sitting on a volcano about to blow. Still, I couldn't bring myself to slow down. The last banked corner before the speed trap approached and despite an increasing sense that I was behaving very stupidly indeed, I kept the handbrake pressed down and, thus, off. Centrifugal force pushed my little death machine right up into the curve and almost shot it over the top but a little braking kept me on track, literally. Then the nose of the sleigh corrected and barrelled down the straight with the speed trap visible to my right. Tom's speed from thirty seconds earlier was displayed on the screen: 45km/h.

All-in. Death or glory. What Torero can do, Krauser can do better!

I leaned back into my most aerodynamic posture and whizzed passed the camera. A fraction of a second later I saw the board register my speed: 55km/h. Even on the level straight the sleigh seemed intent on spinning off into the trees, bucking and thrashing below me. The final corner approached at terrifying speed and I suddenly realised I'd blundered into a literally deadly risk. I was travelling at 55km/h on a little metal sleigh, on a sheet metal half-pipe, and all around me stood vertical steel poles and tall trees. I wasn't wearing any safety equipment. Not even a helmet. You can imagine what smashing into a steel pole at that speed would do to my pretty face.

Imagine the loss to the daygame community.

My insane competitiveness vaporised and I released pressure on the brake for what I hoped was a controlled deceleration. It worked, but not quite well enough. I barrelled into the next curve and rode up high on the upper edge, the right-side rail on my sleigh not quite going over the lip and into air. Had I been racing only slightly faster it would have, spinning out of control and flinging me somewhere into the treeline. My death machine seemed to hang suspended for seconds — probably only micro-seconds in real time — then eased back into the racing line. The rails bumped and threw me forward a little, which caused me to lose grip on the handbrake, suddenly slowing the bobsleigh. That caused my body to lift completely out of the seat and I tipped to the inside of the curve and landed with my chest against the inner lip of the track, bouncing off the metal ridge at about 30km/h before somehow landing back in my seat.

"Fucking OWWWWWWW!" I bellowed.

Luckily, I'd accidentally landed back in the correct position and the final incline of the track slowed me down. By the time I came out of the curve I was in full control of my vehicle. Nonetheless, that was me done with these new-fangled 'adrenalin sports'. I could've literally killed myself there. I'll stick to daygame, thank you very much.

I put a brave face on it as the sleigh rattled up the cable ride back to the starting line. Tom and Samir waited, commenting favourably on my speed record. We'd all finished and went inside for a Czech lager. Halfway through the first pint, the adrenalin wore off and the rib-cage over the left side of my heart throbbed painfully. I'd once cracked two ribs in Brazilian Ju Jitsu class, in 1998. This felt the same. Only now I was seventeen years older and less resilient.

My ribs were so sore as to require painkillers the next four days and remained aggravatingly painful for the next six months. They'd continue to aggravate me in the weights gym anytime I needed to expand my chest or put pressure upon it, such as with a lean-over barbell row on a bench. It took two years to heal completely. The injury made me intimately aware of my aging, and with it my mortality. Six years of daygame had made me feel young again — invincible. Now I'd almost killed myself in a fit of reckless abandon and was carrying the evidence that my body didn't heal as fast as it used to. It put a dampener on things.

I told John about it over the phone.

"Do you think Tom was trying to kill you?" he asked. "Egging you on because he knows you can't let him win." I'm pretty sure he was joking but such is John's dark imagination one could wonder.

"God no, not at all. But I have learned that this flowmad shit isn't for me."

Tom and Samir left the next day, after we finalised the post-production responsibilities. I'd take full control of the *Beginner Daygame* book and Tom the video. We'd keep each other in the loop during production, but we agreed it was best to leave each other to our specialisms. Too many cooks spoil the broth and all that.

I remained in Prague a few more days, flying home on the 15th. I banged Klara again and would've had Oksana over but she was out of town visiting family. I also had two awkward dates with other girls. Readers of *Adventure Sex* will recall I almost banged a Serbian virgin called Ivanna and did have a fling with a Kazakh called Sabira in my Prague trip the previous November. I was able to get them both out again for coffee in the Costa behind New Yorker (which has since between replaced by a wine bar called *The Alchemist*).

I didn't know where I was at with Ivanna. I still wanted to bang her and was no longer in a rush to accomplish the feat. Back in November I'd been riding a crest of abundance, having poked four girls in six days, so my forbearance for the nineteen year old virgin's reluctance to have sex was somewhat lacking then. I'd impatiently cast her off. Three months of no girls over winter had changed my mind. It was rattling the whore in Marbella that finally broke my mind, making me think *what is the polar opposite to these unsatisfying whores?* A timid virgin, of course. So I'd tentatively re-engaged with Ivanna over WhatsApp and she'd responded. We met for coffee not really knowing what the other wanted. I played it slowly, we chatted, and then kissed a little at the end. I didn't try to bring her home. Awkward though it was, I felt she was back on an even keel and would meet me any time I returned to Prague.

Sabira was of a different mind. She looked stunning and dutifully sat next to me at a ground floor table in Costa and made good conversation. We kissed a little, so I knew she still fancied me, but she turned down my invitation to continue drinking. She politely disengaged at the end of the coffee and I took the obvious hint: she'd enjoyed our fling but had no appetite to take a place on my rotation. We talked a little more over WhatsApp until I confirmed her disposition then it faded away. I was disappointed. I'd have loved to have her as a Prague regular. She was achingly hot and fantastic in bed.

It had been a good trip. One week in Prague consolidated two confirmed regulars with Klara and Oksana, a near-miss Same Day Lay, and the raw material of a new product. I'd gotten my 2015 season started.

It's a really good introductory book

I'm sure I'm in the video somewhere

Chapter 8
PUTTING IT IN CRAZY

"Where are you now, Julia?" I typed into Facebook messenger.

"Thailand, still. I just lost my job! My company went bankrupt yesterday."

Julia had relocated from Moscow two months earlier, taking advantage of a job offer from a Russian company operating in a coastal Thai resort. We maintained regular contact and she was thoroughly enjoying herself in the winter sun. Julia was a thrill-seeker with a knack for getting herself into interesting scrapes and I'd constantly badger her to write a memoir, even offering to edit and publish it myself. She'd recently begun dating an ex-pat nightclub owner who hung out with Thai gangsters.

"And I was nearly raped," she added.

"What?"

"Last night. The boss called us all into his office at lunchtime to announce the company closure and lay us off. So, the girls and I drowned our sorrows in the bars. You know me, I got chatting to strangers so by the time I wanted to go home it was two in the morning and my friends had already left."

"Don't say you went home with a random man!"

"Nick! You know I'm not so easy!" This was mostly true, if not entirely. "I flagged down a scooter taxi but half-way home the driver took me into the hills. There were no people there and it was dark! I jumped off the back of the scooter when it was still moving and ran away. I have scrapes all down my legs!"

"Julia, that was more than a near rape. He would've probably cut you into pieces and fucked your skull. You know how brown people are."

"Ooooh, I know! Exciting isn't it!"

We continued our chat, getting up to date on our respective adventures in the fortnight since we'd last spoken. Julia knew all about my PUA identity and had even read (and enthused about) *Balls Deep*. I felt the moment ripe to inquire about my recently received intel.

"Tom told me he banged you in Moscow."

"Yes, if you must put it that way."

"Why didn't you mention it?"

The chat window showed Julia typing, then deleting, then typing, then deleting. Evidently, she was thinking carefully how to express herself on a delicate subject, which surprised me as I'd set the pair up and given overt encouragement for them to hook up.

"Well, I was embarrassed. It was a difficult situation. We met the first time and I brought Veronika with me. It was fun but nothing happened. Tom wanted to see me again but I was going through some problems with my flatmates and didn't want to think about it. Then, one night, I was suddenly homeless in the middle of Moscow. I slept in my car." So far, nothing surprising. Julia always got herself into scrapes. "The next day I cried all afternoon, sitting in my car. Tom happened to message, inviting me out. So I met him. He kept trying to kiss me. Finally, I got drunk and thought *what the hell? Let's do it!*"

"He said he popped a Cialis and banged you all night."

"God no! We had sex for ten minutes and then I sobered up, started crying again and wanted to leave."

I wasn't sure which of the two, Tom or Julia, I should feel sorry for. Equally, I wondered which of the two wildly-varying accounts bore the closest resemblance to actual historical events. Deciding I'd never be sure of the truth, I put it to one side and played video games.

Newcastle couldn't keep me for long. Tom and I planned a return to Zagreb for the beginning of April. Checking through available flights it looked like I might as well go via Prague and spend a few days there first. So, late in March I turned up at Vaclav Havel airport once more and this time I had booked a delightful apartment above a chocolate shop called Gold Pralines on the edge of the Old Town. Logistics couldn't be any better because Palladium mall was a hundred metres to my east and the Chapeau Rouge pub my, favourite venue from which to pull a date home, was fifty metres to the west. Even the weather was agreeable, if a little cold.

Right then, got to get myself daygaming properly, I thought. *It's all well and good swanning around with Tom but daygame is a solo sport. Get on it.*

I put my lucky leather boots on, psyched myself up in front of the mirror, then ventured outside. It was shortly after lunch. I felt like the daygame season began today so I was happy to simply put myself into the mix, wandering around the mall and along Na Prikope waiting for inspiration to hit. The success of 2014 had shifted my mindset. I felt like I'd now climbed the mountain of 'get good with women' and already earned my player card. Jaunting around Europe chasing skirt was now what I did. My calling. I was good at it.

Deep within me grew an overpowering urge to rest on my laurels. Surely the girls would recognise my increased stature in the community. Shouldn't they begin approaching me?

After an hour without talking to a single girl, I ruefully accepted that I would indeed still have to make the effort of opening myself. My internal dialogue wasn't too avoidant, and considering I was only just now looking to put myself about for 2015, I was pleased to notice my approach anxiety was diminished from prior years. At the beginning of every year I need to get over a hump but it seemed that hump was smaller each time.

I had an idea.

Why not record my thoughts, and publish the inner dialogue? My smartphone boasted a voice recording function and my hands-free set was tucked into my jeans pocket. I dug it out, untangled the cables, and plugged it in. What to talk about? *You feel like an advanced player now, Nick. Talk about that.* I rambled on a while, quite enjoying the therapeutic effect of externalising my self-talk to stop it careening around inside my skull, and decided I should do so more often. I could create a podcast out of it. Further rumination led me to conceive of the podcast as a free lead-in to eventually sell my London *Womanizer's Bible* video product, once I had edited it down.

I walked and talked for an hour before finally realising I still hadn't opened. This was just more avoidance.

A pretty girl walked by and I forcing myself in against the mild stirring of approach anxiety. She stopped to chat a little then excused herself. A second girl also humoured me for a minute. The accumulated cobwebs of five months without daygaming solo were brushed aside. I felt good again, like my old self. Whether it was statistical coincidence or due to my heightened awareness now that my state was improving, I suddenly saw more girls on the street. It was as if a theatre director had pulled one set of actors off stage — drab

Girl Junkie

middle-aged shoppers — and hustled a new group on for the next scene. Suddenly, there were hotties out. Not many, but there were definitely sets to be had if I wanted them and I most certainly did want them.

My eyes settled on a dream set.

I hadn't yet fully itemised and categorised my theory of how to define and recognise a dream set. That would come in later material. But I could feel it with this girl. She was a tall brunette, almost my height in her heeled leather boots, and wore tight-fitting blue jeans that made the quality of her bubble butt apparent to anyone walking behind her, as I was. More than that, her mannerisms sold me. She seemed to drift aimlessly, like a leaf blowing in a soft wind.

I opened.

Pavlina was Czech, twenty-two years old, and working a nondescript office job. She seemed to like me. On the downside, Pavlina looked a little crazy. Her grooming and fashion suggested a normal young woman but her eyes were on fire and she seemed checked-out, like she was experiencing our conversation on a slight time delay. I felt like I was playing multiplayer *Call Of Duty* on a lagging internet connection.

"Let's get a coffee, right now," I suggested and Pavlina agreed. We were stood in front of the French-themed boulangerie *Paul* on Na Prikope so I took her inside. We made small-talk in the queue. I ordered a cafe latte and Pavlina wanted herbal tea. There were unvarnished sturdy wooden tables in a row along the large windows as the cafe disappeared into an adjoining mall. Several were free, so we chose one and sat down.

It doesn't matter what we talked about. I like this, oh really? I like this other thing. Blah blah. We were communicating on a non-verbal level. It was obvious she was horny and liked me. I suspected horny was her natural state. It would explain the fire in her eyes which had pre-existed my materialising in front of her ten minutes previously.

After the coffee, Pavlina wanted to show me a different cafe, on the other side of the mall's small atrium. It was of Czech style and sold sweets and pastries. This time we ordered local beer and took our glasses around a corner into a smaller room away from the eyes of the bored staff. We sat across from each other at a round table and continued our inane chat.

I think she wants it. This is a same day lay.

Everything felt right, from the very moment I'd seen her ass and wanted to put my dick into it. Unlike my first two approaches of the day, Pavlina had struck me on a visceral level before I'd even seen her face. I just *knew*. I liked her and she liked me. Even now, as she blathered on about some fancy book she was reading, the sexual tension was palpable.

We were drinking beer at 3pm. Small signals are important.

I tested my hypothesis by finding an excuse to examine her hand. She left it resting heavily in mine as I caressed her fingers. Then I played with her hair. Yes, it was on. We finished the drinks.

"Let's go for a walk," I said. Pavlina nodded her agreement.

Two minutes later we were outside Gold Pralines and I was unlocking the door to my lobby.

"Should I come in?" she asked, uncertain about something though I wasn't sure what.

"Yes, you should."

It was a traditional Old Town two-storey building at least a few hundred years old. The lobby floor was cobbled and doors to two separate apartments opened onto the ground floor. We went up a staircase that folded back on itself to a landing with a door on the right and left. My apartment was to the right, and my landlady's other listing was to the left. Pavlina came inside but wouldn't take off her black leather boots. She seemed to be having second thoughts. We hadn't yet kissed.

My front door opened to a small interior hallway with the bathroom alongside on the right and a tiny study room on the left. Beyond that was a large kitchen and dinning room, and walking still further ahead I came to a lounge with an open plan leading to the bedroom. The apartment was far larger than I needed. I'd only rented it due to an off-season deep discount placing it into my budget range.

Pavlina stood in the archway between the kitchen and lounge. She wouldn't take a step further.

Oh dear.

Same day lays are usually plain-sailing until the moment you start undressing the girl. For a girl to be rattled within a few hours of meeting, while still sober, normally requires her to be very much up for it. Thus there tends to be no resistance until just before you get at it naked. Pavlina's sudden reluctance was problematic but not at all surprising. I quickly ran possible courses of action through my mind before settling on one.

I walked up to her, gently pushed her back against the wall and planted a kiss. She responded hungrily at first but quickly gathered her wits and pulled away. That told me her hindbrain was onboard the Krauser SDL Express — she was horny and attracted to me — but her forebrain was rebelling against something. Probably the speed with which we'd progressed from strangers on the street to being close to fucking. It had been barely two hours.

"No. This is too fast," she said. Then, without giving me time to reply, she turned on her heel and walked out. I followed her out. Once back on the cobbled Old Town streets she relaxed. "I have to go. I have things to do. We can meet another time," she said and we exchanged numbers.

I had much to think about over the next half hour. Best do such thinking while walking the streets. Where did I stand? Things were promising. She hadn't mentioned any insurmountable obstacles to sex. No boyfriend, no leaving town, no moral qualms. She'd been overwhelmed by the pace, that's all. Fair enough.

I've always had a hankering for Prague bratwursts

I approached seven girls that day and the last one was also memorable. It happened outside New Yorker. A very slim girl with curly light brown hair flashed past. She was a good twenty metres away and many shoppers and tourists were between her and I so she seemed to flit like a shadow in a haunted forest, from tree to tree. Nonetheless I felt the unmistakeable sense of purpose deep in my stomach. She was *right*.

It took only seconds to realise this but by then she was already in New Yorker and on the escalator to the first floor. Not liking the increased pressure of opening girls in shops, I gambled it was better to wait until she came out. That entailed risk, not least that she'd spent twenty minutes trying on clothes and by then all spontaneity would have drained from my vibe. Balanced against that, I saw no reason to take the lower odds of success that the high-pressure scenario of 'shop game' entailed.

I waited.

She came back out within minutes and immediately raced off along Na Prikope towards Palladium mall. I'd anticipated that, so I was posted up on that side of the street. She walked past and I got a good look. Long fashionable wool coat in dark pink, spray-paint-tight blue jeans, Converse desk shoes, and a nice leather handbag. She was exceptionally well dressed and her make-up looked professionally-applied. Although medium height she was very slim, yet had real hips and from what little I could surmise through her sweatshirt, she seemed to possess a fair rack. This was a very pretty girl. I could imagine her on a cosmetics advertisement or lingerie poster. She wasn't stunning to the extent men would all agree she was top tier, but she had that 'model' look if not quite being hot enough. An eight, for me.

I sensed rather than saw her check me out. That sealed it. I caught up and opened her.

"You. I like.... this," I said, gesturing my hands to include her whole person. I'd deliberately left it ambiguous whether I meant her body or her style. I liked both, for what it matters.

She smiled. Yes, she liked me. This would go well.

"I'm Nick."

"I'm Lydia."

"You're not Czech are you?"

"No, I'm—"

"Wait! Let me guess." She stopped and waited expectantly, playing along. I checked her out again and pretended to think hard. "Siberia. You're Siberian."

That genuinely surprised her. "How did you know? Yes, I'm Russian. From Siberia."

Girl Junkie

Like most of my daygame cold reads it was a statistical surmise based on my past experience. I'd learned the principle from reading Sherlock Holmes stories as a boy. He would, for example, research every type of tobacco on sale in London and examine the distinctive character of each when burned to ask. Thus should he find ash at a crime scene he could identify the tobacco, and thus inquire at the limited number of tobacconists selling the brand in order to narrow down a list of suspects. I'd been highly impressed by this creative interplay of homework, observation, and deduction. Years later I'd learned about the art of Cold Reading used by charlatans such as mind-readers, fortune tellers, and spirit mediums. There were books explaining how such imposters learn statistical trends in the population (e.g. most popular boy's and girl's names by decade of birth) and typical indicators of life situation (e.g. wedding bands, or untanned skin where a wedding band would've been prior to a divorce). Much like Sherlock Holmes, the charlatans would have a laser-like focus on key indicators to look for in a client, then a wealth of relevant statistical knowledge against which to apply in order to make a probabilistic statement that would impress the client.

I don't think applying this schema to daygame made me a charlatan, mind you. It was just fun and games.

I'd learned from long experience in London and Minsk to recognise Russians. They have a unique facial structure (or more correctly, a limited number of types) and a favoured fashion aesthetic. Once they talk, the national accent can also be identified, as can the typical grammatical flourishes they use when translating into English, which will differ from non-native speakers who speak the Romantic languages. These lessons apply to daygame everywhere. Specifically to Prague, I'd learned that many Russians and Ukrainians came to study at university and that of the former, Siberia was the most common point of origin. I didn't know why. Probably Russians from west of the Ural mountains simply stayed in Russia.

Anyway, the important point is that Lydia was pleasantly impressed and it increased my chances of shagging her. We chatted for ten minutes then I took her number. She had somewhere to be, otherwise I'd have tried to pull her into Paul's too.

That was enough for me. I was tired after an eventful day. I ate some Alaska pollack at the Nordic fish restaurant in the shopping mall food court and then collapsed onto my bed with music running on YouTube. I'd gotten back into the daygame saddle. I felt alive. There are so few feelings that can match the thrill of a good day on the streets. It has the brain-chemistry hit I'd found in kickboxing or extreme sports, but with the added thrill of knowing the very next set could lead to fast sex. There are, of course, other ways to get laid. However I'd always felt like I truly *owned* the success of getting laid from daygame. It was all me. Only me.

Though I hadn't actually had sex, as yet.

I let the fatigue drain out of my limbs then took a hot shower. My mind was still buzzing. I figured it was a good time to get cracking on my edit of the *Black Book* footage. I booted up the PowerDirector editing software on my lovely new laptop. It was a small 13-inch gaming laptop that I'd bought as an 'investment' to edit *Daygame Overkill* but with an eye firmly on taking my video-gaming with me on the road. It slipped neatly into my leather rucksack and I anticipated many hundreds of hours watching YouTube, movies, and games on it over my coming travels.

Two hours of editing later I was mentally frazzled. I slipped into a long deep sleep and didn't wake until noon the next day.

I pinged my leads over my first coffee, sat in the ground floor Costa cafe in Palladium mall. It's a well-known spot for daygamers because it's on the corner with the greatest footfall, between the main entrance and the side entrance to the tram stops. I noticed a familiar face, and tried to place him.

It was a man sitting at the next table. He was my height, my age, and also a skin head. However, this guy looked swarthy, possibly Turkish, and was in tremendous physical condition. He wore a tight black t-shirt which barely contained his muscular frame. His arms bulged, the skin glowing like mahogany, and were dotted with tattoos. *Got to be gay*, I surmised. Straight men don't get that level of condition without being deep into a sport. This guy had an aesthetic bodybuilder physique. He looked fantastic. Not like how Mirco Cro Cop or George Foreman looked good, but more like how Ricky Martin or Luke Evans did.

No, Nick. You're just being petty because he looks better than you.

I observed him for some minutes as carefully as I could without tipping him off. The last thing I wanted was him thinking *I* was the faggot in this encounter. The Costa cafe was a simple rectangle floor-plan with the counter tucked into one wall, a narrow upholstered bench with three tables against a second wall, a line of floor-to-ceiling windows looking onto the mall on the third side, and then a wide-open entrance completing the rectangle. There were a few tables on the mall side of the windows. The possibly-gay possibly-Turkish guy was sitting there people-watching.

Was he daygaming?

He'd claimed the best seat for fishing, with sight-lines of the mall corridor, the escalators, and the tram entrance. He was definitely scanning the crowd.

A few likely girls sauntered past, of the type I'd expect a keen daygamer to at least consider. I'd be able to observe the decision-making process — do I open or not? — etched onto his face in real time. The Turk didn't open. He seemed to stare right through them and only then did I realise he wore earbud headphones. By now I'd finished my coffee so I went outside Costa and began a loop of the ground floor, keeping my eyes open for sets. My loop ended with my walking past the big man and his eyes gave me a brief flicker of assessment, no different than he had any other shopper, before staring fixedly ahead as though I didn't exist.

I did a second loop. Then a third. My focus was on the mall-goers, trying to find a set. It was still quiet so I was soon looping back in front of the man. He still hadn't moved. No friends had joined him, he hadn't taken out a book to read, nor was he checking his phone. His coffee had long since been finished and cleared away by staff. What was he up to? He'd come to resemble a statue. A sentinel perched atop a Gothic cathedral, overlooking the town square.

I was getting unnerved now.

Surely he must be wondering why I was wandering around so aimlessly? He must've noticed me scanning the crowd. Nobody notices daygamers on busy shopping streets but that's because there are streams of pedestrians going about their business, moving from point A to point B. It's different when a people-watcher is staking out an area and you keep moving into his zone of interest.

Against all rules of daygame footfall probabilistic judgement, I went up the escalator to the less-frequented first floor just to get away from him. The last thing I wanted was to open a girl, get blown out, and then have a surly Turkish sentinel log my failure for god-knows what future purpose. I decided I'd do all my day's approaching on the streets outside. The weather wasn't at all bad, anyway.

Both Pavlina and Lydia replied to my pings. They appeared keen. I suggested a late-afternoon coffee to Pavlina and she agreed. Great. It's always nerve-wracking to get a girl into your apartment only to let her leave un-shagged. So many of them simply disappear from your life. Pavlina had cooled off, arranged her thoughts, and considered it wise to see me again. That's what I assumed. She seemed crazy, so who knows what her thought process really was.

When she arrived at New Yorker that evening she looked great. She wore the same knee-high black leather boots but this time with black tights, a tight skirt, and a thick grey wool sweater that was pulled tight across her breasts. She had better make-up than the day earlier too. I was very optimistic. We went off into the Old Town and found a quiet bar. For the second drink I took her to Chapeau Rogue. Plain sailing.

We'd only been out for two hours when she accepted my invitation back to the apartment. This time she took her boots off, sat on the sofa in the lounge, and waited patiently as I poured wine and set up music. The sexual tension hadn't lifted so Pavlina perched nervously on the edge of the sofa with her knees and ankles pressed together, sipped the wine, and waited for me to act.

I didn't hang about. I let her get halfway through the glass then took it out her hand, set it onto the table and kissed her.

All hell broke loose in the best possible way.

She jumped me on the sofa and straddled, pushing her chest into me and grabbed my head in her hands. Soft agonised moans escaped her as she writhed atop of me. Yes, she was definitely crazy. I took firm handfuls of her ass and tits, then set about undressing her. She was naked before I'd removed even my shoes and her body was good, though not toned. Full firm breasts and solid child-bearing hips made me moan a little too. I led her through the large archway leading to the bed and pushed her onto it as I undressed. Then we were fucking.

I raw-dogged her, something still quite new to me. I'm not sure why but it felt appropriate. She was dripping wet and when I pushed my dick into her she let out a wail like I'd stood on a dog's tail. Then she pulled me tight and scratched her long fingernails down my back. It hurt but she could've poured vinegar into the wounds for all I cared. I wouldn't have felt it because I was getting my notch and it's scientifically proven that a man is physically invulnerable during the first five thrusts of a new notch. Just like the first five frames of animation in the *Dark Souls* dodge roll.

Things got out of control fast and I loved it. Pavlina began screaming and panting, completely losing her mind in the sexual act. I hung on the best

I could as she bit my shoulder, squeezed me in a bear hug, and stared wildly into my eyes. Then she started crying.

"Are you okay?" I asked.

"Fuck me!"

I figured she'd probably enjoy being slapped, so I backhanded her across the face and she cried more. Not knowing if that was a good thing, I decided not to repeat the trick. I turned her over and banged her some more and now she was really throaty in her screams. She arched up, bending her head back to look at me, and then theatrically collapsed face-first in the mattress. I wasn't done, so I kept banging away. It resuscitated her so I was treated to another ten minutes of her wailing, thrashing, and moaning. I hadn't heard such a self-pitying racket since watching some Serbian cops eject a gypsy beggar from a restaurant in Belgrade. Finally I pulled out, dragged her off the bed by her hair, and made her suck me off until I came in her mouth. She swallowed and we lay in a helter-skelter of limbs on the bed, exhausted.

It had been fantastic sex. Truly memorable.

I banged her again and we fell asleep. She left early the next morning. Too early for me to get dressed and walk her to the tram station. We kissed goodbye at my front door and she looked content. I quite liked the idea of more Pavlina in my bed.

Chapter 9
BONES

Lydia had maintained a steady text conversation with me the previous day and we arranged to meet the evening after my romp with Pavlina. It was my last before flying to Zagreb to meet Tom. Having expended a year's worth of calories shagging Pavlina and then having the very attractive Lydia lined up for later I judged it reasonable to forego any further street game that afternoon. Instead, I edited more of *Black Book* and spent my final two hours in the cafe staring into space, satisfied.

I met Lydia outside Palladium after the sun had already set. Light from inside the mall cast a glow extending several yards from the heavy swing doors at the entrance, within which a dozen young adults smoked and waited for friends. A few yards further into the rough cobbled plaza each person walking by was just a dark silhouette, impossible to see their faces. Lydia was dressed nice, but I got the impression that nicely-dressed was her natural state, date or not.

She was excitable. That was a plus.

"Have you been waiting long?" I asked.

"No. Five minutes. How are you?"

"It's been a lazy day. I feel good, like a bear waking up after hibernation."

I led her to Chapeau Rouge which was as yet less than half full. We took a table at the back of the main room.

"I'm having a beer. What do you want?" I asked, as I hung my leather jacket over the back of a chair. My latest gambit was to choose a table for four, two seats each side, and then let the girl sit while I ordered the first round. That allowed me to smoothly place the drinks on the same side of the table and slide in next to her. If I telegraphed my intention by sitting down first, a timid girl may choose to sit opposite me, which would reduce my opportunities to create sexual tension early. Everything I did now was about efficiency. How could I get the girl with less fuss, less input, and less beating around the bush?

'Younger, hotter, tighter' had morphed into 'faster, straighter, cheaper'.

"I have beer too," replied Lydia and I sidled up to the bar.

Lydia took this lovely photo of me

Chapeau Rouge is such a good date venue it perhaps deserves a more fulsome description. It would be the setting for many adventures in the coming years. The Old Town of Prague is all situated within tightly-defined city limits. Imagine a large semi-circle with the river as the 'flat' diameter and then the curve as stretching from the East where it touches the river by a road bridge near Palladium and then along the Na Prikope shopping street until reaching another big bridge in the west by Andel. Although all of central Prague is nice, within this area everything is Old Town: Gothic and baroque architecture, traditional restaurants, souvenir shops, and thousands upon thousands of excitable tourists.

There's even more Old Town across the river, but after taking in the sights with Valeria one time I never returned. There's no daygame to be had up there.

The east side of the Old Town has the best nightlife such as a couple of nightclub-bars, my favourite being James Dean. It's where you can see all the late-night tourist pub crawls and shouting yahoos vomiting on each other. There are also a number of nice bars. Across the road from James Dean is Harley's, a rock bar fashioned after the famous motorcycles. It's a decent nightgame venue, for those brave or foolhardy enough to work an environment with five drunken Spanish men for every one female.

Chapeau Rouge is how I'd imagine the Parisian club Moulin Rouge if it was only two rooms, on a tiny budget, and owned by a beatnik. There was a nightclub in the basement but I'd never been down there and I'd yet to see a queue form to gain admittance. The ground floor is what mattered: two rooms only. The main bar was a long high-ceilinged rectangle with a few floor-to-ceiling pillars near the entrance with drinks rests attached, then a long table that could seat a dozen, and then a raised section against the back wall with a wooden bench for four with an associated table and a few stools on the other side. That's where I sat with Lydia. The second room was half the size of the first and had three high tables with high stools, another small bar, and a few wall-mounted televisions above head height.

So much, so bleh.

What made Chapeau Rouge special was its vibe. Prague has a wonderfully sleazy atmosphere in that the streets are all late-medieval beauty not far removed from a Gothic horror video game designer's wildest fantasies. Yet within these streets lie small pockets of sleaze: strip clubs, whorehouses, junkies, and drinking dens. It strikes the perfect balance between civilised beauty and the potential of wild adventure. Chapeau Rouge exemplified this balance being as it was housed in a beautiful baroque corner building several hundred years old. The bar was the usual dark burnished wood with rows of whiskeys and liquors behind it, and multiple lager taps on the front. The bar staff all sported tattoos, piercings, and rock'n'roll t-shirts but none looked shifty. They liked beatnik fashion but they weren't junkie scum.

It was all about balance. Yin and yang. Good and evil. Rock and roll.

Better yet, the proprietor had liberally decorated the walls with mounted skulls and bathed them with subtle coloured lighting, mostly purple and blue. It felt warm and edgy. Absolutely perfect for drawing out a girl's more adventurous side. The very walls seemed to whisper, "go on! Nobody is watching. You can follow your impulses here."

Girl Junkie

I'd not yet learned if Lydia would follow her reckless impulses but the date had started well. She spoke good English and tried hard to be interesting. Now that I'd seen her without a coat I was taking in just how slim she was. I've never seen a girl so skeletal while still retaining a firm round ass and tits weighing in at a solid handful each. She was the healthiest-looking skeleton I'd seen since Bones from the *Super Ted* cartoons I'd watched as a child. And she was awfully pretty. She had that heart-stopping iconic look. The look where you know there's not another girl in the world who looks like her.

Looking at her was pleasant. She was bottled sunlight, condensed gold, packaged honey. She was as Siberian as a girl can possibly be without breaking the law. I kept looking at her even as my hands went through the motions of checking out her rings, bracelets, and hair. My mouth was a kiss away from her right ear.

I took her dainty little Siberian hand and squeezed it. She smiled.

I kissed her before we'd finished the first drink. It was obvious she was a Yes Girl from the very first moment. The only questions were *how far will she go?* and *how fast can we get there?*

"The first thing I noticed about you was not, believe it or not, your lovely ass. No, what I first noticed was your fashion. It's very elegant but looks fresh and young." I was buttering her up like I wanted her vote, dropping in a sexual spike as a test, but it wasn't far from the truth. She blushed excitedly.

"I love fashion. I am building a business as a fashion photographer. I like photography," she said.

"What do you mean? Do you take photos of clothing, or poses, or portraits?"

"I do everything. Sometimes I do artistic portraits, other times it is like fashion shoots in magazines. It is a new business so I'm small. I do weddings also, for money."

I sensed a new gambit coming on. Some of my best material occurs spontaneously on dates. I see something and my inner-PUA immediately logs it as a future regular gambit. God almighty, I felt inspired!

"Are you a good photographer?" I probed, setting up the punchline. "Are you skilful?"

"I hope so. Many clients like my photos." Lydia seemed keen to impress me. Never in my life have I failed to get excited when a pretty girl with a tight ass wants to impress me. Not once. I was already visualising how it would look with her bent over and my dick buried deep inside it.

"Can you make me look beautiful?" I asked, affecting a modest look. She laughed. "You are already beautiful!"

I feigned relief, blowing out a long breath, looking to the ceiling, and leaning back. "Thank God for that! I used to be really handsome. My mum said I was the most handsome boy in the world. But then I did kickboxing and I got all the beauty punched out of me."

"You are still beautiful," she said, and reached over to kiss me again.

I invited her to my apartment at the end of the second drink. She accepted gracefully and accompanied me without a fuss, sitting on my sofa as I did the usual formalities with wine and music. Just like Pavlina twenty-four hours earlier, she straddled me and got hot and heavy. I pulled her sweater over her head and unhooked her bra. Her tits took me completely by surprise.

God, they were perfect. How could such a tiny, skinny girl have firm, high, full-sized breasts. Even the shape was perfect. A million comic book artists at a million drawing boards couldn't hope to produce a single sketch of such geometric perfection. There was no option but to pull Lydia forward and get a mouthful. She rested a hand on the back of my head and moaned softly as I indulged myself.

I was having a great time. If casinos were taking bets on 2015 being a great year, I'd have pushed my entire savings account all-in. First Pavlina, now this! I began wrestling with Lydia's belt and zipper. She wriggled away and the first ominous gust rattled my house of cards.

"No! I cannot today. I have girl's day."

The cry "FUCK!!!!!!" did not leave my mouth but its psychic energy echoed across the distant reaches of the cosmos, bouncing back with the power of a thousand suns. There was literally nothing in the world I wanted more than to bang Lydia. World peace... one hundred stars on Super Mario 64... an ethnically-homogeneous white Europe... nope, none of that mattered. All I wanted was to put my dick in Lydia's delightfully firm ass and then cum across those unfathomably nice tits.

Despite such modest goals, the universe was determined to frustrate me.

I stood up, with Lydia still attached, her legs wrapped around my waist. She weighed less than a McDonald's Happy Meal. I set her down by the window and pushed her to her knees. Then I pulled my dick out. She looked up expectantly, as if waiting permission. I nodded.

Lydia gave a great blow-job. To this day I wish I'd recorded it on a hidden camera. It looked like she'd go all night so I moved her towards the sofa, just for variety, and then pulled out so I could make myself come. She remained on her knees, looking up at me with her mouth open and tongue hanging out. I came on her face at first, but somehow it felt sacrilegious, like despoiling the Magna Carta, so I shoved my dick back into her mouth until the rest of my embryonic Aryan super soldiers were marched down her throat. She gave it a good gulp down and that was that.

I'd have liked Lydia to stay but she made excuses about work and study. We watched some YouTube, had another glass of wine, then I walked her to the metro station by the mall. It had been a thoroughly enjoyable evening. Well, obviously. How could it not?

I had my flight the next day. Both Pavlina and Lydia stayed in touch but unfortunately the latter claimed not to use social media. That meant our messages would be standard SMS and, as any travelling womanizer can tell you, that's a bad omen when you're jaunting around countries with different telephone networks.

Drinks with Klara

Chapter 10
BALKANISED

> "I've soured on Zagreb," I told Tom as we drank a beer in Bulldog pub in the Old Town of Croatia's capital city a few days later. "We daygamers are a superstitious lot and easily swayed by the early results in a new city. We're solipsists too. Ask a daygamer, 'how is City X?' and his assessment depends *entirely* on whether he got laid there."

We sat on leather sofa chairs with our backs to the bar. An open balcony ringed the room above us, the same place I'd taken Petra and Morana the previous Autumn for first dates. Both were tall university students featured on *Daygame Overkill*. I'd banged Petra that night and Morana had sucked me off. Such success seemed a long way off now.

"You don't have any good leads, then?" Tom asked.

"Nothing. There are two girls replying but nothing solid. How about you?"

"Nothing. That artsy girl came back to my flat last night but I couldn't beat her LMR."

We'd only been in town a few days so it was hardly disastrous but I couldn't beat the feeling that Zagreb wasn't the pussy paradise it had first appeared. The girls were very hot but in all the hours we'd traipsed the streets we'd been unable to find any walking around, much less shag them. It seemed Croatian girls had spent the whole winter eating McDonald's and ice cream, to judge by the amount of chubby asses we'd seen.

"Is it because our standards have risen?" I asked. "I'll freely admit that my first couple of years in Game I wasn't too discerning. I took plenty of phone numbers from eights, but I found the sixes far more likely to come out on dates and nothing was gonna stop me shagging them."

"Nah, Zagreb girls are hot. There's just not enough of them about. It's a small town, and the weather is shit. It's only the big busy cities that can maintain decent footfall in shit weather. We got unlucky. In summer it'll be an entirely different story."

We both mulled that over, looking into space and sipping from our glasses of beer. I liked this bar. It had smooth polished wood panelling and shiny brass fittings. I was in no hurry to face the blustery spring wind outside.

Drinking with Tom in Bulldog pub

"I'm flying back tomorrow. Got some coaching lined up."

"How's the business going?" I asked.

"Great. There's an untapped market since Andy and Yad pulled out. I can put together a couple of students in a city and get a good weekend out of it."

We spent an hour that morning sitting in my beautiful apartment by the train station as I showed Tom early ideas for our *Beginner Daygame* book. I wanted to go all-in on a detailed visual design heavy on demonstration photos and graphics so I'd sketched out some ideas. Tom had to rein me in a little, his greater experience of teaching a good counterbalance to my habit of disappearing down theoretical rabbit holes. He opened up his Macbook to show me some early rushes of the accompanying video. It was promising.

"Let me show you how *Black Book* is coming on," I said and plugged my laptop into the television with an HDMI cable. "This is just the early cut, mind. I'm still working on the visual design for the updated slides and I'm getting some music done for a proper intro."

We sat next to each other on the sofa and I double-clicked to open a file covering the same creative opening drills discussed earlier. We watched the video.

"Good idea, I like it," he said. "It's a nightmare getting students to use their brains. They all want scripted stacks. This gives them a good way in to what we do naturally now."

After about five minutes, I felt Tom had a good enough look to give me feedback. "So, what do you reckon? I think it'll eventually be about four hours, so I want to price it at $99. That's half *Overkill* and it's definitely not as deep or as impressive as that."

That's a beautiful apartment

"Daygame fans will pay anything. Even $199. But yeah, it's good for $99. What's next after Zagreb?"

"I've got one week here then I'm getting the bus to Belgrade. The flight back to Prague goes through Belgrade anyway so I might as well bus it. I'd like to give it another look."

I threw in the towel on Zagreb after Tom left. My leads were all flaking and only one came out on a date. She was an artsy girl who smoked thin cigarettes, had a subtle tattoo on her wrist, and every other element of the tedious artsy girl caricature. I'd have liked to fuck her because she was slim and pretty but talking to her was a chore. She felt like a Non Player Character in a video game, repeating the same tired old cliches which had grown stale in

1960s beatnik circles. None of it was offensive, mind. I'd simply heard it all before, many, many times, and there wasn't the slightest spark of originality.

My irony sensor couldn't handle it.

I'm sure there was a period in history when tattoos were a sign of rebellion and when leaning over your crossed legs with a cigarette hanging carelessly from your lip was the height of postmodern cool. This girl reminded me of Marla Singer from the movie *Fight Club*. It was the outsider as a fashion statement.

I still tried to take her home, but she wasn't having it.

"You don't take me very seriously, do you?" she asked.

"Frankly, no."

"I can tell. You are nodding your head and probing with short questions to make me talk, but you really don't care what I say. Why is that?"

My immediate answer was, *because you're a cookie-cutter teenage rebel who can't see she's as much a follower as the normie girls she seeks to distance herself from*. However, that wasn't the whole truth. Even if she'd been the most uniquely interesting girl in the world I'd have acted exactly the same way. She wasn't *that*, as even now I can't for the life of me remember her name.

No, my utter fatigue with pretending to show interest in her in order to bang her arose from some other source, and I wasn't sure where. Pavlina held my attention by her craziness and the roaring sexual tension we shared from the very first moments. Lydia equally enraptured me because I'd found her extremely attractive in a stylish manner than exemplified what I value in women. I hadn't been especially interested in their girlish prattle, but I had been interested in them, fundamentally, as people.

Not this one, though. Nothing stood out. She was just the one girl in Zagreb who'd agreed to a date that week. Notch fodder.

I decided politeness was needed, rather than truth.

"I think it's my mood. I have a few family worries back home that are always lingering at the back of my mind. Sorry."

Walking away from the date I decided I just wasn't in the right state of mind to keep daygaming, especially as the streets didn't present me with any girls I wanted on the occasions I did walk around. So I recorded a couple more podcasts and then retired to a cafe to read a series of John Le Carre spy thrillers. My mood was yo-yoing between the thrill of a new daygame season and a revulsion against the same thing. I couldn't figure it out. I'd have only two nights in Belgrade so it was easy to convince myself not to bother daygaming at all.

The coach ride along the motorway from Zagreb to Belgrade was agreeable enough and I continued to read spy novels. I took my old room overlooking Studentski Square and then messaged my regular girls to see who was about. Vesna was the most enthusiastic so I met her in Hot Spot Cafe across the road then banged her a half hour later. Her body had lost none of its wonder, with her big firm breasts, waspish narrow waist, and superhero-proportioned hips.

Very little going
on in Zagreb

She prattled on about being in love with a new boyfriend. I didn't mind, but her droning on grew tiresome so I eased her out and lay on my bed watching YouTube. Then I had an evening date with Milena. I never tired of her company as she was still the most beautiful girl I'd ever banged and her energy complimented mine perfectly. She enjoyed sitting next to me, looking up through her long eyelashes, listening to me talk about whatever was on my mind. She was also very good in bed.

I declared my first day in Belgrade a success. Milena stayed over then went to lectures in the morning. Suitably refreshed, I took a stroll down the Knez Mihailova high street to see if the urge to open would sneak up on me. It did, briefly. The first girl I opened, a Serb who'd grown up in and now lived in Paris, took a liking to me. She was in town a couple of days visiting family before returning to France. Physically, and in her mannerisms, she reminded me strongly of Vesna but with better hair and a lesser body. The weather was pleasant so we sat outside Aurelio cafe for a drink. After an hour I realised it wasn't going anywhere. She began talking about her boyfriend so, after a five minute grace period so as not to be obvious, I got rid of her.

My other regulars hadn't come through. Marijana was back home in Nis, Sofija was going through the 'hate' phase of her constant I-love-you/I-hate-you pattern, and Nina said she still had a boyfriend so she couldn't have sex with me. I returned to my room, collected my John Le Carre paperback, and sat back down in Aurelio. Looks like I'd close out the trip by reading.

To my surprise, Kalina pinged me on messenger. "Heyyy. You here?"

We'd met a year earlier, an unremarkable street stop near Republic Square. Kalina was twenty-four and worked in a nail salon. Not as well-educated as most girls I seemed to meet, she hadn't gone to university and couldn't speak a lick of English. In her favour, she was tall, leggy, and slim. She looked better from a distance than close up but when dolled to the max it was easy to want a piece of her. Sadly, I'd as yet had no such piece. We'd had two dates in 2014, both with her friend tagging along as translator. On the second date, the friend had left us alone five minutes specifically to let us kiss. Still, I'd written Kalina off. She hadn't put out and she didn't reply to my messages.

A month earlier, in March, things had gotten interesting. She'd sent me a picture of her (unremarkable) tits and drawn me into sexting. It was awkward stuff, as she couldn't understand my English and her replies were literal gibberish. But, she'd appeared to masturbate, to judge by the coy photos she'd sent to encourage me to keep sexting. Then she'd maintained a radio silence. A few days before I arrived in Belgrade she'd popped up again, liking some of my photos on Facebook. So, I sent her a message while still in Zagreb.

"Hey, I'll be in Belgrade this weekend. Just a couple of days."

She replied fast, full of smiles. "Yes. Great! We meet!"

"I arrive late Saturday night."

"Okay, we meet Sunday night."

When Sunday night had come, she cancelled, claiming she needed to go to a party. So I'd had Milena around. When Kalina suggested Monday, today, I agreed but wasn't hopeful. Kalina had a way of pissing me around. So, her message was both a surprise and, logistically, fortuitous. It seemed she was checking in about the arranged date for later than evening.

"Hey crazy," I replied. "I'm still in Belgrade."
"Oh heyyyy! Good."
"Let's meet."
"Okay."
"Today. 6pm."
"I work until 8pm," she wrote in Serbian, which I translated with Google.
"Okay, 8pm."
"8:15"
"Okay."

I didn't know whether to be pleased about this. No doubt, I wanted to bang her. She was pretty, it was a notch, and it would enliven my otherwise mediocre trip. But I was also reminded of the grating tedium of our prior two dates and her flightiness in text. The odds looked grim, but I had nothing better to do. I didn't know how Kalina would irritate me, but I knew she'd find a way.

She's probably going to cancel with a bullshit excuse, I thought. *She's a princess.* The clock inched around to 8pm and I was still sitting in my apartment, utterly non-plussed. My optimism hovered close to zero. The whole day I'd possessed neither vibe nor sexual intent. Stunning girls walked past me all afternoon and I couldn't manage a chubby much less a full boner. Try as I might, I couldn't even visualize banging them. Resentfully, I slipped on my shoes and walked up to Republic Square for the date. *Funny how expectations change everything,* I mused.

Nonetheless, I'm a disciplined player so I needed to formulate a game plan. My mood sucked and I was sick of Kalina dicking me around. This is the last time, I resolved. Either I fuck her or delete her number. No other choices. No matter how far Kalina and I go sexually today, if it doesn't end in actual fucking, I must delete her number. This resolution gave me a purity of purpose. It gave me conviction.

I don't recommend this as a general dating orientation but when you wish to set a limit on how much attention a girl can milk, put a limit on the time wasting, it works fine. Now I needed to work around the expected language barrier. We couldn't sit in a cafe and talk because Kalina's English was bad and my Serbian worse. It would be a horrendous conversation and any sexual tension would fizzle away in a cloud of awkwardness. So, if not that, what?

You have to walk her straight home, I realised. It was the perfect strategy as it not only side-stepped the cafe date issue but it also communicated

Girl Junkie

very directly that I wasn't pissing around: put up or shut up. There was a Maxi supermarket on the way, so Kalina would have an opportunity to raise concerns as I bought wine, and I'd deal with them or cut her loose. The problem, as I could see, was I lacked sufficient vibe to sweep her up in a wave of momentum. When timid girls like you, they can be led if you show force of character. I didn't really know if Kalina was timid or difficult but the solution could be the same in either case. I needed to work myself up into a sexual tornado.

I lacked sexual intent, but I wasn't lacking a dull frustration against Kalina and my poor recent results generally. Perhaps I could work that up, into a sexual rage. I could project my anger onto Kalina, sublimated as sexual intent. That would be win-win for us both. So, as I approached Republic Square I began visualizing banging the girls walking past me. My visualisations were lurid and specific, imagining myself dragging them across my room by their hair, forcing them to their knees, sticking my dick in their faces and slapping them, telling them to lick my balls. I visualised bending a girl over in that part of the Studenski Square apartment where I fucked all those other girls, and then coming on her face.

While I talked myself up, these girls carried on chatting to their friends completely oblivious to the volcano of sexual frustration about to burst behind them. Fortunately, they never looked behind to see the look in my eyes. I felt like an Arab in a Swedish music festival.

It worked. I was very horny indeed. Whatever objections Kalina raised, I would power right through them. My swag was back on. No longer did I shuffle around like a lost soul. Girls noticed the subtle changes in my mannerisms and I received a stolen glance here and there. *I'm gonna fuck her. If her friend comes up I'm gonna fuck her friend too.*

My phone buzzed. It was now twenty past the hour.

"I am late."

I stood in front of the big horse statue at the square and waited. And waited. After that Herculean effort to rouse myself into a notch-winning fury of pent-up sexuality, I felt it all ebb away again like tears in the rain.

"I come." she wrote.

Kalina was now twenty-five minutes late and once more I was the hollow shuffling zombie I'd been most of the past week. *Just go home*, I thought. *Fuck this. She's a time waster.* No. I swallowed my pride, bit my tongue and thought: *lose the battle, win the war*. So long as I could get Kalina in front of me I might yet shag her. Finally, she arrived, walking across the square from the bus stop opposite a row of pizza takeaways. She was dolled up nice: lipstick on, eye shadow. I walked her towards the nearby supermarket down a back alley on the route back to my apartment.

"How do we talk? My friend is not here."

I shrugged and tried stumbling conversation. We'd not walked twenty metres when she dropped a rage-inducing bomb. As if her flaking and lateness wasn't bad enough.

"I go soon."

So she'd just come say hello. The penny dropped. *Hang on, is this just an epic waste of my last night in town? She has suckered me out for, like, fuck all.* I'm maintained a poker face but rage bubbled away menacingly. I was ready to vote for Sharia Law and honour killings. Put the paper in front of me and I'll sign it. The Muslims are right: women should be second-class citizens.

"I have private client," she explained.

"I'll fucking bet you do, you whore," I muttered.

"What you say?"

"I met you, you go," I said.

It turned out her nail salon sometimes booked her private clients at night, a group of women. "I meet girls nine o'clock," she explained. It was now twenty minutes to. I wondered if she could see the steam coming out my ears. *Don't be reactive. Emotional control is a cornerstone of game,* I told myself then countermanded that order with, *hang on it's okay to be reactive when she's a fucking bitch and totally deserves it.*

I wanted to give her a piece of my mind but the language barrier prevented me. That bottled up my rage even worse. I resolved to find a public Wi-Fi spot so I could rebuke her via Google Translate, telling her precisely what I thought. On the way, I ducked into the supermarket to get wine, just on the safe side.

"I'm not happy," I said, keeping it simple.

"What do you mean? Oh, I think I understand."

"Do you? You decided to meet your friends at 9pm and you tell me this now."

"I don't understand". She meant that literally, that the words made no sense to her. I couldn't even tell her off. Now I was trebly angry, unfocused rage rattling around inside like steam in a bunged-up kettle. I needed to get a grip. Stop and think. Apply best daygame practice. I remembered my original date formulation, to simply lead her to my apartment, escalate, and let the chips fall where they may.

"It's okay," I said, and kept walking. Kalina followed. We arrived at the top end of Studentski Square then walked through that small park. It was heaving with small groups of teenagers drinking and smoking.

Kalina stumbled through a few sentences, the gist of which was, "I really wanted to meet you but I am busy, I must meet girls, I have clients."

I let her talk, letting her trip over vocabulary, because it engaged her mind. So long as her legs were walking, it was good for me. Suddenly we arrived at the street door outside my apartment. My rage had mostly dissipated because Kalina had made noises of contrition and had now obediently followed me home. Was I misunderstanding the whole situation?

I checked my watch, reading it as quarter to nine. Did she say she was meeting the client at nine precisely, or just that she needed to leave me at nine? I couldn't remember which, or if she'd even specified. There was frightfully little time to do anything. I unlocked the street door, we walked upstairs, and I opened my front door. Kalina stood inside while I put some music on.

"Can I sit down?" she asked. Her politeness surprised me. Was I completely wrong about her being a princess? When a girl presents persistent difficulties it isn't always clear if she's causing the problems herself, or simply trying her best to deal with complications her own life has thrown up against her will. Perhaps Kalina really was busy. Perhaps she had a boyfriend to negotiate her way around.

"Yeah, of course," I replied and indicated the edge of the bed where she perched.

I sat next to her, pulled her to me, and kissed.

Kalina was reticent at first but I was in no mood for sweet romance. The clock was ticking down and with it my patience with her. I pushed her gently back onto the bed, she let it happen, and I started fondling her tits — the highest escalation I'd yet tried in our briefly-blossoming love affair. I sensed her breath thicken so I put my thigh between her legs then fingered her through her jeans. I fumbled with her zipper, trying to unfasten them.

She looked up at me. "Do you have a condom?"

Ah, the magic words!

"Yes, I do."

Now it was agreed, I stood up and doffed my clothes. The doomsday clock was still ticking and I wasn't about to belabour the process of getting naked. Kalina wore a furry body-warmer jacket over her white blouse and she didn't attempt to remove them. She had an assortment of rings, necklaces and bracelets which she also didn't remove. Rather, she simply kicked off her boots and stripped off her jeans and panties until she was naked from the waist down.

It looked very odd. Naked lower half, and a fully-dressed upper half. Kind of like police crime scene photos of rape-murder victims. Given how murderously angry I'd been moments ago, perhaps that was appropriate.

Kalina wasn't messing around either, was she?

I put on the condom and guided her back to the bed. Just before reclining, she put a resisting hand on my chest and said, "please quick but no hard." I must've looked puzzled because she added, "I see client. My hair and make-up be good."

I stuck my dick in and her phone rang in celebration. She glanced over at the screen and said, "this woman I meet at 9, she wait for me".

Not wishing to keep a paying customer waiting, I rattled Kalina fast in missionary position on the bed then stood her up and bent her over the piano by the wall to briefly do her from behind. It didn't take long to come, and she was evidently hoping I'd get on with it. I checked my watch: 20:58. It felt like I was Tom Cruise in *Mission Impossible*, disarming a bomb moments before detonation.

Kalina pulled her jeans back on and shuffled into the bathroom to sort herself out. I slipped on my boxer shorts and waited. She grabbed her handbag off the table and opened the door to leave.

"I go. You stay. Message me when you Belgrade."

I dare say she looked pleased with herself. From kissing to coming had taken less than five minutes. Evidently girls don't mind a quick knee trembler themselves. She left me standing in my boxer shorts wondering what had just happened. Stupefied, I sat down on the bed and stared at the walls for a few minutes. Then I showered, hoping to clear my head. Kalina was my second notch of the year and it seemed to have blind-sided me in the best possible fashion. While my brain still reeled, I pulled out my phone and recorded another podcast, trying to make sense of the episode to myself.

Zagreb Old Town streets

Headed to Belgrade

If they knew why
I was there then yes

Chapter 11
NEMESIS

I flew back to Prague the next morning, the 14th of April, with my return to Newcastle already booked four days after that. I'd been on the road quite long enough and though much of it had been frustrating, the overall results had been ultimately satisfying. During my usual pre-season winter ruminations, I'd looked back on 2014 with an eye towards learning from my mixed successes and failures. A key learning point had been that one month on the road is the longest I could stomach before growing increasingly antsy and melancholic. Daygame injects high drama into trips but also makes them stressful, setting you up for volatile mood swings, pinballing between hero and zero. Trips tended to be fun retrospectively as memories rather than in the real-time experiencing of them. Perhaps the years were catching up to me, causing me to grow a little jaded and see things pessimistically. I'd theorised that by shortening my trips and moving around more, I'd take better advantage of the "new city, new trip" vibe boost. So, early 2015 had involved only short trips.

Lydia and I had exchanged a few SMS over the week in Belgrade. She seemed keen. I arrived in Vaclav Havel airport once again, looking forward to scoring my next solid Russian notch. The airport was now as familiar as baldness. I walked over to the tourist information counter to buy my 32-crown bus and metro combo ticket, then on to the McDonald's around the corner for a cheeseburger and flat white coffee. I sat on a high stool gazing out of the window, eating until I saw the 119 bus turn into the bus stop outside the terminal. Life seemed smooth and trouble-free. The combination of banging Kalina and arriving in Prague had lifted my spirits.

Gold Pralines was once more blessed with me as their upstairs tenant. I'd messaged the landlady directly for a cash price quote and gotten lucky she had a vacancy and was willing to offer another heavy discount. No sooner had I thrown my rucksack into a corner than my phone buzzed. It was Ivanna, the young virgin.

"Are you back?"

"Yes. I just arrived. Want to meet?"

"Okay, I just finish school."

"Meet now?"

"Okay."

"Let's meet outside Palladium. Message me when you arrive."

I still hadn't banged the teenage Serbian but was very much determined to try. She'd been naked in my bed four or five times so far, without success. Her body was exactly what I look for in a bed partner and her timid quiet character suited me just fine. Even without banging her, I enjoyed having her around. I took a short walk to the mall and had a look around.

The Turk sentinel was at his usual post, gazing fixedly into space.

Oh!

Ivanna was due any moment so there wasn't time to daygame but his presence nonetheless set me thinking. I couldn't shake images from the video game *Resident Evil 3: Nemesis*, an old Playstation title from 1999 and at that point my favourite in the popular Japanese horror series. Players took the role of a SWAT team member exploring the fictional Raccoon City during a zombie outbreak. The key conceit of the game, the mechanic that made it so fondly remembered by fans such as myself, was that the evil Umbrella Corporation sent a genetically-mutated Terminator to hunt you down. He'd pop up at the most inopportune times and force you to run for your life.

This Turk had a similar effect upon me.

He even looked a bit like the Nemesis. A big, overly-muscled skinhead. Relentless.

I turned tail before he spotted me and waited outside the mall for Ivanna. She arrived wearing her usual colourful leggings and big coat. We kissed and I took her to an Asian fusion restaurant across the road for late lunch. Then we hung out in my apartment, most of it with my paws on her naked body. As the bedroom tempo rose, I got my dick out.

"I want to put my dick inside you."

"Yes, okay."

Ivanna lay on her back and allowed her legs to flop open. I shuffled inbetween and pushed myself into the hot seat. Try as I might, my dick just wouldn't go in.

"Try to relax more," I coaxed, softly rubbing her pussy and pushing a finger inside. Ivanna purred and writhed but felt very tight and dry.

"I'm trying. I don't understand. I want this but my body doesn't listen to my mind."

I persevered another ten minutes, already resigned to failure before we abandoned yet another deflowering attempt and settled instead for more grab ass. Ivanna apologised. For all the frustration, I enjoyed having a pleasant sexy Serb naked in my bed as we watched YouTube and chatted about life. I liked Ivanna a lot. She had the same vibe as Milena and before her, Dovile. I like girls who take pleasure from being easy-going and agreeable. She stayed until late.

Pavlina didn't respond to my messages. Lydia agreed to meet the next evening.

Ivanna excused herself to return home for study so, fearful of meeting my nemesis in the mall, I messaged Klara. She agreed to meet that same evening on an hour's notice. It was odd, really. My entire day consisted of either lying around in my apartment with a girl, or popping across the road to bring a different girl back to lie around with. If only my whole life could be whiled away in such circumstances I'd be as happy as a dog with two cocks.

The sky was an inky black and rain clouds threatened. Klara stood outside Palladium wearing retro-style wools and elegant black shoes with thick medium heels and black tights. She'd definitely given her make-up an extra ten minutes. I liked her too. She was a smart bookish intellectual. Banging her made me feel like a caveman ravishing an anthropologist. I always gave her a few slaps to accentuate the point.

"Hello Klara, you look nice."

"Hello, sexy beast."

I took her to Chapeau Rouge, for appearance's sake, but the way she just smiled, listened, and let her eyes glisten it was obvious she was killing time until I kidnapped and fucked her. I took her home after the first drink. We sat on the sofa drinking wine and I was rather amused. Klara was not, and would never be mistaken for, a dumb broad yet she seemed incapable of forming complete sentences. She sat with perfect upright posture, rocked gently back and forwards, while smiling inanely at me. Every now and then she said "yes", or "oh!" when it seemed appropriate.

Was this a Russian thing? Julia and Zaria had been exactly the same way: highly-educated, whip-smart girls who seemed to completely lose all cognitive functions when anticipating sex.

If I'd had a tennis ball, I'd have tossed it across the room and shouted "fetch!"

Vulnerabilities are made for exploiting so Klara's extreme compliance motivated me to try something new. So far, we'd only ever had simple sex in missionary position and a little doggy-style. I'd always worn a condom and she'd never sucked me off nor let me come anywhere but as usual. Klara gave the impression that sex was to follow correct traditional etiquette with nothing outside of expected boundaries. She'd have made a great courtier for Louis XV.

I wanted to test things.

I took the wine glass from her hand, placed in on the low table and then kissed her. She sighed and collapsed into me. So, I walked her around the sofa, bent her over it, and slipped my dick in from behind. She gasped.

"Do you wear a condom?"

"No."

"You should wear a condom."

I kept pumping her. "Yes, I should. But I wont."

"Oh!" she gasped, clearly thinking it preferable to continue getting fucked than to insist I stop and glove-up. I did her extra hard, as I find this usually makes girls amenable to new flourishes of sexual technique. Then I turned her around and pushed her against the wall, fingering her. She wrapped her arms around my neck and kissed me, then I pushed her down the wall until she rested on her haunches and dick-in-mouth height. I'd quite deliberately boxed her in.

She made no movement towards my dick. Rather, she remained on her haunches but looked studiously away, displaying the hint of a smile. I grabbed my dick and waved it in front of her face. She made motions to turn her face this way and that, her lips pressed tightly together like a toddler refusing food. Undaunted, I slapped my dick on her forehead.

She giggled then set her face into a mock stern expression. "Nick! You ask too much!"

I continued dick-slapping her and soon noticed she wasn't attempting to evade or parry the blows of my pork sword. Like a duelling musketeer pressing his advantage against a fading adversary, I rubbed my dick around her face, down her cheek, under her chin, and back up the other cheek. Klara continued to bleat and whine.

"Nick, stop!"

Finally I tried pushing my dick into her mouth. She grabbed it and looked up at me.

"You ask too much!"

"Suck my dick."

She did.

Having made her decision, she didn't hold back. What Klara lacked in technique she made up double in enthusiasm, taking it as deep as her girl-sized throat allowed and then pulling out for a better examination. I banged her some more then stripped her naked. She sucked me off again then I carried her to the bed for a jolly rodgering. For reasons that escape me, I didn't especially want to put it in her arse, so I didn't try.

I regret that.

My stamina wasn't what it had been in years past. After ten minutes my skin had reddened and become clammy with sweat. I put Klara onto her knees and came in her mouth. She swallowed, then playfully slapped me.

"You ask too much!" she repeated.

From that moment forwards, until late 2016, I only ever raw-dogged Klara and she always sucked me off and swallowed my cum. I considered this a successful arrangement in our romantic affairs. She stayed overnight then left early in the morning to do some library-related clever stuff.

I pinged Lydia the second afternoon to arrange a time and place for our agreed date. She was tardy in replying and then finally sent a long message. Even before reading it, I knew from the length that it was bad news. Lydia explained she'd broken up with her boyfriend shortly before I'd approached her and now she'd gotten back with him. Thus she couldn't see me any more. Apparently I'd only just missed out too — this drama had all occurred two days ago, while I was in Belgrade. To say I was frustrated is an understatement equivalent to saying "the Red Army went a little overboard after the fall of Berlin." Had I remained in Prague the whole time rather than visit Zagreb, it's a fair bet Lydia would've come off her period and supplied me with the hot enthusiastic sex that is my human right.

Bollocks.

I couldn't get those firm round tits out of my mind. In a multiverse of one million alternate timelines, my balls should have been slapping against Lydia's bubble-butt in every single one of them. It wasn't fair.

Heroically, I tried convincing her it was still too early in her rapprochement to consider herself morally bound to monogamy with this boyfriend character. I cited Aristotle and Plato to support my case. Lydia begged to differ. So, she dropped off the hook. If I wanted another notch in my three remaining days in Prague, I'd have to bloody well go out and earn it.

Bollocks.

During the previous few weeks I'd fallen into WhatsApp chat with a British player called Brian. He lived in Brussels doing some kind of overpaid project management job with a bank, the type of pointless make-work role that, when finance consulting, I usually recommended management cut back on. He'd read most of my books and left positive reviews on the Lulu sales page, so I was kindly disposed to him despite having never met him. As we chatted it became clear he was a bit of a rascal and at that time had a girlfriend living in Prague.

"I'm in Prague loads, mate," he boasted. "Got this dolly bird there, ain't I? She used to be a television star. Still goes to all the right parties. Long legs, model face. Been in Playboy."

"How old is she?"

"Details, mate. Doesn't matter."

The conversation soon moved towards whether we'd be in Prague at the same time. It looked like we would, as Brian already had a flight booked the very next day. We set up an afternoon meeting at the Costa coffee in Palladium mall. It wasn't until I was walking there that I remembered Turk Nemesis. Would he have staked out the venue?

As luck would have it I bumped into an American daygamer I already knew called Gerard. He lived in Prague, having stockpiled a healthy war chest of savings from sources unknown. I'd heard he'd been a big shot technician in Silicon Valley, but I'd not yet asked him about it. Gerard was half-Asian, half-white I think, but that too seemed too delicate a topic to broach directly. He dressed well in mainstream fashion, like a display mannequin in an M&S store window, and kept himself in good shape, looking considerably younger than his thirty-seven years. We'd winged a couple of times and he did a handful of sets. We got on okay.

I thought of Turk Nemesis, who by now had grown to a nightmare figure in my overactive imagination. Perhaps I should apply the old 'bear rule':

when attacked my a grizzly bear you don't need to run faster than the bear. Rather, you need only run faster than your hiking partner.

"Gerard, mate. I'm headed into Palladium to meet a friend. Wanna come?"

"Sure."

My trepidation was unwarranted as Costa was both Turk-free and Nemesis-free when we arrived. It was not Brian-free, however. I saw a tall muscular man dressed in a cashmere sweater, cotton slacks, and Italian leather shoes. He sprawled lazily in a sofa chair with a small espresso on the table before him. His manner was how I'd imagine Napoleon at rest after conquering Egypt.

"Nicholas," he said, upon catching my eye. "Welcome."

He said it like he owned Costa and I was his guest.

"Brian, right?"

"Yes, Nicholas, that is correct."

Gerard introduced himself then went off daygaming. I stood in line for a coffee then sat down in the sofa chair across from Brian. We chatted a while. He was in town for two days to see his bird. If he could get away from her he promised to have a walkabout with me.

"So you daygame, then?" I asked.

"A bit. I prefer nightgame. Get lashed with the lads and see what the tarts are up for."

It was peculiar, this mix of affected upper-class debonair and a seedy undercurrent of squalor. Imagine Sir Walter Raleigh or Sir David Attenborough rolling around with African whores in a Calais refugee camp. That's the vibe I was getting.

We chatted for an hour then he rose, adjusted his sweater, and informed me he needed to meet the missus at the mall entrance. I shook his hand and we said our goodbyes, then though I needed to go out the same doors, I let him get ten yards ahead of me so that his bird didn't see us together. She was already waiting and fit his description of her exactly: tall, model-esque, a bit past her prime but still hot, and dolled up like Victoria Beckham on her way to a red carpet.

I liked him. I figured we'd see each other quite a bit in future, which turned out to be the case. Now I needed to bring my thoughts back towards daygame.

It was as yet still mid-April so the traditional European daygame season was only two weeks old. The weather was forgiving, with clear blue skies and enough sunshine to force a man to unzip his leather jacket and take off his hat. I paced up and down Na Prikope while giving Palladium a wide berth. At any moment I expected my Turk Nemesis to hunt me down.

Daygame provided me with some leads. I took a beautiful Russian student on an idate to Paul's. She looked exactly like the porno actress Tania Russof, perhaps the third such that I'd dated, all of them Russian. I hadn't yet banged a Russof-a-like so I was doubly keen on this girl although her beauty and restrained feminine manner would've guaranteed her my attentions regardless of how closely she resembled a porno slag. We chatted for an hour, had a small beer in Battalion, then she gave her number and left.

Following this success, my vibe rocketed upward. I was truly back into the swing of things. I took more numbers and two of them turned into dates. Both girls were similar: slim, petite Czech girls studying at university. One was a red-head, the other a brunette. On consecutive evenings I took them to Chapeau Rouge and sat them down at the same table I had Lydia. Feeling rather flush with confidence, I tried kissing both on the second drink. Both girls acquiesced but sadly neither wanted to meet again. You never know where the cause and effect lies. Did I push them too hard? Not hard enough? Would it have mattered anyway?

I was disappointed to lose the red-head because she was an amateur ballerina with a wonderfully lithe body. Sadly, I never got to ravish her. I saw Ivanna one more evening, had another fruitless roll around in the sack with her, then took my flight home to Newcastle. My dad picked me up from the airport and I spent the rest of that evening lying on the sofa watching football with him. I hadn't yet made plans for my next euro jaunt. There was a big project to deal with first: *Beginner Daygame*. I'd chipped away at it for the past month and was now tinkering with the cover design. It was almost complete.

BLACKEST BOOK

CHAPTER 12
GATESHEAD

Chapter 12
BLACKEST BOOK

Now that he was free of Andy and Yad, Tom was devoting considerable effort to building his own YouTube channel. He'd confided that he didn't much enjoy writing but took great pleasure in fiddling around with video editing. I looked upon him as a friend and fellow-traveller so I was keen to help out and I watched all his YouTube content both for pleasure and to see whatever new ideas he came up with that I could learn from. Since my *Rock Solid Game* team had broken up in late 2012, I'd struggled to find like-minded peers of sufficient skill with whom I could bounce around ideas. Back in the old Hampstead mansion I'd been living with my friends and wings. If I had a question or a problem to solve, the answer was quite literally next door. Jimmy lived in the room next to mine, Johnny the next one down, Fernando one floor above, and Mick one floor below. Later, Steve would take over Mick's room when the latter returned to Australia.

We'd grown so accustomed to the convenience that we hadn't appreciated how lucky we were. You don't know what you've got 'till it's gone.

My primary sounding board since then had been John Bodi. We'd lived together right through to April 1st 2014 and travelled together for two months after that. We fell out in Belgrade in May that year. Though we remained on good terms and spoke frequently, I'd resolved to never travel with him again and he shared my opinion. Tom and I had leaned heavily on each other since 2013 and once he finally left Andy in early 2014 he was especially keen to have me on his YouTube channel and to allow his guest posts on my blog while he built up his business.

It worked well. We liked travelling together, talking theory together, and throwing around business ideas. The daygame world often treated us as a unit, like Laurel and Hardy, or Morecambe and Wise. Doing *Beginner Daygame* together, our first joint product, seemed a natural fit. Tom would appeal to fans of video and I to fans of writing. It would cross-pollenate our audiences.

Tom had begun to segment his YouTube channel into several regular strands of content. There'd be the expected in-field recordings to demonstrate his bona fides and whatever technical point he wished to convey. He'd also do theory pieces talking to a camera, and had grown increasingly fond of 'lifestyle' videos where he preened for the crowd showing off the 'flowmad' experience. I liked this content. He'd put out one or two videos a week so it was nice to boot one up while I was chilling with a coffee. It helped reinforce the idea that daygame is fun and I ought to be out doing more of it. Tom then added a podcast series, where he'd waffle on for half an hour about a topic. They were rambling, and I noticed he never did seem to impart any actual information, but it filled the time pleasantly, like watching the daily soap operas *Eastenders* or *Home & Away*.

It was with this positive disposition towards the world that I settled into a reclining chair in my parent's conservatory one morning in Gateshead. My cup of freshly-brewed coffee stood on the window sill to my left, together with a test print of the first draft of *Adventure Sex* that I planned to read and scribble notes into the margin. Sunny skies, birds tweeting, and the prospect of a steak and kidney pie down at the local pub for lunch. Life was good.

I booted up my laptop, opened YouTube, and noticed Tom had uploaded a new video. "Street Improv For Daygame" was the title. *Okay, that'll be interesting, he's good at that.*

I pressed play.

Ten minutes later, one thought, and one alone, dominated my mind: *Tom, you absolute cunt! You total fucking snake!*

I was raging.

Tom had plagiarised the exercises I'd shown him in Zagreb from the *Black Book* less than two weeks earlier. He'd literally copied exactly the theory and exercises I'd created and then offered them for free on YouTube, completely unattributed and not crediting me mind you, as his own ideas. The video showed him wandering around Oxford Street with a spy-cam on his lapel as he kept a running commentary of the labels he put on the girls walking past. He explained to the viewer that good daygame opening requires observing a girl carefully, trying to form an immediate impression that produces a label, then after opening you can expand upon it.

Two weeks after I'd shown him that very exercise.

I had shown him only one five-minute section of *Black Book* and, by the wildest coincidence, precisely that concept had now appeared on his channel. It was bad enough him stealing my material and passing it off as his own, but even worse was he knew I planned to release *Black Book* as a paid product. Not content with pre-empting me with my own material, he was giving it away for free. He was no better than a copyright pirate.

What a back-stabbing cunt.

Another thought occurred to me. When *Black Book* comes out, everyone will think I'm copying Tom! His video was rushed out quickly whereas I was still carefully editing my product. It wasn't the first time Tom had pre-empted my release of concepts, rushing to associate them with himself before I had a chance to release my own products. It was why, in mid-2014, I'd resolved to stop showing him my works-in-progress. All I'd shown him of *Daygame Overkill* prior to release was five minutes of one in-field. I hadn't trusted him with such an important product of mine, one with so many new ideas. Because I considered *Black Book* to be "easy-come, easy-go" from how the BBC inspired it, I'd relaxed my rule and he'd taken advantage.

What a back-stabbing cunt.

"Nick!" my mother called from the sitting room. "Are you alright?"

"Yeah, fine. Why?"

"You were shouting. I thought something was wrong."

I hadn't even noticed. The air fizzed around me, like the aftermath of a volcanic eruption.

My rage gradually subsided. I wanted to remain friends with Tom and that would involve making allowances for his foibles. Didn't Jesus say 'let him without sin cast the first stone'? Admonishing myself that I too had severe character flaws, I talked myself down. *Let it lie*, I rationalised. *You didn't invent daygame. You may have created this exercise, and you may be primarily responsible for the theory of modern daygame opening, but you didn't pull it all out of your own arsehole. Tom contributed to the method too.*

It worked, to an extent, but for a couple of days I couldn't bring myself to work on *Beginner Daygame*. I read through *Adventure Sex* and made copious notes in the margins. It took around a week. While I scribbled in my own memoir, the postman delivered a thick black-bound hardback of Giacomo Casanova's rather more famous memoir. Tom had been evangelical about it.

"Mate, you absolutely must read Casanova. He was the original daygamer!"

Girl Junkie

I'd heard the same stories as everyone else and no more. Dimly, I was aware of Casnova as a legendary womaniser from pre-industrial days who had written an epic memoir of his exploits. I imagined a foppish dandy with powdered face, large wig, and frilly cuffs on his shirts. A larger than life character like an old-time Stephen Fry, minus the insufferable smugness and literal faggotry.

"I read the whole thing," Tom had continued. "Eleven volumes. It's a big monster of a book. One year I made it a challenge and I read tons of it in Moscow one time when I was depressed. Everything we do is already in there. He literally went around Covent Garden approaching women on the street! Just like us! He travelled around Europe chasing girls just like us. But there's so much more. He was a proper con man!"

"That's a bad thing."

Tom screwed up his face but didn't voice his obvious disagreement. "Really, give it a try. It's fascinating."

I'd taken him up on his challenge and ordered a copy from eBay. It thumped onto my doormat around the time my heart rate had settled back to normal after the 'Street Improv For Daygame' episode. I put another coffee on the filter machine and ripped open the heavy cardboard package. That afternoon I spent four hours reading Casanova, getting up to page 99.

I was underwhelmed.

I messaged Tom, choosing not to mention his latest video. "I'm reading Casanova. It's shite. Nothing happens."

"Yes it does. Keep at it."

"Mate, I'm a hundred pages in. Some lass he lives with has been possessed by a demon, and his school master doesn't feed him. That's about it. No shagging," I insisted. "It's shite."

"Hang on. Which version have you got?"

I told him what was written on the first page, together with the publisher. The 1923 version, I think.

"That's the problem!" he wrote. "You've got a bowdlerised translation. They cut all the good bits out. You need the Trask version."

I thanked him and did some internet searching. Much to my surprise, Casanova's memoir had been translated several times. Casanova had written it in French and finished it in 1797. From 1838 (the first English edition) to 1960 it had only ever been published in translations derived from bowdlerised German and French editions which had been heavily abridged and censored in order to cut scandalous sexual content and to tame Casanova's political views. The English version I'd read, a reprint of the Arthur Machen translation of 1894, had been based on one of these inaccurate versions.

No wonder it was shit.

What kind of faggot would write a memoir *without* inserting incendiary political opinions? A scaredy-cat homosexual Hillary-voting globalist, that's who. If I was to write a memoir, I'd be sure to slip casual racism and sexism in. Really subtly.

Winston Churchill had personally ordered the original Casanova manuscript be rescued when an Allied bombing run in WWII had razed the building in which it was stored. That document was later bought by the National Library Of France for almost six million pounds. It was published unabridged and uncensored in French in 1960. Willard R. Trask based his definitive English translation upon this version. That's the one Tom recommended.

```
The original title
   was catchier
```

Eleven volumes of some randy Italian chasing whores? No thanks, I thought. I found an abridged single-volume Folio edition online with delightful art and a handsome slipcase. I ordered that, put aside the Machen translation, and a few days later I was once again ripping open a new package.

Three days later I messaged Tom.

"This is better, but still a bit shit."

I struggled to wade through it. Casanova seemed a deathly dull writer and I was losing my will to live with every page. I'd return to his *History*

Of My Life in 2018 and revise my opinion of Casanova's memoir upwards considerably, but in 2015 I wasn't at all impressed with the daft lad. I figured we were way better at skirt-chasing.

"Nick, bad news. Now that I'm editing the *Beginner Daygame* video I'm realising that the sound levels on our theory pieces are all messed up," said Tom over WhatsApp.

"Messed up how?"

"It's all the background noise from the cafes and malls we sat in. It's hard to listen to."

"Really? The microphone was clipped to our lapel. The in-fields didn't have street noise getting in the way. It's quite clear."

"The streets aren't as loud. Lots of people in the mall, gabbing on. Trust me, we can't use it."

That was unfortunate. Although the primary purpose of March's visit to Prague had been to capture in-fields, I thought we'd done rather a good job explicating the London Daygame Model clearly in those little pieces for the camera. I'd considered it wrapped up. The book was going through its final check for typos and we hoped to release it within a couple of weeks. I'm not patient at the best of times so this hitch unsettled me.

"So what should we do? You're the video expert not me."

"I don't know. I suppose I'll have to re-record them myself in my home studio. At least there we can control the background noise. Trust me, we can't use what we did in Prague."

Reluctantly I agreed. Tom then began to explain he had arranged a one-month long residential training session with a rich American daygamer called Hank. He was an older guy, in his late forties, who had already done coaching with Yad, Andy and a few short sessions with Tom,

"One month? Fucking hell, that'll be intense," I offered.

"We'll be sharing an apartment in Warsaw but the deal is that I take him out two hours a day as a wing. Hank is already pretty good so it's more about having a wingman and giving a little polish here and there."

I'd never been to Warsaw. Locations I've never visited tend to take on a indefinable amorphous shape in my mind. For whatever reason, the idea never truly resonated that one European city is much the same as another. Warsaw may as well have been Mordor to me. This was despite my having been to the Polish cities of Lodz and Krakow in 2010.

"What's Warsaw like?" I asked.

"It's good. I coached a few students there already. Decent size. Okay birds."

I tend to think of the world as one big blur. I don't perceive it as it really is until I've had my feet on the ground and wrapped my hands around it, so to speak. Call me an abstract thinker, but my mind is aloof in concepts and ruminations. In fact I seem to have a real talent for failing to appreciate the richness of life until it slaps me in that face. So, Warsaw to me was what I'd read in the history books: the Jewish uprising in the Warsaw ghetto, that Pact the commies signed there in the Cold War, and a composite of images I'd had from spy dramas on television.

Warsaw was just some cold grey place. Tear gas.

This seemed to me to be confirmed when my old housemates Jimmy and Lee took a trip there in the winter of 2012. Lee's old workout partner from London, Sam, owned an apartment in down town Warsaw and the tenant had moved out. Hoping to cadge a few free nights board and see the sights, they took up Sam on his invitation to visit. Nobody had reconnected the gas heating — and it was the depths of winter.

"All three of us shared a bed with a blanket wrapped around us. I was shivering all night. Slept with my hat and gloves on. Horrible," Jimmy had related a week later.

Given this, I'd decided to give Warsaw a wide berth ever since. Only now, Tom's enthusiasm had tipped the scales back in favour of exploration. I hadn't yet decided where to spend May so suddenly I took an interest. There was a budget flight from Newcastle to Krakow, where my friend and sometime-wing Ash had just relocated a couple of weeks earlier for a new job, and a fast train from there to Warsaw. The idea appealed. It would be as precipitous a time as any to try the city.

"I might give it a look. Do you mind?"

"Err, no. Of course not. But I'll be pretty tied up with coaching."

"No worries, I'm happy to go solo."

The shitty censored edition

Showing Casanova a thing or
two about skirt chasing

Chapter 13
FINAL SOLUTION

It was a simple matter to confirm Ash was around and then place my bookings. I flew out to Krakow on the 3rd of May, a Sunday, with my trusty brown leather rucksack and the excitement of checking out two cities I'd not gotten overly familiar with. Like a sailor loaded down with a pocket full of coin after months on the high seas, I wanted to find beer and slags. The May weather was glorious and Krakow is as beautiful a medieval town as you could ever wish to see. It has a walled Old Town on a par with Prague or Budapest. The centrepiece is a large square with a church in one corner and a large low covered-in market in the middle. Horses pull ornate carts through the cobbled streets and tourists sitting in cafes overlooking the square eating tapas, quaffing wine and being terribly sophisticated.

Adding to my high estimation of Poland, it had so far resisted the Muslim invasion that German chancellor Angela Merkel had foisted upon an unwilling European populous. Not a single Allah was Akbar'd in Krakow the whole time I was there.

My train rattled out of Krakow airport through an ominously darkening afternoon. Quaint old villages raced past the windows. The train slowed up as we pulled into the city and the tracks cut a path through the gleaming new glass towers of a business district. Many well-known blue chip companies placed their back-office data centres in Krakow, hence why Ash had been offered his job. Krakow is a curious mix of the old and new. One minute you're walking past Siemens and Deutsche Bank with clean shaven men in Hugo Boss suits chattering on Blackberries, then next minute you're tripping on a cobblestone and sidestepping horse shit outside a medieval church.

Girl Junkie

I checked into an apartment next to one such churches just outside of the Old Town walls, down a little street across from a kiosk selling tours to Auschwitz death camp. I had no desire to visit such attractions, having gotten quite tired of being told to care about the Holocaust over and above all the other genocides of recent history. Anyway, I'd seen 1970s exploitation movies such as *SS Experiment Camp* and *Gestapo's Last Orgy* so I figured that was enough WWII history for me. They were likely as historically-accurate as the globalist nonsense on The History Channel but with the added advantage of being full of tits and ass.

Ash is an Indian, born in the English midlands. I like the guy but he's still got to go back. That's what I tell him. "Ash, mate. When the day of the rope comes, I won't turn you in. You can hide in my attic, like Anne Frank. I'll forge your diary afterwards too, like her Jew uncle did. When the mob comes looking for a mud to lynch I'll tell 'em *he went that way*, pointing the opposite direction. That's what I'll do for you, a favour risking my own life and limb, to give you a ten minute head start. Because you're my mate."

He took it in good humour. His dad was already buying up property back in India just in case they really did need to leave Europe in a hurry. Except for his physical appearance you'd never have guessed Ash was anything other than English. He talked like a midlander, was a fanatical supporter of Liverpool Football Club, and read about European medieval history for pleasure. He even played 'grand strategy' video games such as *Crusader Kings* to relive European conquests, with himself as the conqueror.

Ash and I had a few beers the first night. He knew a lovely burger bar drinking hole upstairs from the main Florianska tourist street and brought a few of his carousing buddies out with him. We stuffed our fat faces, downed some local ale, then he needed to get an early night. Work tomorrow. I wandered up and down the main drag speaking to a few girls.

The first two were pleasant but no more than that. It was getting dark, around nine o'clock, and the streets were still lively. I noticed a petite girl looking in the window of a souvenir store. She wandered off, stopped suddenly, then looked in another store window. My predatory instincts kicked in. Here was a girl with no plan of action, ambling aimlessly. She had tight leggings to show slim athletic legs and a firm bubble butt. Really, her ass was amazing and completely outsized for her figure, not unlike those popular Colombian Instagram models.

To this day, thinking about her ass brings tears to my eyes.

"Oi!" I said. She spun to face me, not at all startled. "You're wandering around like a crazy person."

That made her laugh and the rest of the chat was easy. After confirming there was nowhere she needed to be, she lived in Krakow as a student but had no plans for Sunday evening, I invited her for a drink.

"I know a good bar. I'll show you," she said, so I agreed.

That bar was literally around the corner, tucked into an alcove in a line of buildings facing the north end of the main square. It was an art deco cafe-bar and we sat at a small circular table made of cream marble flecked with black. We both ordered beer.

Olga turned out to be quite a talker. She wouldn't shut up. That wasn't a bad thing because she was above average intelligence, kept herself up-to-date in world affairs, and studied hard in her economics degree. I tended to disagree with her conclusions but she was only twenty-two, and a girl, bless her, so I didn't voice my objections. I liked her long brown hair and solid figure.

"Do you play sport?" I asked, drawing attention to that figure.

"Yes. I go to the gym and I like yoga."

"So, you are flexible?"

"Yes, very."

After the first drink I suggested we sit in the basement of the same bar because I'd noticed, when going to the toilet there, that it was almost empty and had nice long padded benches. It was thus far more amenable for escalation. Olga agreed and we took our second beers downstairs. The conversation continued to hum nicely. She was putting considerable effort into helping me get to know her.

I tried kissing. She turned her head in a "not now" kind of rebuff.

"I just broke up with my boyfriend. I don't want to get involved with anybody."

Despite this verbal kick-to-the-nuts her body language told me otherwise. She stayed close, let me paw at her, and didn't leverage my display of sexual intent as an excuse to leave. If only I could keep chipping away at her for another hour, and another beer, I'd likely get something out of the situation. She gave me a good in when I turned the conversation towards male-female relations.

Olga liked *Fifty Shades Of Grey*.

"I'm a strong-minded girl. Most men are too weak for me," she said, puffing her chest out so her small firm breasts strained against her shirt. Olga was telling what I needed to do in order to seduce her. I took the hint and began displaying more overtly dominant characteristics in my tone, storytelling, and teasing. By the bottom of our second beer I decided to go for it properly.

"Put that down," I ordered, indicating her drink. Her eyes momentarily popped wide at my tone, then she complied. I sensed she was intrigued, but hid it well. I stood up. "Stand up," I ordered.

She stood. I sensed her quivering a little, trying to control herself.

"This is what will happen," I said, then stretched my left hand out so my fingertips rested on the centre of her collarbone, then I pushed her slowly backwards until the wall arrested her motion. I kept walking in, until my chest touched hers. She was breathing heavily, but not showing any other overt signs of excitement.

"I will fight you," she said. "Don't try to kiss me."

"Shut up."

I grabbed her neck hard enough to matter but soft enough to avoid hurting her. She gasped. Then I tried to kiss. She turned her head away and wormed her hands up between my chest and endeavoured to push me away.

"Stop! I won't kiss you," she said, her head still turned away, looking at the far wall.

"I will kiss you," I said.

Footsteps sounded on the staircase. It was the waiter. He stopped halfway down, realising he was intruding something but not sure what. He lingered a moment, then spoke. "Do you want another drink?"

I still had a firm grip on Olga's throat and she still held her hands pressing against my chest. I did look rather like a rapist caught in the commission of his crime. There was no option but to brass neck it.

"Another beer please," I said, like James Bond ordering another martini.

After a moment, I released the pressure on Olga's throat so she could speak. "One for me too," she said, weakly.

The waiter stood dumbly for a few seconds then turned around and walked back up the steps shaking his head. Olga and I resumed our roles as victim and rapist.

"I won't kiss you. I mean it!" she insisted.

Now I released her throat, grabbed her wrists and pinned them against the wall above her head. Her cheeks flushed. I rested my spare hand heavily on her hip bone.

"I could rape you right now. The barman won't stop me."

"No!"

She stared at me defiantly and I tried to kiss her again. She flinched and turned her head away once more. Footsteps clunked on the stairs and the barman came down with two pints of beer, very timidly I thought, and placed them on the table behind us. Then he slinked away, as if hoping not to be noticed.

"Thanks!" I called after him.

"Dziękuję Ci," called Olga, meaning the same thing in Polish.

I grabbed her face with both hands and forced the kiss upon her while she was powerless to move. That did the trick. She wrapped her arms around me and pulled me in, squirming and moaning. We made out a while and then retook our seats in a manner far more agreeable to me.

"Where do you live?" I asked.

"You're not coming home with me."

"Maybe not tonight. Where?"

She told me the area. It was five minutes walk from the bar. Sadly we were not to go there. Around ten pm, after the third drink, Olga insisted on leaving. I tried more of the dominance but she was resolute, not in the earlier token roleplay sense, so I didn't press the issue. We swapped numbers and she expressed her hope of seeing me again.

As I stood outside the bar, with a church in front of me and the Hard Rock Cafe on the other side of it, I watched Olga skip away home. Three beers with each of Ash and Olga had left me quite drunk. The dynamic sexual tension with Olga had thrilled me so I was now as horny as Freddie Mercury on methamphetamine. I'd already booked a train to Warsaw the next afternoon, and accommodation. My abbreviated Krakow adventure was rapidly drawing to a close.

What to do? Simply going home seemed a waste, but the streets had emptied out.

Breaking the habit of a lifetime, I opened my Tinder app on my smartphone. Like most men I'd given Tinder a try a year or two earlier and, also like most men, I'd been horrified at the low quality of matches I'd gotten. It had made me very grateful indeed that I'd gotten good at daygame.

Perhaps Poland would be different. Perhaps it would be the one place in the whole wide world where Tinder girls were worth fucking. I swiped 'yes' for every girl who looked even vaguely fuckable in my diminished mental state. It took ten minutes until Tinder told me I was out of swipes then I walked home.

I laid stretched out on my bed in a slanty-roofed attic. I'd organised this trip on such short notice that all the nice apartments were already booked. A young woman living with her boyfriend was renting out her spare room so I took it. Lovely little place it was too. It felt lived in, unlike the sterile beige-walls-and-Ikea-furniture prison cells many Airbnb landlords default to. She'd offered me to join her for a drink with friends but I'm sure it would've been either awkward to hit on them or a waste of my time by not hitting on them. Ash had been a more attractive proposition as a beer partner.

I opened my laptop and checked out Tom's channel. We had finalised *Beginner Daygame* and launched it that very morning. We'd synchronised posts so that he uploaded the video to his channel the same time I uploaded it to mine. I wrote a blog post announcing it and included a link to the 130-page PDF which we were selling for ten English pounds. What with the flight, dates, and drinks I hadn't yet settled down to watch Tom's final video production. Now seemed an opportune time.

It started well.

Tom is a talented video editor and he'd put together a cool montage of us approaching girls and stalking around Prague like bad-asses. Then he cut to an introduction where he stood against a white-board facing the camera, explaining to absolute beginners what daygame means. He'd pitched it well, drawing on his extensive experience teaching kids in high school in addition to his hectic daygame coaching of 2011-2013.

It was slick. I liked it.

Tom went on to explain the model in simple terms. I'd already laid out a thoroughly detailed flowchart of the London Daygame Model for *Daygame Mastery*, then a more simplified version in *Daygame Overkill*. Tom had maintained even that latter version was too much for beginners ('they are idiots, mate') so insisted we simplify it further until it could be literally mapped onto the fingers of your hand. Thus we had the five stages, Open, Stack, Vibe, Invest, Close, and in the book we'd adapted it to a photo of Tom's hand. On the video he now counted it off on his fingers. It was both inspired teaching methodology and totally cringe. What man is going to shag girls if he's still using his fingers to count?

I watched all twenty-five minutes of the video and thought, *damn that's slick*. Tom's editing skills far outpaced my own and he'd really put the effort in. It was a perfect introduction. And then I realised why I'd felt a gnawing doubt grow throughout the video. I replayed it all from the beginning, skipping through quickly. Yes, I was right!

I wasn't in the bloody thing! Tom had edited me out.

Well, that's exaggerating things but the overall impression was clear. Tom had indeed re-recorded all the theory pieces, over half of the total runtime, and completely excised all of mine. I only appeared during the in-field segments and never addressed the audience directly. To a complete beginner, that is to say the target audience, this wasn't a Torero-Krauser production. It was a TOM TORERO!!!!!!! (and krauser) production. I was the hired help.

What a cunt!

I'd been scrupulously even-handed in designing the book so that Tom and I appeared exactly equally, with the same number of photos each, the same prominence, and shared credit. In my book we were a team. I couldn't shake the feeling that he'd deliberately diddled me, that his concerns over audio levels were a thin pretext to excise me from the London Daygame Model marketing.

Nick, you're being too suspicious, I reminded myself. *Just because he's stabbed you in the back multiple times before doesn't mean he has this time too.* I was reminded of what Jimmy had warned me about early in 2013, when Tom and I had made up after a big falling out. "Don't trust him," warned Jimmy. "He's a fruit. He'll fuck you over again. He's got a Svengali-like hold over you. Any time he apologises you rush back, believing he's changed his spots. You're like a battered wife with him. He won't change." For nearly two years, Tom and I had gotten on well and it had appeared Jimmy had been wrong.

Okay, he'd drawn me into trouble with Richard La Ruina in Minsk, forcing me to stand against Richard and Yad so they couldn't beat him up. Okay, he'd trashed my reputation by faking his in-field kiss close video. These were all in the past.

But now?

He'd plagiarised my *Black Book* material for his YouTube channel, airbrushed me out of our shared *Beginner Daygame* video as if I was a victim of Stalin's purges, caught my name up by association with his fake kiss-close video, and now appeared to be rebranding daygame as 'street hustle'. Suddenly curious, I scanned his channel back catalogue further. I soon noticed he'd completely deleted a long video we'd recorded about sexual market value a year earlier

Girl Junkie

in Belgrade. He'd actually re-recorded the content himself, implying the concepts I'd introduced were actually all his idea. Scanning further back I noticed he'd removed every single video that featured me as a guest.

He was re-engineering history. I felt like Michael J Fox at the end of *Back To The Future*, when he starts to fade away on stage because his mother doesn't date his father, and thus he's never born. I wasn't at all happy.

I needed a distraction. Betrayal wasn't a fun experience.

I checked Tinder. After half an hour without any of my swipes leading to matches, I concluded Polish Tinder didn't like me any more than English, Czech or Croatian Tinder. No matter what I did with my profile, I never seemed to attract the attention of girls I considered befitting my stature in the daygame community. So when "Sarah, 22, Krakow" pinged me a match and pre-emptively struck up conversation I was taken aback.

What devilry is afoot? It was now almost 11pm on Sunday night.

I've heard the horror stories of men showing up on Tinder dates to find the girl ten years and twenty kilos more than the photos she'd posted to her profile. Sarah had three pictures and looked fine. I won't say stunning, but she had nice thick black hair, strong eyes, and looked, well, she looked okay. Fuckable. Was there a reason all three photos were head shots? That concerned me. Anyway, on the messaging she affected a mild pretence of being reluctant to come right out, the way girls are, but then we agreed a date for eleven o'clock, just ten minutes away. We'd meet outside Hard Rock Cafe on the picturesque main square. Luckily, I still had my boots on.

So, only one hour after I first started swiping I was headed back up to the Old Town. *Perhaps there's something in this Tinder bullshit after all!* Certainly it was less effort than chasing girls down in the shopping malls. I put my biker jacket and woolly hat back on, and out I went. In my drunken haze I'd presented myself as a bad boy in our chat, so figured I should keep the illusion alive.

Two hours earlier it had seemed the whole world was out getting drunk in the main square. Lithe young lasses in tight trousers and lurid make-up were striking up chat before handing me flyers for whatever nightclub they touted for. Every other minute a horse-drawn carriage drew past, its occupants of a more noble intent than I. Those crowds were long gone. When I approached Hard Rock Cafe, it was as empty as a Hillary Clinton book signing. Finally, at a minute past eleven, Sarah turned up.

She was rather chubby.

I hadn't even said hello before I'd decided not to fuck her. She must've seen my expression change because a flash of anger lit her eyes for a moment. I was caught between a Hard Rock and a hard face.

Now, I know what you're about to say. "Turn around. Walk away. If she doesn't present fair photos on her profile, you have no obligation to stick to the date'" The thing is, for all I run my mouth about being a bad ass, I'm a gentle sort. I don't like upsetting people and I can't see how an abrupt about-turn could do anything but cut this lass to the quick. So, I swallowed my pride — and dare I say, a little bile — and introduced myself. I figured if she's meeting me this late on she's got to be awfully keen.

We went to the nearest bar that wasn't the (overly expensive) Hard Rock Cafe, a little English-themed place composed of many high stools around one long horseshoe bar. It had a name like *Bulldog* or *Churchill*, the kind of name that made me patriotic enough to punch a Frenchman and spit in a Scotsman's porridge.

"I'll get the first round in. Take a seat. What you having?"

"Whatever you're having."

"Do you like bitter?"

"If you do, yes."

Sarah seemed awfully demure, like I had a puppy following me around. There was a bachelor party of six English lads in custom-printed rugby jerseys propping up the bar. To read the lettering on those jerseys, it appeared that Bazza was a wildman and the fathers of Krakow's young women would be well-advised to lock up their daughters before his mates Kev, Sparksy, Davey, Matt, and Brownsy smashed the town. Britain's small expeditionary force was now somewhat depleted by booze and accumulated fatigue, as all six were quietly watching a Champions League match on the wall-mounted television.

The barman pulled my two beers and I sat down next to Sarah at a corner table. It pleased me that she'd picked a spot far from the windows, lest anyone I knew walk past and judge me harshly for my quality standards.

My heart really wasn't in it. All winter I'd been waiting for the moment I'll be let loose upon the girls of Europe and now that I was sitting opposite my third (potential) notch of the year I couldn't muster the slightest interest in this chubby young student. Olga was way fitter. Almost a different species, she was so much better.

Sarah seemed to sense it, so she made the conversation.

This lass really wants to get boned, I thought. *I'll just amuse myself with a little test.* I'd talk about video games. Nothing but video games.

"The thing I like about *Dark Souls 2*" I said, leaning back on my stool like I was educating the whole world, "is that unlike the somewhat labyrinthine structure of the original's levels, with all their inter-connectivity and shortcuts, the sequel is all linear runs to the end-of-level boss. This frees up the art director to lavish variety upon the locations."

Sarah nodded like I'd said something of value. "Oh, that's great!"

I kept going.

"Many people view it as the weakest entry in the *Souls* series, below *Demon's Souls*. Some fans object to the graphical downgrade between the atmospheric visuals of the E3 announcement trailer versus the rather plainer Playstation 3 release. Granted, the dynamic lighting was reduced, the shadows mostly removed, and many textures were simplified or tiled. It's certainly a less attractive game than the customers were initially led to believe."

In this I felt a parallel to my current experience with Tinder.

"Yes, I see," said Sarah.

"However, the place where I think the *Souls* YouTube community is mistaken is in their critique of the game mechanics. Simply put, they were too invested in the sequel being a continuation of the original. They didn't appreciate its attempts to forge its own identity with new mechanics. The use of stackable healing stones over-and-above the first game's limited-use Estus Flask is perhaps the most gregarious example."

Something unexpected had happened. By the time I was halfway through my beer I'd come to enjoy myself. I had no intention of getting laid. I merely drank my beer and ran my mouth to an enthusiastic audience of one. By the end of the first drink, Sarah wobbled a bit. She sensed my lack of sexual intent.

"Look, we don't need to get a second drink. If you want to leave you can. Dates don't always work" she said.

"No no no," I said, hand-waving away her objections. "It's a nice night and I'm enjoying myself. Let's get another."

She went to the bar, I went to the toilet, and I looked at myself in the mirror. I was sloshed out of my mind having put six pints down my neck with Ash and Olga before even starting with Sarah. *Nick, what are you doing?* I asked myself. I lacked the perspicacity to give myself a reply.

I returned to sit with Sarah. Towards the end of our second pint my mood had soured and I was looking for a way out.

"Look" I told her, raising my finger in the air as an exclamation point. "I'm getting the train to Warsaw tomorrow and I probably won't be back. There's not anything in this date, I'm afraid."

If I was expecting her to take the hint, I was sorely mistaken.

"I don't mind" she said, looking intently into my eyes, hard enough to unnerve me. "There's nothing wrong with casual sex."

Had she bewitched me with world-class eye mesmer, or was it just the booze and blue-balls from Olga? Suddenly I started thinking I'd quite like to fuck this chubby girl. I drew myself up straight and gave her my speech.

"I've enjoyed these drinks, but I don't want to see you again. However, my apartment is five minutes walk away. If you want to come back, I'll fuck you."

"Okay. Let's go."

That's how we found ourselves walking back while I kept my eyes peeled in case Olga re-emerged and saw me humbling myself with a Tinder tart. Sarah struck up a monologue, the gist of which was she'd been seeing her boyfriend a few years and he'd gone off to Greece on a study exchange program. He'd claimed the situation warranted loosening up the bounds of their monogamous relationship such that he was now entitled to a fair crack at Greek women without Sarah getting onery. Sarah had reluctantly agreed but now decided that if he was allowed to fuck around then surely so was she. Thus she created a Tinder account a few days earlier and I was the first man she'd met.

I didn't know if I bought her story, but it was certainly an interesting little speech.

"So, we'll fuck. I hope it's good. And then I'll leave" she said, offering herself up cheaply.

We snuck into my room without alarm, as my flatmates were still out partying. I put some music on and we kissed. I didn't really want to, as I knew she really wasn't very attractive. Sarah understood this and dropped straight to her knees to suck me off. Now, I'll grant that she was very good at it and I don't doubt she'd done a lot of that kind of thing in her short time upon God's green earth. So with me swaying on my heels all drunk, and looking down at Sarah's big round eyes looking up while my cock filled her mouth, I started to develop a finer appreciation for my predicament. The old fire returned and I wanted to do some damage — to speak figuratively, you understand.

Girl Junkie

Now, there remained a problem.

I couldn't strip her naked because who knows what unpleasant surprise I might've gotten if she sported a spare tire around her waist. Her tits looked fine pushed up into a bra but I'd learned the hard way many years back that you don't ever want a fat lass to take her bra off. There was no choice but to bend her over the study desk, rip her strides down, and do her from behind.

She let me raw dog her, though I'm not sure that was wise on my part.

How can I describe the appeal of this sordid encounter?

I didn't fancy Sarah at all. She was easily the least attractive girl I'd banged in my entire life. Now, that doesn't mean she was ugly — she had a pretty face, clean skin, good hair, decent proportions. But all that was subsumed under ten, maybe fifteen, kilos of meat. She was a seven who'd eaten her way down to a five. Shame on her letting herself get like that by the fresh age of twenty-two and shame on me for poking my dick into her. And yet, the strange thing is, I was really enjoying it!

I turned her over and did her normal missionary, still careful not to allow my eyes to wander from her face, the one area where she was eminently respectable-looking.

"I'm going to do you in the ass, you slag" I told her.

"Yes!" she said.

So I did.

Finally, I pulled out and came all over her upturned face and she licked me down. I heard what sounded like the front door being unlocked.

"Best get yourself to the bathroom now and wipe that mess off your face," I told her.

Five minutes later, Sarah slipped silently back into the bedroom, closing the door softly. She put on her boots and jacket, wished me a good evening, and snuck out without me needing to insist.

I lay back on my bed, bemused. A few minutes later the landlady called through my door to ask if I've had a good evening.

I dare say I had.

Chapter 14
ROLLERCOASTER RIDE

It shouldn't have come as a surprise, but I found Warsaw to be a pleasant city with electricity, WiFi, and even hot running water. The train ride up from Krakow was delightful. Polish railways ran a modern express train coloured in subtle greys with modern seats, wide windows, that streaked through the lush countryside with easy grace. Warsaw central train station was underneath a shopping mall. Tom had given me directions to the main daygame area, of which that mall — Terasy — was the westernmost tip. Upon leaving the mall, I walked through a sparsely-turfed park surrounding an imposing Stalin-era hall of culture, a gift from the genocidal Georgian himself, and beyond that was the main shopping street. Only a few hundred metres long it nonetheless sported branches of H&M, Zara, C&A, TJ Maxx and several other popular Western brands.

I was to be quartered in the street behind that, called Chmielna. It's a long narrow pedestrian avenue flanked on both sides by assorted cafes and restaurants. Thus in beautiful sunny weather like this day, it is thronged with idle wanderers and friends sitting on patios drinking coffee, wine, or beer. Several hundred metres down it bisects Novy Swiat, a wider and more upmarket avenue also dotted with meeting venues. Turning left out of Chmielna into Novy Swiat would take me to a university campus. For now, I checked into my apartment fifteen floors up a towering block tucked just behind the aforementioned shopping street. The view from my window took in all of Warsaw, it seemed.

"Tom, pal. I'm here," I messaged.

A few minutes later, he replied. "I'm nearly done with Hank. Meet in an hour on Chmielna?"

Girl Junkie

There was a pleasant Caffe Nero directly across the road from my lodgings so I settled in at a patio table with coffee and a baguette, watching the world go by. Warsaw has a wonderfully lively energy, not unlike Krakow, but with considerably less tourism. Perhaps it was my new-town vibe, or perhaps the wonderful weather, but I felt very spritely indeed. Lots of young people milled around and my early observations suggested there'd be plenty of girls to chase.

Tom arrived full of smiles and sat down at my table. He'd only been in town for three days.

"It's ace here. Already had three dates. Look at this bird here." He pulled out his phone and scrolled through the WhatsApp Profile Images folder of his gallery app. He then thrust the picture of a pretty brunette at me. "Had a drink with her last night. Made out with her."

Steady on, I thought. *I just got here. Let me breathe.*

"I'm even getting matches on Tinder. It's Shangri-La here. Tonnes of birds and they're all up for it."

Ah, my mind made the connection. I was reminded that Tom was always excitable about new cities and every single time he'd rhapsodise eloquently about unlimited opportunities. He'd been the same with Oslo, Minsk, Kiev, Istanbul and on. Each and every time the city in question would turn out to be no more magical than the last. No matter how much early promise, when the final scorecard was tallied, most capital cities were about the same.

Still, his enthusiasm was contagious. It was one of the reasons I liked winging with him.

"I've finished my coffee. Let's have at it, then," I said.

We took a walk along towards Novy Swiat and I jumped into the first set I could find, shaking off the shrink-wrap of arriving in a new town. The girl was a brunette, a student, and she chatted pleasantly enough and gave up a number. Sun, girls, new town, Tom's enthusiasm.... it was too much.

My vibe exploded. I was *on* it.

Tom and I kept up a chat about business, our joint venture, and his coaching of Hank. Everything hummed along nicely. I opened girls as we walked. There was a memorable chat with an elegant Russian tourist sitting outside a cake shop on Novy Swiat. She was tucked between the exterior wall and a fancy white-washed metal table but I ran quick 'how best to open' calculations and slid in very smoothly indeed, thank you very much. Tom hung around at a discreet distance on the pavement, scanning passing pedestrians for a set of his own.

Almost as soon as I stood up to leave the Russian, who'd explained she was happily married, I almost bumped into a stunningly voluptuous blonde Pole and opened her. She was giggling excitedly before I'd even finished my first sentence.

"Are you always giggling? Only crazy people do that," I remarked. She giggled and couldn't answer. "You can talk, though? I can't imagine you go through life only giggling."

Kesia explained, eventually, that she was a nineteen-year old freshman student at the nearby university and she was from some shitbox little village in the south, though she didn't use precisely that term. From the corner of my eye, I could see Tom shuffling uncomfortably. I was committing the mortal sin of daygame wingmanship: value-tapping.

My vibe was so outrageously strong that it was shutting Tom down. Suddenly, I realised I'd done five sets to his zero. Even his face seemed to melt a little under the pressure of my vibe. Tom is an experienced, strong-minded man but when a good daygamer is fired up on value-tap superchargers, it's hard not to be shaken. And, dare I say it, there's nobody in the world can cope with my value-tap when I'm firing on all cylinders.

Poor Tom.

If it was any consolation to him, my ribs still hurt like buggery from Prague's bobsleigh run.

I consciously restrained myself for the next half hour, passing up opportunities to open so as to at least give him first dibs. That seemed to do the trick and Tom got in some sets of his own. While reflecting on this eventuality as I watched him chatting up a curvy redhead, I began to get an odd inkling: the past few sets I'd done weren't anything like my *Daygame Overkill* technique of the prior year. Nor were they like the sets I'd done in Prague. I couldn't yet elucidate why they were different, I just knew it was so. Nor was it radically different because I was still following the sequential stages of the model I'd drilled all these years.

It was like moving from Johnnie Walker Red Label up to Gold Label. Or from supermarket value-ice cream to Ben & Jerry's.

No, that didn't quite capture my feeling. It was more like waking up in the middle of the night and pulling on the wrong boxer shorts in the dark. Instead of feeling the expected Primark polyester, you feel the cool soft comfort of M&S 800-thread Egyptian cotton against your skin.

Or something. I didn't understand. I'd need to monitor future sets and think about it.

"There's a good daygamer here you might want to meet," said Tom. We were now up by the university, sat in another Caffe Nero. "He's called Tomas and he's a fan of yours."

"Oh God."

"No, no, no. He's a proper daygamer. Solid. I've met him. He's got your fashion and style but he's legitimately intermediate level. Getting laid. He told me he wants to meet you." I agreed, in principle, and Tom passed on his phone number. "Look, I've got to go back to Hank now. More tomorrow?"

"Yep."

I ended the first afternoon with five phone numbers and all of them replied to my initial feeler message. I went to sleep full of optimism. Daygamers are eternal optimists.

The next morning I was refreshed and looking forward to a solid day at the office — that is, on the street. I pinged Tom but he said he was busy with Hank, a fact soon confirmed by my eyes as I took my apartment block's elevator to street level and walked out onto Chmielna to see Hank talking to a tall blonde MILF in high heels, almost outside my front door. Tom was loitering by a wooden bench twenty feet away, listening in to the conversation through a headpiece connected wirelessly to a big flashing microphone on Hank's lapel.

I walked over, shook Tom's hand, and left him to his coaching. Novy Swiat had already been good to me, so I headed that direction, stopping off at my local Caffe Nero to boff down a baguette and first coffee of the day. It was shortly after lunch, as I'm a late riser. Once again, the daygame gods smiled upon me in supplying ideal weather. I wore only my brown leather boots, ripped blue jeans, and a rock'n'roll t-shirt. Many of the passing girls showed maximum skin under hot pants, denim cut-offs, or short skirts. Straight away, my vibe roared off into orbit.

Somehow I made it all the way to Novy Swiat without opening. Every girl on Chmielna was somehow inaccessible, be it she was in a large group of friends, or holding hands with a boyfriend, or some other barrier. I turned left and made for the university. It was mid-week so doubtlessly some hot flange would be milling around between lectures. I passed a pizza restaurant when I noticed an extremely hot girl rush past.

Extremely hot. High-eight territory. Some could make a claim for a nine. The quality of girl you can go several weeks without seeing alone on the street.

There was more to her than mere boner-inducing hotness. An alarm bell was ringing deep inside me. Not only was this girl a blood-bubbling perfect match for me but her manner screamed out 'open me'. Words can't explain it, but every experienced daygamer knows what I mean. One moment you're walking along scanning the streets, and the next you are blind-sided by a freight train and every particle of your being screams "OPEN THAT GIRL! NOW!!!!"

She was a tall brunette. Long naturally curly hair, light skin, and thick eyebrows over her deep brown eyes. She was as close to a perfect Serb as I could hope to find in Poland. Not only that, but she had a fine rack. When my blood pulsates with this perfect intersection of DNA-tug and spider-sense indicators of approachability, nothing stops me. Even her fast walk, headphones, and imperious facial expression couldn't dent my motivation. My feet were moving within seconds.

I ran after her, got in front, and said hello.

Her immediate instinctive reaction was to glow with pleasure. Hook point.

"I like this," I said, indicating her body and style generally, as was my usual opener these days. "Wild curly hair, nice pins, carrying your books."

"Nice what?"

"Nice pins. Legs. Of this whole street, from down there," I gestured expansively to indicate the length of pavement, "all the way up to the university. On this entire street, you have the second-best legs of all."

"And who has the best?" she asked. I smirked with a self-satisfied grin of the type that gets you punched by men, but often pleases girls. "Oh! I understand!" She laughed.

"Are you going to university?"

"Yes, I will study in the library. I do an entrance examination soon." I must've looked a little confused. "I'm seventeen," she added.

For a moment that disclosure caused me to second-guess myself. Seventeen is right on the borderline of what I'm willing to chase, possibly below. I hadn't as yet resolved in my mind what I considered fair game and whether below eighteen was morally acceptable. Then I looked at her tits. She looked all woman to me.

"Boring. Let's get a drink. Right now. There."

The pizza restaurant was behind us. Red and white checked table cloths were spread across each table. It looked nice. She thought for a moment, shrugged, and agreed. We sat down.

Girl Junkie

"I forgot to ask your name. I'm Nick."

"I'm Paula."

I ordered beer and she perused the cocktail menu for a minute before ordering some big red thing with an umbrella. Probably a tequila sunrise. I couldn't believe my luck. It was my second day in town, my first real day trawling the streets, and after my first approach of the day I was sitting at a restaurant on a picturesque little street under a clear blue sky with an extremely hot young lady who seemed very much into me. Paula knocked her drink back quickly and made quite an effort to keep the conversation going, despite stumbling English skills.

She ordered a second cocktail.

Oh my! Was Paula a dirty-birdy in disguise? From her fashion, she presented like a bookish introvert, but her eyes held the spirit of adventure. Had I put the spirit there with my loquacious charm? Was it always there? I could feel my legs shake under the table. Paula seemed to be really up for it.

We chinked glasses and I examined her nails. Her coy smile suggested she knew exactly what I was up to. So, when we finished the drinks I paid the check and walked her along Chmielna.

"This is my neighbourhood now. I'm the King of Chmielna." I continued to spout colourful nonsense until we were by the entrance to my apartment block. "I'm living here. I'll show you."

I'd made as good a show of nonchalance as I could manage despite my heart beating faster than a death metal bass drum. Paula seemed calmer than myself. She walked in ahead of me, came up to the fifteenth floor, and sat next to me on the sofa as I found my preferred YouTube videos for this stage of escalation. My sole concern was she'd left a few inches space between us when sitting down. I'd have to pull her over soon. I mulled over when might be the best moment. We'd only just arrived and the most important part of the extraction, that is, the actual extraction of her to my apartment, was already a success. There didn't seem any need to immediately jump her like a slavering rape demon.

No matter how much I wanted to.

A bottle of cheap 'bounce-back' wine chilled in my fridge. Usually, I'm not so disciplined in that side of daygame preparation. I poured us a glass each and found cringe 1970s Polish pop videos on YouTube to tease her with by proxy.

"I like Polish music," I announced.

"Really? You know our music?"

"Yeah, of course. Everyone does. You've got some of the greatest bands of all time. The Beatles, The Rolling Stones, the.... wait. No. That's England isn't it. *We* have the greatest bands of all time."

I'd cribbed that tease from Jimmy years ago and it never failed to make me chuckle. Paula showed me a song she liked and I used that opportunity to reach across over her thighs and slide her up alongside me. She stiffened momentarily and stared at me thoughtfully. There was no possibility of her misinterpreting my intent, and she had to have been expecting it.

"I need a cigarette. Can I smoke in here?"

"You can use the balcony," I said, indicating a tiny outside area where the air conditioner outlet opened to the street. There was a washing line strung at head height.

Paula turned away to rummage in her handbag, found her pack of cigarettes and lighter, then stood up, rearranged her skirt, and went out to smoke. I wanted to follow because I was getting a familiar sinking feeling, that things might be slipping out of my control. Paula clearly had an important decision to make and had shuffled outside to reflect in the fresh air with a Warsaw city view.

Standard PUA procedure in these situations is clear: resist the urge to chase. You can't force the girl into sex (as a white Christian) and crowding her at her key moment of decision will, aside from its obvious moral dubiousness, usually lead to her beating a rapid retreat. Paula was so achingly hot and circumstances had already heated up so quickly. We'd spent a grand total of thirty minutes together since my approach. It wasn't even 2pm. My resolve was weakening. I very much wanted to tug at her sleeve and whine, "please, let's have sex. We've come this far, you can at least let me slip you a length. It's only fair. You won't even notice it."

Steeling myself to remain disciplined, I busied myself with YouTube, watching her out the corner of my eye. She was puffing on her cigarette and occasionally turning to glance at me, as if to inform her decision. It was like waiting for your final lottery ball to come up. I judged a reasonable time to have passed then I joined her on the balcony, getting up close enough that she could feel my presence, but not pawing at her. She mumbled something and stubbed out the remaining half of her cigarette and walked back inside.

"Okay, I'm ready," she said, sitting on the sofa once more.

Score!

I say down next to her and pulled her in. She shuffled away and looked at me. "Okay, you can pay me."

Denied!

I couldn't believe I'd heard those words. Their meaning didn't sink in right away. Never before had I street-approached a girl, brought her home, and then been asked for money.

"What do you mean?"

"You pay, you can kiss me."

"Kiss you?"

"Yes."

Paula had poor English so I wondered if she was unsure of the nuances in propositioning me for paid sex, and thus had defaulted to the less-risky word 'kiss'. My own mood was rapidly worsening but I figured she was just being silly, trying it on. I was confident I could impose my stronger character. To do so, I'd need Google Translate.

I typed a short message on my phone and showed her. "I don't understand. Are you telling me I need to pay you money to kiss you?"

She nodded.

Well, this was certainly a novel situation. I couldn't imagine Paula was still a virgin because her mannerisms all suggested a highly-sexually-charged woman. She may not necessarily be a slut, but she undoubtedly thought of sex often and I'd have bet a year of *Daygame Mastery* royalties that she masturbated at least every other day. Nope, Paula was no frigid sourpuss. Her instinctive reaction to my approach had been unmistakeable: feminine satisfaction at being recognised as a sexual creature, by a man she liked.

"Are you serious? Nobody pays to kiss."

She shook her head, to imply I was wrong and this does in fact happen in Poland. I remain convinced it doesn't. I typed some more. "Don't be silly. You like me. I like you. Kissing is the most natural thing in the world."

More head-shaking.

She meant it. I was getting very angry. I began to wish I lived in the then-existent ISIS caliphate. They'd have let me slap her across the face and throw her out the fifteen-storey window. That's what I wanted to do. I was so disgusted by Paula that I wouldn't even rape her first.

I typed again. "You know what I wanted. We had a drink. We chatted. We know each other now."

She folded her arms. I swear she thought *I* was the cunt in this little drama.

"I don't pay for sex. I certainly don't pay to kiss," I wrote.

"Then I go," she said, and stood up.

"Yes, you go. Fuck off."

She fucked off. Good riddance.

I was shell-shocked. Every daygamer rides the emotional roller coaster where success and failure turn on a dime. Many, many times I'd had girls sit on my sofa, fool around with me, and then somehow leave without putting out. I'd had the reverse situation too, where I'd given up a girl as lost and she suddenly launches herself at my dick like I was Donald Trump walking free of a divorce court. Kalina and Sarah were vivid recent examples of such pleasant surprises.

But this? A smoking hot seventeen year old girl being extremely keen during a fast instant date, coming up to my apartment whilst giving me the eyes, and then demanding money just to be kissed? That was new. That was a whole new level of emotional roller coaster.

It had genuinely shaken me.

I ran the last half-hour's events through my mind as though replaying CCTV security camera footage. Paula had definitely not been wandering around actively soliciting an approach. I'd spotted her walking quickly up Novy Swiat with headphones on and her eyes fixed forward. She was going somewhere, no doubt to the library she'd told me about. This was not one of those entrapment scenarios like tourists experience in Riga and Budapest, where girls slowly walk the streets shucking their hips and smiling at stag-do clowns so as to "suggest a good bar" to have a date in. I was certain if I hadn't approached her, Paula would be sitting in the library this very moment, studying.

I suppose I'm glad I got her buzzed on cocktails and ruined her study vibe, I thought.

Her instinctive reaction to my approach had been pleasure. There's no faking that. I'm not a zero-approaches chode who falls for a stripper's fake IOIs. I'm *Nick Fucking Krauser*. I'm the King Of Daygame. I'd banged over a hundred girls by this point. I can read a girl's instinctive reaction. I know what disinterest on the street looks like because I'd seen it approximately three thousand times in the past seven years.

But when did Paula decide to try it on? That was the big question.

I assumed it was while smoking on my balcony. Perhaps she'd thought, *I like this guy, it's going well, but he's forty years old and told me he works in finance. I'm a hot young chick. I think he'll pay for it. Might as well get something for the sex.* Thus she'd come into my apartment quite amenable to a roll around but made the dumb only-a-seventeen-year-old-could-think-that'll-work decision to thrust out an open palm. Such things happen all the time in Havana, Cuba. I'd seen it with my own beautiful blue eyes.

Now I was reconsidering the recent timeline.

Paula had ordered two cocktails and knocked them back quickly. At the time I assumed she was nervous and was thus pre-emptively fortifying herself with alcohol, but what if she was just rinsing me for cash and prizes? That would be something to tell her friends, "I rinsed this English tourist for £10 in cocktails just by smiling and letting him grab my hand. Aren't I clever?" Had those IOIs at the restaurant been false? It had seemed too good to be true at the time, but I'd chalked it up to my having moved to the next level of game.

I'm just that god-damned attractive!

Oh dear! This was becoming quite a humbling experience. Maybe I wasn't quite so awesome as I'd believed ten minutes ago. I was just another daygamer. Girls were still reluctant to acknowledge my status in the Seduction Community. Shaking my head, I slipped on my thin leather biker jacket and went back downstairs and to street level. Whatever my final conclusion on the Paula debacle, some fresh air and a walk around would clear my head.

It would seem the day was being personally choreographed by meddlesome daygame gods because the moment I stepped out of my building onto Chmielna, I bumped into Tom and Hank outside Caffe Nero. I checked my watch and couldn't quite believe it was still, technically, lunch time. Tom introduced Hank, who I'd previously only seen from a distance in set, and I shook his hand. There was no keeping the story bottled up.

"Mate, you will not fucking believe what just happened to me, literally ten minutes ago."

I related the story and while Hank laughed, Tom didn't look at all happy to hear it. While friends, wings, and now business partners, Tom and I were also skirt-chasing rivals. That's a highly competitive business. Or, at least, the men who gravitate to skirt-chasing are highly competitive men. I'd let my exuberance get the better of me the previous day and now I was doing it again. In my mind, I was retelling a funny failure story. I think Tom heard it differently, as an "almost fucked a smoking hot seventeen year old" humble-brag.

Maybe I'd intended it that way. Who knows what dark motives skulk in the depths of my subconscious?

"Look, mate. Nice one. Brilliant. But Hank and I aren't finished the official session so we have to run. Have a good one! And don't forget Tomas!"

The duo smoothly escaped my presence and I was left increasingly bemused. With no better idea, I ducked into Caffe Nero for another baguette and coffee. I pinged Tomas a short message on WhatsApp to explain Tom had passed on his details and I was happy to meet.

"In fifteen minutes? I'm out today too," he replied.

I weighed up trawling the streets solo in an unsettled mental state versus a chat with a fellow daygamer. The latter was far more appealing. I didn't yet have the stomach to get back into the daygame saddle. I agreed and we met outside TK Maxx soon afterwards.

Tomas won't like me saying this, as we are good friends nowadays and he's his own man, but the first time we met my immediate thought was, *he's my mini-me.* I refer of course to the famous *Austin Powers* spy comedy series in which international criminal mastermind Dr. Evil has a midget dressed up in his own fashion as a combination pet/jester.

It's not so odd as it sounds.

Well, perhaps it is. But I swear there's a sensible reason for it.

Men learn through a process of imitate, assimilate, innovate. When entering the Seduction Community an ambitious wannabe-player will usually find a successful player whose style or situation resonates with him and then he'll shamelessly copy everything about him. The rationale is a good one: *what he does is working for him, and he's sufficiently similar to me that I can reproduce that and thus get equivalent results.* I had shamelessly copied many things from my *Rock Solid Game* friends Jimmy, Mick, Fernando, and Johnny. By leaving an extremely detailed documentary record in writing and video, I'd made it possible for new daygamers to copy me exactly.

There was now an army of leather-jacket-clad skinheads sporting short beards, biker boots, and rock'n'roll t-shirts. Many, many girls were now accused of being tall like a giraffe, giggling like a hamster, or walking like an angry cat. Girls were increasingly bemused that these men frequently asked them not to tell their mum they were a bad boy. Strange as that may sound to you, imagine how it felt to me as the person imitated. I didn't know if I should leverage the flattery as narcissistic supply to puff up my ego, or be creeped out and avoid these people.

I suppose it didn't matter either way so long as they bought my products.

Fortunately, for all our stylistic similarity Tomas immediately impressed me as a solid bloke. He looked good, was in shape, and impressed me with that detectable strength of character all experienced daygamers eventually acquire. He couldn't help be excessively polite to me, I think, but it was within the bounds of normality. I'd likely be a little effusive if I met my hero too.

"Chmielna and Novy Swiat are good, but this street and Terasy are probably better. More footfall," he explained. I submitted to his greater local knowledge. These were Tomas' streets and I wanted to know all the best places. We walked to the mall. Terasy is a large circular shape where the main aisle loops around so shops are on both sides, not unlike an Indy Car circuit. If you spend an hour inside it can make you dizzy, as if your steering wheel was on an anti-clockwise lock just like a Daytona 500 driver. Tomas and I entered through the large glass revolving door entrance and hung a right. It was a pleasant early afternoon shopping day so the footfall was lively.

Within twenty metres I noticed a pretty girl standing outside a shop, by a large pillar. She wore faux-retro fashion of a long wool coat, a scarf, and neat trousers. I could imagine her sitting in a poetry recital, notebook in hand. Her blonde hair fell to her shoulders and she was slim. My ongoing conversation with Tomas had shaken off all lingering frustration of the money-grubbing 17yr old so I felt good about opening again.

"You look strange," I said to the blonde. "In a good way. Your fashion is like from another era."

She smiled in thanks.

"I like your blonde hair and blue eyes. You look good."

She realised what I was up to, and smiled again to indicate she was receptive.

"I'm Nick."

"I'm Lala."

We chatted five minutes then I suggest we go to the Costa cafe by the entrance. As we walked off Tomas took note that I was on an instant date and went off to do his own sets solo. Terasy has a large atrium by its entrance that is lit by sunlight through a curved glass facade reaching from the floor to the fourth-floor domed ceiling. Lala and I walked past that and to the large escalator complex leading up to shops and down to the train station. Costa cafe was on a corner directly overlooking the escalators. Much like Palladium in Prague, the outside tables of Costa in Terasy were popular fishing spots with daygamers because of the wide field of view they offered and the chance to catch a girl's glance as she came up the escalator.

I walked Lala inside and ordered coffee. "Go get that table by the window," I indicated and she nodded and took it.

Like most instant dates, I didn't have especially high hopes for Lala based on long-established probabilities. She was certainly pretty and once she hung up her coat, I took a good look at her figure. It was just right: long Slavic legs, wide hips, ample ass, flat stomach, a handful of tits, and slim rounded arms. She seemed awfully agreeable and enjoying the opportunity to meet me. For all those positives, all instant dates carry a catch. It's quite possible to cast a spell over the girl on the street and on into the cafe, but when you take her phone number the bubble will burst. You simply don't know how she'll react upon cooling down. Girls outside the bubble are far less predictable than girls still inside the bubble. Many, many times I'd spent an hour with a girl on an instant date and walked away thinking, *she absolutely loves me, this is completely on*, only for her to ignore my follow-up messages and never see me again.

That's the tough reality of daygame when you chase skirt half your age and two points hotter. All you can do is invest the time, roll the dice, and hope for the best.

"I love coffee in the early afternoon," I blathered. "The smell of coffee beans relaxes me. There are few things better than stretching out in a comfortable chair by the window, with a paperback novel and a cup of coffee. It's living the dream." This was standard nonsense I'd say early on a date, to fill the space with positive energy and let a girl gradually loosen up.

Lala nodded and smiled. "I like coffee too."

"Tell me something about you. So far I know the following—" I held up my fingers to count off a list of facts, "You're called Lala, you're from a city in Western Belarus, you have nice blonde hair, and when you smile you look like a chipmunk. What else?"

She told me she was nineteen years old and had come to study at university with the aim of qualifying for residency and ultimately Polish nationality. I'd soon learn this was a very common dodge in Warsaw. Over the next few trips I'd meet many Ukrainians and Belarusians with precisely that plan. Considering the geography, it made sense. Poland was the nearest European Union member to them. Lala's English was good so we fell into a comfortable groove. She didn't give much away in terms of overt signs of excitement but it was obviously she liked me. That was good, because I really liked her. After half an hour it was time for the next big move: either take her number or bounce her to a second venue.

Let's see how far I can push it, I thought. My spider-sense wasn't tripping out, and our interaction didn't feel strongly sexual, but there was enough simmering below the surface that I felt something might happen if I keep Lala in the bubble.

"Do you know Chmielna street?" I asked.

"Yes."

"It has many nice cafes and bars. Let's go to one of them."

"Okay."

Such words sound unremarkable but for an instant date that's a key moment. The girl has had a look at you, satisfied her immediate curiosity, and has likely made up her mind whether you make the grade, at least initially. So, asking Lala for a second drink was quite a come on. The energy shifted from 'casual coffee' to 'potential romantic adventure'. You'll lose a lot of girls at this point, hence my relief that Lala signed up.

We walked through the park by the big imposing Stalin tower, then down steps into a small open-air plaza below ground level leading to a metro station. Beyond that we walked through an underpass and onto the main shopping strip, turned right by TK Maxx, and on to Chmielna. We passed my apartment block and I glanced wistfully at the entrance. There was a chic bar restaurant called Pictures, themed after old Hollywood movies. Given the sunny weather, we sat at one of the outside patio tables.

I ordered beer. Lala did likewise. Another good sign.

"What do you do in Warsaw?" she asked.

Questions like that were hard to answer. The literal truth, unvarnished, was out of bounds: "Well, I have dedicated my life to travelling the world in order to pick up girls such as yourself, in malls such as Terasy, and try to bang them as quickly as possible. Being alone and timid-looking, I thought you were a likely candidate so now I'm getting alcohol into you and will turn the conversation towards topics that lower your inhibitions towards casual sex and raise your horniness. To be frank, Warsaw is simply as good a place as any. I've never been before and a friend of mine who lives a similar lifestyle suggested it might be a good place to get laid."

I have, on occasion, experimented with that route, with mixed results. I've also tried many less sexual variations ranging from 'travelling businessman' to 'reckless adventurer' tropes. My difficulty lay in my refusal to tell lies. I needed to find an explanation that was substantially true but which emphasised elements conducive to casual sex and blurred those elements that didn't. For Lala, I answered thus:

"I have a Polish friend in London who studies in Lodz but spends lots of time in Warsaw. He told me I'd like the city, as he knows I like things like this," I gestured expansively at the cafes and pedestrians around, as I'm apt to do. "Another of my English friends recently moved to Krakow for work. It all fit together nicely. So I decided to visit Krakow and then get the train here for a look around."

Like I said, all absolutely true but not quite the whole story.

"How long will you stay?"

"Probably for a month."

"A month!?" she spluttered, in a restrained lady-like manner of reserve. "Do you have work here?"

"No, I don't need to work. I work in London three months over winter, collect all my money, and then travel for nine months."

"Oh, that sounds so nice!"

Frankly, yes it does. I'm a lucky man and I don't ever forget it. The girls I meet usually have study and work. Typically they are so young as to have not yet had opportunities to travel the world or seek adventure. I wanted to play that angle, that I am an International Man of Mystery and a girl's ticket to freedom and adventure. The conversation turned to travel and I probed for Lala's hopes and dreams.

An hour passed. We had two beers each. I still didn't know whether to take her number of keep things going. Ultimately, it was a spontaneous desire to roll the dice that decided me.

"Let's go watch some YouTube. My apartment is right there."

"Okay."

Now it hit me. My legs trembled as they always do at this moment: the precise second when you realise she knows what you're up to and is quite happy to be extracted to your den of iniquity. It still wasn't a slam dunk, as my lunchtime failure with *the slag* had recently proven, but a betting man would start looking at his chip stack and consider it wise to push it all in. That's what I did.

It was a short walk. I used the security fob to buzz us into the lobby and then we took an elevator up fifteen floors, walked along a dark hallway, and I let us into my apartment. We still hadn't kissed, so a doubt lingered. Some girls are so naïve as to think men invite them to their apartments for a friendly chat. I'd scoff at that thought had I not been stung by such time-wasters many times before. Once indoors, I faced a choice of two strategies.

Option one suits only if the preceding date has been hot and horny, such as kissing in the bar, a girl climbing all over me, and perhaps some squeaks, moans, and rattles issued from her vocal chords during the process. Such girls will stare with wide sparkling eyes and simmer like California scrubland waiting for a careless hiker to drop a cigarette to provoke the conflagration.

Lala wasn't any of those things. She was composed, amused, and still playing the role of an elegant and only slightly-adventurous girl. So, option two called for the patient approach: relax her. I indicated the sofa.

"Take a seat. I need to go to the bathroom."

I looked at myself in the mirror to psych-up and review the available evidence. We'd met ninety minutes ago, she'd agreed to everything I had suggested, and her mannerisms suggested sexual interest. She wasn't flirty or suggestive, nor did she appear especially horny or dirty, yet the simple fact was she'd walked up into my apartment. It *had* to be on. Had to be. Forget that silly 17yr old tart. Not every girl is a chancer. Some simply like you and hope you'll bang them. Lala was likely such a girl.

I gave it another minute, purely to let Lala acclimatise herself to my place and thus not feel pressured. Then I joined her on the sofa and opened up my laptop. We watched the usual nonsense. I think I still used the 'Trololo stack', a series of four related viral videos featuring a Russian singer from the 1970s, and then clever edits putting his singing onto funny videos of cats and dogs. It didn't really matter, it was just something light to fill the space while our non-verbals carried the weight of seduction.

After the fourth video finished, I did one last mental recap to ascertain if now was a good time to make my big move.

"Come here," I said, scooping Lala by the hips to bring her right up against me. She giggled softly and let me do it. Okay, that confirmed things. I picked up her legs by the ankles and draped them over me. She readjusted, turning towards me, and then I kissed her.

And that was it. Jackpot!

She tore my face off in sexual hunger, pressing in and grabbing at me. I pulled her into my lap and she straddled me, grinding softly. I stood her up and walked towards the far wall, her legs wrapped around my waist, and up against a tall wooden closet. She disentangled and I pressed into her, kissing. I roamed my hands around her tits, ass, and then rubbed her between the legs. Thunderbirds were still Go!

I unbuckled my belt, got my dick out, and guided her hand to it. She tugged keenly so I put light pressure on her shoulders with my fingertips and she dropped to her knees. Then she sucked me off for a minute or two. All my pent-up frustration from the earlier near miss evaporated. I had a beautiful teenage Belarusian girl on her knees with my dick in her mouth. Life was good.

I pulled her up, undressed her roughly, spun her around, bent her over, then stuck my dick in her. I rattled her from behind as she braced herself against the closet and moaned. Her ass was great, so I slapped it and kneaded it like pizza dough. It felt like I could spend the rest of my life pounding her pussy from behind like this without ever growing bored. However, I like my variety. I grabbed a handful of hair, pulled out, and dragged her next door into the bedroom and pushed her roughly onto the bed.

She collapsed in a flutter of pillows, duvet, and jiggly young curves. I got on top and smashed her some more. The mattress was extremely soft so it felt like bouncing atop a wagon full of hay.

"You like this don't you?" I said, returning to my favourite SDL patter. "You like that I saw you in the mall. I thought, yeah she's hot, I'll fuck her. Then I picked you up, brought you here. And now I'm fucking you."

"Yes!"

"My hard dick is deep inside you. I'm smashing you into the bed. You love it, you dirty girl."

"Yes! More!"

It's at times like this I really regret society giving women the vote. They are just too easily led.

We were having so much fun that I wanted to string it out a while. I brought her into the kitchen and banged her doggy-style over the bench, then finally pushed her back down to her knees and came in her mouth. She swallowed, like a trooper. Then we showered and chilled out on the sofa.

I was extraordinarily pleased with myself. The past two hours had been a vindication of everything daygame related. I'd shown up in a new city and gotten laid on my second day. Not only that, but with a very attractive young lady half my age whose personality also fitted mine well. The cherry atop this particular pudding was soaring to such heights immediately after the crushing disappointment of throwing another hot teenager out of my house barely two hours earlier.

Few things are as volatile as daygame.

My phone buzzed. "How was the i-date?" asked Tomas.

"+1" I replied. That was almost as satisfying to the ego as cumming in Lala's mouth.

There was no chance of me hitting the streets again that afternoon. My body was drained but it was my mind that really suffered. I felt hungover, like I'd woken up after an all-night drink-and-drugs bender. I scoffed a pizza across the road then lay on my sofa with a bottle of whiskey, watching daygame videos on YouTube. Tom had been posting content again so I listened to one of his podcasts, announcing the launch of his FlowMad product. *Good on him*, I thought. He'd already sent me a free login to the product but I'd only skimmed it so far.

I had a look at what else was on his channel. There was an odd podcast from two weeks earlier called *Street Hustling*. What on earth is 'street hustling', I wondered? I listened and it sounded like he was just describing normal daygame but putting his own label onto it. That struck me as odd, not unlike how Real Social Dynamics would invent silly proprietary terms for concepts other people had already invented and named. He seemed to be framing daygame as a kind of rebellious activity, drawing parallels to other hustlers such as pool sharks, card sharps, pickpockets, and bank robbers. To Tom, they were all 'hustlers', a band of brothers chiselling a living from between the cracks of society. He was thus wrapping up daygame with such dubious glamour. We were Billy The Kid, Jesse James..... Ted Bundy.

Tom and I had many conversations about how best to frame daygame both in our own minds and in the girl's. A normal ambitious man would simply call it 'chatting up girls' and leave it at that. On a Saturday afternoon he might call his best mate and say words to the effect of, "let's have a walk around town and crack on with the birds." I'd done it myself, briefly, in my pre-game youth. However, we were not normal men.

We were relentless optimisers.

Once you understand the concept of 'frame', you understand its power. If you can direct your mind with the correct metaphors, that imagery will fill in all the blanks for you and power you through self-doubt. Just consider the difference between conceptualising skirt-chasing as 'fishing' or as 'hunting'. Completely different imagery springs to mind. A fisherman sets up in a bountiful spot, throws out a lure, then hopes to reel in a catch. It's a relaxing and passive approach. A hunter strikes out into the wilderness and looks for spoor. He tracks a specific target and sets up for a kill. That's an aggressive and pro-active approach. Both work, but they encourage different thoughts and emotions. We wanted a frame that was optimal.

"I like what you wrote in *Daygame Mastery* about 'respect the hustle'," Tom had explained. "It's like what Jon Matrix and I did with *Date Against The Machine* for Andy, and it's still his best-selling product. We are beyond the pail of normal society. Nobody likes PUAs. There are societally-approved methods for men to meet women and we are doing an end-run around them. Every man who gets lots of girls has a system. We have ours, but it's only one possible system. Beckster had a different one, with his nightclub VIP table game. Good-looking gym guys have their own hustle. Like you said, don't get mad. Respect the hustle."

"I'll agree that far," I said.

He hurried on enthusiastically. "A couple of years ago in Minsk I remember feeling like I was in *Oceans Eleven*, robbing Las Vegas casinos in the middle of the day. All the Belarusian men were at work or university and there was me walking down the street hitting on their women, totally uncontested. It was liberating." Yes, I'd felt the same way. I understood the lure of winning the game by side-stepping the competition but it didn't sit well with me. It felt like cheating, even though I didn't feel strongly enough about it to actually turn down the resulting trophies. Tom continued. "We're hustlers, mate. We are like Paul Newman in *Cold Hand Luke*. Like door-to-door bible salesmen cold calling on housewives."

We discussed at length and while I certainly saw the appeal of this frame, of taking more than you deserve and of cheating the system and getting one over on 'the Man', I couldn't shake the sense that it was antithetical to my own beliefs. I didn't want to bang girls because I'd bamboozled them so effectively that their judgement was impaired. I wanted the girls to look at me and think, *he's my best option. I want him.*

I wanted to deserve my lays. I wanted to earn them.

The reason SDLs felt so vindicating was *not* from a sense of having successfully swindled a girl out of her chastity. Rather, it was the craftsman's joy of creating something special out of nothing, that an end-user would value. I was creating a seductive adventure in which the girl was a knowing and willing participant. That seemed a frame far more conducive to my long-term mental health.

"Tom, I'm not so sure I consider myself a kindred spirit to pickpockets, con-men, and burglars. We aren't stealing anything. It's the opposite, we are building up something special and offering girls an opportunity. I don't want to be the Jeffrey Dahmer of seduction."

So, watching his *Street Hustling* podcast I began to realise that Tom and I subscribed to world-views more different than I'd previously thought. He'd put up a few more videos in which old daygame moves were re-named for Tom's new brand. Comically, he had invented *the Maradonna move*, which meant simply shaking a girl's hand. I wondered if he'd next invent *the Torero Curve*, a wheel-shaped appliance that turns on an axle and can be used to drive along roads.

Deep down, I knew something was up. It seemed clear that Tom was doing a 'soft-next' on me, that is to say to disassociate from someone without telling them. He'd scrubbed me from his channel, from most of our shared promotional video, and was now re-branding a model created by many men (the LDM) as his own creation with his own brand name. It seemed he wanted his YouTube channel to be a walled garden, viewers discovering daygame for the first time through Tom would think he's all there was. He'd used Andy's *Daygame.com* platform to raise his profile initially, then used association with me and my large blog readership to further raise it. Now that he had ten thousand YouTube subscribers he finally felt strong enough to discard me and push on alone.

That's what I thought at the time, anyway.

It was while in this foul mood that I checked out *Street Attraction*'s channel. They were rising names in London who had built a strong subscriber base with infield and travel videos. The team was a three-man band, being the leader Eddie, his younger friend Richard, and a Polish guy in his thirties called Maciek. Eddie had introduced himself to me in November the previous year at my *Balls Deep* launch event in London. He'd shaken my hand, said he'd enjoyed my material, and wished me luck. That made a positive impression on me, as a solid masculine man who could probably be trusted. Richard was a stark contrast in energy, though equally likeable. He was in his early twenties and seemed hyperactive. Many of *Street Attraction*'s best infield videos were of Richard doing crazy things in the street and pulling off bold gambits. He had a few street kiss-closes on video. Maciek was a back-stage man, rarely appearing on camera.

Eddie had just posted up a long video of a talk he'd given in Poland a few weeks earlier titled something along the lines of 'How To Get A Same Day Lay — With Infield'. I clicked on it. My first surprise was how big the hall was, there must have been two hundred men in the audience, because Eddie was speaking as part of a larger event organised by Polish PUAs. Eddie stood at the front and patiently explained his version of the LDM while pausing to show clips of an infield video of a same day lay he'd gotten from Trafalgar Square that year.

I immediately understood the subtext. It is extremely hard to get SDLs on video not just because of their rarity, but also due to the logistical challenges of recording the whole thing from street, to date, to apartment. If the video or audio cuts out at any time, YouTube monkeys all begin screaming 'Fake! Fake! Fake!' Just imagine how many hours you need to pound the streets, how prepared you need to be with your microphones and cameras, and how disciplined your cameraman must be, in order to capture the elusive unicorn of an SDL video.

Eddie had done it. He'd banged a pretty blonde teenager in about two hours. She was English, too.

I understood his excitement as I'd have felt the same way. Towards the end of his instant date, as he was bringing her home, he must've been quivering with anticipation. Not so much for the sex, as for the video recording. As soon as the girl left his house he'd have been calling his cameraman: "Did you get it? Did you get everything?" They'd have watched the raw footage and thought, *this is money!* So, I surmised that Eddie had mulled over different ways to use the footage and settled on this one. He'd created a product called *Approach To Lay* and was in Poland promoting it with a free seminar speech.

I was impressed. Eddie wasn't just showing good skills in getting the girl, but also a wise head in having it recorded and marketed. I watched his whole seminar then sent him a WhatsApp message congratulating him on a solid piece of work. He replied thanking me.

There was one sticking point, however. Something which aggravated me as acutely as seeing a Muslim in an English city. Eddie's talk had essentially outlined the LDM that I'd spelled out in *Daygame Mastery* and he had even used jargon that I'd specifically invented, such as "the fire escape move" to describe a way of testing if a girl's last minute resistance is real or token. He hadn't given me any credit nor mentioned my name once. To the Polish crowd, he'd invented this stuff.

Now, it wasn't flagrant. Eddie had a right to revel in his recent accomplishment, and the LDM was created by more people than just me. You could make a strong case that the Model was public domain now, such was its ubiquity within daygame circles. So, in a different mood I'd have likely felt more flattered than annoyed. But this was coming so soon after uncovering Tom's shady moves and I was piqued at the idea of another popular YouTube channel airbrushing me out of history. And, I won't deny, I can be quite jealous of other people's successes.

I messaged Tom. "Check out *Street Attraction*'s new seminar video. They literally outline the whole LDM and don't give us any credit."

To my surprise, and not without inspiring in me a sense of irony, Tom was more angry at being 'disappeared' than I was. He suggested we send a stern email demanding *Street Attraction* stop passing off our material as their own. That seemed to me an over-reaction.

"We can make this win-win," I wrote to Tom. "Eddie seems like a solid guy so I'm certain he's not trying to mess us about. I'll bet you it simply didn't occur to him that we'd be this bothered if he didn't give us credit. How many times have we used Mystery or 60YOC material without specifically crediting them? Loads! *Street Attraction* are legit daygamers and I think probably good people. We should befriend them. Bring them in, not start a beef with them."

To his credit, Tom quickly agreed. I wrote a polite message to Eddie and Tom sent it from his account. We congratulated him on his recent good content, wished him luck, and asked if they'd consider crediting us sometime just so people knew the theoretical antecedents to the Model. Eddie replied the next day in friendly tones, promising a special video listing their influences. True to his word, a few days later *Street Attraction* posted a video of Eddie and Richard specifically naming Tom, myself, and some other intellectual pioneers in the community.

Now I felt embarrassed at having asked for it, because it made me feel awfully vain. Eddie and Richard had acted impeccably to our request. That was enough for me. The storm had now blown over the teacup. I messaged Eddie thanking him for the video and we struck up a chat that culminated in a plan to meet for coffee at the earliest opportunity. There was now a track record by which I could judge him, and my conclusion was I'd like to be on friendly terms with him.

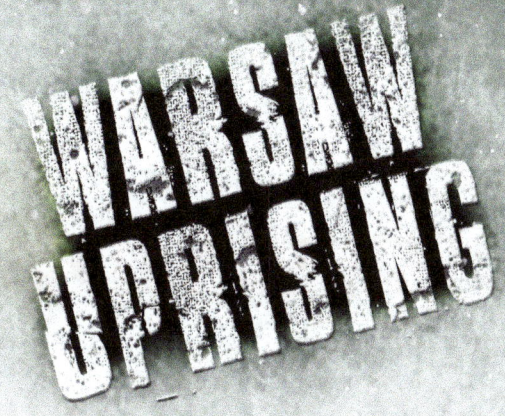

Chapter 15
WARSAW UPRISING

My daygame had changed. I wouldn't realise it until much later, with the added perspective of hindsight, but my learning process progressed through distinctive stages which seemed to conclude each time I created a product. Having followed up *Daygame Overkill* with a winter hibernation, I'd inadvertently undergone a process of reformation. The ugly maggot of Old Krauser was emerging from his chrysalis in the bright spring sunshine as New Krauser, a beautiful butterfly bringing colour and joy to Warsaw's streets.

At a core level, the change was best expressed as my feeling let off the leash. It was like the Model had been a corset constricting my freedom that was now suddenly cast aside, no longer demanding I follow the specific sequential stages of daygame. I was the jazz guitarist throwing aside his sheet music and improvising from moment to moment. It felt like all I needed was to allow my vibe to switch on and then all the right moves would present themselves unbidden.

Tom noticed this and he didn't like it much. On our second day walking between Terasy and Novy Swiat he became increasingly uncomfortable as my vibe overpowered his. I couldn't blame him, frankly. Most days I was a good wing, well drilled in the wing rules set up in my *Rock Solid Game* days with Jimmy, Mick, and Fernando. Now, however, my style had switched. With the Model receding into the background, and with it the various mental supports we all used to prop up our motivation and overcome approach anxiety, I was now powering myself on vibe. Pure, raw, uranium-enriched vibe.

My daygame engine was hungry for fuel. What I couldn't generate internally, I took from the girls themselves, feeding off their happy excitable reactions. When that proved insufficient to feed the beast, I sucked additional vibe from my wings. In this case, from Tom. New Krauser was an exuberant, carefree, happy-go-lucky force of nature on the streets. It made my sets excellent, but it also made me insufferable to be around for longer than an hour.

Tom felt himself wither and die. He made his excuses and went back to Hank.

Judged purely from a technical point of view, a keen observer of my sets would say I'd become high-energy and made heavy use of sexual spikes and touch. Rather than standing at a polite distance engaging in conversation on a get-to-know-you topic, I'd be right in a girl's face teasing her, checking her out, and playing with her hair or prodding her stomach. When it hooked well, which was rather often, girls seemed to heat up. It was like overfilling a balloon, watching it get bigger and bigger and bigger.

It was also incredible fun. Every good set was like hitting the crack pipe. Dopamine flooded my brain and sent my vibe soaring ever higher, leading to better sets and even more dopamine. Nobody can remain that high forever. After a few hours I'd crash back to earth and find myself incapable of constructing simple sentences for the rest of the day. I'd acheived something I thought ought to be recorded in the annals of scientific history: I was the world's first producer of natural bio-cocaine. I could get high from daygame. From talking. The only raw materials I needed were sunshine and girls.

If word got out, the illicit drugs industry could collapse. The CIA and Vatican would lose their primary sources of funding.

I was dangerous.

Tom became scarcer, understandably, but I had the good fortune to meet a new wing that same day, a Danish man called Lars. He'd contacted me on my PUA Facebook page a few months earlier and happened to catch me in a good mood so I'd given him a free online consultation. We'd hit it off well so upon realising he'd be visiting Warsaw the same time as myself, coffee seemed the natural plan. Like every other meeting that month, it was in the Caffe Nero across the road from my apartment. I was sat poking at a roast beef baguette when he showed up. My first impression was *bloody hell, he looks exactly like action movie star Jason Statham.* There was an unmistakeable resemblance: skinhead, short stubble, big muscles, and similar face. Additionally, Lars dressed very well, just like the popular Instagram male models.

Surely I was the only daygamer who looked a bit like Jason Statham? It was a little chastening to see Lars pulling it off considerably better than I. Anyway, it didn't matter. He looked cool. We shook hands, he sat down, and we navigated the awkward early moments of meeting someone you'd only heard about online. Like a Tinder date.

"How on earth do you struggle with women?" I asked. "You are built like an action movie star."

"Well, it's complicated. I'll explain. Are you okay for coffee? I can go and get you another one."

"I'm fine. Please explain. I'm genuinely intrigued."

"Like I said in our Facebook chat, it's easy for me to get Tinder dates. The problem is that, in person, the girls all seem to fade away. Often my dates begin with a hug and I walk them to a bar. We sit talking and the girl is all smiles and sparkling eyes." He looked at my empty cup and plate. "Are you sure you won't have a coffee? I can get you a sandwich too."

"I'm good." Though I appreciate the sentiment, receiving gifts feels icky. I resist the guru-acolyte dynamic as much as I can. I'd rather meet men as equals.

"Are you sure you want to hear this? I don't want to bore you with my issues. Okay? Well, after about an hour I go for the kiss but by then the girls have gone cold. Something switches off inside them and what was previously a long, engaging conversation crumbles into small snippets and short sentences. It's infuriating. Some of these girls are hot. I don't get it. They like how I look, often saying it at the beginning of the date. 'Wow, you are handsome' and so on."

Frustrating, no doubt, but the reason was clear to me It was early afternoon and the sun shone fiercely through the large cafe window, directly into my face. I squinted. Lars noticed my discomfort.

"Is that too bright? Would you like my chair? We can swap."

Yes, now I was certain.

"Lars, you're too nice. I've seen the Tinder profile pictures you sent me. In those, you look like a Viking badass what with the beard, scowl, and the cool beanie hat. Girls match you *precisely* because you present online as a bad boy. Then you show up with your big muscles and action-movie star posture and the poor girls think all their dreams have come true. Then you start talking and the illusion breaks. It's all 'are you comfortable?' this and 'can I take your coat?' that. They came out hoping a gruff masculine arsehole would bash 'em over the head, drag them home, and fuck them. Instead, they get a gentleman."

"Oh."

"You have to be more of a cunt. Like me."

"Ah yes, that's a little difficult. I was brought up in a devoutly Christian household, taught to respect women and always be polite."

"Be a cunt."

"I shall try."

"Okay. Consultation over. You owe me £200." His eyes widened, then he realised I was joking. "See, like that. I was being a cunt. It has a salutary effect, like adding spicy wasabi sauce to bland sushi rice."

We hit the streets together. There is a busy road between the Stalin tower and Terasy mall with a pedestrian crossing covering it. Hard Rock Cafe is on the corner. The streets had filled up and as we waited for the green light the pavement grew thick with shoppers. As we crossed, my eye flicked to several girls. All were pretty but none grabbed me emotionally. I wanted to *feel* it. When my vibe was on I no longer had the patience to grind out sets. I wanted them to spring spontaneously into my consciousness, for the girl to impress me so instinctively that I was opening her before I even realised it.

Those girls weren't right, but I needed wait only twenty more seconds for one who was. Just as we approached the large revolving doors at the mall entrance, a lovely girl came swanning out in the opposite direction, towards us. She had long blonde hair and what I call the 'amateur female tennis' figure. That means bronzed vibrant skin, generous bust and hips framing a flat stomach, and curved thighs and calves like she works out but not too hard. I'll take that figure over catwalk-skinny every day of the week. Seeing as today was, strictly speaking, one such day of the week logic thus compelled to take her.

"Oi! Girl in stripy blue and white dress." She turned and smiled. "Right! Stop. Good! I'm Nick."

"I'm Mileena."

Mileena, eh? I'd already had one of those in Belgrade.

She looked especially good close up. I soon found out she was a university student visiting for the weekend from some out-of-the-way city. Mileena wasn't an especially engaging talker but my trousers couldn't have stirred more had I been listening to Winston Churchill tell me I should fight 'em on the beaches. I wanted to shag her on the beaches, on the landing grounds, in the fields, and in the streets. Actually, in one particular street — Chmielna — in an apartment fifteen storeys above. Whatever the cost may be.

We chatted a couple of minutes before I invited her for coffee. The staff of Caffe Nero were perhaps surprised to see me back so soon, but they were getting used to my odd habit of showing up with a different person every time. Mileena and I sat outside, enjoying the sun.

I wish I could remember what we talked about, but it was certainly gibberish and no different to my usual patter. Sets have a way of blurring into fudge over time. We quickly hit a comfortable groove of mutually-recognised attraction. Mileena let slip that she'd get her train home the next morning so I knew my only option was to keep blowing up our little love bubble and then hope for the best.

"Let's get a beer next door," I suggested, indicating Pictures bar. She agreed.

By the end of the first beer we'd been kissing. Mileena had the excitable spark of a girl who knows she's on an adventure and loves being swept along. I couldn't quite believe how hot she was. Not that she was a head-turning stunner from Stunnerstan, mind you, nor that I hadn't already banged a bunch of broads as good or better, but because this was the day after the previously-related exhausting roller coaster ride that had ended with my dick in Lala. It seemed too good to be true, repeating the feat the very next day. Same Day Lays just don't work that way. The Daygame Gods don't allow it.

"My place is over there. Let's go up and watch some YouTube."

To my surprise, she agreed. We hadn't seemed that far along in the seduction dance. So, I found myself rinsing out the wine glasses left by Lala and pouring what was left of my bounce-back booze into them. It had taken three girls to finish the bottle. I took the glasses over to the sofa, where Mileena was watching baby pandas tumble down a slide.

"Cheers."

"Cheers."

Kissing and escalation followed, like economic ruin follows socialism. Mileena straddled me, let me roll her onto her back, and seemed to be having a giggling, exciting time of it. I felt her tits and came up against her limit. She gasped, realised what I was up to, and drew her line in the sand. I was able to pull down the straps of her dress and bra, freeing her upper body to enjoy the cool summer breeze. She seemed uncertain whether that was a good thing.

Her tits were a good thing. Two good things. My two favourite things in the world.

I alternated between kissing her mouth, her neck, and her tits. I was having a whale of a time. So much so, if I could've put it to the vote I'd have legislated to get more of it every afternoon and twice on Sundays. Mileena moaned and writhed but occasionally stopped, bit her forefinger gently, and stared at the ceiling. That didn't bode well. Plotting my next leap in escalation, I waited for another of her moaning/writhing episodes and worked my hands up under her skirt from the rear, to grab some ass.

Ass-grabbing was Mileena's line. I could kiss her on the lips, I could kiss her on the neck, and I could kiss her on the tits. But with growing confidence and growing strength she would defend her ass, she would never surrender, and even — which for a moment I did not believe — her will was subjugated and starving — she would carry on the struggle until in God's good time with all His power and His might stepped forth to the rescue and the liberation of her chastity.

Or something.

In less Churchillian terms, she shut me down. Tits, yes. Ass, no. I was not to get laid.

Mileena's moans gradually conceded ground to fully-formed syllables, which became sentences. These sentences informed me she must go because friends were waiting. I took a farewell run at her tits before she pulled her dress straps up and disengaged. We exchanged Facebook details and, had she lived in Warsaw, I'm sure I'd have seen her again. She seemed absolutely happy with our dalliance, resisting only because it was too much, too fast.

Too fast? I scoffed internally. It had been *one whole hour* since we'd met! What did she want, love letters and long walks down the beach?

I walked her back down to Chmeilna street level and kissed her goodbye outside TK Maxx. We chatted online over the next few months but my trips to Warsaw never coincided with hers. Our connection wasn't strong enough to risk my making a trip especially for her. Had she let me build up solid long game, or sent me naughty photos, I'd have reconsidered. But she didn't, so I didn't.

That evening I dated the blonde teenager from the first day out with Tom, on Novy Swiat. We arranged to meet near our initial encounter, at a corner bar next to the world's most delicious ice cream kiosk. I didn't like the date bar at all. Inside it was all velvet walls, shiny lights, and godawful dance music. However, outside was all curved plush chairs and tables. In such good weather, anything outdoors on Chmielna or Novy Swiat was pleasant by default. So, I chose a place that wouldn't confuse the young lass.

Dominica was the epitome of bubbly. Her figure was as pneumatic as Mileena's and she positively glided across the pavement to reintroduce herself. She ordered a cocktail to my rum and coke. Then once more, for the fourth time in short succession, I went through my usual first date routine. She told me about her university course, home town, hobbies, and her favourite music. It was interesting because I was interested in her. Nonetheless, it went in one ear and out the other, my brain tissues soaking up the information only as long as needed to analyse and fine-tune the direction of seduction. Then, like a bath sponge, my brain squeezed out the facts to make room for more.

"Really, you do economics?" I queried, feigning surprise. "You don't look smart enough."

"Oh! I'm quite intelligent, I think," she replied, laughing.

"I'd have thought all those graphs and equations would frighten you. You're only a girl."

Half a drink later I began my primary escalation. A sensible man would've waited considerably longer and established more rapport. Mystery himself instructs us that 'the game is played in comfort'. But, then again, Mystery also advocated the Seven Hour Rule of time spent on dates before attempting to extract a girl to a sex location. My combined time with Olga, Sarah, Paula, Lala and Mileena before extraction added up to less than seven hours.

For a week I'd been flush with a flurry of furious action. I was not to be forestalled by following the fancies of a former philanderer. I began verbally escalating.

"What part of your body do you think is the most sexy?"

She pretended to think about that, though she obviously already knew. It had to be her ass. Nobody with an ass that good would ever think otherwise.

"My ass," she said, her smug satisfaction softened by a light, girly smile. "How about you?"

"What do I like on your body or my own?"

"Of my body."

"Well, I haven't had a good look at your ass. I was waiting until you stood up to go to the bar. Hmmmm, let me think." I then made a production out of thoughtfully checking her out, like the Big Bad Wolf assessing the building materials of a little pig's house. "Tits. You have nice tits."

She blushed and took a quick sip of her cocktail. "And on your body?"

"Apart from the obvious?" I queried, crooking my finger slightly to indicate my crotch. "My neck. I have a strong neck from wrestling and boxing. A girl needs something to hang on to."

Dominica's mood exploded like a chain reaction levelling an oil refinery. She'd clearly fancied me from the beginning, as was evidenced by the sparkling quality of our street chat and her readiness to come on an evening date. Added to that was my bold escalation timed to match the alcohol from her second cocktail, heating her up. She was awfully giggly and her cheeks reddened in pleasure.

I walked her back to my apartment. At the street door, I took out my keys nonchalantly and prattled on about nonsense to distract her from the line she was about to cross. I got as far as opening the door before she stalled.

"Wait. Are we going inside?"

"Yeah, this way."

"Uh.... um.... Let's stay outside."

Every player understands the conundrum. You've met a silly young thing who is absolutely thrilled to meet you. Through long-practiced and hard-won skill you can make the seduction flow effortlessly smooth, letting her soak it up as though sinking into a hot deep bath. She experiences it as silky rippling velvet but actually creating that impression requires a series of complex calculations on your part, not unlike an intricately complex music box whose whirring cranking gears can create a deceptively simple and beautiful melody.

The velvet carpet had run out of fabric at my front door. Beyond was a harsh marble lobby floor and linoleum hallways. Dominica returned to reality, her feminine instinct warning her things were about to get very real, penis-in-vagina real, and she hadn't yet decided whether that was a good idea.

A player has a few options at this stage and he can only hope he chooses optimally.

If you correctly judge the girl is a bubbling kettle about to boil, you simply hustle her inside. "Come on, don't be such a girl," you admonish and shove her indoors, playfully. She'll giggle, stumble inside and you'll be balls deep within ten minutes. That also works if she's already decided to fuck but needs you to offer her a fig leaf of plausible deniability so she doesn't appear a brazen harlot.

If the girl is merely nervous, you take another tack. Mumble something that limits the adventure to a safe level, such as, "It's just for ten minutes. I'm tired and need to wake up early tomorrow." When a girl's hindbrain has already decided in your favour, throwing that bone to her forebrain will get her upstairs. Then it's game on again. Ease off for ten minutes in the apartment, but the game is almost won.

A third option is to play for time. Things are headed towards Balls Deep City but she needs to be walked around a park or sat in a nearby bar for another drink or two. Having planted the extraction idea, it will grow. She'll probably become more comfortable with it, the initial drama having dissipated. While she acclimatises to the thought of sex, the alcohol and rapport continue to strengthen your hand. "Okay, it's no big deal. Let's go for a walk," you say, shutting the door and affecting a nonchalant inner calm that you most certainly do not feel. *Bastard! That was close!* you really think, sympathising with The Hooded Claw feels when Penelope Pitstop narrowly escapes his clutches once more.

None of these strategems are a sure thing. Like everything else in game, you calibrate to the best of your ability, make the optimal percentage play, and hope for the best.

We stood on the threshold of my apartment building with me halfway inside and Dominica standing resolute on the pavement outside, her handbag held delicately at her belt buckle in both hands. She looked awfully cute and timid. Her manner quite belied her fantastic wide hips and bubble butt.

"I'm a virgin," she said. I wasn't expecting that confession.

"Okay."

"I can't come in."

We looked intently at each other for five seconds. She was timid but firm. My eyes naturally softened because I liked her. I wasn't faking my empathy.

"Look, that's okay. Let's have a walk."

I took her to the small grassy park at the north end of the Stalin building. It was shrouded in trees and boasted many park benches. The teenagers of Warsaw had long since pre-empted me in using it as a necking zone. I intended to join them there.

"I'm sorry, but I'm not what you think. I don't really know you."

"It's fine, really. Let's have a nice walk and sit in the park. It's a warm night with clear sky. Believe me, I'm enjoying this."

"Are you not disappointed?"

Yes, very much so. I'd been a whisker away from banging my second nineteen-year old in consecutive days. I'd already chosen the fireworks to fire overhead as I ran my victory lap around Warsaw.

"No, I'm not. I never expect anything. I just want to enjoy our time together."

The hour we sat on a park bench was the longest I've ever held an uninterrupted boner — even longer than during Donald Trump's election night win a year later. Dominica, bless her silly virgin heart, wasn't in control of her swirling emotions. She'd vacillate between climbing over me and panting in my ear, then skidding away and gazing at the stars. Who knows what fiery emotions were stirred up underneath those ample-but-not-quite-remarkable breasts? It's easy to forget that I'd been in precisely this kind of scenario a few hundred times already whereas it may be quite a novel experience for her.

I exhausted my stock of closing techniques. We'd go two steps forward then one step back. We'd break off and have a heart-to-heart on an issue dear to her in the moment. I told short evocative stories and mused philosophically upon starry nights and our place in the universe. Dominica wasn't to be moved. She'd protected her maidenhead this long and wasn't about to lose it tonight.

"Wow! That's amazing!" I said, pointing across her towards the main road.

"What?" she said, turning her head to follow the line of sight from my finger.

"This" I said, and put my hands up her shirt.

She had a laugh, and I had a grope, but it didn't advance my cause. She bleated about needing to get the last train so I walked her to the Metro and kissed her good night. I'd see her one more time but by then momentum had died. Dominica enjoyed surfing my tidal wave of seduction but that wave had broken upon the reef of chastity. No doubt she parcelled up the experience, put a ribbon on it, and set it on a shelf marked 'happy holiday memories'.

Happy holiday memories, as I'm sure my dear reader agrees, are not as satisfying to a man as honest-to-God banging.

Dominica made it two near misses in one day, and three in two days. Grimacing, I felt another dopamine hangover coming down the pike. That said, I wouldn't swap places with anyone else. Not for the whole world.

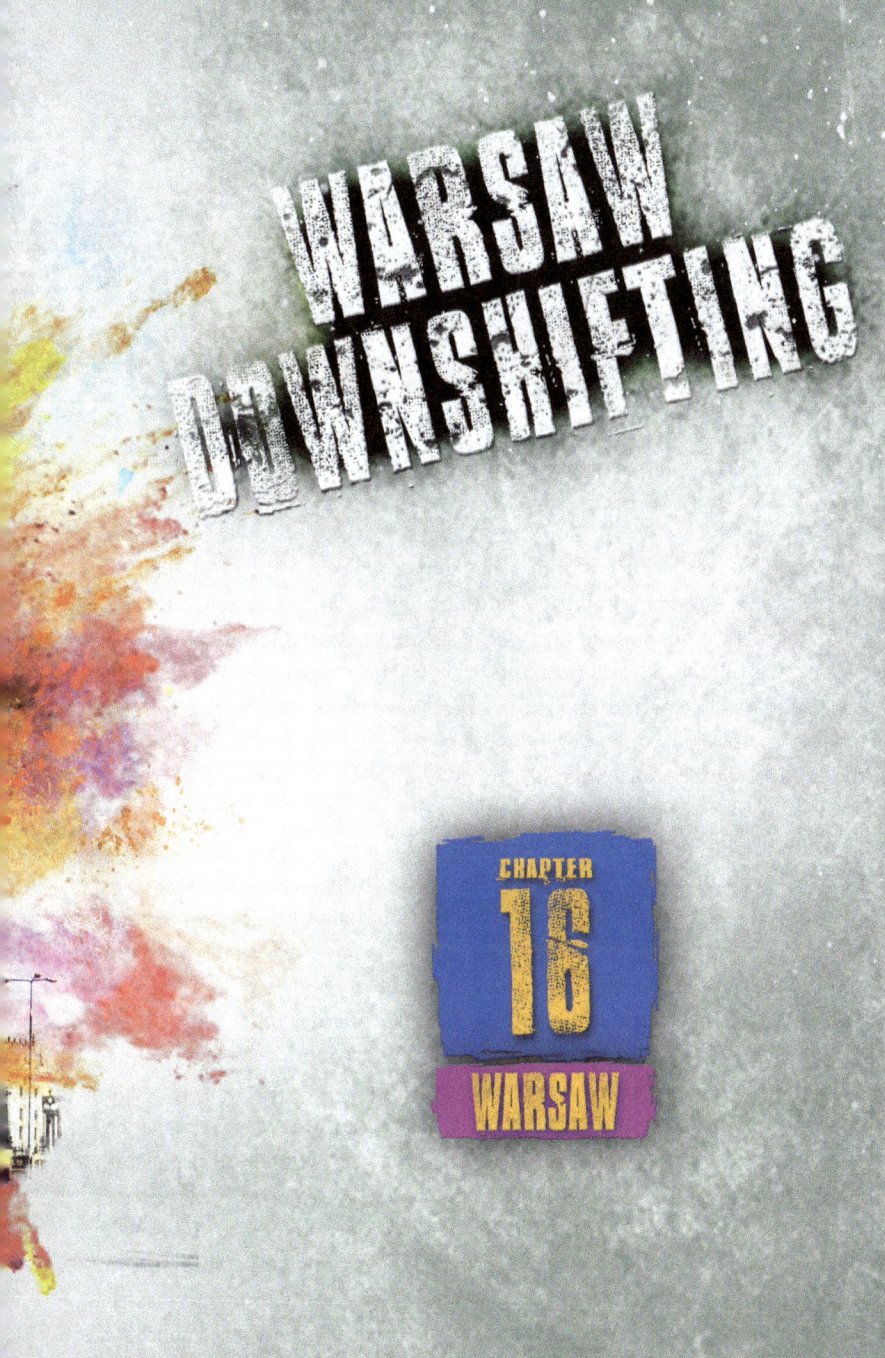

Chapter 16
WARSAW DOWNSHIFTING

Tom wouldn't come out any more. He sent a polite message explaining he was too busy with Hank and thought it better if he daygamed solo outside of coaching hours. That disappointed me because Tom is a very good daygame wing. He has a cheerful and adventurous approach to the streets and knows all the wing rules and possible permutations the streets can throw up. Winging with him is like being in a safe pair of hands and most people find the experience pleasant.

My style is rather more volatile, so my own wingmen tend to find their experiences with me either astonishingly good, or painful to endure. There wasn't much middle ground, back in 2015. I could wow men with my street game, but also shut them down with my overpowering vibe. After sessions they'd often relate they hadn't believed some of things I did, and reactions I got, were even possible. So, there was a big upside to winging with me. More so because I'd developed a keen eye to spot my wing's weaknesses and then offer them small tweaks that brought large rewards.

For all that, I could be quite tiresome to be around. I always seemed to end up with the largest share of the daygame pie. Tom had, wisely, edged off stage and into the shadows. I couldn't blame him. Warsaw represented a permanent end to our wing relationship, as we'd grow increasingly distant and soon fall out.

So, on my fourth full day in Warsaw I struck out alone with a spring in my step, walking two inches above the ground on a magic carpet powered by an emerging sexual abundance. Would this fourth day be as productive as the previous few? It would seem the answer was 'yes' because on my third approach, outside H&M, I found myself in conversation with a curvy young brunette.

Very curvy. Big firm tits, mashable ass, tennis-player thighs, and a flat stomach.

Very young. "I'm eighteen," she said.

Wanda was beginning university and extremely introverted. I'm surprised she stopped for me at all and for the first minute she remained skittish, keeping a no-man's-land of several feet between us as she looked around nervously. My carefree vibe carried the day. Eventually, she relaxed and let me step in closer.

"You seem very shy," I said, mirroring her mood so as to demonstrate empathy.

"It's not normal. I don't talk to men."

"You never talk to men?"

"Of course I sometimes talk. There are boys in my school, and we talk. I mean this. Talking to strange men. I don't do it."

"How do you feel now?"

"Scared."

"Is it a nice feeling."

"I don't know. Something about it is nice."

Though she reminded me of a frightened rabbit, frozen to the spot only long enough to decide which rabbit hole through which to bolt, I knew Wanda liked me. Natural feminine curiosity was defusing her instinctive programming to run away. If I could only put her at ease, things might go somewhere.

"You know, I've never kissed a boy," she offered, unprompted.

I'd been handed a mission from God. This poor damsel had not yet bitten from the forbidden fruit and, in what we must all agree is almost certainly divine intervention, fate had now placed her directly in front of precisely the right man to remove such a terrible burden from her shoulders.

"That's too bad," I said. "Let's have a coffee right now, on Chmielna."

"Okay."

She followed a step behind me, meekly, just how I like it. I ushered her to a table on the outside patio of Caffe Nero and was even gentlemanly enough to pull out a chair. Knowing her heart must be beating trip-hammers at what was, to her, an outrageously bold adventure, I left her alone a few minutes to ease the pressure while I ordered our coffee. I told the barista to make both coffees small size, thinking I might find the table empty upon my return and end up drinking them both myself.

Wanda was still there.

A few minutes isolation had done wonders. She seemed considerably at ease. Her English stumbled here and there but we could make good conversation for ten minutes. It was approaching 4pm and still a beautiful day, after a run of equally beautiful days and beautiful women. Rainbows, unicorns and world peace sprang to my mind. I felt so generous, brimming will goodwill to my fellow men. I'd have likely signed off a planning application to build a mosque in a European nation.

Who should I see walking along Chmeilna, on a date of his own, but Tom?

Wanda and I were sat up against a metal rail fencing off the patio area. I faced west, towards the Stalin building and thus with a wide field of view for pedestrians coming from the shopping district. Wanda sat opposite, facing the university zone. Footfall had picked up so I didn't notice Tom through the throng until he was almost passing us. He walked with consciously good posture, gesticulating authoritatively, and looking upwards at the sky. No doubt he was spinning some yarn, as we all do in the moments between meeting a girl and sitting her down at the first date venue. With him was a scraggly little beatnik girl who looked like an archetypical art student. She'd shaved the left side of her head and her unwashed dyed-blonde hair above it was pulled into a loose pony tail. Pieces of metal disfigured her face, pushed through her nose and one eyebrow. Her bare arms sported a few small girly tattoos.

On the plus side, she was petite and slim.

Tom glanced over, noticing me for the first time, and momentarily interrupting his monologue. At first, he showed pleased recognition. His eyes lit up, one daygamer on a first day noting a fellow rascal also on a first date. We both knew exactly how we'd found our girls and how we'd proceed with them without needing to tell each other. Ours is a secret society.

It's natural in these moments to check out your fellow's women. We are all interested in the quality our friends are pulling. He instinctively scanned Wanda, taking in her pretty face, thick brown hair, big firm tits, and though his view was blocked by a Caffe Nero advertising board, he couldn't help but conclude her lower half was equally tantalising. Wanda was probably an eight, and an obvious good girl. While this was occurring, mere fractions of a second, I was sizing up his girl towards the conclusion narrated above.

Tom had the shit end of this stick. His face fell.

He nodded imperceptibly, his street etiquette always was impeccable, then carried on. The girls remained oblivious. He'd only interrupted his own patter a short breath. I smiled. I liked Tom, despite knowing our friendship was currently strained to breaking point. I didn't trust him in the slightest, but I did like him. There were other times where, as my seduction rival, he'd win a round from me. However today, and indeed this whole week, the scorecard marked each round to me. This one I was winning 10-7 with two knockdowns.

If it was on Pay-Per-View, the commentators would be begging the referee to stop the fight.

Vain, puffed-up scoundrel that I am, I smiled.

"What's funny?" asked Wanda.

"Nothing. Nothing at all. I'm simply in a very good mood. I like this. Your energy pleases me."

Wanda smiled now.

Ten minutes later I walked her to my apartment building and up to my room via the elevator. She trembled the whole way up. For reasons I couldn't yet determine, she wanted to tag along with me despite swells of rising panic. I briefly reflected on why a timid eighteen year old girl who had been too shy to kiss a boy was now allowing herself to be led to the mystery apartment of a forty year old foreigner who was so obviously a player. And in only thirty minutes since first saying hello, at that! I didn't have an answer, but so long as these things kept happening I wasn't going to shit a gift horse in the woods.

Once upstairs, YouTube got another workout but my wine glasses stayed on the kitchen sink's draining board. Girls had been coming into my apartment with such unexpected rapidity that I'd not had time to replace the bounce-back booze. Wanda remained nervous but made what conversation she could.

I kissed her.

She took a few seconds to process my onslaught before her lips parted and she fumbled her way into kissing me back. Her body softened and the air seemed to leak out of her like a flat tire. A further thirty seconds of sloppy mouth action invigorated her, flipping girlish surrender to womanly passion. So hot did she become that I swear that in a dark room you'd be unable to tell her apart from a Filipino street whore. Overwhelmed by her own display, she gasped and pulled away.

"Oh!" she exclaimed, looking sheepishly at the floor. Her manner was a cartoon caricature of bashfulness, which I loved.

"How was your first kiss?"

"I like it."

We kissed more. I gently pushed her back onto the sofa. She wrapped both arms around me and one leg, for good luck. The other I pinned between my thigh and the sofa cushion. *It's on*, I thought. *I do believe it might be on!*

Immediately, my mind's computer ran all possible algorithms. Tapes whirred, transistors buzzed, and memory banks heated up. My mind simulated several seduction chess matches from opening gambit to check mate, then ran them again with changed parameters. Move and counter-move were plotted. Probabilities assigned. I hadn't expected Wanda to enter my building, nor to let me kiss her, which is why I hadn't formulated a strategy in advance. I'd stepped into the jungle without a compass.

Should I ease off, make a cup of tea, and then suggest we watch YouTube together and occasionally snog on? The goal there would be to build more rapport, get her comfortable, and date another day. Alternatively, should I run the train right now and take advantage of her raging tempest of emotions, leveraging dramatic momentum?

There are no right answers. All you can do is calibrate then roll the dice.

I decided she had already let herself go way further than her forebrain would ever knowingly allow. Her writhing, gasping presence on my sofa was entirely due to her succumbing to the pleasure of seduction. If her buying temperature should drop one degree, she'd revert to the timid girl who doesn't kiss boys that she'd been half an hour earlier. It was a gamble based on incomplete information.

I decided to go for it.

But you knew I would, didn't you?

Wanda was my fourth teenage bounce-back in four days. I was bulletproof.

I took hold of her breasts, elated to find them as easy on the touch as they'd been on the eye. Firm, buxom teenager breasts. My favourite type. She blinked excessively upon my first grapple, not surprisingly considering her sheltered existence so far, then let nature takes its course. Emboldened, I reached under her sweater and traced my fingertips along the skin of her stomach before closing in on her breasts, skin-to-skin. She liked that too, but sadly it broke the spell.

"No."

"Mmmmmm."

"No!"

She broke off the kiss but remained comfortably sprawled beneath me. My hand still cupped her right breast, something she was either temporarily oblivious too or didn't much mind.

"Are you okay?" I asked.

"Yes, I'm okay. But I should go."

"Yes, perhaps," I agreed. I gripped the lower end of her sweater and slowly lifted it up to expose her bare stomach. I kissed around her belly button. Her abdominal muscles visibly contracted, released, and then quivered. The poor girl was midway between ecstasy and terror. My boner raged. The sweet smell of Wanda's young flesh threatened to rend my mind, unleashing a demon inside. I felt such powerful forces despite being an old hand at seduction, with over a hundred notches. I could only imagine the drama Wanda felt.

"Mmm... Yes... No. I should go. Aaaah!" she explained, helpfully.

I rolled her sweater further upward, exposing her breasts. Her bra was white. Somehow I knew it would be. My mouth roamed higher, kissing the twin mounds her bra had so generously pushed together into deep cleavage. She possessed quite a rack. I applied light pressure from my forefinger to pull the bra cup away from her right breast. A hard brown nipple sprung up to greet me. It was only fair I make my acquaintance more intimately.

"No. I can't," she wailed.

Wanda scooted out from under me, hurriedly pulling her sweater down. She looked terrified though, oddly, not terrified of *me*. There wasn't a trace of anger, or even disapproval. Her pale face looked like a soldier who'd been shot at and missed. She grabbed her bag and made for the door.

"Okay, let's go outside," I said and opened it for her, as if it had been my idea all along.

We took the elevator downstairs and I kissed her before we reached the ground floor. She liked that but broke off as soon as the doors opened.

"I'm sorry, I must go," she said and then literally ran away. I stood at the elevator doors, bemused. In a small security cubby hole by the rowed letter boxes, a porter sat in his swivel chair reading a newspaper. He hadn't even looked up.

I returned to my room.

Later than evening I pinged Wanda with some gay nice-guy fluff about how lovely it had been to meet her and that I hoped she enjoyed the rest of her evening. She replied with a long polite message saying she was glad she'd met me, would remember the experience, but had no wish to see me again.

Easy come, easy go. I wasn't nearly as disappointed at the time as I am now, writing about it. When you're knee-deep in flange, even when just rolling around with them and not getting any shagging done, you can absorb any amount of near misses without blinking. Though I'd only done three sets that day I was exhausted. YouTube got another workout but this time it wasn't baby panda bears on slides, but video game reviews.

I remembered Lala, the lovely Belarusian blonde I'd banged a few days earlier. It now felt like months ago. Well, I hadn't ever forgotten her but luring her onto another date hadn't been a high priority, due to my other pressing interests. I pinged her and was pleased she got back to me. That's always a worry with fast sex, that the girl files the experience in a box marked 'fun one-time adventure' and declines a sequel. It seemed, however, that Lala was rather keen to see me again. I too was keen. We arranged a date later in the week.

That evening Tom texted me: "+1. Came on her face."

Oh right, the shaved-head girl.

I judged that was Tom's way of hitting the ball back into my court, to prove to me he was doing well himself and hadn't been at all bothered getting busted with a sub-par bird at precisely the same moment I had almost bagged a hottie. Frankly, I thought he should've have texted me: "-1. Wish I had higher standards."

Ah well, like I hinted earlier, our relationship had become strained. I wasn't feeling charitable towards him.

It turned out that Eddie's seminar in Poland was not an aberration and he did indeed frequently visit Warsaw. He messaged to say he was flying over imminently so we arranged a coffee. It was now the fifth day of my eventful trip. He already knew my local Caffe Nero so we met there, at lunchtime.

We got on well immediately, without any of the probing and sparring PUAs will sometimes subject each other to. I was confident of my abilities and contribution to the Game, as Eddie was confident of his. So, we skipped the bullshit and chatted like normal people. He explained he'd been around since 2005, having read Neil Strauss' *The Game* and immediately tested his advice. As a young man he'd tried street game in Leicester Square before 'daygame' even existed. Even more to my surprise, he had met with then-popular and comically-incompetent London daygamer Johnny Berba back when he was fifteen years old when his family first moved to West London.

"Berba was a good guy. Really funny and girls liked him when he was doing Game," Eddie opined, "but then he abandoned the principles and did his own natural thing and got weird."

"Are you still mates?"

"Nah. Haven't even spoken to him in three years."

I didn't realise *Street Attraction* had been around so long, since 2010, and that Eddie's experience of the game exceeded my own. There weren't many people who could claim to have pre-dated me as an effective daygamer: Yad, Andy Yosha, Sasha, Russ Snakeskin, Keychain, Jeremy Soul. That was about it, and only if you considerably relax your definition of 'effective'. It's a bad habit of mine. I assume if I don't know about something then it doesn't exist. I'd only become aware of *Street Attraction* six months earlier and thus concluded, solipsistically, that they were a new outfit.

"How did Richard get involved?" I asked.

"It was through friends, not Community. People never believe it but Richard used to be socially-awkward. I met him when he had a job selling mobile phones from a kiosk in a shopping mall in Harrow. He was only just coming out of his shell after having been bullied and ostracised through high school. He's a good lad so I taught him up and he really took to daygame. Once we saw how good he'd gotten, we brought him in as a coach."

It was quite an understatement to say Richard was merely 'good' at daygame. He'd already developed his own style and did things no-one else could. Putting him infield was like letting an Energizer Bunny loose with a broken wheel: it spins around madly, creates an awful commotion, and every now and then magic happens. When that magic is caught on camera, you get great YouTube content. Unlike *Street Attraction*'s rivals in the closely-related 'social prank' genre, Richard was real and the girls weren't paid actresses. He was the infinite-material generation machine. Put a camera on him, pump his state, and then wait for the infield footage to roll in.

Speaking of infields, I wanted to pick Eddie's brain on two men whose videos had recently made a buzz in daygame circles that spring. He knew the London scene inside out, being based there, whereas I'd lost touch with all but my close friends and wings there.

"What do you think of Daniel Blake?" I asked him.

Daniel was a tall husky man in his mid-twenties with a wild mop of curly hair and good facial features. He came to my attention one morning in March when an infield video of his had popped up on my recommended viewing sidebar on YouTube. I'd never heard of him at all. "Same Day Lay with Hot Ukrainian" boasted the title, or something like it. I clicked.

Sitting in my parent's conservatory wearing my dressing gown and monster feet slippers, I had a familiar experience: mixed feelings. Ostensibly, the video showed Daniel performing a typical front stop on a hot brunette. I recognised the streets as Krakow. The girl hooked very strongly immediately and then Daniel proceeded to follow textbook LDM game. And I mean literally textbook. All of his lines and moves were ripped directly from *Daygame Mastery*, so far as to use my own assumption stacks and comparing the Ukrainian to small furry animals.

No harm in that. I wrote the book precisely so as to share my material with the world. If anything I was flattered, even though I was growing increasingly agitated by people using my content uncredited when marketing themselves as coaches. Daniel bounced the girl to a cafe and then back to his apartment. The video faded to black as he unhooked her bra.

Good infield. Finally a daygamer catching a solid SDL end-to-end with good camerawork, I thought.

My gut didn't like the video anywhere near as much as my brain did. Everything felt off. Faked. Like a Barack Obama smile.

I watched it again and the tension between brain and gut worsened. Were you to read a transcript of Daniel's conversation you'd find it hit all the right notes and followed the stages of the LDM faithfully. That's how girls get picked up. Those are the things that get said: you open, stack, throw in a tease, flirt a bit, ground the interaction by sharing a bit about who you really are, then restate your interest and invite them for coffee. However, actually seeing it acted out on video was like a bad porno scene. There were awkward pauses in the wrong places and Daniel seemed extremely disengaged mentally, like an autistic child.

You're just jealous, Nick. It's a good infield with better production values than your own. You knew young guns would come along and surpass you. You even said as much in Daygame Overkill. Daniel is such a man.

I inspected Daniel's channel with greater scrutiny. This was the first and only video on it. He already had over thirty thousand views in just two days, and his channel boasted ten thousand subscribers. Such numbers didn't ring true at all. How does a brand new channel attain such prominence so quickly? There was no reason at all for YouTube to elevate it, they hate PUA channels and often ban them, and his search parameters were no different to other infield videos with a fraction of his views. Nobody famous featured in it. Who subscribes to a channel with only one video? Daniel had as many subscribers as *Street Attraction*, the latter having been around five years and uploading dozens of quality videos in the same niche.

The truth was obvious. Daniel had bought fake subscribers and fake views. PUAs are like that. They call it pre-selection. Normal people call it fraud.

But he's a tall, above-average-looking white guy. He's young. It's not at all unlikely that a pretty girl would sleep with him. It's the natural order of life. Catching him in underhand marketing shenanigans doesn't mean the whole infield is fake.

Many blog readers had asked my opinion so I gave Daniel the benefit of the doubt. You can't go calling out people publicly as frauds without evidence. It's a serious charge in the industry and my opinion carried weight within the daygame world. So, I replied telling readers the video looked okay to me, if a little goofy. Still, it didn't sit well. Every previous time I'd seen the same red flags, subsequent events vindicated my gut feel and the fraudster had been exposed. I was too willing to give people the benefit of the doubt. I was overcompensating in order to neutralise my self-admitted tendency to not give my rivals the credit they deserved.

It was in this context that I asked Eddie's opinion. He was experienced in the ways of the streets. He also knew the word on those streets, as it were, in London. Who was Daniel Blake?

"Yeah, I've heard of him and his mate Ed Lopez but don't know much about them."

"You must. He's based in London."

"I know. I saw the video and people say his name but I don't know anyone who knows him. Never seen him on the streets of London. All I hear is that he's often out, but rarely in the usual hot spots like Covent Garden so he's never seen in-set."

"That's odd. A beginner could be unknown but not a lad capable of pulling an SDL like that. Also, ten thousand subscribers isn't consistent with being unknown amongst your peers. Back when I lived in Tokyo, I used to say there wasn't a single good MMA fighter I didn't know about. That's not as boastful or as unlikely as it first sounds. Being obsessively into MMA and watching every show, reading the websites, and checking the records of fighters, I knew a lot. Becoming a good fighter takes time and requires experience. You have to fight an increasing level of competition in order to accumulate ring experience. It's not possible to get genuinely good if all you do is steamroll a dozen nobodies. By this logic, when a fighter steps up to a competent level of opposition then, even if I don't know him, I'll know his opponent. If the new guy wins, I get to know about him specifically. Thus it's actually quite easy to know of every good fighter."

Eddie followed my chain of reasoning but hadn't quite drawn the parallel I intended. I expanded.

"Daygame is the same. There's a path everyone follows from beginner to expert. Nobody runs out into Covent Garden, does their first hundred sets in secret, and is suddenly good. Beginners all go on forums and find wings. They comment on blogs and YouTube videos, sharing their experiences. You see them at boot camps or seminars. New daygamers try to mix with the community and then the higher-level lads bring them along. Word gets around and thus by the time a man has reached the same-day-lay-a-hot-Ukrainian level he's already well-known."

"And yet, no-one in London knows him," said Eddie.

"Precisely."

"I did meet him, though."

"You said you hadn't."

"No, no, you misunderstand," countered Eddie, shuffling forward in his seat and raising a finger in preparing to clarify. "I haven't seen him in London. However, I was in Krakow last month and bumped into them both. They'd relocated there after watching our How To Get Laid In Poland video." Now I was very interested. Eddie continued, "What a weird charmless pair! Low in confidence. Daniel's slurred speech was jarring, like he's permanently drunk. They copied your material word-for-word and took ideas from our *Street Attraction* videos. Daniel and Ed worked as a team, filming each others supposed 'same day lay' infields. They only started dropping SDL footage onto YouTube after we uploaded one onto our channel. Whatever we'd put out, they'd replicate it a week later. They even copied the shout-out video we did which credited you and Tom."

"Yeah, I left a message on his channel saying that if he was gonna use my material he should at least credit the source," I said.

"The main thing I'd add is that I was immediately suspicious about both of them after meeting and gaming with them briefly in Krakow. They did not come across as successful seducers at all. Their footage is suspiciously stable, always in focus, and too close to the action. Too good to be true. I know how hard it is to get solid camerawork in something so unpredictable. They're just opportunists, trying to make a quick buck with scam infields."

We'd get a final judgement on Daniel six months later but I'll come to that in due course. There was a second name I wanted to run by Eddie.

"What do you think of Deepak Wayne?"

"Fake as shit."

"Yeah, that's my read but I haven't spotted any smoking gun yet. My spider-sense says fake."

Deepak was an Indian immigrant to Germany, based in Berlin. He'd run a YouTube channel for a couple of years and sold pick-up coaching programs but I hadn't heard of him until he appeared on, of all places, philosophy lecturer Stefan Molyneux's YouTube call-in show. It was a big deal too because Stefan had nearly a million subscribers. Deepak had called in to ask Stefan's opinion on brown immigrant men dating white European women, a topical question due to the stratospheric increase in rapes caused by some of those immigrant brown men. Deepak complained that the rapist refugees had poisoned the well for other immigrants and made daygame harder.

Being racist and anti-immigration, I wasn't at all sympathetic.

That conversation with Stefan had quickly become the stuff of internet legend as the non-native-speaking and stubborn Deepak tried desperately to avoid answering Stefan's main counter-question: why are you so interested in white girls? Deepak squirmed, obfuscated, wheedled, and dissembled. He kept mentioning he was a dating coach and it became increasingly obvious that Deepak's initial choice of topic was a ploy. All he really wanted was for Stefan's one million subscribers to hear his marketing pitch and perhaps be inspired to hire his coaching services. It backfired spectacularly and when the right-leaning daygamers of Europe got wind of it he became a laughing stock.

That same spring, Deepak's infield videos had begun surfacing in my YouTube viewing recommendations. Most had clickbait titles designed to titillate or offend, such as "Ugly Man Dates And Sexes Hot Woman" or "Best Same Day Lay — Must See." I detected a spiteful undercurrent with some videos race-baiting such as "Immigrant Brown Man Sleeps With Hot White Girl." I didn't know it then but the Wayne Dating company he was then a partner of had race-baiting as their central marketing pitch: all the coaches were ugly ethnics who boasted unconvincingly of their prowess in stealing white women from local men. I watched a couple of his infields. Some were shot in Berlin and a few in Warsaw. It was grim viewing.

Deepak re-enters our story in more dramatic fashion a year later.

Eddie and I had gotten on well. We were soon discussing a possible euro jaunt together. He'd never been to Riga, Latvia and I hadn't been back for almost two years. It's a beautiful city in summer, the girls are hot, and I'd been laid on both prior trips. We reached an agreement in principle, with the schedule to be determined later.

After a week in my Chmielna hight-rise apartment I was forced out to make way for the next booking. I'd gotten one more hot teenager back but had also failed to shag her which meant I was 1-for-5 in closing bounce-backs in the four days I'd been chasing skirt. Excessive volatility had exhausted me. It felt like I'd been holding a tiger by the tail five consecutive times. A vague sense of unreality clouded my thoughts as I tried to determine how close I'd actually come with the four girls who'd ultimately escaped my clutches. A serious technical game question needed to be answered.

Had I come close to banging these four girls, or had I merely pushed them further along the seduction path than usual even though the eventual outcome had already been pre-determined a failure?

What counts as a 'near miss', anyway?

That isn't the trite question it first appears, or at least not to an ambitious daygamer obsessed with fine-tuning his technique to extract the maximum excitement from the streets. If a tree falls in a forest and nobody heard it, did it really fall? If a bird lets you get your hands up her shirt but you don't bang her, was it really close?

Three cups of Caffe Nero latte fuelled my deliberations.

The crux of the problem, as I saw it, lay in in divining a woman's decision-making process. PUA theory trended towards the myth that Game is unbeatable and a player in form is omnipotent. Women themselves owned very little agency, according to PUA theory, and were instead buffeted around by the irresistible mesmerism of the pick-up artist. I'd learned of this intellectual orthodoxy the hard way by posting online accounts of my failures. Immediately following such public admission of a failure, my blog comments were swarmed by anonymous advice-givers telling me my technique was shit and if I'd only inserted such-and-such a routine, or held my frame, or pushed harder, or..... bollocks.

Yes, bollocks.

Girl Junkie

It was all bollocks.

Keyboard warriors are like cultists. So steeped are they in PUA ideology, and ideology it is, that you simply cannot tell them it wasn't possible to bang a particular girl on a particular occasion. To a noble knight of the PUA table round, every single girl can be shagged on the first date if only you apply the perfect date formula. If you failed to bang her then, ergo, you fucked up. Cultists believe that because they *must* believe it. You're more likely to persuade Muslims that Mohammed was a paedophile than a PUA cultist that some girls can't be banged on the first date — or in my case, a two-hour bounce-back.

I've banged some girls in little over an hour while others took six or seven dates. What factors determined the difference? Could I accurately predict them ahead of time in the case of any given girl? And most importantly of all, could I massage those factors so as to turn the outcome toward a direction more preferable to me? This was the Philosopher's Stone of daygame. How does one improve one's chances of a same day lay?

One such lingering doubt had long since dissolved under the corrosive weight of my own personal experience: I knew SDLs were highly dependent upon the skill of the player. It wasn't dumb luck. I'd blundered into a couple in my early days but now SDLs happened increasingly regularly, as did the near misses. Sure, luck still mattered. The girl needed to have strong sexual attraction, feel horny, and be sufficiently available. Her character must possess some amenability to adventure and to casual sex. Assuming such a girl was stood in front of you, it was indeed skill that determined if you capitalised on the opportunity.

The very first sufficient condition — recognising there even *was* an opportunity — required skill. A player develops his spider-sense over time, that little voice buzzing in your head: *she's available, she might be up for it.* Sometimes my body would respond first. A minute into a street approach I might have a boner and my heart fluttered like a faggot watching gladiator movies. That's how Lala had affected me early on. My body reached conclusions ahead of my mind. There were times I'd see a student of mine walk away from a set and I'd immediately chastise him: 'why did you just let her go? That was totally on!' and he'd look at me with a mixture of befuddlement and agony at tossing aside his winning lottery ticket.

Skill mattered, but how much? Could you ever really know how 'on' a set was?

During my third cafe latte I resigned myself to what I now called the Daygame Uncertainty Principle: Even when you bang a girl, you don't really know whether it was *because of*, or *in spite of*, your game techniques. If you don't bang the girl, you have even less information on what you did that helped and what didn't. Like a famous brand manager once quipped: *half the money I spend on advertising is wasted. Trouble is, I don't know which half.*

I was vexed.

My vexation hadn't abated when Lala met me outside the tower block containing my new apartment, a few dozen metres north of the Stalin building. That part of town is blighted by fifty-storey concrete monstrosities from the Warsaw Pact era, which sucks for the people of Warsaw but offered me low-cost accommodation in a logistically perfect location. Lala stood outside my front door, smoking a cigarette. She wore skin-tight leggings above thick heels and below a thigh-length tightly-wrapped black skirt. A thin wool cardigan was pulled across a low-cut plain vest. She looked very nice. She hadn't lost any appeal through my having shagged her, as a less attractive girl might.

"Hey fancypants, been waiting long?"

"No, just a minute. And I'm not fancypants."

She said it playfully. I assumed she'd looked up the term after I'd called her that in recent texting. The online definition hinted at a negative nuance, of being too pleased with oneself.

"That's good. Okay then, crazypants, lets go up."

It was evening and Lala didn't seem at all concerned that we weren't going through the motions of a restaurant or bar date first. I'd invited her to watch a movie on my laptop so she knew the score. The elevator disgorged us and, I'll say this, I had a gorgeous view across the city. We drank wine from my new bounce-back bottle. I didn't mind depleting it because deep down I already sensed my will to approach more girls entering into steep decline.

For half an hour Lala and I lay together on the sofa watching a movie and making small talk. Evidently that bored the both of us because as soon as I pulled her into me for a kiss, she leapt at it. Clothes came flying off and I saw her tights were actually above-the-knee lace with suspender straps attaching them to her garter. Her bra and panties matched. The girl had gone all-in on sexy lingerie. Good on her!

I rattled her across every piece of furniture in every room, except for a white plastic chair that felt aesthetically grim and out of place. The dramatic tension accompanying first-time sex was long gone but I thoroughly enjoyed seconds and realised I wouldn't get bored of banging Lala for a long time to come. Afterwards, as we once more lay on the sofa, I probed her decision-making. Hopefully she'd relieve my vexation.

"When did you decide to have sex with me, that first day?"

"In the Costa, during out first coffee in the mall."

"That quickly?"

"Yes, within half an hour. I wasn't certain, but I looked at you and thought: I can have sex with this man."

"When did you realise we would have sex?"

"As soon as you invited me to your apartment."

This was all valuable information regarding my quest for the Philosopher's Stone. Lala had not been bamboozled, befogged, nor bewitched. Not even beguiled. Quite the reverse. She'd consciously and knowingly let me lead her along. It supported my preferred theory that women were acting with full agency, co-operating in their own seduction. Sure, a man could tempt a girl. Game mattered. But it was more like the smell of McDonald's tempting a drunkard after midnight. He's fully able to pass up on a late-night Big Mac and probably will do if he's not already feeling the munchies.

"How many men have you had sex with?"

"You are the second."

"Wait... That doesn't sound right. You seemed very comfortable following me home for sex. I didn't detect any nervousness. How could you be so calm if you're so inexperienced?"

"I was nervous. It's the craziest thing I ever did."

"But, even so-"

"I've slept with some girls. I'm not completely inexperienced."

Colour me surprised. "Are you bisexual?"

"I thought I was," she mused, "but after sex with you, I think I only want boys now."

Colour me flattered. You can bet I'll remember that reply until the moment I draw my last breath on this earth. Lala opened up only a little more, explaining she'd kissed a bunch of girls in the past few years and rolled around in bed with a couple others. Her comfort with fast seduction came from transfering that experience to me, but she insisted it was a one-off because of the novelty.

"Even with the girls it was never the same day," she said.

Lala had no tattoos, no piercings, and she dressed like any normal girl who buys her clothes on the high street. Right up until the moment I'd first stuck my dick in her I had no reason to suppose she was 'dirty', and I still don't. I spoke to her just recently and she's been in a relationship over two years, with the boy she met after me.

So, could I have predicted the same day lay with Lala while still in set? I don't know. The best I can say is I knew the possibility was there. But what about the other four girls?

I realised there were two different possible interpretations of my crazy first week in Warsaw, representing opposite ends of the same spectrum. The conventional view was this, based upon the standard chronological analysis that the closer a girl gets to being naked in your bed, the closer you are to fucking her: I'd almost banged five girls, but four had wriggled off the hook in the closing phase. The alternate explanation was I'd only really been 'on' with one girl: Lala. The other four were never going to have sex but through my pumping them up and leading them forwards I'd gotten considerably more action from each than I'd had any right to expect.

It's likely that if I'd simply taken the phone numbers of all four girls and said goodbye on the street, all four would've failed to reply to my first message. My new style of daygame had almost succeeded in extracting blood from a stone. I'd gotten bounce-backs and tomfoolery with four girls who should've, by rights, been mediocre number closes.

That was one way to look at it.

Or had I simply blown four good leads by pulling too hard?

Too good to be true
with Paula

Meeting Lars

There were flash storms

Chapter 17
ASHEN ONE

I did Lala in the ass a few days later, in yet another apartment.
We had settled into a comfortable routine whereby every few days she came over for the evening, sometimes staying overnight. She'd follow me around quietly and listen intently whenever I spoke. Add good tits onto that combination and you're talking Perfect Woman. Lala was no dummy, so when called upon to make conversation she was eminently capable of it, but for the most part she was happy to chill out and get herself fucked.

I made an effort to return to daygame, walking around with Tomas for a few days. No matter how I wrestled with my hindbrain, things didn't happen right. There was only one day where I got going and even then only after I'd already mentally thrown in the towel. I opened perhaps twenty-five sets that afternoon, an outrageous multiple of my usual work-rate, and gained almost nothing for my labours. As rush hour approached, Tomas and I sat on a low wall at the end of the central park, next to a set of steps leading down to the entrance of a Metro station. I opened every solo girl who walked by, one after another, despite feeling almost zero sexual intent.

It would've been too much effort to chase, so I sat on the metal rail in the middle of the steps and simply grabbed at the girls. It was funny in a self-defeated way, like watching a football team 5-0 down throw everybody forwards in the final five minutes of play. One girl hooked strongly, a blonde metal chick wearing dark lipstick. She stared wide-eyed as I pulled her in and worked some mesmer magic. She bit her lip and swayed into me, then gave up her number.

Not that it mattered. She never came out for a date.

"I'm done," I declared. "Something has snapped inside. I simply cannot daygame any more."

Maybe a change of scenery is in order? I wondered. Olga was still messaging keenly from Krakow and had taken to sending dirty pictures. The memory card on my smartphone had filled up with various poses showing her ass to good affect, plus a few with her tits out or shoving some fingers up her pussy. They were good photos, if somewhat deficient in lighting, focus, and composition. Olga was the proud over of a fantastic gym body and her ass was especially memorable. Looking at her photos was like mainlining cocaine. I broached the topic of hanging out and she seemed keen. So, keen to escape my Warsaw funk, I planned two nights back in Krakow.

It's a fantastic ass though, don't you agree?

My apartment stood on the eastern edge of the Old Town, within the historic walls. Olga came out to meet me the same evening. Once more she showed herself to be struggling with the same issues that had limited our idate. Raw animal desire battled against her own moral code. She recommended a shisha bar conveniently located around the corner, one street behind the main square. For most of the date she kept her distance from me, making good conversation but edging away any time I tried to paw at her.

Nonplussed, I decided alcohol may be the solution.

"Bollocks to this place. Let's go to a proper sleazy pub," I suggested.

"I know a good one. It is very close, in a side-street from Florianska."

We paid the shisha bill and stepped outside into the warm night air. It was dark. Olga slipped her arm through mine and we set off across the cobbles. Halfway across the square I heard a shout behind me.

"Krauser!"

For fuck's sake, what's all that about?

"Nick Krauser!" I heard again. Someone was insistent upon attracting my attention and there would be no ignoring him.

I turned my head to see an enthusiastic young Indian man waving at me twenty yards distant. He was about the same age as Ash, and too looked British-Indian. You could make a case he was as well-dressed too. What he definitely lacked was Ash's social calibration. What on earth was he playing at, hailing me when I'm so obviously on a date, and using my PUA name? He looked too happy and excitable to be harbouring bad intent.

I gave him a nod, hoping he'd fuck off, then kept walking.

"Who was that?" asked Olga.

"I've absolutely no idea. Must be a friend-of-a-friend."

Fortunately, she either hadn't caught my PUA name, or else hadn't registered Krauser as an odd surname for a Brit. As if to remedy that oversight, the man called out again.

"Krauser PUA!"

I gritted my teach and prepared to have a go at him but he was already striding off in the other direction, fist-pumping, no doubt pleased with himself.

Olga led us down a seedy side-street full of questionable bars and clubs. On the right side was a large black door, propped open beneath a black sign with the bar name — which I forget — written in white. We stepped inside and immediately headed down a concrete staircase into the basement. I'd asked for sleazy and the vibe didn't disappoint. The walls were bare brick and the woodwork features painted dark. Dim lighting made it a struggle to get around but seemed a fair trade off for the grotty vibe. The main bar area was a long low room with the bar itself against the back wall. To our right, a rickety wooden staircase twisted in on itself leading up to a mezzanine room full of tables.

So far as I could tell, there was only one other punter drinking in the entire place. He was a husky middle-aged local man of evidently low social status. Clad in cheap ill-fitting casual clothes, he was propped himself against the bar on a stool and nursed a pint of beer. The staff seemed to be ignoring him. I sidled up with Olga.

"What are you drinking?" I asked her.

"I'll have beer."

"Two beers please," I told the barman, indicating a pump crested with a large black bull and the beer's Polish name. As he pulled the pints, the odd man next to us attempted to get my attention, speaking in Polish. As politely as I could manage without showing weakness, I tried to fob him off.

"Sorry, mate. I only speak English."

He didn't like that and muttered darkly under his breath. Then, as I turned away to pay the barman, the drinker began talking to Olga. Naturally, I didn't understand a word. She answered a few questions, without enthusiasm, but politely enough the man sensed his opening to pester us. Recognised the tell-tale signs, I smoothly intervened.

"Have a good night!" I said cheerfully, holding my beer glass up to the man, then pulled Olga away. "What was that about?"

"He was complaining that I am drinking with a foreign man. He tried to tell me I'm a slut."

If he'd known how deftly you've rebuffed my escalation so far, he'd have never claimed that, I thought wryly. Players know full well that, should a strange man strike up conversation when you're on a date, it is always with the specific intent of fucking it up. Some interlopers are ambitiously attempting to AMOG you and steal the girl. Others are whiny white knights burning with envy that you might shag a girl above their own class. This drunk seemed to be the latter. One easy tell that the interloper is acting in bad faith is they'll address the girl in her native tongue, specifically to freeze you out. I had chosen to pull Olga away politely, but I'd have been absolutely within my rights to tell him to fuck off.

Burn it into your brain: If a man interrupts your date to make conversation, no matter how innocuously his opening gambit, he is harbouring evil intent. Every. Single. Time. My standard response nowadays is to shut them down immediately: "Sorry mate, we're busy," then turn away.

The drunken Pole reaffirmed my resolve to get Olga somewhere quiet so as to break through her resistance. She hadn't even let me kiss her yet. Strange that, considering the dirty photos. I led her up the rickety staircase and was pleased to find the mezzanine room empty but for a quiet couple in the corner. Shadows shrouded the room. A wide brick supporting pillar stood in the middle of the room. Holding that pillar between us and the other couple to block sight lines, we sat at the opposite side.

"Come here, woman," I said, pulling Olga's chair towards me. Her knees came against mine. We sipped out pints then I pulled her in.

"No."

"Yes."

"No. I can't."

"Can't what?"

"Can't kiss you. I told myself no."

"That's stupid. Come here."

I brute-forced it and as soon as Olga's lips met mine it was game over. She rose up out of her chair and straddled me, panting into my ear. My hands found their way to her tits, after brief diversions across her thighs, ass, and hips. It felt great, having a pretty tight-bodied girl writhing around on top of me in the dark. I briefly considered whether I could bang her in this very room, and should I wait for the other couple to leave first.

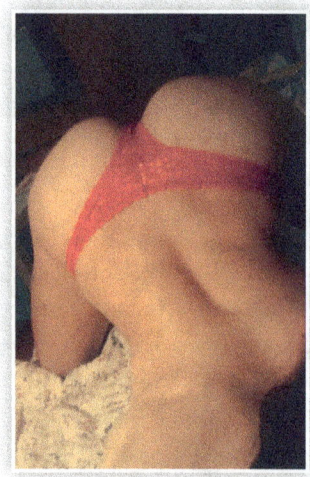

This is what was at stake

Heavy steps clattered on the staircase. Someone else was coming up.

Olga disengaged quickly and returned to her chair, fstill lushed and breathing heavily though the darkness hid her shame. My eyes focused on the staircase as it sounded ominous. I noticed a bald head first, then broad shoulders covered with a thick seal-like covering of fat. It was the same obnoxious drunk as earlier, at the bar.

Girl Junkie

He saw us and made a bee-line. He sat down at the table next to us, turned his chair as if we'd invited him to parley, and stared. I've often wondered how so many people get themselves murdered in pubs, but I wonder no more. This ill-mannered oaf was actively seeking out mischief from strangers. He created problems where none existed before, likely with men with tempers far shorter than my own.

He ignored me completely, again, addressing Olga in Polish. His body language and vocal tone suggested conventional daily chit-chat but I wasn't fooled. Olga replied politely but aloofly, making clear she didn't appreciate his company. He persisted several minutes, trying ever harder to draw her into conversation.

His strategy was simple: he was a spoiler. No amount of beer could furnish him with the hope he'd ever get near to a hot young woman of Olga's calibre, so, he hoped to smear enough shit on the walls that everyone felt sick. Once more I toyed with murderous fantasies, less abstractly this time. It's very difficult to get murdered in Europe.

Almost every newspaper report of murder I've ever read makes it obvious the victim co-operated in their own death. Examples flashed through my mind:

A silly tart dates a succession of obviously-violent boyfriends. She waits until he returns home drunk and then agitates him, riling him up. He raises a hand, telling her to shut up and leavet him be. "Go on! You're too fucking scared to hit me, you pussy!" she goads, so he clouts her. The tart rushes into the kitchen a yanks a knife from the block, waving it around, shouting and screaming. "You're a faggot! A loser! Keep away from me!" she wails, half-scared and half tauntingly. She slashes at him, drawing blood from his forearm. The drunk, violent, recently-enraged man grabs the knife from her and plunges it into her heart, then calls the police to turn himself in.

The world is relieved of one tart and one scumbag. Win-win. Karma.

My point is that violence is usually easily avoidable. Don't go to the notoriously violent bars. Don't eye-challenge violent men. Don't argue over whether it's your bar stool or his. Don't call someone a dickhead when they accidentally spill your pint. Most violence comes with prior instructions on how to avoid it, usually of the "stop doing that or I'll hit you" variety. Taking the most elementary precautions can almost entirely eliminate your risk of being murdered.

This Pole hadn't received the memo. The one that says: Don't harass a stranger on a date. Don't call his girl a whore. Don't follow them around the bar.

"Tell this guy to fuck off," I told Olga. "Say it's from me." She obliged. I expected a confrontation but instead he looked stung, like I'd pulled his pants down on a school stage. He shuffled off downstairs muttering what I took to be insults on his way out. I was relieved. Olga was more than relieved. The episode had turned her on, both the frustration of being interrupted as she was heating up, and then at my willingness to face down an interloper.

She straddled me again, dry-humping, grinding herself up and down my dick. Sadly, our jeans denim was in the way. I reached a hand down between us and unbuckled my belt. Time to fuck her here and now.

"No!" she gasped.

My belt was loose. I unbuttoned my jeans and unzipped. Out came the Krauser dick.

"No!" This time, she scuttled away, back onto her seat. My dick remained out but she steadfastly refused to look at it. Ten seconds of stalemate slowly elapsed, Olga endeavouring to keep her eyes level with mine. It was cold in this bar. I put it away. She explained, "we can't have sex. I don't know you. I'm religious and this is wrong."

We had another pint and then she invited me to her apartment, a ten minute walk across the railway lines, in a newly built complex. It sported unusual cubicle allotments, like child's play bricks stacked atop each other. It reminded me of a *Call of Duty* multiplayer map, for some reason. As we walked and talked, Olga asked my opinion of the European Union. She held sentiments opposite to myself, believing Poland benefited hugely from financial subsidies and economic freedom, and that this outweighed the loss of sovereignty and constant globalist pressure to admit migrants and promote homosexuality to children.

Just keep talking, I implored her telepathically, as I steered around several conversational landmines. She invited me inside but soon declared she had study early the next morning and needed to sleep. We got into bed together, Olga wearing her bra and panties. Not to be discouraged, once we'd settled into a spoon position I began feeling her up.

"No, I need to sleep," she moaned, swatting my hands away.

I continued. I grabbed her ass and squeezed it like a squeaky toy. My hands roamed up and down her legs, my fingertips dragging across her stomach until she pulled it tight in reflex, then I took a handful of her breasts. She moaned, writhed, and swatted my hands away.

Seeing as I was already stripped to my boxer shorts, I pulled my dick out and pushed it against her ass, trying to find her pussy. Olga dodged left and right more artfully than Floyd Mayweather Jnr in a boxing ring, not letting me find the target but only half-heartedly rebuffing my attack. I sensed indecision. It was in the balance. I grabbed her shoulders and rolled her towards me. We kissed more then she rolled around, turning her back. I ran my fingers inside her panties and tried to pull them aside and slip my dick in, in one smooth motion.

"No!" she said. "If you don't let me sleep, you'll have to leave."

Her voice was different now. Firm. I recognise a firm 'no' when I get one, so I shrugged and shut my eyes. I too was very sleepy. There'd be another chance.

I slept badly and left at 8am with Olga, saying goodbye at the tram stop. There wasn't much to do the rest of the afternoon so I popped home to shower, collected my laptop, then sat at a cafe on the North corner of Florianska street. The time had come to begin re-writing *Adventure Sex*, volume four of this 'umble memoir. The *Beginner Daygame* project with Tom was done and the docket was clear. Time to move on to the next book.

I'd begun writing *Adventure Sex* the previous November when in Prague to close Ivanna. That was during a cold spell and the accumulated fatigue of the year had sapped me of the will to approach. So, when not hanging out with the buxom Serb, I'd killed time in my usual Costa Cafe in Palladium. My mind had been too frazzled to write. I hadn't blogged any of 2014's stories and thus didn't have the skeleton structure of a book ready made. Nonetheless, I was committed to produce a fourth memoir. My plan was simple. I dictated all my year's stories into an audio recorder without a care for narrative structure or any literary niceties. Then I hired a transcriber and a ghost writer from UpWork, paying them to sort it all out, turning my ramblings into a real book. It was a genius plan, or so I thought. The dictation took a week sitting in Palladium and then I handed the audio files to a transcriber. Two weeks later she returned a whopping 200,000 word transcript.

My first thought was, *damn! I don't half waffle on!*

I passed that transcript on to a ghost writer, an English man living on the Portuguese south coast who had impressed me with his writing samples. Roy, for that's his pen-name, agreed to trim the fat, re-organise it, and re-write the transcribed speech into written prose. He had delivered the manuscript in March of this year. One week of talking then $1,500 of fees had netted me a complete memoir volume! Wasn't I a smart boy?

Sadly, there was a problem: the book was no good. It was dull. I didn't blame Roy as he'd done well with the materials at hand. The problem was in my original plan. Using a ghost writer for a memoir is considerably less effective than using one for fiction. Fiction is easy: outline the plot, sketch the characters, and write a chapter or two as a style guide. Your ghost writer can fill in the blanks with his own imagination. Not so with *Adventure Sex*. A memoir must stick to the facts. Roy could only include whatever information I'd given him and if it's not already in the transcript, he must ask. But how would he know there was something to even ask about? Therein lies the territory of unknown-unknowns. How does he know to ask about a story I might've forgotten to make him aware of? He can't rack his own memory to recall my experiences. Additionally, a memoir needs to be written in the authentic voice of the subject, something only the subject himself can do.

So, I wasn't quite the smart boy I'd congratulated myself as. Now, sitting in a Florianska cafe in Krakow, I needed to go through Roy's 99,000-word *Adventure Sex* manuscript page-by-page and rewrite the whole thing. It would become an entirely different book, and on this afternoon after striking out with Olga, that intimidating project kicked off. Three coffees (it's always three) and four hours later I'd bitten into the opening chapters.

Olga texted throughout the day. She be free again that evening, my last before returning to Warsaw. We agreed to meet outside Hard Rock Cafe at 8pm. She explained over text that she wanted to walk along the riverside, no doubt hoping that by indulging in gay romantic nonsense she'd break down her own barriers regarding sex. I agreed. Olga was absolutely gagging for it and likely as frustrated with her LMR as I. There was still an hour to kill before the date. I dropped my laptop at the apartment and tried to persuade myself to daygame again.

It was an uphill struggle.

I walked up and down Florianska and around Galleria mall. There were plenty of girls to accost but I didn't have it in me to accost them. A few times I forced myself to open but I felt like a photocopy of a photocopy of the real me. Where had the charismatic Nick Krauser gone to? The sky darkened and it wasn't until walking up Florianska one last time that I had a bit of luck.

A curvy red-head was slinking towards me. She wore tight blue jeans and a black biker jacket unzipped. That latter detail clearly wasn't an accident because her white t-shirt was so tight that her full breasts threatened to break out of their fabric prison. My spider-sense immediately picked her out from the crowd, that combination of buxom body, figure-hugging clothes, and her hip-swaying slinky style. As she passed to my left she turned her head slightly and held me with a long stare. The slightest hint of a self-satisfied smile formed on her lips.

I opened. Of *course* I opened. Lack of vibe never enters into the equation when a sexy girl gives me a come-on. Her interest floods rocket fuel into my daygame machine, with an extra line of cocaine for the driver. This redhead was a walking crack-pipe daring me to take a hit.

"Hi. I'm Nick."

Words weren't necessary, which is just as well because her English was far less impressive than her chest. We stared deep into each other's eyes. I stepped close so as to brush closer to said chest.

"I'm Ana."

Ana was a cat, according to my daygame typology. These girls slink around waiting to be petted. They soak up sexual energy like a sponge, purring contentedly. Cats are absolutely confident of their feminine sexual appeal. It wouldn't cross their minds to be intimidated by male attention. To them, it's the elixir of life. We only spoke a few minutes. I invited her for a drink there and then, calculating I'd have a little over half an hour before Olga showed, and I could always push her back a bit longer. I wanted Ana in front of me with beer.

"No. I go friends now. Take number."

Were it possible to exchange contact details by the mere crackle of sexual electricity, we'd have made scientific history. That breakthrough still eludes us, so I reached into my pocket, swatting my boner aside, and pulled out my smartphone. Ana leaned into me with her head over my shoulder to check I'd taken the number correctly. I gave her a peck on the lips and let her go. That too was a test, if she'd returned my kiss with an open mouth I'd have made-out there and then, and tried to drag her into a bar. The fact she told me she was seventeen made me more, not less, motivated.

She slinked off, shucking her hips left-to-right for my benefit.

Olga arrived a bit later, meeting me outside Hard Rock Cafe.

As planned, we walked to the south end of the Old Town and on to the waterfront. It was romantic, with Olga linking arms and resting against me each time we stood still. A metal sculpture of a dragon rose up at the foot of the castle wall on the river-facing side. Every hour it breathed fire, bringing a cluster of shrieking tourists to watch. We patiently waited for just that and Olga squeezed my arm tightly when the dragon obliged with a jet of flame.

I kissed her. Everything seemed good.

We walked an hour more and though Olga had excellent English, and a motormouth, I found myself growing bored. My subconscious had assembled all Olga-related facts, computed, and returned the conclusion that she probably wouldn't have sex tonight. My interest level nose-dived accordingly, forcing me to go through the motions and put a brave face on it so as not to be impolite.

"I can't stay long," she said. "I have an essay to write for tomorrow."

"How long?"

"Maybe half an hour." We'd been together a little over ninety minutes on this date.

"Okay. Let's chill out at my place. It's close."

"No, not tonight."

My optimistic PUA brain was determined to overrule my pessimistic subconscious. *There must be a way to fuck her. Think, Nick!* Attraction wasn't lacking. Olga seemed dripping wet just looking at me. My woes were caused by her traditional upbringing in a conservative stable family. Though only lightly religious she'd absorbed all the Polish church's attitudes towards sex. She'd already told me she'd never have an abortion and would rather bear the child of a mistake than kill it. That made her great wife material but it was a strike against her as a source of casual sex.

How could I fuck her? Seeing as she wouldn't come into my flat and refused to take me to hers again, where could I fuck her?

My eyes roved the surrounding area. I looked around the rock face supporting the castle foundations for any hidden caves or defiles. Nothing. I squinted my eyes and looked across the river in the vain hope some inspiration would present itself from that side. Nothing. I racked my mind for disabled-access toilets in cafes and untraversed back streets winding around the Old Town. Each time I visualised a potential sex location, I performed a mental dry-run, calculating lines of sight and potential sources of interruption. It was no good. There wasn't anywhere in the centre of Krakow, that I knew of, where I could have public sex with Olga. My mind cast back to 2010 when I'd rattled a young art student in the toilet of a grotty pub at the north end of the Old Town but I'd been unable to relocate that pub when searching on the previous day.

"What are you thinking about?" she asked.

"Batman."

Olga and I walked back around the castle, along the street leading to the main square. She was prattling on about the European Union again. It turned out this wasn't monomania but rather the subject of her next essay for university. I nodded, made soothing listening noises, and then I had it!

I fucking had it!

The castle.

It was a big beautiful bastard of a fortress atop a hill of rock. Afternoon had passed into evening so it was no longer open to tourists. A wide road zig-zagged up to the main gate and I noticed three things there of interest to a degenerate daygamer seeking rapid sex. First, I hadn't seen a single car go either up or down the road, nor could I see the silhouette of a single pedestrian. The entire road from street level up to the very castle gates was deserted. Second, unlike most tourist attractions in Central Europe, the castle's lower walls were not fitted with display lights to prettify the building at night. Or if it was, they hadn't been turned on. Lastly, the walls were built with ramparts and protuberances such that there were many dark crevices further hidden from view.

I ran the mental projection. If I could walk Olga up to the foot of the castle walls, if I could pull her into a dark corner, if I could heat her up, then shagging was entirely feasible. The risk of interruption was almost nil. In the unlikely event a car or gaggle of tourists approached, we'd see and hear them long before they us.

If, if, if.

"That castle is amazing," I waxed, as lyrically as I could feign. "Every Englishman loves his castles. I hope to own one, when I'm rich and famous. Let's go take a closer look."

Olga followed. She'd already let me maul her in public spaces, so if she suspected my plan she wasn't yet resistant to it. Mind you, I doubt many people outside of the Seduction Community would seriously think of having sex outside a popular tourist location on a raised platform observed by clear sight lines from half the city. Even if it was too dark for those sight lines to matter.

Halfway up, a car passed us on its way down. That was the only interruption.

I pulled Olga into a shadowy nook, the walls towering above us on two sides as we stood in the angle of intersection. We kissed. I began mauling her again and finally she realised my intention. Her familiar vacillation ensued: desire vs values.

"No!"

I reached down her shirt and pulled her tits out. They were firm, pert but also no more than a small handful. Thus I withdrew my hand and changed the angle of attack to below, pushing her sweater up towards her face to expose her that way. She bit my ear and clutched my shoulders as I sucked her tits. My hands found her pussy, from the rear, and I fingered her through her jeans. The plan was simple: heat her up as much as possible in the hope her resistance would crumble. I bit her neck and pulled her jeans down to mid-thigh.

That she allowed it surprised me. I'd expected to be rebuffed the moment I fumbled with her buttons. But no, she stood next to me with her bare ass hanging out and her panties crumpled near her knees along with her jeans. I got two fingers in, reaching around her ass to get them in from behind. She continued to allow it, moaning only half-hearted appeals to stop.

I got my dick out.

"No!" she gasped, her eyes wide. This time, she couldn't help but stare at it.

I put her right hand on it, like Obi Wan teaching Luke to handle a light saber. She began furiously tugging me off. I pushed her head down and she almost put her mouth around it. At the last moment she popped up, shaking her head gently as if in physical pain from the temptation. My reaction was to frig her harder.

She bent over again, her face just inches from my dick, her left arm around my waist for balance and her right hand wanking me off with increasing vigour. Her ass pushed back so I could get a smooth action with a few fingers in her now soaking-wet pussy. I turned my head to scan the road and the city we overlooked. Nobody was coming. This went on at least five minutes. Olga kept looking up at me with a pained expression, her eyes startlingly wide and full of fire, and she bit her lip. Then she'd sigh and put her head down as if intending to suck me off, only to lose her nerve at the last moment. A few times I pushed her further down, trying to nudge her over the hump. The whole time I kept frigging her.

She looked to be absolutely gagging for it, but couldn't make the leap, like a first-time bungee jumper who holds up the queue yet refuses to retreat. I figured some strong-arm tactics might work.

I dragged her further into the corner and spun her around, pulled her hips to bring her ass towards me, and tried to slide my dick in. Olga reached her hand back to block the thrust, then spun back to face me.

"I want to fuck you, right now," I growled.

"No."

"I want to put my hard dick into your wet pussy. I want to make you scream my name."

She bit her lip hard enough to draw a spot of blood. Her eyes looked sad, distraught at being desperately horny for sex yet unable to actually follow-through and seize her rewards.

Just as distraught as me, then. And for similar reasons. If a charity had run television appeals showing our sad faces, I'm sure sympathetic donations would've poured in.

Finally, Olga pulled her jeans up, forcing me to pull my fingers out of her pussy.

"That's unfortunate. I love your bare ass," I smiled, taking a handful and squeezing her now-denim-clad rear end. She laughed, confirming she hadn't realised my quip was a diversion so as to wipe her pussy juice off my hands onto her clothing.

We walked back down to the Old Town square.

"Tonight was lovely," she coo-ed, linking arms again.

It was certainly memorable, I'll grant her that, but I retired to bed intensely frustrated. That was my fifth near-miss in less than ten days. The next morning, I took the train back to Warsaw for my final week. I was defeated. Except for knobbing Lala some more, I wanted nothing to do with women for a while. So I sat myself in a Caffe Nero with a view of the Stalin tower and then, under the soft loving shadow of communism, continued re-writing my draft of *Adventure Sex*.

Chapter 18
NORMALITY

The UK was now shitsville as far as I was concerned and I had no desire to hang about. I flew home by way of Krakow on the 22nd May, the direct flight getting me into Newcastle late at night. My frequent absences from the country of my birth made things increasingly complicated. My bachelor pad in London was long-since demolished and all my possessions were crammed into a small lock-up on an industrial estate near Brent Cross. That forced me to make my parents' home my base though, truth be told, I quite enjoyed being back home and reconnecting with my roots.

As the day after arrival was a Saturday, a small family get-together was planned by the North Sea coast. My brother used to run a market stall there, in Tynemouth, on weekends selling rare second-hand books. The market was held inside the large metro station which retained it's Victorian era architecture and was thus delightful to be around. My parents would drive over, then usually my dad would go off to his model-building club meeting and my mum walked along the seaside. That would leave my brother Lee and I to browse the market stalls and sit in a cafe built into the former station master's office. Usually I'd pick up a couple of old paperbacks to read the following week.

That week I bought an old memoir of a British soldier captured in World War 2 and held in the notorious Nazi concentration camp at Dachau. It sounded pretty bleak and, unlike the Holocaust, it was probably based on true events. The lurid cover was awesome.

Lee went off to pick up his kids from football practice so I took my usual stroll into Tynemouth village which by now was a-flutter with summer decorations. There were paper Union Jack flags hanging on streamers between lampposts and many coloured banners. Tynemouth is an upper-middle class area situated at the point where the river meets the North Sea, hence the name. The main shopping street has a small thin park flanked on either side by single-lane roads. All along both sides are independent cafes, craft shops, and patriotic-named pubs. Usually I'd sit in *The Priory* pub by their old log fireplace and read one of my recently-acquired paperbacks until my parents came back with the car shortly after lunchtime to return to Gateshead. Sometimes I'd walk out to the cliffs and the ruins of the old priory that dominate the skyline.

It was nice. It felt like home. My relaxed and wholesome home town life stood in an increasingly stark contrast to my adventuring overseas. It felt like one was the real me and the other a superhero costume donned at special moments. Only now, I spent more time in the superhero costume than I did in normal life.

Just like Superman.

I shook my head and gazed out over the churning waves of the North Sea. It really wouldn't do to keep comparing myself to Superman. That can go to a man's head. For much of 2014 I'd believed my own press clippings — that is to say, I was getting so much effusive praise for *Daygame Mastery* and *Daygame Overkill* that I'd forgotten the two most important facts in my life: first, that it was still an uphill struggle to get laid, and second, that I was still a bit of a cunt.

The next afternoon, Sunday, the family met at my aunt's house in the countryside. Each of my aunts, my dad's sisters, had bought a small terraced house in a former mining village. They lived in the same street and took turns hosting us each Sunday. We'd have tea and biscuits then, weather permitting, take their two dogs for a walk in the nearby forest. Simple, earthly pleasures. It never failed to unsettle me. I enjoyed feeling the soft mud crumble underfoot and to smell crisp forest air. Watching the dogs running, jumping, and barking brought a smile to my face. It wasn't unsettling due to a lack of enjoyment but rather my increasing inability to place the experience within my mental map of the world.

When chasing skirt in foreign climes, I'd miss the groundedness of nature and family life. I'd miss the certainty of routine and the patient progress of gradually feathering one's nest. At the same time, I knew living conventionally, and only that way, would bore me to tears. My younger aunt's house looked out over a series of allotments that gave way to rolling hills and a view across the valley for several miles. It's beautiful, like the windswept landscape of a *Wuthering Heights* or *The Hound Of The Baskervilles*. The greens and browns of nature inspired mental images of waxed Barbour jackets and deer-stalker hats. I wanted to fill a tobacco pipe and take a sheepdog for a walk. I wanted to sit on a rock overlooking a bubbling brook and sketch pencil art of the trees and flowers. I would be lord of the manor. Count Krauser of Old Heworth. If I'd a whip, I'd lay it across my indolent servants' backs.

I felt terribly English, looking over the moors. Colonial. Cecil Rhodes had said, "to be born an Englishman is to win life's lottery" and I agreed.

Yet I knew I'd tire of the stable life. My heart yearned for adventure. There was more of the world to see. It wasn't enough to live in Japan, or stay for months in Brazil, Mexico, Thailand, Serbia, Lithuania or wherever else. There had been a time I could read adventure stories and lose myself in escapism. For the past few years I took such stories not as fiction but as guidebooks in how to have my own adventures. I was no longer a spectator. I was a do-er.

There was no getting around it: I was falling between two stools. My home life and my travelling life each provided satisfaction but stood in opposition. Neither was good enough on its own, so was I condemned to flit from one to the other, loyal to neither? Like Italy with its wartime allies.

I was increasingly troubled. It rumbled away deep inside.

The next afternoon I received an unexpected call from Derrick, my old school mate. The same Derrick who I'd sat next to in class through most of my secondary school, and whose girlfriend's flat I'd lived in for a couple of years before moving into Château RSG. They'd since sold up and taken their London-priced home sale proceeds to a small rural town and bought quite a big old house. Derrick's parents still lived in Gateshead a few hundred metres from my own and like me he tried to visit frequently. This time, our visits had coincided.

"Fancy a drink?" he messaged.

"Sure, where?"

"*The Fiddlers*?"

"Okay, how about seven this evening?"

Thus I made the short walk down the bank to the pub situated at the edge of the sports field of my old secondary school. Every day I used to walk past *The Fiddler's Arms* to and from school so it felt odd to have a drink there now I was an adult and somewhat disassociated from the region.

Derrick and I hadn't met in nearly a year so I curious if he'd changed. As a teenager he'd looked astonishingly like the lead singer of Aussie rock band INXS, so much so it had always mystified me why he'd never done well with women. He'd had a pretty Greek girlfriend in London, called Magda, but then shacked up with his current wife and mother of this children who was ten years older and nowhere near as pretty as the Greek. That said, watching them together they had a comfortable balance and appeared happy enough.

I'd gotten divorced from my wife, so I wasn't in a position to evaluate their more successful marriage.

Nonetheless, it mystified me. You can't always figure out what people see in each other. Now that I was making a profession of male-female relations, I tried to put a Game frame of reference onto it. I recalled that Derrick had always been lacking in self-esteem and socially odd, although well-liked by his peers because he was kind-hearted and funny. The times I'd met his parents they struck me by how little personal force they projected, appearing to merge with their furniture. Nice, friendly people but you could forget they were there.

As a young adult Derrick was tall, athletic, facially good-looking, extremely smart, and kind-hearted. Put him in the right environment and you'd expect him to be banging fashion models. More than once in the past few years I'd thought, grimly, how much easier my pick-up career would be if I had Derrick's natural advantages. And yet he'd aimed low, choosing the safe option. It had worked out fine, he was happily married with two young boys, but I wondered if he didn't consider he could've gotten to the same place but with a smoking hot girl.

I decided today was not the day to ask him about it. Anyway, he'd grown very fat these past few years, boozing heavily. If there was anything he wished to confide in me, he'd bring it up himself. Failing that, I could tease him on being a lard arse.

As I ruminated, I pushed open the doors to *The Fiddler's Arms* and stepped into the smaller of the two bar rooms. It was no bigger than a school classroom. A pool table rested in an area towards the far wall and a line of circular dark brown wooden tables stood on the side by the entrance, with a long bench of cushioned green leather. The bar was off to my left, a continuation of the same long bar area that stretched into the other, main, room.

Derrick was at the nearer bar, paying for his pint of Guinness. He turned with two pints in his hands, handing the second to me. He was always thoughtful like that.

"Pool?"

"Sure," I agreed. "Though I'm rubbish at it."

We didn't need to talk much, having known each other for over three decades. A word here, a look there, and it wasn't until two games of pool and a pint later that we sat down at a table and chatted properly.

"I've got something to show you," I said, pulling a paperback of *Balls Deep* from my large outer pocket. "I'm a writer now!"

Derrick took it and perused the cover, flicking through the pages. "What is it?"

"My memoir, of doing pick-up."

"You always did like writing. Remember in Mr Boardman's class when," and then we steered away into reminiscing of school days. After half an hour a couple came in and I recognised the man though I hadn't laid eyes on him in over twenty years. He glanced around the room as if searching for someone, saw Derrick, and smiled.

"Is that Paul Andersen?" I asked.

"Yep. I told him we were coming to The Fiddlers so he said he'd come down with his lass."

Readers with a keen memory will recall Paul and I spent a year or so walking down to secondary school together before we had a mild falling out. I'd never disliked him but we'd drifted apart then and hadn't hung out since. So this reunion was quite unexpected. There was a table next to Derrick and I so the two newcomers bought drinks and joined us. A few brief introductions followed, for the girl's benefit.

"Nicky, lad. I haven't seen you in years! What have you been up to?" I gave him the short version, omitting the sleaze. "Nice one, mate. I always thought you'd end up in London with a good job."

"How about you, Paul?"

"It's funny you ask now. Everything changed in the last year." He looked over at his girlfriend and smiled. She squeezed his hand. "I was a bit of a bad lad. I'd started TWOCing [Taking Without Owner's Consent — the official name for joyriding in stolen cars] the last couple of years at school but got bored with it. Then we got really into football, going to the match. I fell in with a firm of football hooligans. Always fighting and having scrapes with the law. Then, I was labouring on building sites and drinking too much."

His eyes were wistful, like the famous old pirate Captain Morgan looking back on his buccaneering days, long after converting to Christianity and settling down in a quiet country home.

"Anyway, to cut a long story short I was all a bit out of it, wondering what I'd done with my life. And then I met Leslie here. It was funny but she'd lived only one street over from me for ten years and we'd never met. Then, well, we got together and I've straightened myself out. It's been eight months now," he said it like an Alcoholics Anonymous member logging the days since his last drink, "and we are very happy."

Paul seemed completely sincere. Derrick raised a glass and we chinked them in cheers.

"What's this?" said Paul. He'd shuffled a little on his bench seat and accidentally sat upon the corner of the book I'd given Derrick. He lifted up Derrick's coat and saw the bright red cover. "Haha, that skinhead on the cover looks like you." He narrowed his eyes, looking at me then at the book.

"It is him," said Derrick. "He just gave me a copy of his memoir."

Paul picked it up with visible curiosity. "*Balls Deep*, eh? You were well into books at school weren't you. What's it about?"

I felt embarrassed. Not at the content, but that Leslie was listening and seemed equally interested. Perhaps they expected the memoir to talk about my university days and time in London. It's not every day you find out your old school mate is an author. I'd have been equally curious if Paul had revealed a career as a singer, or pro fighter. Hell, even his unofficial career as a football hooligan had intrigued me. But I didn't really want to explain what a Pick-Up Artist is.

Not in front of the skirt.

"Oh, it's a little vanity project," I said dismissively, if not entirely inaccurately. "I happened to have a copy lying around in my parents' house when Derrick invited me out."

Leslie was reading the back cover now. I felt like a paedophile in the defendant's dock waiting while the judge reads the jury's verdict. I wasn't at all ashamed of my skirt-chasing ways but rather, my discomfort was caused by the clash between my life now and the old image of me that someone who'd only ever known me at school would still hold. I imagine porno actresses feel something similar when the kids at their children's school discover mum's videos on PornHub.

"It looks nice," said Leslie diplomatically and we talked of other things.

I was back home almost two weeks in total. Much of that was spent enjoying the big new television on my bedroom wall, watching movies and playing video games. The familiar travel itch had kicked in after a week. Fortunately, my next trip was already planned: Eddie and I were headed back to Riga.

WANTON AND GETTING

CHAPTER 18
RIGA

Chapter 19
WANTON AND GETTING

A week before departing for Latvia, I happened to find my old flame Tatiana online in Facebook chat. We fell into conversation.

"Hey fancypants. How is the CCCP?" I opened, adopting my usual tease of assuming all Russians are card-carrying communists.

"Nick! It is nice but I'm sad."

"Well, that's understandable. You haven't seen me in over a year."

Tatiana soon expanded upon her woes, key amongst them being she was approaching her thirtieth birthday and didn't have any marriage candidates sniffing around. She lived in a city a few hundred miles from St. Petersburg doing some kind of IT teaching at a private college.

"My life is boring. I don't know why I bother dieting and going to the gym. No interesting men talk to me."

She was serious. When I'd first met her in Trafalgar Square, almost two years earlier, she'd been in fantastic shape. She was a regular gym rat and competed in ballroom dancing in her home town. Tatiana fell hard for me and, after realising I was a dead-end as a potential husband, she'd allowed herself to have some fun with me. That had included visiting me for a long weekend in 2014 while I was in Belgrade the previous summer. It was the last time we'd met.

"I'm depressed."

"Well, how about this for an idea…. I'm going to Riga next week. That's not far from you, is it?" I was remembering that she'd taken a coach to see me there the last time I was in Latvia. "Come and visit. I'll cheer you up."

"Thank you Nick. I'll think about it."

That thinking took two hours. She confirmed and we arranged logistics.

My logistics were horrible. There is no easy way to fly from Newcastle to Riga, which surprised me considering the latter's popularity as a bachelor party destination for drunken Brits. The main issue was my tight purse-strings. Finally, after an hour on price comparison websites, I booked an early morning flight to Dublin. The airport layover was seven hours before flying on to my final destination. With naïve enthusiasm, I guessed I'd spend the layover writing or something equally productive. At worst, drinking Guinness and chatting to leprechauns. Eddie wasn't due into Riga until two days later. We booked a big shared apartment near the train station.

On the appointed day, my alarm woke me at 5am and I wasn't at all happy. "Fu---fu--fuck off!" I groaned, swatting at it. Sounds of shuffling and plodding feet reverberated through the walls and then my mother knocked on my bedroom door.

"Get up, lazybones!"

It was still dark outside. I was desperately tired, having slept only a few hours. I'd been playing *Dying Light*, a zombie survival game, until the wee hours. Fortunately I'd packed my rucksack before sleeping. I stumbled into the shower, then sat in my dressing gown drinking coffee. My mother continued to pester me.

"Get ready! Your dad is giving you a lift in thirty minutes."

"I'm already packed. It'll take only five minutes to get dressed."

She wandered off to do whatever unnecessary things she'd gotten out of bed for. They seemed to consist mostly of clattering around in the kitchen cupboards. Five minutes later, just as the caffeine had quietened my mind into an early-morning bliss, she came back into the lounge brandishing a Ewbank carpet sweeping device. Much to my astonishment, my mum was determined to clean the floor at 5:15am. It looked clean enough already to me.

It was aggravating, which I'm sure was the point of the exercise. She pushed hard, leaning her weight onto the handle so that the device's rollers ground into the carpet noisily.

"Can't you wait till I've gone? I'll be away ten days, which is ample time to clean the carpet."

"Move your feet out of the way."

"What's wrong with you? I'm trying to relax with a cup of coffee before my flight and you're deliberately making a racket. There's no reason at all to do this now."

She stopped suddenly, straightening up, hands on hips. I could see indignation rising.

"Well, if you want to tidy the house *be my guest*. Don't have a go at me for clearing up your mess after you!"

"There is no mess, and it's not after me. You've got ten days to be after me. Right now, you are doing this *through* me."

My mum's cheeks reddened and her eyes narrowed into cold evil slits. I'd triggered her narcissistic rage again, as I knew I would. I stood up and walked into the kitchen to clean my coffee cup.

"Where are you going? I'm talking to you."

"No, you're not. You're deliberately aggravating me. I'm getting out of the way. You're disturbing my peace of mind with all this hectoring."

"I am not hectoring you. I'm just making sure you're not late. It's not fair on your dad after he promised to give you a lift. Or on me getting up early to see you off."

I could hear my dad walking around upstairs, his footsteps audible through the ceiling. He didn't seem to be in the slightest rush, as was to be expected when we weren't due to leave for another twenty minutes.

Tatiana drew this for me

"There's no point you getting up. My dad is giving the lift not you. And I've never missed a flight in my life."

My mother continued to splutter, moan, and threaten. Then she preceded to lie, and finally to guilt-trip me. I was thoroughly disgusted. Her machinations were transparent but what I couldn't figure out is why she was trying so hard to alienate me. These flare-ups had become increasingly common over the past five years and were a 50/50 bet in the final twenty-four hours before a flight. There were no such problems with my father.

I stormed off upstairs absolutely furious at my mother for engineering a fight and ruining my peace of mind. I'd now fly off to Riga on a sour note. My dad came downstairs at the last possible moment — quite deliberately, to evade having to take a position — and got the car out the garage. I placed my rucksack on the back seat. My mother came out to give me a hug and I pushed her away.

"Fuck off. I'm not talking to you," I said.

My dad pretended like nothing had happened. He dropped me off at the Newcastle Airport departures lounge and I thanked him for the lift.

Riga was warm and sunny. Our apartment was clean, modern, and very white. Like me.

I met Tatiana in town the next afternoon, a Saturday, and was surprised to see she'd dyed her black hair to a peroxide blonde. She looked a little older and fatter than I remembered, suggesting she'd not been joking about letting herself go a little while depressed. That said, she still looked good. She was pleased to see me but her eyes held a touch of melancholy, as if her excitement to be in Riga was offset by the knowledge it was nothing more than a weekend of fun.

"I only stay one night," she informed me. "I can't get time off work."

Given the weather was amenable, we walked around the central park by the canal and had coffee in the Old Town. Our conversation hovered around light-hearted nonsense as I wished to distract her from her troubles. Towards early evening I steered towards my apartment and she came upstairs agreeably.

The lounge was a large white-washed room with a big grey sofa pushed up against the windows on the side facing into a courtyard. On the right of this was an en-suite kitchen area and at the opposite wall was a dining table. Two doors to the left opened onto bedrooms. Tatiana and I sat on the sofa chatting, not mentioning the obvious subtext.

"I want a husband but it is so difficult. The men in my city are not interesting."

"Go to another city."

"That too is difficult. I have a good job and I like it. It's not easy to change."

I hadn't yet been to Russia so my imagination conjured up dimly-formed images of the country. Mostly they involved the massive wrestler Zangief from the *Street Fighter* video game series and a procession of dangerous KGB assassins from James Bond movies. The Russian girls I'd met in London gave me the impression the whole country was chock full of hotties and thus even a girl of Tatiana's good looks would be up against stiff opposition in the local marriage market.

"Come to London, then. I always say to men that if you want better women, you should head East. It works the other way for women. Move West and your options expand."

"What do you mean?" she asked, sitting upright and turning towards me. This was a topic dear to her heart. She loved London.

"Well, you've been to London. You know how it is."

"Nicky, I was there less than one month. You were the only English man I met. I was at school every day."

"Okay then, I'll explain. Have you ever wondered why I always travel to central and eastern Europe to chase women? It's because as an English man I am dissatisfied with my options in the English dating market. Put bluntly, English women are shit. Fat, badly-dressed, ill-mannered oafs. The women of your country are so much better. It's like they are a different, superior species."

"So you like Russian girls. I still don't understand."

"If men of my quality are ignoring English women in favour of Russian women, what does that tell you about supply and demand of men?"

She thought about that for a few seconds. I took the opportunity to refill her wine glass. A drunk Tatiana would be more fun in bed. Comprehension dawned and she smiled, to answer my question.

"By economic theory, it suggests there are more good men in England than good women. Wait!.. And in Russia it is the opposite!"

"Precisely. Whatever man you can get in your little communist hellhole city, if you go to London you can get better. Simply moving to London changes your position as if you were five years younger and two points hotter."

Tatiana liked that idea. Hope lit up her eyes. All she wanted was to find a husband, have children, and be loved. I wasn't offering even one of the three. I did have an offer of a different type, which I now explained.

"Look, I've thought about this and I have a plan. Find a way to get into London whether on a tourist visa, as a language student, or a job transfer.

Girl Junkie

From there, it's simple. Once a week on Thursday evenings I'll take you around the financial district: St Pauls, Liverpool Street, St James' Square. I know these places and the people, because I used to be one of them. After work, small groups of smart, affluent professional men go drinking in bars. These men never meet pretty women. All the girls in their offices are fat secretaries or hatchet-faced man-jaw career women. Same for the few women who go into the bars. I know how these men live. They get an early train to the office and work hard all day. They eat lunch at their desk and take the late train home, exhausted. Their few free hours each evening are spent in the gym, or watching Netflix, or studying for the next professional exam. At the weekend they get drunk with colleagues, watch football, buy some expensive gadget, then sleep it off on Sunday."

Tatiana was just about following me. She seemed surprised at my suddenly passionate oration. I continued.

"The point is this: these men are perfect husband material and yet they *never* meet women as pretty as you. I spent years in this milieu. The luckiest men will marry the least-ugly receptionist or waste thousands buying jewellery for strippers. If a girl like you shows an interest and acts femininely around them, they'll fall in love within weeks."

"That sounds great Nicky, but how will I meet such men?"

"I'm coming to that. It's simple. I'll take you out once a week. We'll go to the bars together. You point out a man you like and I'll contrive to start a conversation with him. At first he'll think you're my woman but if the interaction goes well, I'll let him know you're single. It won't take long until you are stacking up dates and choosing your man."

I was deadly serious. I liked Tatiana and wanted to marry her off. She thought about it a while then our conversation moved to other topics. Finally, I decided to fuck her.

"Come here," I said, pulling her in to kiss. She resisted, pushing me away.

"No, I came to Riga just to see you. Not for sex."

"Bollocks. I'm having you."

I persisted and she let me push her flat onto the sofa and make out with her. She continued to resist so I put my hand between her legs and rubbed her up. Her resistance faltered and she relaxed underneath me. Soon she was kissing back explosively, like a hungry demon let loose from hell.

I always liked that about Tatiana. Once switched on, she was a hellcat. Zero to a hundred miles-an-hour in seconds.

I pushed her to the floor and got my dick out. Her eyes opened wide and then she grabbed a hold and sucked me off. Sucking, slurping and popping noises abounded, Tatiana acting as though this was the happiest moment of her life. Perhaps it was. *That escalated quickly*, I thought to myself. It was such a good blow job I wasn't the least inclined to stop her but after a few minutes I felt I ought to contribute something to the interaction so I pulled her to her feet, bent her over the kitchen sink, and stuck my dick in from behind.

Tatiana was as good as I remembered.

She writhed around, grabbed hard onto the cupboard edges until her knuckles went white, and all manner of nice guttural sounds escaped her pouting mouth. Thoroughly enjoying myself, I carried her over to the dining table, laid her out flat on it to banged her some more. Then I ordered her to her knees again and made her suck me off. Assumed I wanted to come, she began pumping me hard, like trying to get the last squirt of toothpaste out of the tube. However, we'd only been going ten minutes and I wasn't done.

I took her into the bedroom, picked her up, and threw her several feet across the room so she landed heavily in the middle of the double bed.

"Turn over. I'm going to fuck you in the ass" I said.

"Oh, Nicky!" she gasped, and obeyed.

She perched on her knees and elbows with her ass pushed back into the air. I pulled a condom on and buried my dick in. She yelped and shivered like a dying deer. I pounded her. The following five minutes were possibly the best sex of my life. Tatiana screamed the house down, gasping and yelling like a madwoman, absolutely wanton. She clawed the duvet and pillows and even climbed her hands up the headboard, scratching at the wall like a Jew locked in the gas showers. The whole time she gurgled and roared in a paroxysm of unbridled lust. I slapped her ass and pulled her hair.

It was fucking brilliant. I've had many, many good sex sessions with a whole assortment of beautiful and sometimes crazy women, but this one particularly sticks in the memory.

Finally, I put her on her knees for the third time and let her suck me off. I came on her face, aiming for the eyes. Then I collapsed on the bed while Tatiana went next door and showered. Sex had been so much better than expected, despite the high standards set by Tatiana's prior efforts in bed with me. Should she find and marry a London finance chode, he'll be a very lucky man.

We lay together an hour, then she sucked me off and straddled me.

"You lie still. I'll do this," she said. It suited me fine. She rode me for ten minutes then got off and sucked me off again.

I rarely bang a girl twice in one session. My preference is to make the first time long and satisfying for us both, so it'll often take up to an hour. I tend to get sleepy and lethargic after sex so by the time I'm interested in banging the girl again, I'm too comfortable to move.

I fell asleep.

The following morning we woke up late and took a short walk into the Old Town for coffee and lunch. My mood had darkened. Tatiana had only a few hours before catching her bus and though I was usually comfortable having her around, this time I felt disconcerted. Our long discussion of her romantic frustrations made me feel guilty for using her as a fuck buddy. Of course she was an adult and knew full well this trip was only ever about casual sex, so I hadn't deceived her. Still, I couldn't shake the feeling she was vulnerable. Had I done a good thing providing escapism and happy memories, or a bad thing in reminding her of what she couldn't have?

I had trouble focusing on our conversation. I wanted to look away. Preferably, I'd find a cafe and sit alone staring into space for a few hours. My reveries were of increasing frequency and duration. Something deep in my subconscious wasn't happy with my life's trajectory.

"Are you okay, Nicky? You don't talk."

I believe a man shouldn't burden others with his problems. Part of being a man is carrying weight on your own shoulders. Nobody likes a whiny bitch. It can be a tightrope with girls, to share enough of your inner world that they feel connection but to close off those insecurities and frustrations that would undermine her assessment of your confidence. Suspecting I'd never see Tatiana again, I decided to share. These worries had been bothering me for months.

"I too have my romantic frustrations."

"Tell me, Nicky."

"I don't know what I want in life — in my romantic life. The way I live now is lots of fun but it's very wearing on my body and soul. From the outside it looks amazing, travelling all across the world with my friends and sleeping with lots of women."

"You sleep with lots of women?"

"Yes."

"I guessed so."

"Have you heard of PUA? It means pick-up artist. There is an underground community on the internet of men who create a system to get girls. We share tips and the skilled men teach lessons to the other men."

"We have something like this in Russia, for women. There are websites and chat groups on how to find a rich husband."

"Something like that. I'm a pick-up artist. That's how we met in London: I was using my system. For a few years I've been travelling and sleeping with girls. Up until last year I really enjoyed it but now it often seems futile. When I started, I was unhappy because I wanted pretty girls but couldn't get them. Then I got lots of them and was happy, and now I have the same but I'm unhappy again."

We were sitting on slatted wooden chairs facing each other across a low table in a cafe restaurant. Our table was in the outdoor beer garden, facing the cobbled streets. Tatiana sipped on a cocktail and I drank cappuccino. She was intrigued but hardly sympathetic.

"My problem is I got what I wanted but found it wasn't what I expected. I'm like the dog who chased cars every day and finally caught one. Now I feel like my life is scattered across four corners of the earth. I last felt this when I lived in Japan, when half my life was in Tokyo and the other half in London. Settling in one city or the other would mean giving up half of the things I love. My life today is like that, but scattered across a dozen countries. There's not a single place I'd be happy to settle in. I'm certain wherever I settled, I'd always be thinking of what I left behind in the others."

"What is wrong with Newcastle?"

"If you'd been there, you'd know. It's more communist than Russia. There are many nice people, of course, but the average level of Newcastle people disgusts me. They are parochial, poorly-educated, slovenly savages. My brother lives in a nice area and all his neighbours and friends are communists. He's always complaining on the phone about them, and about never being able to say what he really thinks. For years I've avoided that problem by being on the move with a small group of like-minded friends. When I settle, I'll have to learn to get along with people whose values I despise."

"Is Newcastle really so bad?"

"You're Russian, so you wouldn't know. You think England is still the country of Sherlock Holmes, Queen Victoria, and Winston Churchill. It's not. It's a communist hellhole. It's full of fat, lazy parasites who eat McDonald's and swill beer. Saturday night in the city centre is like an African civil war. It just.... disgusts me. And each year, we get fuller of third world immigrants and, worse, the English people actually welcome them all. They want to virtue signal to everyone how they aren't racist."

"Are you racist, Nicky?"

"Yes. I hate the third world. I want to gun them all down at the border."

"Nicky, you really mean it don't you?" she laughed.

I did. The calm even-handed Krauser you know and love today wasn't always the paragon of brotherly love.

"This is my romantic frustration. My country is going to shit, so I can't settle there. I can't even talk to the people there. Every other country has its problems, not least of which is that it is *another country* and thus I'd be a foreigner who is on the outside. I had that already in Japan, even though I spoke the language. It's great for a couple of years, until you realise you'll always be just a guest. So, I'm tired of chasing skirt across countries and equally unenthusiastic about choosing one skirt and one country."

She sipped her cocktail through a straw. "Yes, Nicky. We all have problems." I stared into spare for fully five minutes before Tatiana piped up again. "I'd like you to make me pregnant."

That snapped me out of my reverie. It was the second time this year a Russian girl had said it to me.

"What?"

"I want your baby. Listen to me, it is not so unusual. My life in Russian is okay but for the man problem. I have a good job, a nice apartment, lots of money, and many friends. I am comfortable. The problem is the men are not good. I want a baby and you will make a very good baby." I looked as uncertain as when Zaria had made essentially the same pitch. Just as Zaria had, Tatiana rushed on to assure me how little I'd need to contribute. "I don't ask to marry you and you don't need to be a father. I just want to be pregnant with your child. I will do everything else."

Having received a similar pitch a few months earlier I was ready for it this time. My shock lasted only thirty seconds. Then I patiently explained the reasons I couldn't agree, principally that I considered it child abuse to willingly sire a child knowing he will be fatherless. Tatiana was disappointed but didn't press the issue. An hour later I walked her to the bus station and kissed her goodbye.

Her offer had only made me more disconsolate. It had exacerbated my sense of unreality with what my life had become. How ironic that I couldn't find a palatable solution to settling down, and yet two very hot Russian women were offering to bear my children for free.

That night I had an unexpected meltdown. Since first beginning my Player's Journey, I'd experienced periodic nervous breakdowns which had, at first, greatly puzzled me. The process always began the same way, with a slow build-up of anxiety over the direction of my life. This took several days, sometimes weeks. I'd become increasingly distracted and thoughtful, often losing track of time as I stared into space for hours on end. My doubts were mostly existential: was I on the right track? Was there any meaning to life? What is the Good Life and is this it? Subsidiary to these big worries were more practical concerns on whether I'd succeed in attaining my goals. In the first couple of years I'd experienced frequent doubts whether I'd ever become good with women. Once those doubts were put to rest by consistent real-world successes my existential anxiety turned inwards: was I a good person? Was I fundamentally broken in some irredeemable way? By 2015, I was mostly over those doubts and my anxiety had lately turned towards pure competitiveness: am I good at pick-up? Do my achievements on the street and in the bedroom justify my growing public reputation as an 'MPUA' (Master Pick-Up Artist)?

It was important to me that my public image accurately reflect my real-life situation. I was utterly contemptuous of all the bullshitters and charlatans infesting the Community. Possibly this was an overreaction to my having being taken in by some of them when I first began. There was also a tinge of envy, because the charlatans tended to aggressively market their brands and thus usually outperformed me in brand awareness and sales. It was frustrating to see forum discussions lauding men who I knew — from direct experience as well as the 'word on the street' — were utterly incompetent seducers.

My last meltdown had been in November the previous year, ironically within days of logging the highest peak of my seduction career, when I'd cycled four hot young women through my bed in one Prague day, banging three of them. Meltdowns were not a reaction to failure. They were as likely to happen following success.

This meltdown was long overdue.

Looking back now, I realised pressure had been building since my first week in Warsaw. There were unresolved issues. I'd considered my upward ascent

Girl Junkie

towards 'getting good with women' to have ended with that aforementioned peak in Prague. I'd climbed the mountain. I'd succeeded in reaching my goal and now I didn't have any idea where to go next. Aimlessness plagued me. Without a goal, I was just treading water. It was awful.

Banging Tatiana tipped me over the edge. I don't know why.

I lay in bed and the dark night of the soul overcame me. I curled up into fetal position and shivered. A succession of images whizzed through my mind, like a film strip snapping on the projector spindle and spinning at uncontrollably high speed. I remembered the happy times of my marriage and then its crumbling toward divorce. I felt the aching loss of loneliness and its replacement by the hope engendered by my first few dates from daygame, in 2009. Images continued to overlap each other, like photos stacked into a pile one by one. There appeared to be no logical connection, the heady highlights mixing equally with the depths of despair. I remembered travelling with the *Rock Solid Game* gang throughout the Balkans, of parties at our London mansion, and the pleasure of solo adventuring abroad.

One question continually recurred: what's the point of all this?

I began to think of friends I'd seen recently. There was my friend Ash who claimed outrageous success since moving to Krakow but I felt like he wasn't giving me the real story. Tom Torero had recently uploaded a podcast in which he claimed to have banged nine girls that month. Though theoretically possible but I didn't believe it for a moment. I'd seen him three times walking around on dates with sub-par women and his messages to me, and his keeping a distance, suggested he was avoiding me so as not to be triggered. A man swimming in fresh pussy *never* gets triggered. He'd also used turns of phrase that made me suspect his recent podcast was designed specifically for my ears, rather than his five thousand YouTube subscribers.

These ruminations heightened my anxiety. If my natural inclination was to suspect my friends of constructing elaborate frauds specifically to trigger me, what did that say about my own personality? Was I really so self-important? Did I really think the world revolved around me?

For two hours my mind bounced pinball-like between the twin poles of distrusting my own inclinations and of taking red flags seriously. I'd recently read a book by Gavin De Becker called *The Gift Of Fear*. His primary message was to trust your instincts. He postulated that many victims of violent crime report having felt stirrings of unease and fear long before the attack. Their survival often hinged upon following instinct even when their conscious mind rationalised away the seemingly illogical warnings. We have evolved survival instincts, and many criminals exploit our more fallible logical reasoning to bullshit us into ignoring them. The lesson had stuck and I now tried to listen to my subconscious in all things.

What was it telling me now?

It was too murky. I was grasping in a deep fog, the shapes around me blurred and indistinct. My subconscious was telling me something was wrong, but what? Was the problem with myself, or with my life's trajectory, or with my trusting certain friends? It was maddening. On paper, I was living exactly the life I wanted. I was living comfortably on book and video royalties, travelling the world, banging some pretty young girls, and was held in esteem by friends whose opinions I respected. Shouldn't I be content?

Eddie was due to arrive the next day and I was looking forward to seeing him. I needed somebody to lean on and he seemed to be a solid guy.

There are some killer memoirs out there

Interview with Eddie

Not bad considering what I'd just done to her

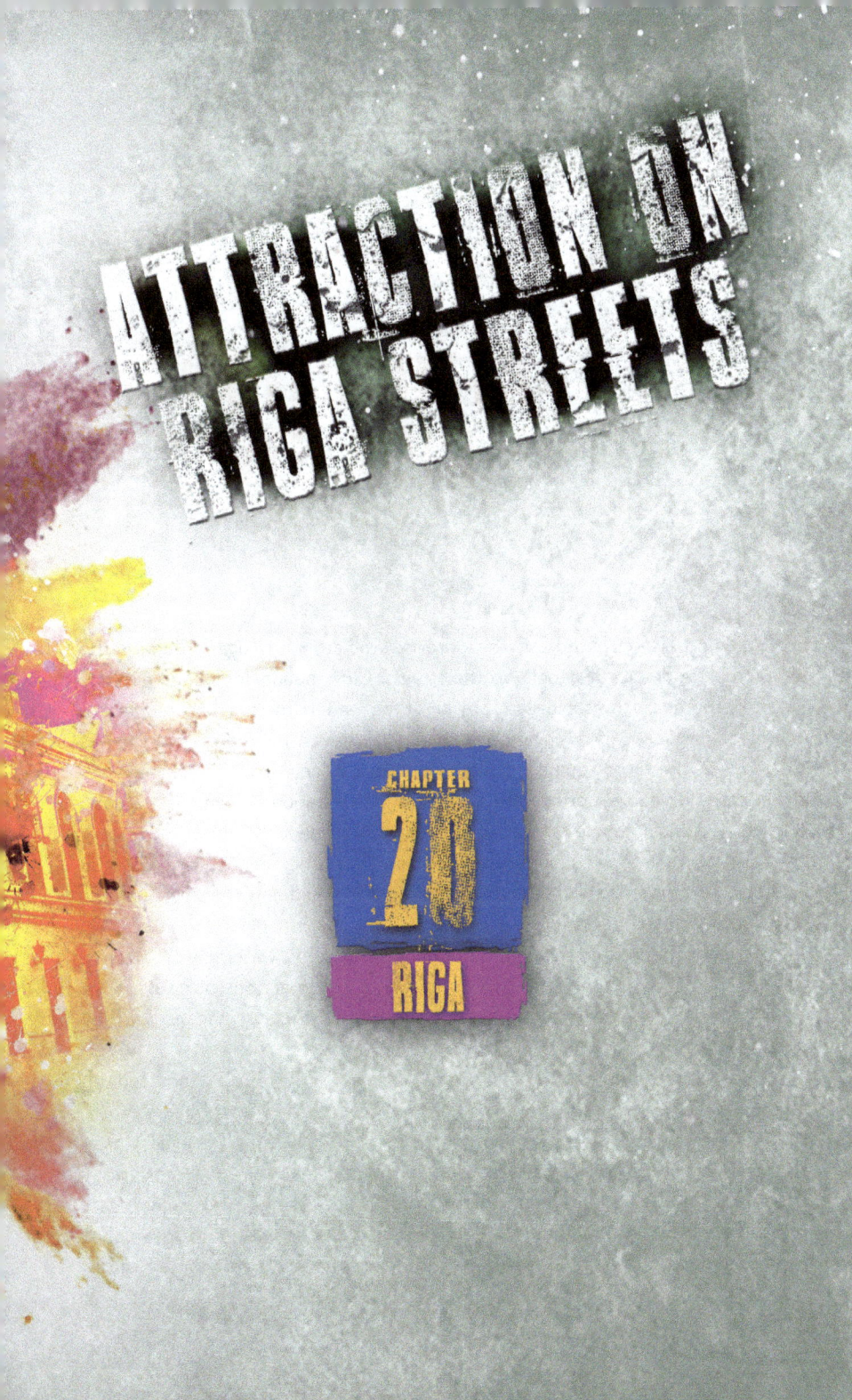

Chapter 20
ATTRACTION ON RIGA STREETS

Eddie and I soon found out the primary problem with Riga in June is the complete dearth of people on the streets. On a pound-for-pound girl-for-girl basis the quality was excellent but any time we left the main thoroughfares we might not see even a single pedestrian. Our search for footfall soon led us to prioritise the large square outside the train station, which fortunately had the excellent Double Coffee cafe tucked into the station building and a patio outside. The main cobbled street of the Old Town, leading from a bridge over the canal on to an open square, then finishing at another large square, was also reasonably trafficked. Still, it was disappointing. We could only manage a handful of approaches each per day.

We spent much time sitting around in outdoor cafes, watching the streets. It felt a waste of energy to walk around with so little action to motivate us. It was in one such cafe that Eddie interviewed me on video for his YouTube channel.

There were some memorable sets. At the train station I chatted up a leggy Uzbek who was in town only a few days. During rush hour a crowd of commuters would stream to and from the station, walking up a short busy shopping street towards a line of bus stops. Beyond that was a pleasant grassy park. I met a hot young Ukrainian there and Eddie found a few willing girls of his own. Being a video guy, Eddie had a good camera with him so we shot clips of each other hitting on the girls, with a view to editing a montage later.

After two mostly fruitless days we'd at least gotten the lay of the land. The centre of the Old Town was fairly reliable after work hours, as was a small shopping mall on the edge of it. That mall was long and thin with continuous glass windows several stories high. A hallway ran from end-to-end, where we did most of our indoor sets. Once up a floor or two, it became harder to find girls. We ventured into some side streets and another mall, mostly without result. So, the Old Town, the mall, and the station environs provided most of our entertainment.

"Where's everyone gone?" I wondered aloud.

"Was it busier last time?" asked Eddie, having never visited Riga before and thus having no standard of comparison.

"I can't say first time, in 2011, because it was minus twenty degrees so we only did nightgame in the Old Town. In 2013 it was way busier, but that was September, I think. Perhaps everyone is out of town on holiday."

Filming our daygame montages

Next door Lithuania's capital Vilnius could be like that, with many locals taking long trips down to the beach resort of Palanga. Eddie didn't seem to mind the lack of action as much as I did. I'd soon find out he was more laid back and patient than myself in most things.

My most memorable set came when walking by the park with Eddie. He wanted to shoot some video of approaches so I made an extra effort to open. I did a few fun sets on a stretch of busy pavement alongside the little park. Some college somewhere had closed for the day, we guessed, because there were more student-aged girls around. One such girl approached, walking her dog on a leash. It was a little cute thing. The girl, that is, though I suppose the dog was too.

"Hey, stop there, you!" I called playfully and the little lady came to an easy rest. She looked up at me with gentle anticipation. I noticed her hair was tinted with dark red, as if she had a hint of natural ginger mixed with her brunette colouring. She was only an inch or two taller than five feet and pleasantly curvy.

I can't remember what I said to her. The three things on my mind were: firstly, she looked pleased to be there; second, that Eddie was across the road with his video camera running; and third that her little dog was yapping contentedly, busying itself sniffing my ankles. We made small talk and I remember feeling rather emboldened, so I tweaked her nose, patted her on the head, and chucked her chin. Playing up for the camera, you may conclude. There are clips of the set spliced into the aforementioned interview on *Street Attraction*'s channel. I do remember she was called Valda, was eighteen years old, and a native of Riga. We exchanged numbers and I walked away thinking it quite likely we'd meet again.

Picking up Valda

That evening I endured a time-waster date with another local girl. It was bright sunshine until late so we lay in the park chatting. She let me paw at her and rested her head in the crook of my arm, but refused all kissing. When she insisted on not doing anything that could upset her boyfriend, I let her go. On the plus side, Eddie had been hiding behind a tree videoing some of the date. Luckily the park wasn't busy, so it's unlikely anyone would report him to the police for suspicious behaviour.

For all the slow progress with girls, Eddie and I were really in Riga to get to know each other better. That element of the trip went smoothly as we got on very well and chatted freely over beers in the Old Town bars. Eddie filled me in on the backstory of *Street Attraction* and his future plans for the business.

"How is business?" I asked.

"It's alright," he responded in his usual understated manner. "We don't really have any big-selling products. There's the VIP video area but that's only £20 so it's not a money-spinner. *Approach 2 Lay* is selling decently."

"Does the channel make any money?"

Relaxing in the park

"Not really. It's very hard to monetize YouTube even when a video goes viral. We had the *How To Get Laid in Poland* video pick up steam and get a few hundred thousand views. Lots of people talked about it, but the share of advertising revenue is so small it doesn't really make a difference. The main business value of the channel is the sign-ups it brings for boot camps."

This was as I'd suspected. I'd followed many video game YouTube channels who had ten times the subscriber base of *Street Attraction* and those content creators often stated they needed viewers to donate to their Patreon account in order to make a living. Within the world of pick-up, only live in-field coaching is a reliable living. My own good luck with

Daygame Mastery notwithstanding, nobody seemed to be making a living from products alone.

"Does coaching bring in much?"

"Enough that Richard, Maciek and I don't need real jobs. But it's up and down, depending on sign-ups."

This kind of discussion fascinated me because I'd never intended to make a living from pick-up and couldn't possibly advise anyone else on how to do so. When first writing *Daygame Mastery* I'd intended it to be an underground book, not for sale at any price. My initial vision had been to print up only ten copies to present to my friends. Looking back, I realise that would've been extremely dumb. It's a certainty somebody would've ripped off all the ideas and claimed the money and credit for them. In the age of the internet and digital production, nobody can keep material secret any more. Nowadays, I had a few friends able to turn their backs upon office work in order to scratch out a living from daygame coaching. Steve was getting by on products and coaching, as was Tom. I could add Eddie to this short list.

Midway through the trip, Eddie discovered another unexpected benefit to running a popular pick-up channel. I was sitting in our lounge editing together my infield footage for a short YouTube montage. Eddie was in his room checking mails.

"Nick," he called, picking up his laptop and carrying it into the lounge to sit next to me on the sofa. "What do you think of this?"

He pointed on his screen to an email he'd just received. I read it. Taken at face value, a girl from a small Polish city had seen his *How To Get Laid in Poland* video and enjoyed it. She'd begun following Eddie's work and developed a crush on him. She was now emailing to compliment him on being an attractive masculine man and expressed her wish to meet.

"Is that real?" he asked.

I re-read it. "It sounds too good to be true. Some random girl decides to throw herself at a YouTube pick-up artist? My guess is she's either a busted-up single mum, or it's a put-up job and it's really some *SlutHate* character trolling you."

"Yeah, that's my first thought."

"You won't lose anything by replying. Just be careful what information you let out. If it's *SlutHate*, they'll be social engineering, trying to pump you for anything that can attack your business or dox you."

Eddie mulled that over. "I agree, but something about the mail rings true. It doesn't feel fake."

"In that case, ask her for photos. Certainly get her on Skype video chat before you commit to any plans."

I returned to my editing. My idea was to time the cuts to the beats of the background music, a cover version of The Kinks *Dedicated Follower Of Fashion* that I'd had re-recorded with amended lyrics. Half a year earlier when producing *Daygame Overkill* I'd learned how cheaply I could get custom music from the website Fiverr. It had become something of a hobby, writing silly songs and getting contractors to record them for me.

The next morning, at breakfast, Eddie was very excitable indeed.

"I was chatting all night with that email bird. She's for real. She's a student, eighteen years old. Told me she's a virgin and pretty much propositioned that I deflower her."

"Crikey."

There wasn't really much more that could be said in response, now was there?

"She sent a couple of pictures, including a nude. She's hot."

"I want a YouTube channel," I moaned. "Here's me chasing skirt the old-fashioned way while you sidestep all this daygame nonsense through the miracle of modern technology."

"Mate, I'm as surprised as you are. It's the first time it's ever happened. Anyway, how are your leads? Has anything come through from Riga."

"As it happens, yes. That little dog-walker girl wants to meet tomorrow evening."

"Ah, my flight is in the morning. I won't be able to record it."

"No worries. I'm checking into a new apartment for the last three days, anyway."

Chapter 21
TEENYBOPPER

With Eddie gone, my mind turned towards Valda. She agreed to meet after college at the square in the Old Town by the bridge. I waited outside the McDonald's at the corner overlooking a canal that snakes through the central park. The sun stayed strong and locals seemed keen to take advantage, milling around aimlessly enjoying the weather. Valda showed up on time wearing tight faded blue jeans and white trainers. Together with her light orange cardigan she looked about twelve years old. If not for her womanly hips and sizeable breasts I'd have questioned whether she'd told me the truth about her age.

"No dog this time?" I asked.

"He's at my grandmother's house. I have to pick him up around eight o'clock."

Given it was now already six, it seemed the little Latvian was trying to give me a hint that we wouldn't have a long date.

"Then lets get started. How about the odd-shaped cafe over by the canal," I said, pointing off across the rolling green banks.

"Sure."

The cafe to which I refer was my favourite in the city. Picture, if you will, a long narrow canal that winds snake-like around the East side of the Old Town. On each side, carefully-landscaped grassy banks rise to street level and a flat park full of trees and pedestrian paths. This is Bastejkalns park. A keen walker can stroll for hours back and forth taking in the cultivated slice of nature on one side and the preserved Old Town architecture on the other. That walker will notice small museums and public buildings, as well as open plazas and theatres. All of it is compressed into a small area befitting such a small capital. It's like a bonsai Paris.

One bend in the canal is straddled by a footbridge overlooked by a teashop shaped like a large cafetière instrument. The six-sided two-storey building is constructed mostly of glass and wooden supports, with a surrounding canvas canopy that protects the outdoor sofa seats built into the ground floor exterior. On summer days these seats give a delightful view of the park and the fresh air from sitting outside. Inside is the counter and serving area. A staircase winds up to the first floor, a single airy room into which sunlight streams through the large glass windows. More sofa chairs face outwards at every angle. It was here that I led Valda.

We sat together on a sofa, a low glass coffee table before us where I rested my cappuccino and her tea. The teapot suited her well: small, curvy, and of as yet unrevealed contents. For the first ten minutes our conversation was stilted. Valda's English was excellent but our conversation faltered more because I couldn't get a handle on how to treat her, and she too seemed uncertain. Gradually, we settled into comfortable chat and got to know each other better. She explained she was entering university after summer and was interested in foreign travel, though as yet she'd only visited Spain. Her high school had a link-up with a Spanish city and she'd been able to attend multiple school trips there and a couple of family holidays in other parts of the country. She was learning Spanish and hope to study there on an exchange program.

As Valda relaxed, I became increasingly confident she was into me. Her conversation grew animated as she expounded on opinions and gestured frequently. Due to her youth and petite frame I couldn't shake the feeling she was a shy, inexperienced girl even though her mannerisms suggested she was rather more adventurous than that. Certainly something had compelled her to come on a date with me, a man twenty-two years her senior. She pressed me on that very issue.

"How old are you?"

"How old do you think?"

"Oh, I don't know. Old! You have some white hairs in your beard and no hair on your head."

"I'm forty," I said, truthfully.

She seemed to like that, but it silenced her for a few seconds as she processed it. "Yes, I thought something like that. You are older than my mum."

"What do you think about it?"

"It's okay."

That seemed to me a big signal. She was talking as though it was already agreed that we liked each other. Not one to miss an opportunity to escalate, especially at that time in my life, I pulled her toward me. She snuggled up, leaning her head onto my shoulder. I tipped up her chin with my finger and kissed her.

For the next half hour there was only one thought on my mind: her appointment with her grandmother to pick up the yappy dog. It was now after seven, and she was due at eight.

"Does you grandmother live in the centre?"

"No. About fifteen minutes walk away."

I saw Valda had finished her tea so I suggested a walk through the little park near the train station. More importantly, it was near my new apartment. Time was running out. We walked downstairs and out, crossing the main road that marked the border between Old Town and New. Our conversation was now all superficial frivolities as we gently strolled through the park, Valda at ease following me.

Too much at ease, I thought. If she knew I was walking her to my apartment, surely she'd show some trace of nervousness. Perhaps she was intending to politely glide away at the crucial moment. Still, I was committed. This was likely my only shot at Riga sex because I was leaving town soon and it had taken a few days to get her out this first time. We turned two corners and then, sandwiched between a women's fashion boutique and an Italian restaurant, we were at my front door. As nonchalantly as I could manage, I put my key in the door lock.

"I'll show you here," I said, not caring to specify what 'here' entailed.

Valda followed me in, walked through the courtyard, and came up the stairs. We kicked our shoes off in the hallway and she sat on the sofa while I took my bounce-back wine bottle out of the cupboard and poured us a glass each.

"This is a nice apartment. I've never been inside a building in this part of town. It's very exclusive," she cooed.

Well, it was costing me £35 a night, which was rather over my budget. Still, having been on God's green earth for forty years I'd grown accustomed to occasional stays in nice places. Back in my finance days my business trips always included five-star hotel accommodation. I reminded myself Valda was just eighteen and never had a job. At her age, I'd never stayed anywhere nice either. Unless you count the Butlins leisure park at Skegness.

"It must be very expensive here," she continued. "It's very nice though. I want to see the view." She got up and stared out the window a few minutes. I figured her fascination was aiding my cause. I walked up behind her, up close, and handed her a glass of wine. She took it and let me kiss her neck. Her breath quickened and I felt her shudder against me.

"Come, let's sit together," I said and led her back to the sofa, pulling her legs up over mine. We continued to chat and sip wine. My mind was still on the clock.

"Will your grandmother mind if you're a little late?" I asked.

"Oh, that's fine. I'm not going there. I just made that up in case I didn't like you and needed an excuse to leave early."

"Ah!"

She smiled, as if to say she wasn't as naïve as she looked. I took her wine glass and put it on the floor.

"In that case, you naughty minx, I will have my wicked way with you."

I pulled her onto my lap and we made out. It was as though I'd turned the ignition on a car and revved the engine. Valda shifted up several gears and pushed into me. Rapidly, I pulled her cardigan, vest, and bra off leaving her topless. Her breasts were a very pleasant surprise, being pert and a solid handful. Though medium size per the tape measure, on her small frame her breasts had the effect of two basketballs glued to a plastic drinking straw.

She did what I had wanted to do myself. She placed both her hands on her breasts and squeezed them together, creating a deep cleavage. Her eyes were misty.

"Hey, I'm the one who is supposed to do that," I complained, pulling her hands away and having a good grab at them myself. She chuckled and pulled my head in, encouraging me to get more intimately acquainted with her bosom.

I flipped her over onto her back and began fumbling at her jeans. She seemed hesitant. As I unbuttoned the top button and slipped my hand down the front of her panties I realised why. I felt a panty liner.

My party was pooped.

"I just finished my period. I hope it's okay."

"It will be, don't worry."

To my relief, when I pulled down her jeans and then panties, there was only a tiny spot of blood on the inside of her panty liner. Less than you'd get from squashing a ladybird. The idea of period-sex disgusts me.

Not disgusting enough, however, to forego notching a pretty eighteen year old, mind.

I rolled a condom on and fucked Valda on the sofa. Cushions slipped and my left calf ached from bracing myself in an awkward position, but I wanted to slip her a few lengths while seduction momentum was on my side. Only after she gasped and pulled me closer did I risk pulling out and shifting to a more comfortable position.

There go Valda's clothes

That more comfortable position involved bending Valda against the wall, where she braced herself with both hands while I pulled her ass towards me and slipped it in from behind. She began moaning and squealing now, raising her tempo. I was struck by how good she looked in this position because her hips were wide and womanly but her waist was waspishly narrow, creating an extremely appealing contrast. Briefly I wondered where nature found room to squeeze in functioning internal organs in such a narrow stomach area. Valda's thick reddish hair was loose and she flicked it around. I took a handful and slapped her ass hard with my free hand.

She screamed in pleasure. Actually screamed. My instinctive reaction was to check if the window was open, because the house rules on my Airbnb reservation specifically forbade making a noise after 7pm. *Fuck it, what are you thinking?* I chastised myself. Enjoy it. *You always preferred the screamers.*

Valda was outside of my usual catchment demographic due not so much to her youth (Lala had been only a year older) but more her overall *impression* of youth. She was so petite in figure and mannerisms that banging her felt illegal. Yet, to see her bouncing on the end of my dick and screaming

Girl Junkie

in pleasure, I felt God intended this outcome. He moves in mysterious ways. Nonetheless, as often happens when I bang a girl of unusual type or circumstance, I had a reflective out-of-body experience. I was reminded of an old joke:

> My friends bought me a sweater for my birthday. I'd have preferred a screamer or a moaner, but I guess a sweater will have to do.

I pushed such ideas out of my mind and focused on the tight naked form in front of me. To take her screaming reaction to my ass-slap as a guide, I guessed Valda liked it rough. Good, because rough was precisely what I intended to deliver. I slapped her again, yanked her hair, and tried to hip-thrust hard enough to pancake her against the wall.

"Wait..... arrrrgh!..... too hard!" she gurgled.

I ratcheted down a little, puzzled.

"I don't like it hard," she said.

"Yes you do. Look!" I said, then slapped her ass and gave a strong upward-angled thrust that lifted her feet off the ground. She squealed in pleasure.

"Oh God! I think I do!"

Evidently Valda was learning something new about herself. Ever the enthusiastic educator, I resolved to impart more of my accumulated wisdom. I pulled out, grabbed a handful of her hair, and bodily dragged her to the bedroom. She struggled to keep up, hanging onto my arm to stay upright as her feet stepped quickly in time with mine. I threw her onto the big double bed.

"Be careful with me. I've never had hard sex."

"I know what I'm doing."

"I should tell you, I'm very loud. I like to make noise."

"That's great. Be as loud as you can be." To emphasise this, I went over to the far wall and opened the window. She giggled at that, realising I intended to disturb the neighbours and wishing to play along.

I stuck it in her again and Valda delivered bigly with the screaming. She was about as loud as Tatiana had been a week earlier but for entirely different reasons. Tatiana lost herself in sex. The Russians' guttural screeching was an expression of her feral nature coming to the fore. Valda was more controlled, screaming for the pleasure of making a noise, just as a singer may project her voice on stage purely to display the limits of her vocal talent.

Either way, I liked it.

I smashed her as hard as I could. "You like it hard, don't you?"

"Yes!"

"I'm going to do you in the ass."

"Wait... what? No. I've never done that."

"Now is the time to learn."

Valda wasn't play-acting. She looked genuinely concerned. I slowed the tempo a little, still lying on top of her as she lay in missionary. I looked into her eyes. "Do you trust me? Do you trust that I know sex, and I know what I'm doing?"

"Yes, I think so."

"Then believe me. Girls like anal sex."

"Isn't it painful?"

"Only for the first thirty seconds," I lied. "Then pain stops and then it's only uncomfortable. After another minute, it's pleasurable. After five minutes, you'll wish it could last forever."

I wasn't entirely bullshitting her. I'd initiated several girls into anal sex and in each case this was exactly the progression. The only question was whether Valda would take to it immediately or writhe around in pain for five minutes before finally relaxing enough to enjoy it.

"Okay," she said, and let me roll her over onto her stomach.

It took a few minutes to squeeze my dick all the way in. She groaned, winced, and finally gasped as I felt myself sink in until my hipbone was set against her ass. Slowly and gently at first, I pumped in and out until I felt her relax entirely. I'd come to know that moment, when the last tension is gone and a girl's body has surrendered to the experience. From there, you can pound them as hard as you like.

Valda found out that I liked to pound very hard.

I rattled her for ten minutes, sometimes launching myself bodily into the air with both my feet and knees fully clear of the mattress in order to dive-bomb into her like an overly-suicidal Stuka pilot over Stalingrad. Valda left an ever-deepening body imprint in my mattress as she absorbed each shock. I suspected the memory foam would remember her shape for several days to come. I slapped, grabbed and choked like a madman while Valda went through her entire vocal range of screams much like a choir singer practising scales. Finally, she wilted.

"That's enough. I can't take any more. My ass hurts."

I pulled out, slowly, then we rested a few minutes.

"How did you like it?"

"It was better than I expected. It's nice but I prefer the normal way."

Having pulled the condom off, as I always do after anal, I rummaged around for a new one. Midway through my search I decided I'd rather raw-dog her. So I stuck my dick in her mouth and let her suck me off a bit. Then I slid my dick into her pussy.

"Are you using a condom?"

"No."

"I don't want to get pregnant."

"I'm going to cum on your face."

She thought about that and seemed to find it not disagreeable.

Valda had a deeper store of screams than a tantrum-throwing toddler, keeping up a satisfyingly long racket for another ten minutes. Then I pulled her to her knees and made her suck me off again. I came in her face, a little in her mouth, and then managed a bit more onto her tits. She knelt there a while, looking dazed.

"Do you want the shower first, or me?"

"You can go first," she said, then collapsed backwards onto the bed.

Whatever existential doubts I'd held the over the past week seemed entirely washed away. I was exceedingly pleased with myself on multiple fronts. Valda was young, buxom, great in bed, had let me anally deflower her, and it had all come a little unexpectedly on the first date. All things considered, I was drinking life from a glass half full. Valda showered while I dressed in my bedroom. Then we lay together chatting.

"How many men have you slept with?" I asked, expecting a low number.

"You are the ninth."

"That surprises me," I said, truthfully, careful to keep judgement out of my tone. I'd expected a couple.

"I've never slept with a Latvian man. Riga is a small city and word travels fast. I don't want to get a reputation. The other men were all Spanish. I had some fun on my trips there."

"So, if a Latvian men met you like I did, would you sleep with him?"

"No. It is good you are English. It makes it safe, and more interesting."

Valda soon made excuses to leave. I'd have kept her overnight if I could but she lived with parents and didn't want to risk being exposed. She said she'd like to meet again but wasn't sure if she could because of her exams. We kissed, swapped Facebook details, and she left.

Later that night we exchanged messages. I had a question I wanted to resolve. I can quote this chat verbatim, as I kept a screencap.

"Do you think you'll ever develop a taste for older men?"

"Service provider," she wrote, harkening back to my quip earlier in the evening that I'm a service provider of adventure sex. "Well, what I thought after I left was: god, it will never the same with guys me age.

"Now you know why I'm confident."

"Yep, now I see. To be honest, I always thought I like when guys are being soft and sweet with me. But you kinda turned my world upside down. Guess I'm not the first who said that!"

I do like it when girls say such sweet nothings.

"You can thank me for teaching you."

"Yes. I know more about myself now. Thank you!"

Killing time
after Valda left

Montage footage

My vibe was certainly good

Chapter 22
RADICAL HONESTY

I'd come to realise that my enthusiasm for daygame was increasingly volatile. My moods too were volatile. Since my early days on the streets of London I'd evolved the concept of 'the emotional roller coaster' to describe the wild swings I'd feel from zero to hero, mostly depending upon how a particular girl responded to my approach. A run of consecutive blowouts, especially the dreaded 'eye-roll' type, could grind me into the dust. Then the very next set could see a girl giggling, blushing and patting my forearm. For my whole pre-game life, I'd considered myself a man of steady mood, so it came as quite a surprise to find myself buffeted around on the wild seas of daygame.

That described the ups and downs of a given day, but across the medium term my mood remained constant. In the early days, that constant was 'mildly depressed'. The spikes and troughs of a single daygame session were no longer so extreme but my medium-term mood oscillated between extremes. I looked back on the year-to-date and realised I had only two emotional states: either bubbling with enthusiasm or struggling with a prohibitive lethargy. What on earth was going on?

It took several coffees and long walks around Riga to get a grip on these recent changes. My working hypothesis was that ego no longer fuelled my skirt-chasing. For six years I'd tied my feelings of self-esteem and life progression to my continued success with women. I'd set the goal to become a pick-up artist. I'd taken steps towards that goal. Committed to it. Although psychologists, especially limp-wristed soyboy psychologists, might criticise a man for allowing ego to fuel his actions, I felt it had been a wise move. Ego is the engine of self-improvement. It's the First Cause that sends a man into the world to claim what is rightfully his. It's the ego, the sense of your being the centre of creation, that allows a man to stand against a cold, hostile environment and make himself feel important enough to do battle.

Ego had, so far, produced a smoothing effect on my daygame. It had balanced out the peaks and troughs. If I went out for five hours and did fifteen sets, my ego would log that as progress even if I'd been unable to acquire sticky phone numbers. Even failure represented forward momentum because I was *learning daygaming*. I was *perfecting the process*. In those cases where I did get laid, it felt like winning at life. However, midway through 2014 I clocked my one hundredth lifetime notch and suddenly my ego dropped out of the Player's Journey. That's not to say I'd ceased to be an ego-fuelled monomaniac, as I clearly still was rather full of myself, but that the burning fire of ego had been directed away from the process of daygame.

Put simply, I was a player now. I'd succeeded.

The grand over-arching sense of progression through my Player's Journey had evaporated. I was no longer on a mythical journey, a modern-day Hercules or Theseus. I was just a forty-year old man chasing twenty-year old skirt. Nobody builds statues on Mount Olympus to such a man. Homer wrote no poems about it.

What I was left with was simply my day-to-day appetite for chasing skirt. It was no longer meaningful.

I hadn't quite formalised this change of orientation to my mind's satisfaction, but my subconscious was pushing me in this direction if only I could interpret its signals. It's why I'd had my meltdown in Riga and why I was now inordinately concerned with indexing myself against the performance of other daygamers I knew, and non-Community seducers in the wider world and in history. My ego was at a loose end. It needed something else to get hot and bothered about.

My flight from Riga took me home via a week each in Warsaw and Prague. I touched down in the Polish capital on June 15th and rented a cosy private apartment high up a sky-rise building a few streets north of the Chmeilna cafe area. I was in no mood to open new girls but I was keen to see Lala again. I pinged that I was back in town and she came over that evening.

The Belarussian and I had settled into a comfortable routine and she was extremely agreeable. The apartment was on a corner with windows overlooking the city centre on two sides, including a balcony. There was a small lounge area and the bed was tucked neatly into an alcove with shelves at the foot. A television was thoughtfully attached to the wall so I plugged my laptop into it with an HDMI cable and lay in bed with Lala as we watched movies.

There was the usual fooling around. Looking to add a little variation to sex, I spent a while sitting behind her, fingering her while my free arm snaked around her chest to hold her tight against me. Then I pushed her to her back, perched so her head fell back off the mattress, so I could face-fuck while she was upside down. Oh yeah, I did her in the ass too.

It was a pleasant way to spend a balmy Warsaw evening.

The next morning, over coffee, I told her about my Nick Krauser alter-ego and writing career. Even as I said the words I knew it couldn't help matters but I was growing increasingly frustrated with having to keep the secret. It was like I couldn't share the most important side of my life. Imagine the hypothetical conversation, when keeping things secret:

"I'm a writer. I make a comfortable living travelling the world, based on book sales."

"That's nice. Are you good at it?"

"The consensus within my little pond is that I'm a big fish. My main book is considered the best ever written on the subject."

"What's it about?"

"I can't tell you."

"Why do you travel?"

"I can't tell you that either. I've dedicated the last six years of my life to mastering an extremely difficult skill. Doing so has completely changed my personality and opened my eyes to an entirely new way of seeing the world. I'm very proud of it. It was tough."

"What skill is that?"

"I can't tell you."

It was an unusual position to be in. It was already ironic that I'd sometimes meet girls on the street who had already been opened by men using material from my books. The girls sometimes acted like *I* was the cheap plagiarist, using lines I'd read on the internet (rather than that *I'd written first* on the internet). Pressure was building. Just as I'd felt compelled to share intimate truths with Tatiana in Riga, I felt that Lala and I had grown sufficiently close that she should know more about me.

We were in a nice Caffe Nero next to my apartment building, the same one overlooking the Stalin tower that Lala and I had hung out in before. I explained to her that my freebooting adventurous lifestyle was funded by my pick-up writing. She was intrigued but not exactly enthusiastic.

"I knew something was up," she said. "You were too good at it. It was obvious you picked up girls a lot, but I didn't realise it was your job." Not long after that, she asked the obvious question. "So, what number am I?"

"112," I said, knowing to what she referred.

Whatever she thought about that was hidden behind a straight face and short "oh!"

She asked a few more questions and soon I felt I'd sufficiently unburdened myself. Lala now had enough information to make an informed decision about her future relations with me. She went to the bathroom, returned, and we finished our coffee in silence.

"I must go to class now," she said. "But I do want to ask you one thing."

"Yes," I said, slowly. Here it comes.

"Will you send me a copy of your book?"

For the time being, Lala was happy to remain a regular. She liked me, it suited her purposes, and I hadn't pretended to offer a relationship. I remembered I had a copy of *Balls Deep* in my luggage back at the apartment so I made a mental note to give it to her next time we met.

After three nights in the nice apartment I moved into another further down the road. My afternoons were spent writing or hanging out with Warsaw-based friends but I could only manage a half-dozen sets. I felt like a car running on fumes. My interest in banging Lala remained undimmed. She came over to spend the night and I banged her on my last morning before getting the train to Krakow, from where I'd take a flight to Prague. As a leaving gift, I gave her a signed copy of the book, the inscription reading, "to my very dear #112."

She laughed at that.

Things on the Krakow front had suddenly livened up. That week the red-headed slag Ana had begun texting me. I'd pinged her speculatively, that I was returning to her city. She'd ignored my previous few texts.

"When u arrive?" she replied, unexpectedly.

"Thursday evening."

"What u want to do?"

"Drinking, flirting. Normal stuff."

"You have apartment?"

This seemed an unusual question. I remembered the hot eyes she'd given me a few weeks earlier. Rather than show excitement, I conveyed the essential logistics without fanfare.

"Yes, I always rent a private apartment when I travel."

"I want to have bought sex with you."

That gave me a moment's pause. Things had taken an interesting turn. Who knows what goes on in the heads of large-chested seventeen-year-olds?

"Explain in more detail."

"Fuck me so hard, I want to be your slave and pay for this."

So this chick was going to pay me to shag her? Well then Eddie, with your Polish groupie, I'll see you and raise you one. Mine is a year younger and money is changing hands in the direction signposted *Pimp*.

These ass cheeks

Ana sent a few dirty pictures with her ass-cheeks hanging out of a thong and her breasts spilling forth. Call me an old-time romantic but I'd have condescended to bang her for free. We arranged a time and place for the next evening in Krakow.

"How much you pay?" she texted.

"Wait! You want me to pay you?"

"Yes."

Girl Junkie

What is it with hot Polish seventeen-year-olds? The only two daygame sets who'd ever asked me for money were such girls. At first I thought Ana was soliciting a sexual fantasy and the money was only a token of the role-play.

"Twenty euros," I replied.

"Fuck you! So cheap!"

"It's a token amount for the fantasy. I don't pay for sex."

"Fuck you! You think I only worth twenty euros?"

"I can't believe a whore is calling me cheap, frankly."

"I'm not a whore!"

This conversation wasn't going anywhere. It looked like I'd be spending my one night in Krakow alone. Or would I?

The train dropped me off by Galleria mall at lunchtime and I checked into a nice apartment just across the main paved square in front of the main entrance. Having nothing better to do, I went walkabout. I'd barely had time to shit in the McDonald's toilets and take a McCafe coffee to the Old Town square when a man approached me.

"Hey, Nick Krauser?"

He was a German in his early thirties. Average height, a little muscle, and a face that reminded me of Homer Simpson without being actually comedic or misshapen. Just a resemblance, is all. He struck up conversation and, for once, I didn't mind. Having nothing better to do I suggested he wing with me. We did a few sets.

Late that evening it grew dark and I was running out of steam. To my surprise I'd done some sets and had a long idate. The German looked equally tired so we mulled over calling time on the session. At that moment we were walking back towards Galleria mall, exiting a pedestrian subway complex to reach the main plaza. As luck would have it, a pleasant-looking blonde was sitting on the low wall, checking her phone.

I sidled up and opened. She liked me. Ten minutes later I walked her into my apartment. The German lad saw the writing on the wall and went his own way.

I remember very little about this blonde except that she was nineteen years old, had straight blonde hair almost to her waist, was a little chubbier than I'd like, and claimed to be a virgin. She hadn't shown any reluctance coming into my apartment, perhaps a little naïve over the kind of things that happen to women left alone with men. We kissed on top of the bed and

I cajoled her under the covers. She let me strip her to underwear but was resolute in preventing any fucking.

I did try. Many times.

"Look, I'm happy to stay overnight but you must stop trying to sleep with me," she finally said, exasperated.

"No problem. A man must try."

"Yes, that is okay. But a man must also know when to stop."

I figured I'd probably fuck her in the morning, as often happens when girls come close the night before. We fell asleep. Perhaps wise beyond her years, the blonde rose early. That spiked my guns.

"I go to university now," she chirped.

Sunlight streamed through the curtains. I felt awful, so it must've been early.

"What time is it?" I croaked, blinking painfully.

"Eight."

"Jesus! What's wrong with you?"

"My class begins at nine."

I was in no condition to stand up, much less wrestle the girl back into bed. Preferring the cozy warmth underneath the heavy duvet, I pulled it up to my chin.

"Classes are gay. Come back to bed."

"No, I must study."

She was pulling on her boots now. Though hardly an unattractive young lady, the daylight didn't flatter her. The soft mattress seemed intent upon swallowing me like quicksand. Nope, I wasn't moving.

"If you don't come back to bed, I can't fuck you."

"Yes, you are right," she smiled. Then she bent over to give me a kiss on the cheek and bounded away. I heard the door close behind her. Only then did I realise I'd missed my chance to grab her.

I went back to sleep. Check-out wasn't for another three hours.

How I feel
after a near miss

Taking my writing seriously

But I'd turned
to the dark side

Chapter 23
SCATTERBRAINED

Sodomising Valda and Lala had somewhat lifted my mood. I entered the manic phase of my bipolar daygame disorder. I arrived into the centre of Prague with uncharacteristic determination and enthusiasm. My apartment was a grotty two-bedroomed affair just outside the south-east edge of the Old Town. Rare for me, it had both a lounge and a bedroom. No sooner had I dropped my bags off than I headed out passionate for daygame.

It was lunchtime and cracklingly good weather. Nothing was going to stop me. I could feel bubbling in my blood, the likes of which I hadn't felt in years.

"Get laid or die trying," I muttered to myself, leaping into my first set at the bottom of my street only moments after locking my front door. The first six sets were so-so. My vibe was light and playful so girls chatted to me, but the usual random dice rolls came up on 'boyfriend', or 'busy', or 'I don't give my number to strangers'. Those rejections were delivered pleasantly and rolled off me like criminal charges from a Democrat.

I found myself in Wencelas Square eating a roast beef baguette. An enormous sense of well-being filled my breast. If the Mexican Cartel had synthesised a potent mix of heroin and cocaine I imagined this is how it would feel. Standing outside New Yorker were three lads I'd met in Warsaw, being Tomas, a German man my age called Daniel, and a third person whose name escapes me. They too had only just arrived in town, doing a jaunt of their own from their Warsaw base.

"Hey Nick, how's things?" said Tomas, striking up conversation.

"Good. Good." I muttered, looking around at the busy streets.

"When did you arrive?"

"Good. Good."

That stumped him. I wasn't paying the slightest attention because my brain circuits had fried. I'd become hyperactive. My eyes darted from girl to girl. I ran off and opened, made a girl laugh, took a phone number, then rejoined the group.

"That seemed to go well," said Daniel.

"Yeah. Good."

Realising I was incapable of conversation, they left me to it and talked amongst themselves. I stood at the edge of the group and continued scanning the street. God only knows how I looked, all shifty-eyed and distracted.

"Gotta go," I said, and ran off after another girl.

I soon found myself in deep conversation with a French tourist on her way to the riverside to check out an art gallery. We walked there together and I hit on her as fast as was practicable when walking side-by-side along a busy pavement. She undoubtedly got the message because once arriving at the gallery she politely disengaged and declined my invitation for coffee.

Unfazed, I patrolled the riverside promenade with high intensity. Perhaps saliva dribbled from my mouth. It's usually a dead spot for daygame because of the high concentration of tourist groups and families. I quartered the area methodically and squeezed out five sets. It was hard work, like squeezing humility from a Jew, but I got two phone numbers and enjoyed it. I'd now done twelve sets, the upper end of my range for a typical day out, and it wasn't yet three in the afternoon. The sun continued to shine, girls continued to walk, and I continued to hunt. *Get laid or die trying*, I reminded myself. My route threaded through the winding Old Town streets to come back out at Wencelas Square and it's high concentration of viable sets.

I ate ice cream with a Ukrainian student who then told me she had a boyfriend, after I paid. I approached three different girls in the same H&M store. I approached another girl by pointing at her bratwurst and demanding a bite (she laughed and let me have some).

Twenty sets.

"Palladium mall! You haven't even been to the mall yet," I recalled. That wasn't inner dialogue. I was now talking out loud to myself. I walked along Na Prikope, doing a few brisk sets on the way. It was really quite remarkable that I found so many girls I liked and had so little compunction in opening them. All the skills I'd carefully polished over the years regarding target selection didn't matter. I simply opened any girl I liked. There were many such girls.

I got a few more numbers in the mall, but my Turk Nemesis was stationed on guard at the Costa so I left rather than risk his all-seeing eye disrupting my precious vibe. It was five o'clock and I'd now done thirty sets. Racking my brain, I couldn't recall any other day in my life where I'd reached the magic three-oh. This was the hardest I'd ever worked on the streets and, miraculously, I was still bubbling with energy.

Something was odd. Very odd indeed. I'd done more sets in four hours than in ten days in Riga.

Daygame is often compared to poker because the mix of skill and luck is analogous. You can never control the random variation amongst girls on the street: who has a boyfriend, is in a bad mood, doesn't like your type, and so on. All you can do is present yourself to maximum advantage and hope the girl takes an interest, much like in poker you play the hand you're dealt and hope for the best. You can't control your luck but you can outwork it. The harder you work, the luckier you get.

I was now thirty-five sets into the day. My average open-to-lay ratio hovered around 35-to-1. I was due a Yes Girl. So, would you believe it, that my thirty-sixth approach was my Set Of Glory?

Karma delivered as I stood opposite the entrance to Palladium mall, on the opposite side of the tram tracks where they curve around towards Florenc. A young lady busker sat on a stool playing famous songs by rubbing the rim of glasses filled with different amounts of water, thus creating different notes. Another busker was dipping two large sticks connected by string into a soapy bucket then spinning around to create large bubbles. Little kids chased after the bubbles to pop them. It was a pleasant atmosphere.

A blonde girl walked towards me up the gentle incline from the river. From thirty yards away I noticed her slim proportions and long golden hair. She wore black leggings, a short skirt, and a thin jacket. As she came closer I realised I liked her rather a lot. Very pretty. At this stage in my madcap day, opening felt as easy as breathing. Perhaps my vibe was on-point, or perhaps I just got lucky with the right girl. She stopped and smiled.

"You look like the girl from *Game of Thrones*," I said.

"I know that show. Which girl?"

"The dragon lady. Now, if you've got some dragons circling overhead protecting you from villains, tell me now. I'm having a great day and the last thing I need is to be set on fire."

It was nonsense but that didn't matter. Frankly, I was surprised I could form coherent sentences. It turned out that Angelina was from Russia, twenty-six years old, and studying Czech language in Prague. We chatted five minutes then I suggested we have a coffee in the theatre bar on the corner.

"Where?" she asked.

"Right there," I said, pointing to the outside patio with tables just twenty yards away.

"I don't do this," she said, shaking her head. Her eyes said yes.

"You do today. Come on."

Then I carried her away with my glowing vibe. She followed.

It was pleasant to finally sit down after four hours walking along cobbles in my new biker boots. My feet ached. Though the boots looked awesome — brown smooth leather with brass accents nailed into front and back — they were designed for riding a motorbike, not actual walking. The pedometer on my phone told me I'd walked twenty kilometres.

Angelina and I chatted for twenty minutes while the waiter brought out americano coffee in tiny porcelain cups. I struggled to unwind my brain from it's hyperactive state so at first my patter was trivial and retarded. Set against that, the previous thirty-five sets had so broken down my social inhibitions that I was now as free as Icarus soaring towards the sun.

I don't remember anything we talked about. Truth be told, I forgot her words as soon as she spoke them. There had been too much social stimulation and my brain was full. It didn't matter. She liked me. I was struck by how gorgeous she was. If I banged her, she'd be the best of the year so far. Top five lifetime. She really did look like Daenerys Targaryen from the hit TV show, before the actress got fat in the later seasons.

Exhaustion finally set in, now that I was seated. My legs felt forty years old. I decided I'd have to go all-in on Angelina, my final set of the day.

"Let's go to Chapeau Rouge. It's a great beatnik bar," I suggested.

Angelina agreed that sounded like an excellent idea. She agreed also to order beer to match me, a great sign. We had a drink there and by now the barriers between a man and woman meeting for the first time had dropped away. She was laughing, giggling, and making jokes. I'd finally unwound and could speak normally.

"Tell me something. What part of your body do you think is most sexy?" I asked, having decided it was time to really hit on her. Angelina's tongue briefly darted out to lick her lips. She played with her beer glass, sloshing the drink around inside.

"My ass, I think," she replied, grinning mischievously. To her, this was quite the heady height of naughty adventure.

"Well, I don't know if I agree. I haven't properly checked it out. Next time you go to the bar I'll take a look." Her eyes widened in mock indignation. Hastily, also in humour, I added, "Oops! Did I say that out loud? I only meant to think it. I don't want you to know that I'm a pervert."

"What do you think is most sexy?"

"About you, or about me?"

"About me."

"Your hair. It's long and golden, like the princess in Rapunzel. When you're not walking around the Prague streets you belong in one of the Gothic towers, waiting for a prince to rescue you."

This kind of playful patter was coming naturally now and Angelina's eyes flashed with anticipation. *This guy really is charming*, her face seemed to indicate. I dare say I was.

"So, what's the sexiest part of my body?" I asked. "Apart from the obvious," I added, pointing carelessly at my crotch.

"Hmmmm. The first thing I like about you are your boots. I like a man with rude shoes." That, at least, made me feel my aching feet weren't suffering in vain. "But that's not your body, is it?" She let her eyes rove over me, boldly. "Your shoulders. You have strong shoulders."

That seemed to conclusively answer the *does she fancy me?* question. Rather than labour the point I soon moved back into deep rapport. I was gunning for the same day lay. Deciding this, it was time to change venues. There are two crucial elements to an SDL: rapid consumption of alcohol, and rapid venue changes. Add those together and a girl's inhibitions are lowered and her sense of time distorted. From there — assuming she likes you — it's easy for her to rationalise making another mistake in her life.

"Have you been to Batalion Bar?" I asked. This was my second-favourite bounce venue and it was closer to my apartment than Chapeau Rouge.

"No. What is it?"

"It's a cool American diner in style, but it's actually a bar. It has comic book art all over the walls. It's very striking."

That comic book art is all hot birds with big tits wearing skimpy costumes. Great for sexualising an encounter without doing anything yourself. Angelina

Girl Junkie

agreed so off we went. It was there that we finally kissed. Her reaction made it clear she was very much enjoying the experience. After a pint of beer each there, I took stock of the situation.

A same day lay is meant to be experienced by the girl as a smooth, unexpected, opportunistic encounter in which Cupid lends a hand in putting all things into harmony so sex 'just happens'. This is an entirely artificial impression. From the aspiring player's side, it is a nerve-wracking and carefully-crafted sequence of events in which probabilities are calculated, logistical issues overcome, and anxieties dampened. I liken it to when a toddler is ever so proud at having ridden her bicycle down the back lane, oblivious to the stabilisers on the wheels and the parent holding the seat to maintain balance. That's not to say Angelina was unaware of what I was intending, girls always know, but I doubt she appreciated how consciously I was probing for data and feeding her replies into my decision tree.

The only thing I could think of

We'd had three drinks in three venues. Two of them alcoholic. We'd been together almost two hours and just recently kissed. Looking across the table, I saw Angelina's eyes shining in excitement as she rolled a stuffed olive on her tongue. She was happy, horny, and a little buzzed.

Time to extract.

"Let's go for a walk," I suggested.

We walked along Na Prikope and stopped at an off license to buy a few cans of beer. I turned her up the steep lane that ended in my apartment.

"Where are we going?"

"My place is up here." Ten metres up here, to be precise.

"No, I don't go in."

"It's a nice place. We can watch YouTube and drink the beer."

"No," she repeated, clutching my arm and pulling me back towards the main street. "Let's walk more."

This was a decision point. Do I try to cajole her through the door, knowing that the chances of sex rise dramatically the moment she steps inside, but taking the downside risk that the mood is soured and I lose her entirely? Or, do I shrug it off like it wasn't a big deal and then try again later? It was an easy decision.

"Let's walk to the Old Town square," I suggested, as if that's what I'd wanted all along. "It's beautiful in the evening."

Angelina smiled, relieved. Hopefully, she had only demurred over the speed of my bounce-back rather than the implied final end-point. It was still on. We walked through the cobbled streets with Angelina linking her arm with mine. Dusk had passed on into darkness. Bright lights glowed from souvenir shops selling matryshka dolls and Fabergé eggs. I could smell beef goulash in the air.

We sat on benches in a tiny park behind the cathedral and opened the beer cans. Angelina put her feet up, draping her legs across my thighs. More conversation followed, all of it slipping my mind in an instant as I couldn't help ticking off the minutes until I felt the time ripe to try and take her home again. I was heartened to see she hadn't slackened her drinking pace. We drank two cans each, kissed a bit, and finally she seemed to indicate ever-so-subtly that perhaps now was the right time.

"Let's walk," I said. She nodded, got to her feet, and then as I strode off she linked arms again and leaned into me.

There was no trouble getting her indoors this second time. We sat on the sofa and I regaled her with a YouTube music mix. We kissed more and, finally, I channelled the spirit of Captain Cook and other great British explorers of the unknown. I let my hands go boldly into uncharted regions.

"This is so fast," she said, amongst other things.

It took about half an hour of patiently pushing against her resistance and allowing her to gracefully surrender each base. Finally, I had her naked on my sofa. She looked fantastic. Visualise, if you will, "hot Russian blonde with long golden hair, big blue eyes, and a slim athletic figure". Now add decent tits and a firm ass. That's Angelina.

Unfortunately for you, it was my dick that went into her.

It was great. You'd have enjoyed it.

We only remained on the sofa long enough to get my official two strokes in to claim the notch. Then I carried her into the bedroom and got down to the proper business of a Great British Rogering. She'd clearly pushed her chips all-in, giving as good as she got. She sucked me off a bit and when I banged her from behind against the wall she kept yelping "Da! Da! Da!" over and over. I quite liked that.

I came on her tits and dozed off.

An hour later I woke up and banged her again. She stayed overnight but left early the next morning so I was more interested in falling back into deep sleep than in giving her thirds. We'd already swapped numbers. It was a very nice situation. I'd been in Prague only one night and already bagged a very high quality Russian blonde. Perhaps my year was finally hitting terminal velocity.

I once more considered the instability and unpredictability of my life's trajectory. Two weeks earlier I'd been so depressed as to shiver with existential angst, and now I had a cracking bird on the go and felt like Big Chief Awesome, leader of the Awesome Tribe in the legendary kingdom of Awesomistan.

Chapter 24
THE RUSSOF MUSE

Banging a bird is usually enough to completely dissipate my skirt-chasing energies, so after waking up late I sat in a cafe reading. Tomas and his friends were hitting the street hard. No surprise there — they were only in town a few days. I eked out a handful of sets, what would in normal circumstances feel like a decent day's effort. However, compared to the searing madness of thirty-six sets the day before, I somehow felt like a slacker.

There was one memorable girl. Vera was a Ukrainian brunette who reminded me a lot of the retro Private porno actress Tania Russof. She wasn't quite as hot, but the resemblance was striking and Vera was still a very pretty girl. Her English wasn't very good but she looked at me with quiet interest and seemed keen to give up her number. That set happened on the cobbled square outside the main entrance of Palladium. I walked on into the mall, saw Turk Nemesis staking out the corner Costa and then promptly turned one-eighty to ply my daygame trade outdoors.

Tomas invited me out for a drink that evening, a Saturday, and we arranged to meet in the basement nightclub area of James Dean bar. The ground floor is a 1950s American diner with which I was familiar from the prior year. Downstairs can get wild on the weekend as competing groups of Spanish, Indian and Italian chodes one-up each other on how thirsty they can appear to the half dozen or so unattractive women who attention-whore on the dance floor.

"Maybe we'll do some night game," Tomas had enthused.

"You may be disappointed," I replied.

Having gone home and slept off her previous night's rogering, Angelina was still talking to me over WhatsApp. I took that as a positive evaluation

Girl Junkie

of my bedroom performance. There's always the worry with SDLs that the girl files her experience under "one-time adventure" and never replies to further messages. Sometimes I'm the party who fades away gracefully into the shadows. In Angelina's case I was very keen to tap more of her fine ass.

I invited her out to join us in James Dean later.

Angelina was waiting for me outside Palladium with a big smile on her face. Her long blonde hair flowed right down to her ass. It was the kind of hair to make a monk break into a convent. *Did I really bang her?* I wondered. She seemed too cute for an animal like me to dare lay his paws on.

"I hope you weren't waiting long," I said, kissing her softly.

She pushed up onto her toes and pressed into me. "No, I just arrived."

I put her on my arm and walked down to James Dean. It was rammed. Under any other circumstance I'd have walked right back out again. There was a short queue at the door as security were already operating a one-in-one-out policy. With some satisfaction, I looked down the queue and through the windows across all the seated diners. Angelina was far and away the hottest girl in view. Evidently ego still fuelled the Krauser Express as it barrelled through the seduction wilderness.

After five minutes queuing, the door-man, a big burly skinhead, opened the door and waved us in. Instinctively I sized him up, as I do most men, for whether I could take him. He was only an inch taller than I but his head seemed to be twice the weight of my own. His was the kind of cro-magnon skull that archaeologists would never discover in a mass grave because no stone age axe could ever crack such thick bone. He was polite, well-mannered, and even smartly dressed in a black suit that seemed to be painted over his rippling muscles. If I held a gun on him, I'd have been frightened to fire it in case the bullet ricocheted back at me.

Shelving these odd thoughts, I took Angelina inside. We threaded our way past groups of inconvenient Italians loitering on the staircase, positioned so as maximise the disruption to passing patrons, as Italians always seem to do. Turning a small corner into the nightclub area I was hit almost physically by a wave of sweat and bass. Fortunately, James Dean isn't a dance or hip-hop club so the DJ tends to play real songs: compositions involving actual instruments, melodies, and singing rather than some African shouting about how badass he is over the top of someone else's music. Occasionally, they even play a song I like.

I scanned the crowd, spotting the shaved head of Tomas at the far end towards the long bar against the opposite wall. Taking Angelina by the hand, I pushed through the crowd as she slipstreamed behind me. Call me juvenile, but I enjoyed it. I enjoyed leading the hottest girl in the club by the hand through a crowd of thirsty euro-chodes.

"Alright chaps," I greeted them. It was Tomas, Daniel, and that other lad whose name I still don't remember. I suppose he felt underappreciated, like the band members in Oasis who aren't the Gallagher brothers. Let's call him Ken.

Angelina smiled and greeted everyone, then hovered close. It was so crowded she couldn't help but push up to me. We had a drink, chatted, and I sent her off to dance a few times. My friends tried opening a few sets but there was very little to shoot at. After an hour I'd tired of the place. It was obvious from looking at Angelina she was just waiting for me to take her home and fuck her. This agreed with my own desires.

"We're headed off," I said, making my farewells. I briefly reflected that the first time I'd met Tomas in a new city, Warsaw, I'd gotten an excellent SDL with Lala. Meeting him the first time in another city, Prague, I'd gotten another. It's enough to make a man believe in fate.

Sex with Angelina was very good. We fell asleep and she stayed over.

Sunday was my final night in town before returning to Newcastle. Angelina wanted to come round again and I'd have eagerly agreed if not for one small detail, the Ukrainian brunette Vera had confirmed our date. So, I held the Russian at arm's length. Her texting became a little sore, as she quite reasonably argued that we should take advantage of the short time we had together in Prague before my next, as yet undetermined, trip.

Yet, I scented a notch. Something about Vera felt promising though she hadn't committed herself to anything but a drink. My spider-sense told me it was worth risking Angelina's ire to have a crack at Vera. We arranged to meet outside New Yorker at 8pm.

Vera was patiently waiting with her feet together and hands demurely grasping a small handbag in front of her belt. I scanned quickly, noting her black tights clearly displaying slim athletic legs to advantage, her hair down, and more make-up than the previous afternoon. These all suggested a promising date.

"I hope you weren't waiting long," I said, kissing her cheek in greeting.

"No, I just arrived."

I had a flash of deja-vu.

"Let's go to Batalion Bar. It has a great sleazy vibe and cartoon art on the walls. You'll like it."

"What is sleazy?"

"Everything, darlin'. Everything."

Batalion was only a hundred yards away and, being a Sunday, we easily found a seat. I'd like to say the conversation was interesting and that I dazzled Vera with a skilful presentation of wit, wisdom, and mystique but, frankly, I can't remember anything of it. Dates had long since become a blur. My brain had reconciled itself to a never-ending succession of new girls taking the seat opposite me in a cafe or bar. It would retain a memory of their utterances only as long as needed to interpret and respond to them. I'd form impressions on what mattered to me: her keenness, her availability, her character type, and anything else that could be leveraged to increase the probability of a successful seduction.

The one thing I was incapable of was giving a shit about anything a girl said to me.

This is not meant as a critique of Vera, as it had been the same situation with Angelina two days earlier, and Valda before that. I was numbed by the overload of female novelty. It felt like there was only so much room in my head and any new piece of information about a girl would force out some other important titbit. Things had changed from only a year earlier, when I would really dive deep into a girl's psyche, genuinely intrigued by whatever made her unique among girls.

Perhaps that was my problem. Harsh experience had shown me girls aren't unique. It was the very same-ness of my dates that made them difficult to remember. I'd tried hard to create a model of interaction that reduced seduction down to its essential elements, and fashioned techniques and gambits to best handle each eventuality in turn. This had made my dating life akin to a fitter on a factory production line. It was efficient but deadened my soul.

I still enjoyed dates. It's hard not to enjoy the will-I/won't-I drama of trying to rattle a new girl. It's equally hard not to enjoy drinking in a girl's beauty and her own coquettish attempts to impress. But trying to remember anything we talked about? No chance.

After the first drink I'd confirmed Vera was indeed keen. She passed all my little tests with flying colours: letting me examine her fingernails, brush out her hair with my fingers, and gleefully contributing to an increasing intimacy in conversation. That made it time to change positions. Seated as we were on stools over a high table, it wasn't ideal to bring her to sit alongside me. Making matters worse, a large organised pub crawl had shown up. They were led in by two shouty Scottish girls wearing Prague Pub Crawl t-shirts and purple baseball caps. These were the chode-wranglers working for whichever tour company organised such piss-ups. Behind them, following like doped-up sheep, was a line of twenty young men and a few chubby girls, their customers. As expected, the customer girls were shamelessly milking the men for attention, screeching nonsense, grabbing at any man not paying sufficient homage to her vagina-ness, and from time-to-time making as if to kiss other girls.

Usually such groups are led straight into the basement bar but today they bought their first drink upstairs and milled around near our table.

"Let's have a drink downstairs," I told Vera and spirited her away from whatever chaos might break out on the ground floor. It was unlikely the pub crawl would interfere directly with my date but it was an uncontrolled environment so I saw no reason to take a risk. Vera seemed to agree.

The basement was a long cavernous room broken into three sections by pillars and archways that allowed a comfortable flow from end-to-end but give the feeling of distinct rooms each with a slightly different character. I sat Vera as far from the spiral-staircase entrance as possible, at a sofa bench at the far wall. Then I bought two beers and sat alongside her.

It was all rather easy.

We kissed. Vera cupped my chin and exhaled with obvious pleasure, tipping her hand that it was very much 'on'. Neither of us cared much to talk now, having reached an understanding of mutual attraction and all necessary etiquette having been observed. We drank, kissed, and gazed idly into space. After twenty minutes we'd finished our beers. The pub crawl chose that moment to file downstairs, jamming the wrought-iron staircase. I waited for them to be herded against the bar, thus clearing our path of egress.

"Oh, here come the crazies!" I said, in mock dread. Vera laughed. "I think this is a good time to leave."

Vera didn't ask me where to. She found out ten minutes later, when I unlocked my front door. She didn't evince the slightest surprise. This girl had come out hoping to get laid. I felt it my moral duty to assist her in achieving her goal. There were still two cans of beer in the fridge from

Friday night with Angelina so I opened those and walked Vera into the bedroom.

Sex with Vera was good. Her body was great. She wasn't blessed with big breasts or a bubble butt but she did have the tall rangy athleticism of a volley-ball player. Her skin was smooth and her muscles supple. I wrestled her around the bedroom as if she was a BJJ opponent who'd talked smack about my gym. Halfway through I was reminded of her resemblance to the porno slag, Tania Russof.

Russof took it in the ass in most of her videos, I recalled.

"I want to fuck you in the ass," I said, turning her over to butt-up position.

"No!" she yelped, scrambling away.

I manhandled her back into a vulnerable position and tried to get my dick in. She scrambled away again. I took that to be a firm 'no' and one passionate dream died there. Fortunately she wasn't at all soured on further sex, riding me with vigour. Then she sucked me off and I came on her face.

Vera went off to shower and I checked my phone. Angelina had left a few messages over the past two hours that I'd not read or replied to. She was still trying to invite herself over for the night. I thought about that, hearing the shower water through the doorway as Vera cleaned herself off. I sent a non-committal "hey, crazypants" message to Angelina then waited for Vera to return.

It was a simple decision: If Vera wanted to sleep over, she'd win the battle for my services. If not, Angelina could take her place. As it happened, Vera stayed. I fobbed off Angelina. I lay on my back on the mattress staring up at the ceiling, the edges of the room invisible in shadow. A soft yellow glow snuck around the curtain edges from the street lamps outside. Vera lay naked with her head on my chest. Once more, I was struck by the volatility of my recent life. A couple of weeks ago I'd been so lethargic — not to mention unlucky — that I'd given up on daygame in Warsaw. With only one girl, Lala, to bang I'd spent several days sitting in Caffe Nero writing a book. Now I had one very pretty Slav in my bed and another fuming at the other end of a phone because she couldn't booty call herself over.

Feast or famine, it would seem.

Vera sucked me off again in the morning and then went to work. I caught my flight home.

Chapter 25
FREEDOM PORN

The *Street Attraction* lads had a boot camp in Belgrade scheduled for July. It was part of a grander Balkan tour taking in first Slovenia, Croatia and Bosnia. There would be Eddie, Richard and Maciek travelling together with a handful of students. Eddie planned to shoot lots of video for the channel, adding the elements of freedom and overseas travel to their usual pick-up content. Euro-jaunting was increasingly popular not just for us lucky few able to restructure our lifestyles around it but also for a vast army of internet voyeurs who enjoyed the escapism.

Personally, I blamed Tim Ferris and his bestselling *The Four-Hour Work Week*.

I'd never read the book but that didn't stop me having opinions about it. My first encounter with Ferris had been way back in 2007 upon the book's original paperback release. I'd been working in Blackfriars in my finance job and noticed it on a promotional table display in the local Blackwell's book shop, on the corner where Fleet Street crossed into Ludgate Circus at the Thameslink train station. I'd often wander up there on my coffee hour because there was a Starbucks cafe I used for my lunchtime nap.

I picked up Ferris' book, read the back-cover blurb, and skimmed through in five minutes. That seemed sufficient to grasp his key message. Ferris himself called it a "compass for a new and revolutionary world." I'll say this, he's an excellent self-promoter. This next paragraph really leapt out at me: "Forget the old concept of retirement and the rest of the deferred-life plan—there is no need to wait and every reason not to. Whether your dream is escaping the rat race, high-end world travel, monthly five-figure income with zero management, or just living more and working less, this book is the blueprint. You can have it all—really."

His scheme revolved around outsourcing your administrative tasks, streamlining unavoidable tasks according to the 80/20 rule, and if possible creating a passive income stream through entrepreneurialism. I put the book back on the table and went for my Starbucks nap, fully intending to read the book sometime but never quite getting around to it. Considering I still haven't read the book, it's surprising Tim's message stuck in my mind so long.

I was now living according to what (I presume) were Ferris' principles. Like him I'd tired of an overworked office life and quit the rat race. First had been a period of rapid downshifting with *Rock Solid Game*'s fortuitous move into Château RSG in Hampstead. We'd been there three years and fully acclimatised to a time-rich cash-poor lifestyle. Then I'd begun self-publishing my daygame books and very carefully set up that business to be fire-and-forget. The Lulu platform handled orders, printing, and shipping such that I needed only log in to my creator's dashboard to see sales, and then receive a bank transfer of royalties once a month. Kajabi was equally hands-off in hosting my video products.

Ferris' sales pitch had turned into a reality for me. I was experiencing my greatest and most pleasurable freedom on a daily basis: earning money whilst sitting on the toilet.

One thing John and I had noticed in Chiang Mai — a digital nomad hub — in 2012 was how solitary and boring the free life was for most people. Every Starbucks cafe in the city had scores of young Westerners staring into Apple Airbook laptops, sipping coffee. They were all in a daze, neither moving nor speaking. If someone had slid removable partitions between their tables, Starbucks would've resembled the office cubicle farms they'd once escaped from. In this respect, the London daygame crowd were different.

We had something to do with all our free time in these foreign climes: chasing skirt.

My château housemates, Jimmy, Mick, Fernando, Lee, John, and Steve had all ranged across Europe and beyond. We'd drank the bars dry and tried to bang the prettiest local girls we could find. It had been the time of our lives and we'd been far more successful than we'd ever dreamed. To me, this is what *The Four-Hour Work Week* was really about: a platform to enable adventuring.

Maybe it is about that. I still haven't read it.

The Four-Bird Shag Week would be how I'd re-write it.

Once reason my blog had caught on was this melding of disparate mindsets. On the one side was my 'unplugging from the matrix' and rejection of the conventional life. But what then? What do you replace it with? That's where the skirt-chasing with my own Rat Pack entered the picture. We weren't simply escaping from wage slavery. We were pursuing a dream.

The Good Life.

Sightseeing in Prague

Tom's YouTube channel reinforced this message with his *Flowmad* branding. He was inspired by more established channels created by back-packers, adventure travellers, and suchlike. These e-celebrities weren't chasing skirt but they were taking advantage of the modern economy to travel the world, see varied vistas, eat odd foreign food, and engage in whatever sky-diving, bungee-jumping, pot-holing whims that occurred to them. It was a DIY version of the travel shows my mum and dad used to watch on television. Tom had always felt the call of the wild, so he merged his off-the-beaten-track journeys with his daygame in cities. Viewers liked it.

Now I'd met a new group of lads doing their version, *Street Attraction*. Whereas my recent travel partners — Tom, Steve, John — were each lone wolves like myself, the antics of *Street Attraction* reminded me of my *Rock Solid Game* days. They were a high-spirited group travelling in a pack, sharing messy apartments, and getting drunk every other night. And of course, the daygame.

This was all in my mind when Eddie and I talked in late June, considering future plans. His schedule was tied into ticket sales for boot camps whereas my own was completely free. We thought it a good idea if I'd join them on the Belgrade leg of their Balkan tour, a city I'd been meaning to return to. It would be a change of pace for me. More raucous.

I had a week back at my parents' house then flew out to Prague again on the 10th of July, stopping over a couple of nights before flying on to Belgrade on the 13th. The way geography, airlines, and prices lined up it was easier than the two-leg Newcastle-Paris-Belgrade route that wouldn't give me the benefit of a run around the Czech capital. It was also a chance to see Angelina and Vera again, plus girls I'd met the previous year, Ivanna, Klara, and Oksana. The biggest obstacle to maintaining a rotation of Euro-girls is the simple logistical problem of being away from their country for long periods of time. I intended to pass through Prague as often as possible on my way to other cities.

Angelina had calmed down since being snubbed a couple of weeks earlier. We'd remained in contact over WhatsApp so she came over on the first night. The jollies made me feel welcome.

The next day I tried some daygame. The magic of my previous Prague trip was gone but I got a little done. The highlight was an astonishingly pretty Ukrainian with long legs and bushy blonde hair. I accosted her as she walked out of the Old Town by Wencelas Square and immediately upon my open she gave a knowing smile.

"Let's have coffee, you and I," I suggested.

"Yes, you have an interesting idea. Where do we go?"

"You said you read Kafka. How about Kafka Cafe?"

She agreed so I walked her back into the scrum, across the Old Town square, and into the Jewish Quarter. Keeping one hand tight on my wallet, I threaded through the back streets until we were outside the aforementioned cafe. It's a quaint old place.

Viktoria and I sat against the back wall under a large mural, drinking coffee. Her English was good and she informed me she was in Prague only two months to study Czech. She was nineteen and, should she pass the language exam, would enter a university there as soon as possible. Viktoria was level-headed, softly-spoken, and possessed of endearing natural grace. I liked her a lot. I wasn't so sure what she thought of me.

My decision-making process was greatly eased by the circumstances I found myself in. I had but one day in town, almost zero enthusiasm for further daygame, and was in the company of an exceptionally high-quality woman who indicated she had nothing better to do these next few hours. She was almost daring me to keep the bubble blown.

"How about a walkabout?" I suggested.

"There is a medieval party here. I'd like to see it."

"A party?"

"No, not party. What is the word? Festival?"

I was born centuries too late

"You tell me."

I wasn't any the wiser over the next ten minutes as Viktoria lead me across the river to the side of the Old Town to which I rarely ventured. We turned a corner and the buildings seemed to disappear. We'd walked into a small forest, in the middle of the city. Low hills rose up, thickly wooded with trees, and a small valley dropped away ahead of us. Ancient walls blocked off our entry, with a metal gate at the corner where the city seemed to end.

Clearly it was a tourist attraction. Large throngs of slants, wops, gooks, huns, squareheads, and niggers milled around like the United Nations. Cameras clicked and maps were consulted. I was the only proper white man. I felt like I should take charge.

"What's going on here?" I asked.

"It is the festival," replied Viktoria.

That didn't enlighten me so I wandered over to a local dressed in colourful medieval dress. He showed me a pamphlet with photos of sword fighting, jousting, and beer swilling. I realised the festival was an historical re-enactment of Bohemian medieval tournaments.

I love that kind of thing.

Viktoria and I bought tickets, and she snapped off pictures of me posing with behind a suit of armour, like I was wearing it. The local goon checked our tickets and pointed us to a descending stone staircase. Down we went, to a large pavilion.

Having shagged a bird who looked like a *Game Of Thrones* character that very morning, I was now enthralled by an afternoon's entertainment lifted right out of the early seasons. A quartet of mounted knights simulated jousts. I'd have rather they clattered into one another rather less timidly, but I guess they got enough bumps and bruises as is, doing it every day. An archery display followed, and the finale was a grand melee involving two football hooligan firm's worth of scrappers.

As the pagga ensued below us, Viktoria and I drank thick mead from tankards. She let me kiss her.

"Let's go to a bar," I suggested afterwards.

Something about Viktoria's manner suggested she wasn't to be easily swept along. She seemed fully in control of herself, as greyhounds usually are. Our chat was interesting and involved but the few times I tested with sexual innuendo she neutralised the vibe I was attempting to build. She wouldn't let me paw her either.

The smart play was to burrow deeper into her hopes and dreams, while sparingly doling out DHV stories. That's the smart play. My actual play was to keep pawing at her legs and ass. It wasn't as dumb as it sounds, as I'd already begun to sense Viktoria had played along with me so far only because she'd been bored wandering around alone.

Perhaps I should've played the longer game and kept her keen while I was away in Belgrade. But, beautiful though Viktoria was, I just couldn't be bothered. Vera came around that night and I banged her. No fuss. The next morning I had a flight to Belgrade and bigger fish to fry.

Chapter 26
MISERABLE BELGRADE

I'd soured on Belgrade over the previous year, for reasons I couldn't quite explicate. Just as with Warsaw and Krakow, the Serbian capital was the site of both happy memories and sustained periods of frustration. For the previous two years it had been my prime feeding ground, supplying me twelve supple young women all but two of whom had been very hot. The turning point had been at the end of May 2014. I'd just knobbed six girls that month and had another three regulars on the go from previous trips. My usually modest self couldn't help but publicly crow about my own awesomeness. I called my landlord and turned four weeks into six. The logic had been obvious, so it seemed.

It was a big mistake.

Those last two weeks were spent alone and I quickly fell into a depressingly regular daily pattern, not unlike Bill Murray's character in the popular movie *Groundhog Day*. I'd fallen out with John a week earlier and Tom had been and gone. So each day it was just me, staring at the same four walls every morning. Same cafe for breakfast, same walk through Studentski Square up to the same Knez Mihailova. Same familiar battle between the ego ("get more notches") and the hindbrain ("who gives a fuck, you've had enough"). I had a few near misses but game results are measured in notches. Those last two weeks were a bust.

It was no longer fun.

Just as generals are determined to fight the previous war, I went back in September that year for another month to see if I could recapture the magic. Same apartment, same cafes, same streets. Socially, things went well this time — my old buddy Steve was in town a while — plus Adrian who we'd met in Budapest the month before. I also met an American dude in the gym and we got on well. No homo.

It was a disaster for girls.

My rotation collapsed. A couple of regular girls had new boyfriends. A couple more were out of town all month. Yet more were just mysteriously uninterested. Try as I might I couldn't motivate myself to open new leads. Every day walking around the city centre I bumped into a girl I'd already dated or fucked. Staff at the different restaurants recognised me. I realised I was feeling the dreaded "spotlight effect" — that awkward feeling of having a bullseye painted onto your back and that everyone is watching your sets, disapprovingly. Belgrade is a deceptively small town. It was no longer that place "over there" that I'd raid like a horny Viking. It was now "over here", a place I knew well and it knew me. In the second week of September I suffered intense toothache and required a difficult wisdom tooth extraction. Further complications meant it wasn't until February 2015 that I finally had my teeth sorted and the pain alleviated.

We humans feel things emotionally. On an intellectual level, Belgrade remained a top tier daygame city for me. Emotionally, it was a source of distress. The conflict between head and heart meant I felt discombobulated just being there. That's poison for a man's vibe and can easily lead to a downward spiral of feeling shit, doing shit sets, then feeling even worse. So far in 2015 I'd steered clear of the place, except for a two-night layover on my way home from Zagreb, described earlier.

That September of 2014 I did same-day-lay a virgin inside one hour, but that was a rare glimpse of glory completely against the run of play. Kind of like Wigan's cup-winning header in the last minute against Manchester City in the FA Cup final. The reality was my vibe and game were in the shitter every time I breathed Serbian air.

So when Eddie had mooted my joining *Street Attraction* there at the very worst time of year in the Balkans, the searing heat of midsummer, I'd needed to think it through. Were I to decline a trip with such good company it was highly likely I wouldn't visit Belgrade at all. The last thing I wanted was to suffer *Groundhog Day* again just to fuck another couple of Serbs but..... damn they *are* rather hot in the Balkans, and, well — it wouldn't do any harm to get a few more hottie-notches, right? Fuck it, I didn't have anything else lined up for July. Even if I spend all month in Belgrade cooped up in my apartment playing video games and reading detective novels that would be no different to what I'd do if I stayed in Newcastle. *Might as well keep myself in the game*, I thought.

I booked ten nights and told Eddie I was coming. I declined my usual apartment, on the north-east corner of Studenski Park, even though it boasted the world's greatest logistics and was cheap as chips. I was determined not to fall into old habits. Instead I rented a brand new apartment on Strahinica Bana, the up-scale nightlife centre popular with insufferable status whores. Dismal though it was at night, the street magically transforms in daytime to a pleasant mix of cafes and restaurants.

I arrived from Prague on the 13th, a Monday afternoon, and stepping out of Nikola Tesla airport was immediately hit by a blast of stifling summer heat. The little shuttle bus to Slavia Square didn't help matters as the vinyl seats stuck to my arse and smelled like burning rubber. On the positive side, the streets weren't as deserted as I expected for the season and time of day. A few leggy girls milled around here and there. I did a set on the way to my new apartment, just to break the duck. It was my second of the year in Belgrade.

The landlord checked me in and upon seeing my new abode I was very pleased. It was a long open-plan studio with modern see-through shelving separating the kitchen from the bedroom. A large memory-foam double bed faced floor-to-ceiling glass sliding doors that led onto a large private courtyard. Every was brand new and painted white. The shower was an expensive walk-in fitting shining in chrome and glass.

"Nice," I told the landlord and immediately agreed a cash price for the few extra days before my flight home.

It was unbelievably hot and humid. I was exhausted just standing upright. Within moments of collapsing onto the bed, I nodded off and slept through until 8pm. The following day I tried to start a number farm, willing myself into the usual routine of cold-approaching girls in the hope of turning up some good luck. My first nine sets were deplorable. My misgivings about being in Belgrade weirded my vibe, unsettling the girls. My tenth set was with a stunning tall brunette who joined me for coffee but, ultimately, flaked without coming out on a real date. Still, it reminded me that hot girls in the Balkans sometimes liked me.

Progress.

Satisfied at my work-rate, if not my results, I called time on the day's session and sat outside a new Boutique cafe restaurant at the fortress end of the Knez Mihailova pedestrian zone. The waiter put a menu in front of me and I stabbed a finger at the beef steak without needing to think. The mid-afternoon heat had gone, replaced by a cool breeze from the direction of the river Sava. The locals responded, bursting out of their hiding places to promenade along the main street. My table looked onto it all, now filled with happy couples making their daily pilgrimage to Kalemegdan fortress.

The steak was delicious. I washed it down with a glass of Montenegrin dark beer. The sky was still light and clear. Warmth spread from my stomach into my limbs and I leant back in my red metal chair feeling at peace with the world. Perhaps Belgrade would be kind to me once more. Eddie's gang were due the following afternoon so I looked forward to a quiet night in, reading an Edgar Wallace paperback I'd thoughtfully packed.

The waiter brought the check and I stood up to better withdraw my wallet from my jeans pocket. I pulled out some notes and, as I waited for my change, happened to look out over the street. I locked eyes with a short blonde girl dressed in tight denim cut-offs. Her legs were slim and bronzed, and her face pretty. Then I recognised her. It was Sofija, the virgin I'd deflowered the previous May and my last notch of that fruitful trip. Her last message had been telling me to go to hell, and she'd since unfriended me from Facebook. Sofija was as surprised as I, a shocked expression freezing her face a moment. Then she sniffed contemptuously and turned away.

Just like that, every spotlight in Serbia was turned onto me. The target was on my back again. I shuffled off down the hill to Strahinica Bana and didn't leave my apartment all evening. I finished the paperback and went to sleep.

I was running through Kalamegdan fortress with a horde of angry Serbian men in pursuit. They screamed threateningly at me. My legs grew weary and it was a struggle to lift each foot. I seemed to move at a snail's pace, letting the lynch mob draw closer. I felt heavy. Why? Looking down at my chest I released I was encased in heavy armour. A shiny colourful shirt of mail was inlaid with jewels and gold leaf. My legs bore thick metal plating. No wonder I felt sluggish and tired! Then I realised what had angered the locals: I was wearing Ottoman battle dress. The Serbs had expelled their Ottoman conquerors centuries before and seemed determined to do it again. Magically, my pursuers were now mounted on horseback, wickedly-curved sabres held in white-knuckled fists. A siren blasted, a repetitive loud beeping. The whole city was alerted!

The beeping continued.

I woke up. The beeping was from a stream of text message notifications. I lay bathed in sweat, one part dream-induced fear, one part summer-induced flush. At least I hadn't been strung up. Not yet, anyway. I rolled over and checked my phone. It was 3am. There were six messages on Facebook from Kalina, the nail-salon tart I'd banged earlier in the year. Half of them were written in Serbian and the other half were smileys.

"Good evening," I wrote. "How are you?"

"Meet tomorrow," she replied.

"Yes."

"I come early work. Where you?"

I sent a Google Map link and my address. It was an awfully truncated conversation, but then again, she didn't speak English.

"I be 9."

"21:00?"

"9 morning."

"Okay."

I forced myself to stay awake another ten minutes to ensure the earlier nightmare had been completely erased from my subconscious. Opening my Twitter app, I amused myself posting humorous diatribes against Islam, ISIS, and terrorism. Since turning to Twitter I rarely tweeted about pick-up. It's a platform uniquely suited to short rhetorical extremism, rather than sober debate. By posting incendiary opinions I was generating lots of angry feedback which energised me.

I needed it. Pick-up no longer motivated me. I needed my dopamine spikes from somewhere and soliciting death threats from Muslims and Leftists lifted my mood. Satisfied that I'd moved one step closer to a Twitter ban, I fell asleep.

My alarm woke me at five minutes to nine. Kalina knocked on my front door moments later. Sleep still crusted my eyes and I answered the door wearing only my Incredible Hulk boxer shorts. Kalina was dressed in jeans and t-shirt, with a light jacket hanging open. I smiled, she smiled, then she walked past me into the hallway.

"I thirty minutes" she said, tapping her watch. "Work."

I gestured her to sit on the bed, then walked into the bathroom to complete my morning toilet. After a piss, cleaned teeth, and quick shower I felt ready to face the world. Only a coffee was lacking. I love my first coffee of the day

Girl Junkie

but, upon seeing Kalina looking very impatient indeed as she sat on my bed, I knew coffee would have to wait.

She already had her boots and jacket off. We kissed briefly then she undressed herself and got into bed. I suppose she just wanted to be fucked. She certainly didn't seem interested in talking, and impatience hung heavily in the air. So, I banged her. It wasn't especially enjoyable. Earlier in the year she'd seemed slim but that had been short sex and her undressing then had been limited to pulling her jeans down. I'd never really gotten a look at her naked before now.

I wasn't impressed. She wasn't ugly by any man's standard, but her leanness was too close to skinniness for my taste. Her skin was milk-bottle white. While I accept that is the highest-status skin-colour and exactly what you want in your neighbours, friends, and children, I didn't find it especially sexy in a bedmate. I prefer a gentle tan. Her ass seemed a bit bony too, like she'd lost weight since the last time I'd slapped my balls against it.

Ten minutes in she began indicating I should hurry up. I finished on her tits, knowing she'd resent the extra time needed to sponge off. She gave an indignant grunt but I could tell she was still enjoying the experience. Then she dressed in a hurry, kissed my cheek, and rushed off to work. I went back to bed.

"We're here. Are you out?"

That was Eddie. I replied, showered, and headed up the bank towards Republic Square to meet the lads. There were six of them in total, of whom I'd only met Eddie so far. I knew all about Richard from having seen the *Street Attraction* YouTube channel and heard the word on the street. He presented a wild attention-deficit child-like energy in his infield videos, as innocently happy seeing a set as a dog is at seeing a bowl of dogfood. It was a good public persona, quite different to the serious and sometimes irreverent vibe I projected, or the cheeky chappy persona Tom showed.

Eddie and Maciek were standing in front of the large horse statue in the square, where we'd arranged to meet. We were introduced and hands were shaken. There were three students: a young Japanese lad called Takahiro, an equally young Albanian called Misim, and an older Polish man called Ziemowit.

"Where's Richard?" I asked.

"In set."

Eddie pointed towards the water fountain. There were two young women giggling and staggering around as Richard stood between them gesticulating manically. I had no idea what he was saying, but it was going over well. The trio seemed to glow. We watched a while.

"Are you not recording this? It's a good set."

"Nah," said Eddie. "He's always like this. Can get material any time."

Richard finished by high-fiving the girls, then hugged them, then fist-bumped. They walked off on weak legs, as if laughing had tired them out.

"Richard, this is Nick. Nick, Richard."

"Eh up. Krauser, my man," he smiled, pumping my hand like I'd walked onto his used car lot.

"Good set. How did it go?"

"Good, man. Very good. Both had boyfriends though. Man these Serbian girls are *hot*! I was just saying to Eddie that-"

And then he streaked off, running across the square towards the bus stop. I heard him shouting "Girls! Girls! Wait!" He'd seen another set. Eddie grinned and we chatted about their previous two weeks, in Ljubljana, Slovenia and then Zagreb and Sarajevo. Takahiro had gotten an unexpected SDL in Zagreb with most of the approach and idate caught on video by Eddie. He was excited, at having the content for his channel.

"I'm happy to hang out with you lads," I told Eddie. "But I don't want to get in the way of your coaching, so don't feel obliged."

"Nah, it's all good. The students know about you, they'll appreciate it. Besides, I'm totally worn out. Four weeks of Balkan heat and daygame coaching has run me down. I just want to put my feet up."

With that we hung around the immediate environs of Republic Square looking for girls. The vibe was great: high energy, and fun. It rubbed off on me and my vibe was as good as it had ever been. I took some numbers. I got recognised by another travelling PUA (an American) and bumped into another girl I'd fucked the previous year. It was worrying that there were now seven lads opening in the same streets, especially as Belgrade is always noticeably quieter in summer than spring or autumn. Somehow the potential pitfalls never quite trapped us. We didn't fight for sets and the girls didn't seem to mind that we were obviously just standing in a scrum, peeling off to hit on them as they entered our field of vision.

Eddie and Maciek didn't open much. In fact, Maciek didn't come out of the apartment much. Apparently, he had a girlfriend and preferred to work on the business back end. Hanging out with us would've no doubt been tantalising and frustrating. During a break, I sat down for coffee with Eddie at the outdoor tables of Aurelio cafe.

"How come you're not opening?" I asked.

"I'm not feeling it. These past couple of months I haven't had the drive. I've got a few regulars in London, and then I shagged that Polish bird who'd messaged me in Riga. I just don't feel the need. It's nice to relax."

I could relate to that, though I lacked his calm resignation.

"I swing between love and hate of daygame," I said. "For weeks I can be happy sitting in a chair reading novels, then the urge builds up and I have to hit the streets. Lately, it feels like hitting a crack pipe. Too long away from daygame and I miss the buzz. I think I'm addicted."

"Richard is absolutely addicted. We can't walk to the corner shop together without him doing a set. He's out all hours day and night."

"His game looks good. Highly volatile, but his vibe is excellent and he gets the fundamentals. I thought you just cherry-picked his best infields for the channel but it seems he's always that high."

Eddie grimaced, like a father being told his child is a supremely talented thief. It was a mixture of pride and consternation. "He's always like that," he replied, enigmatically.

The harsh Serbian sun didn't let up on Thursday. We saw two new lads working the street, German PUAs who had arrived the night before. Added to ourselves and the American, that made ten active foreign daygamers infesting the same small daygame area, like a swarm of locusts. Somehow it didn't matter and I pulled eight numbers from a procession of hotties and idated an eighteen-year-old ballerina who starred at the theatre across the road from Republic Square. She was a real stunner but I couldn't get her out on a date again.

Most importantly, deep inside I felt the accumulated multi-year Belgrade weirdness crack, splinter and collapse. The town felt normal again. I was relieved.

Of course it isn't normal to have ten obvious foreigners running up and down the same street hitting on girls in the most obvious manner. Belgrade has a tiny city centre where you see the same faces over and over. A few girls eye rolled me when I hit the "I just saw you and..." line. Eddie and I discussed it over coffee mid-afternoon.

"The streets are getting burned out. The coaches aren't spamming but your three students are. They are probably doing twenty sets a day each, minimum."

"Does that bother you?"

"Yes, but I can't blame them. I don't own the streets, and I've done eight sets a day these past two days. I spoke to one of the Germans. He said a Korean guy ran a massive forty-man bootcamp here last month, and then *The Natural Lifestyles* did one last week."

The Natural Lifestyles are a pick-up company of Australian origin based in Budapest. Their leader is James Marshall, a look-a-like for Aragon in the *Lord Of The Rings* movies. I didn't like him at all, as I couldn't detect any 'game' in his approaches and he was associated with the scam-marketing USA West Coast crowd. His lieutenant, Liam McCreae, was equally hapless and full of shit. They seemed to me to be *Rock Solid Game* without the ability.

"Fucking hell," groaned Eddie. "Forty PUAs. No wonder it's burned."

I'd find out later that bootcamp was an outright scam. The Korean was an American-born slant on the run from the FBI for money laundering. While hiding out in Serbia he'd set up the bootcamp, took the ticket money, and then run off after the first day. I never quite found out all the details but there was a long thread on the RooshV forum investigating it and their conclusion was he'd ripped everyone off. Not only that, but he'd started his PUA company in Budapest after logging a grand total of *one* notch, and that from a girl who studied Korean language at university and was desperate to bang a slant.

Such is the PUA industry.

I didn't consider *The Natural Lifestyles* much better, though it would be a few years before I'd find out about their rather more complex scam. I didn't know then that the company was little more than a front to scam chodes into paying for the instructor's Ukrainian hooker bill. They'd even hire actresses to walk by and give good 'reactions' when the instructor's 'opened' them to demonstrate their skills.

Sickening, but I'd grown used to it. My industry was infested with fakers.

The icing on the burned-streets cake came when we noticed a group of Serbian PUAs doing daygame so badly even RSD cultists would feel embarrassed for them. They literally followed girls down the street trying to high-five them. Eddie and I watched them open seven sets in rapid succession. They failed to get a single hook point. I turned my back in disgust.

We continued to open for the next few days getting the usual mix of hits and misses. Then, when it was time to follow up leads with text messaging, we all noticed a tremendous flake problem, in addition to the common "I have a boyfriend and I love him" problem. I'd daygamed Belgrade nine times before this one and I'd never yet had so many promising leads amount to nothing. The *Street Attraction* lads were having the same problem.

Belgrade had finally been burned.

This was confirmed when one pretty girl challenged me from the opener, "are you one of those foreign guys who runs up and down Knez Mihailova trying to fuck girls?"

"Um.... yes. I kind of wrote the book on it....."

So that's how the first week in Belgrade looked. On the plus side I'd broken out of my one-year in-my-head Belgrade weirdness and was now opening and getting lots of hot girls into my phone book. Offset against this was the negative. Belgrade was burned and I was suffering immense frustration from flakes. The low point was getting recognised yet again by yet another foreign PUA, an American, who then spent half an hour spinning tall stories that, had they been true, would make him the Usain Bolt of daygame.

"I just arrived a few days ago from Montenegro," he told me. After he'd stopped me on the street I'd foolishly suggested we sit outside at a cafe. My legs were tired.

"How was it?"

"I was only there a week. I banged five girls. I only open eights or better."

"Okay."

"Yeah, I walk along the beach and outside the clubs in the evening. Lots of hot girls."

"Sure. And Belgrade?"

"Oh, I don't open here. I got a smoking hot blonde on the first day. She comes over every day and I bang her."

"Well done. Show me a photo."

"Um," he shifted awkwardly in his seat and looked down. "I left my phone in the flat."

Because *of course* every daygamer of such outstanding calibre would leave the house without his phone. It must've been the wildest coincidence that he didn't have his phone the one time he was challenged to produce evidence. I didn't see him again, either on the street doing sets or in the cafes on a date. Presumably he was too busy banging his blonde ten.

Fifty sets and four days in, I still hadn't been laid. Like everything else in 2015, I had mixed feelings. It was a relief to get back into opening and I was intoxicated by hitting the daygame crack pipe so often. Nonetheless I had the nagging feeling that my unbroken four-year streak of getting laid with a new girl every time I visited Belgrade was to be snapped.

Chapter 27
PROMISING BELGRADE

During my peak of high vibe on Thursday I'd taken eight phone numbers and begun filtering them, to see what stuck. The most enthusiastic lead was a short curvy hamster girl who'd told me she was then on her way to meet her twin sister. When I asked for her number I got the usual "I have a boyfriend" defence which I brushed aside. Generally, I try not to rate the strength of a lead based on the street interaction. You can't help getting a sense of it but I'd had too many cases where girls who loved me on the street didn't reply, and the flip side of mundane interactions leading to solid texting and eventual sex. Rather, I suspend judgement until a girl replies to my first message. Her first response (or lack thereof) is the strongest single signal of how likely she is to fuck.

Maya responded great.

She co-operated in the banter until a date was organised. She wasn't the hottest girl that Thursday but I like large-chested nineteen year olds even when their face may be a little below my normal standards. We met at the big horse statue in Republic Square one evening and she walked her twin sister past me, no doubt to get a second opinion. Maya wore a tight summer dress. It probably wasn't cut to a tight fit but with her cartoon-character proportions it couldn't help but strain around her hips and bust.

The date went well but felt like an uphill struggle. I walked her downhill towards Blaznavac, that I'd been calling The Moustache Bar on account of it's interior design being based on that symbol. The famous man it was named after had an admiral's admirable whiskers too. Rather that jump right in amongst the moustaches, we took our first drink in a corner bar across the road from there, sitting outside in balmy summer weather. Maya struck me as a dominant characters. She continually snatched the reins of conversation. *Let her talk herself into my bed,* I judged and leant back to listen, offering occasional remarks. She waxed lyrical about her travels and before long we'd moved into deep rapport and shared our inner thoughts.

After one drink there we moved on to Blaznavac, going inside and upstairs to a loft conversion furnished like a 1940s jazz cafe. The outrageous humidity scared everyone else away from such a stuffy room. Maya and I both seemed keen to trade comfort for privacy, so we stayed upstairs. It was the same cubby hole I'd taken Milena and Dragana in prior years. Before long a film of perspiration lent a slick aspect to my shiny bald head. I could feel sweat in my arse crack.

I'd chosen the sofa pushed against the far wall of the attic. The roof slanted such that it wasn't possible to stand up straight in walking toward it. Maya plomped onto to the sofa next to me and let me pull her in. She refused the kiss.

"I've been with my boyfriend for a year and I won't cheat on him. I just decided to come here because I enjoy flirting," she stated.

That was not going to stop me, obviously.

I knew Maya fancied me so I kept laying it on: prodding her thighs, playing with her hair, grabbing her breasts, dirty talking. These are all little ploys designed to increase physical arousal without forcing a girl to make the mental determination that she's cheating on her boyfriend. *I just sat there, he did everything,* they can rationalise. Maya sat there, showing no inclination to leave. Finally, after two hours, she took a phone call.

"My sister is waiting outside for me. I must go."

"Tell her to go away. You're busy."

"No, I must go." She fumbled in her purse so we could settle the bill.

While she was turned away to grab her handbag, I unzipped my fly and got my dick out. She hadn't expected that, to judge by her open-mouthed shocked expression. I took her hand and put it onto my dick. She allowed it to happen, silently, then, after five seconds suddenly withdrew her hand.

"Don't! I'll go crazy!" she whimpered.

She'd already told me she was possessed of a high libido and had gotten very wet. My dirty talk had escalated along with the pawing and prodding.

"I want to fuck you," I said. She was standing up now, putting on her jacket. My dick was still out.

"I want to fuck you too, but I can't."

"Ok. Enjoy your evening!"

"Bye!"

She rushed down the tight spiral staircase and I zipped myself up. I finished my whiskey, paid the cheque, and went back to Republic Square, where the *Street Attraction* boys were gutter gaming.

"How was the date?" asked Eddie.

"Alright. Got my dick out. It's fifty-fifty that she'll reply to messages."

"I think she knows your intent."

I pinged Maya later that night and she responded. That told me all I needed to know. When you pull hard and let the bubble burst, a girl re-blowing the bubble tells you a second bite at the cherry is highly probable.

I was almost a week into my trip and couldn't help doing a little coaching of Eddie's students, having cleared it with him first. We stood by an ice cream kiosk at the intersection of Knez Mihailova and Republic Square. That spot had clear sight lines ahead and to both sides, making it a fantastic fishing location. It was rather obvious what we were up to, not least to the two young women serving the ice cream, but so long as we spotted girls before they did us it was plausibly deniable. We cooled ourselves down with ice lollies. It was 5pm and the temperature had finally dipped enough for the girls to venture outside in decent volume.

The students brimmed over with excitement. It was their fourth week of a Yugoslavia daygame immersion and they'd all been laid once each, before getting to Belgrade. Who could blame them for a little exuberance? A huddle formed around me while I licked my pineapple lolly and expounded my theory of pre-open calibration.

"It's good daygame to build a quick mythology about a girl before you open her. You scan the streets for the girls you like and when your eyes rest on one, you immediately pick out what made you notice her and use that to build a little mini-story about her."

"Yes, I saw Tom Torero talk about that! Street improvisation," enthused a student. I grimaced, remembering how Tom had stabbed me in the back on precisely this point a few months earlier.

"You might only get as far as a quick label, such as 'slow dreamy short-shorts' or 'busy office girl', but the important thing is it gives you *something*. Once in set you can expand it into some verbal bamboozlement."

I wasn't sure if my advice was going in, or over their heads. They were smart enough lads but daygame is deep and you must absorb it slowly, in layers, over the years. Not that it mattered. Once I begin expounding, I'm not about to stop.

"You'll also find over time that some girls are more interested in you than others, and you can detect the patterns. For example, fashionable girls adorned in many brand names — Prada, YSL, Jimmy Choo etc — rarely like me. I've fucked a few but normally they aren't interested. Conversely, slightly quirky girls usually do like me. More generally in daygame, slow wandering girls open easier than determined fast-walking girls."

I believed all this. I still do.

"So, as you begin to identify patterns you can narrow-down your potential opens to focus on the higher-probability targets. I advise you don't take it too far and start weaselling girls just because they are low-probability. Even the hundred-to-one shot comes in from time to time."

The pineapple juice was melting and running down my hand. I licked it off and began throwing out example mythologies for the girls walking past. A girl in a black and white striped dress caught my eye.

"She's dressed like a bar code. I wonder if everything beeps when she goes into a supermarket." Then, a different girl, "she looks like she's sneaking away from the scene of a crime. Probably a shopaholic."

This went on a while and the lads tried a few of their own.

"She's tall."

"She has a nice ass and heels."

It takes a while to get the hang of it. One girl emerged from the crowd, suddenly attracting my attention. My spider-sense throbbed. I knew I'd found a good set.

"This girl looks like she'll probably be into me," I announced and plotted a course to intercept her by the water fountain. She was a slim, curvy red-head of university age or close to it. Not surprisingly, she took my open very well. I knew she would. I'd felt it in my bones.

I teased everything I could think of, from her hair colour to fashion style to mannerisms. The girl, Jelena, threw it all back at me, thoroughly enjoying our banter. The air buzzed with familiar electricity and sparkle. It felt on. Massively on. I don't remember much of the set, just that I was in the moment, bobbing and weaving, having a lot of fun while the students watched. Then I took Jelena's number and sent her on her way.

The next day's texting was solid. From her very first reply I knew something was going to happen.

"Hey rebel. It was nice meeting you," I wrote. "I'm roasting in the sun. How about you?"

"Haha why am I rebel? Is it too hot? I am doing crosswords and drink coffee… like a grandma." This reply came two minutes after my ping, and was supplemented with many emojis. The moment I read it, I began counting my chickens.

"I guess after the crossword, you'll feed some cats and then start knitting."

"Haha don't go that far. I don't have any cat, but I do know how to sew. Where are you? Sightseeing?"

We had a solid back-and forth. I invited her out that evening and she said she was busy that night and the day after, but free the next day — a Wednesday. Our gang checked out Ada beach for the afternoon. It's an artificial beach constructed on the banks of the river and lined with dozens of open-air bars and restaurants. I'd been with Tom a couple of years earlier and didn't like it at all. It reminded me of the Greek island resorts full of drunken Brits. Drunken Serbs were hotter and better behaved, but no easier to open.

Down at the beach

"All the girls will be in groups, or with boyfriends," I'd warned. That turned out to be the case. Richard managed a couple of half-arsed sets then we all sat at a bar and drank beer under the afternoon sun. It was fun, to get away from the Game for a few hours.

Wednesday arrived. Jelena stood waiting for me at the horse statue and I was greatly pleased to find her hotter than I remembered. I'd first caught her coming home from the gym when she wore almost no make-up. Now she was dolled up and looked fantastic. God bless daygame — girls are frequently hotter than you first imagine.

"Let's go to the moustache bar," I suggest, my breast swelling with optimism.

"What's that?"

"A bar full of moustaches. I don't know the name, but I can find it."

Remembering how damp my sweat-sodden boxer shorts had gotten a prior evening with Maya, I suggest to Jelena that we sit outside in the open-air beer garden. Her eyes sparked, she talked without drawing breath and we were soon touching each other.

"I don't want a boyfriend. Serbian guys are always trying to lock me down. I think I just want fun now, so I can be free to focus on my language study".

Ker-ching!

She continued. "I'm a young woman and I'm in the prime of my life. I like to experience the world."

Not one to waste an opportunity, I reached into my bag of tricks and pulled out the script marked, 'adventure sex rationalisation'. I waxed lyrically about society being too restrictive for girls, with too many people watching. London is so great because it's anonymous, I explained, whereas I imagine Belgrade can feel cloying and dampening to a girl's mood.

"Something funny just occurred to me," I said, mid-way through a script that had actually occurred to me two years ago and been carefully refined through practice ever since. "Isn't it interesting that nobody even knows we met? It's, like, everything we say and do is one big secret."

She nodded in whole-hearted agreement. "I like that."

We were kissing within half an hour. Jelena was obviously horny and ready to go. I begin plotting an extraction.

"My friends are having a party very close by," she said. "Why don't you come along?"

"Whereabouts?"

"There's a bar towards the river. It's very popular in the traditional style."

I didn't like the sound of that. Other girls had explained Serbia's traditional style to me and it involved large mixed groups sitting at long tables with loud music and much chatting, not unlike a small wedding reception. I future-projected how that might turn out: loss of anonymity, additional delays, a path diverging from my apartment, surrounded by people she knows and I don't, language barriers excluding me....

No.

Fuck that. Way too many uncontrolled variables. This girl was keen and the window of opportunity had opened. I ran the percentages in my head. Jelena was currently sitting in a bar one hundred metres from my apartment, horny, tipsy, and in my frame.

"It sounds good. We can join them later. Let's hang out at my place for a drink first," I insisted.

I finished off the rest of her beer and stood her up. She followed happily. Less than hour into the date, we walked into my bachelor pad of depravity. I did move fast them days. Too fast, often. Dates had devolved into running down the clock, waiting for extraction, rather than an enjoyable experience to be lived and breathed in the moment.

Jelena stepped over the threshold without a quibble but once inside she became nervous and babbled incoherently about the friend's party. I showed her out to the back garden, figuring the open air might reduce any lingering sense of her being trapped. I left her staring at the stars while I had a piss. We chatted superficially for quarter of an hour before I brought her inside onto the bed. She was tense but compliant. We made out. I pushed her back onto the bed.

"No, I can't. Stop."

"Shhhhhh. Relax."

We kissed more and she writhed underneath, pushing her crotch up against me. Clearly, she was heated up and ready for boom-boom.

"No. It's too fast. I want to go."

I tried my usual ways of busting token resistance. I fingered her through the sides of her hot pants, two fingers rammed in knuckle-deep. Jelena clutched my back, moaning and shaking her head.

"No, not tonight!"

I kept it going and got my dick out. She stood precariously at the edge of the sexual cliff. One small step would send her tumbling into an abyss of wanton sexual fulfilment, if I could only nudge her forwards.

"No!"

She pulled back. The shutters slammed down and I knew the lay was gone for tonight. With enough experience in both beating and failing against last minute resistance, you can spot when a firm decision has been made.

"That's okay, I understand," I reassured her, forcing my disappointment down where it caught in my throat like a KFC chicken bone. We chatted and she wanted to go for a walk. I took her around Studenski Park then wished her a good time at the party. I walked home tail between my legs: until I realised it wasn't a tail, but my hard dick throbbing with the pain of the nearby blue balls. Jelena had looked so sexy tonight and success had been snatched away at the last moment, two nights out of three.

"Where you at, big man?" I messaged Eddie.

In a pub with the lads, he replied. I joined them for a pint. Richard joined us a half hour later, his face flushed red and dried sweat glistening. He'd just banged a Kosovan brunette he'd met a couple of days earlier. He looked extremely pleased with himself.

"I was wondering how many sets it would take," he said, already looking around the room for any groups of girls. "I've been grinding it hard since Slovenia. I had a good start there banging two birds, and one in Zagreb. But I couldn't make anything stick in Sarajevo or here. I was starting to get worried that it wouldn't come."

There was one more memorable set for me while the *Street Attraction* lads were in town. We were plying the usual route on Knez Mihailova when I found myself outside Zara, in late evening. Most locals were walking home from the cafes and bars. I opened a tall brunette student called Petra who was exactly my type and she bubbled over with positive energy. It was just a five minute chat but she replied to my messages the next day and came out on a date at Blaznavac. We had a few drinks in the upstairs attic area, which was mercifully cool this time, and it seemed to be going really well until she refused my kiss attempts.

"I won't kiss you," she said. "Not on the first date, at least."

Petra struck me as the introverted greyhound type, and thus perfect for me. The date felt like deja-vu, reminding me of an almost identical situation with Milena in 2012. They looked very similar, I'd met them at their same ages, and we were even sitting in the same seats. Milena too had opened up well in conversation and refused a first-date kiss close. She had gone on to be perhaps my all-time favourite girlfriend. Naturally, Petra was unaware of the similarities but they hung over my head the whole evening.

I probably took things too far in the verbal escalation.

"How many men have you had sex with?" I asked.

After a long delay, she admitted to one previous sexual partner and then turned the question back onto me. You could say she was shocked when I gave her my real number. Still, I felt good about it. I liked Petra and Petra liked me.

A few days passed. The *Street Attraction* boot camp had ended and everyone was flying home the next day. One of the students had a late-night flight so rather than hang around in cafes all day with his suitcase, I agreed he could leave them at my place and pick them up before his taxi to the airport.

The next afternoon was Tuesday, and my flight home was Thursday afternoon. I'd been in town over a week and still hadn't been laid. There were just two evenings to try to get a lucky lady into my bed. I was still having trouble with flakes, likely a consequence of the town having been burned for a month straight. Jelena was talking to me, and Maya had been that one date, but aside from that there wasn't any action in my phone. What to do?

Open more sets.

That advice solves many problems right there. Roll the dice and give yourself a chance to get lucky. My Belgrade success streak didn't need end ignominiously on the tenth trip. I wasn't feeling particularly enthusiastic but my familiar determination to get *something* had resurfaced so I planned to hit the streets shortly after lunch. It was roasting hot — again — and not many girls braved the sunshine. I had no choice but to do so because the clock was ticking. If I wanted to make things happen I had to just get on with it.

I need to get into the mood for a fast pull, I decided, just before leaving my apartment.

I tried visualisation, but that didn't work.

I tried meditation, but nor did that. I still felt flat.

Grasping at straws, I browsed PornHub for a scene I remembered from a retro porno video from 1996 which simulated an Old Town central Europe same day lay. It was on Private Triple X video magazine 10 with a blonde Swedish slag called Linda Thoren. It's an amateurish production in which a tourist girl wandering around outside the Paris opera house is picked up by two seedy Euro-twats who take her to a restaurant, and bang her. Stupid porno bullshit, but tolerably close to a real-life SDL to get me in the mood. I watched it and, resisting the urge to relieve the tension, hit the streets.

I did a few sets on the walk up towards the Slavia Square roundabout. I was sleepy, worn-out, and feeling sunstroke. Rather than force myself into a fake happy vibe I recognised my state for what it was and matched my game to the same low energy: chill and laconic. Finally, as I crossed past Hotel Moskva and headed into the plaza above Republic Square my spider-sense buzzed.

Funny how it happens. You just *feel* it. Words and logic don't count.

A leggy brunette was ambling towards me.

At first sight she seemed a typical Belgrade girl: long legs, dark hair, denim shorts, Converse deck shoes, tight white vest. There was no reason to choose her over any other, nor any reason to expect a better result. But, my spider-sense had tingled. My daygame sense, finely tuned over six years, was telling me to pay attention to this leggy slag.

Why?

She was still ten metres away when the reason came to me: her earrings. They were coloured feathers like you'd expect to see in a craft market rather than a high street store. I'd noticed her "softener".

What is a softener? You ask.

You can only perceive so much from a person's outer appearance. I judge books by their covers because, in the modern consumerist differentiated world we now live in, everything is a choice. People are no longer constrained to dress a certain way by their profession or social class. Etiquette no longer binds their behaviours tightly. Thus, people are always signalling who they are and what is important to them. Such signalling is often subtle but when your whole life is dedicated to picking up strangers from the streets, you will pay attention and gradually spot patterns.

The type of girl most amenable to daygame has one foot outside of the mainstream. She need not be an outcast nor an outsider, but she must not be so strait-laced as to get a touch of the vapours because a strange man approaches her.

Girls can be "of the type" to be daygameable generally, and they can also be "in the mood" to be daygamed right now. If you can spot that with any degree of reliability above random chance, your results will improve. Much of my past six years had been spent theorising how to do so and then testing my hypothesises in-field. I'd gotten good at it.

Should a girl be of a slightly quirky or offbeat mentality she'll usually find a way to signal it. Often a single item of clothing or accessory will imply, "I'm not just a standard mainstream girl". Perhaps she has patches on her bag indicating her favourite band, or a little metal badge. Perhaps she wears novelty socks. Perhaps she's carrying an unusual book. Girls who are fully in the mainstream (and therefore choosing to seek the protection of the herd) are usually head-to-toe mainstream in dress. When I find a softener I know the girl is more likely to enjoy my daygame, and I'm more likely to enjoy chatting to her.

It's art, not science. It's just one of many possible ways of narrowing the field. There are big fat grey areas of randomness and misperception.

This leggy brunette had feather earrings and, added to her lackadaisical saunter, it had tripped my alarms. She was hot. My height, in athletic trim, and boasting a pretty face. Twenty-two years old, I'd soon find out. I stopped her.

"Tall girl. Stop! I want to tell you something."

Sometimes a girl's instinctive reaction is so positive that you can't help boarding a rocket ship to the moon. Thunder rumbles, lightening cracks, and leprechauns throw handfuls of gold over the rainbow. You just *know* it'll be good.

Mina was such a girl.

She liked me immediately, purring like a cat. After a minute she said, "I'm going this way, to eat, do you want to join me?"

I nodded my assent and we walked a few dozen metres to a pavement cafe before the short walk up to Hotel Moskva. "I just ate so I'll only have a drink. Since you're eating, why don't you choose," I told her.

We sat under a canopy at the end of Knez Mihailova and I spread out into my chair. Conversation flowed without the slightest stumble and Mina didn't give me any trouble.

"I'm dating a university teacher. He's about your age," she said. Based on her earrings, that didn't surprise me. Call it a leap in logic if you will.

The clock was ticking. My flight was on Thursday. I'd be forced to either SDL Mina today, or get a date tomorrow. I moved fast. We traded intrusive questions. Her ham and cheese toastie was only half-eaten by the time we'd already gotten into deep rapport and I'd shared some funny stories. Was the SDL on?

"I will meet my friend at Slavia Square in thirty minutes," she said, wiping her lips with a paper napkin and carefully folding her disposable plate before tossing them into a trash can.

No SDL, then.

"I'll walk with you halfway, until I find an ice-cream kiosk," I said and away we went.

Where was I at with Mina? She had a boyfriend: bad. She was dating a man my age: good. She needed to meet a friend now: bad. She'd taken time to hang out with me: good. Things were moving in the right direction but not quickly enough. I needed to shake the tree harder.

The street was empty, the pavement colour appeared bleached out to an insipid light grey by the blazing sun. We passed the famous Hotel Moskva and reached a row of benches above a small park that clung to the hill as it dropped down towards the train station. There was a small ice cream kiosk there, a gnarled old lady sat on a stool. She'd laid a reflective silver mat over the top of her freezer to fend off the heat and prevent her wares melting.

I bought a watermelon flavoured ice lolly.

"Come sit with me," I said to Mina and we perched side-by-side on a metal railing at the edge of the park. Despite her pressing appointment, she didn't seem at all keen to leave me. That settled me on my course of action: to swing for the fences, verbally.

"Tell me the sexual thing you've never done, and maybe never will, but you think about it," I asked, licking my ice lolly nonchalantly as if I'd asked the name of her favourite My Little Pony.

"Sex with two men" she replied.

"One at each end like this?" I said, gesturing to describe a spit-roast, "or one dick in your ass and the other in your pussy?" Somehow it didn't sound as outrageously familiar as the words suggest.

"The second type" she said demurely, if the concept can be expressed such. This was less than an hour after we'd first met and I now knew she fantasised about double penetration. I remained chill and non-judgemental, partly as strategy and partly because I was tired and the sun had brought on a throbbing headache. I expounded a little on sexual openness, in a similar vein to what I'd told Jelena and Maya about society being too restrictive toward girls. Mina turned the question back onto me.

"How about you?"

I was ready for that. I'd field-tested numerous answers over the years.

"Well, this answer is half-joke and half-serious. At the moment it's just a silly idea but I think I'll probably do it some time. Next time I suddenly come into some cash, I want to rent the penthouse suite in a hotel, buy lots of cocaine and gin, and hire ten hookers. Then I'll run amok all night until I have a heart attack and wake up in hospital."

She liked that. Smiling, looking up and into the sky, she briefly patted my forearm. We continued the sex talk. We discussed women being dominated and how I like to fuck. It wasn't about titillation, on my side, but strategy. I needed to shake the tree and see what dropped. I wanted to gauge her sexual proclivities and whether her teacher boyfriend was an insurmountable obstacle. There was also the "inception" angle: such sex talk functioned as a preview for her, to give her an idea of what she'd get from me. I hoped it would grow in her mind and perhaps make her horny that night.

Plant the seed and hope for the best.

It was a long shot.

We swapped numbers and Mina wandered off to her rendezvous. I felt strangely confident that I'd see her again. She definitely liked me. However, time was running out. Later that evening I pinged her on Whatsapp but the app marked her as offline and she didn't reply.

That same afternoon, Maya unexpectedly agreed to a second date. Well, by "agreed" I mean we exchanged pleasantries by WhatsApp and when I told her "7pm by the horse again" she didn't say no: she simply didn't reply. I decided to show up anyway, just in case. It was hardly an imposition to wait around for fifteen minutes.

She came.

Maya was dressed in a tight dark-red satin dress and rather well made-up. I wasn't sure if she'd made the effort for me, or some party after our date. Her breasts, my favourite thing about her, threatened to burst out at any moment. She'd pushed them up to form a mighty cleavage peeking through her low-cut neckline. Despite the artifice, what was left below the cleavage line was still a pneumatic bulge that most girls would kill for. I estimated each breast as a double-handful.

I couldn't wait to get them out. Nineteen year old big breasts. Is there anything better in this world?

"I'm meeting my sister and my boyfriend this evening," she informed me, ominously. That set the clock ticking once more and made me wonder where I stood.

My plan was to take her back into the Dorcel bar district near my apartment and work her towards my bed one venue at a time. With this new information about her schedule, that plan seemed too patient. She explained her sister was waiting in Studentski Park for her to hand over a spare phone she'd forgotten. So, we made a detour and there was the rather odd circumstance of saying hello to her identical twin sister who knew Maya was flirting with someone behind her boyfriend's back.

They really did look identical. Same size tits too. I briefly wondered if they'd played switcheroo on me. I wouldn't have minded.

We didn't dally. The phone was handed over, a few words were said, and her sister let us go without interfering. Sensing an odd window of opportunity, I walked Maya directly to my apartment.

"I need to charge my phone. You can smoke in the garden while I sort it out," I said by way of pretext.

She came in without protest, walked through to the courtyard and sparked up a cigarette.

My objective was to keep her smoking in the garden until her momentum towards the bar had died. The moment she ceased to think about our time in my apartment as merely 'popping in', I'd have consolidated the extraction. We sat drinking water on two white plastic garden chairs as Maya smoked. For twenty minutes we made easy small talk. I didn't push hard, I didn't touch her, and didn't try to kiss.

Finally, she seemed settled.

She ground out her second cigarette in the ash tray.

"Let's go inside," I suggested.

Lacking a lounge or dining room, the only place to sit was on the bed. Maya sat with her knees and ankles pressed together, accentuating her undulating curves. She seemed hesitant yet here she was sitting on the bed of a man whose dick she'd already seen. I went for the kiss and she turned away, softly pushing me back with both hands.

I tried again and she continued to squirm and scuttle away.

She wasn't putting up a very convincing fight. *She wants to be overpowered*, I concluded. *That will remove her feelings of guilt with the boyfriend.* I grabbed her by the throat and threw her roughly back onto the bed. She flopped heavily with a satisfied gasp. We made out and she blew hot and cold, alternating between grinding against me or pushing me away, not unlike Jelena had.

The prospect of seeing those magnificent tits tantalised me. I'd gotten my hands on them through her satin dress but so far she'd been swatting my hands away. They felt good. Firm. Firmer than they had any right to be at that size.

"No, we can't do this," she whimpered.

I pulled her dress down off her shoulders and the bra straps with it. Her breasts bounced free with a satisfying jiggle. Somehow, I expected a drum roll and cymbal crash to celebrate the occasion. Internally, VE Day fireworks were blasting off in my head, heart, and trousers. Damn those tits were good!

Then I fingered her.

"No, stop. I need to meet my sister. Oh! Aaaaaah!"

Her feeble protests weakened as animal spirits took hold. All strength leaked out of her hands as she gave up pushing my shoulders off. She let them drop to the duvet by her head in a symbolic gesture of surrender.

I got my dick out and put her hand on it.

"We're not going to have sex" she said, tugging rhythmically up and down. Her body was completely disassociated from her mental processes, the forebrain unable to restrain the hindbrain.

It was time to get sneaky.

I knelt between her legs, fingering her to distraction. With my free hand I pulled my trousers off, careful to ensure the in-out fingering action never stopped and thus Maya remained with her eyes closed, biting her lip. When I judged her to be at maximum arousal, I slipped my dick inside raw-dog. Pausing to slip on a condom might've ruined the moment.

Ruined it for me, that is.

"Don't!" she squealed, her eyes briefly expanding like saucers as she felt me inside.

Then I pumped in and out, fucking her. Within ten seconds she was all-in, arms and legs wrapped around my back, pulling me closer. Dirty, raw, hard sex. Fucking awesome.

After a minute of that we disengaged long enough to strip entirely naked and got right back to it. Maya was short and buxom, the type I find looks best in bed. I smashed her missionary, then wrapped her legs up and pile-drived her. I stood her up against the wall and did her from behind, and finally came all over those wonderful breasts.

Victory. In Europe. Today.

We showered off and lay together a while. I interviewed her.

"When did you know we'd have sex?"

"I thought we wouldn't. I just enjoyed flirting and didn't plan it. It wasn't until you put your dick in that I decided I liked it."

"How did you like it?"

"I loved it."

"What score did you rate it?"

"Oh, let me see... Maybe nine out of ten. I can tell you've slept with many girls."

"Be sure to tell your sister," I joked, wondering just how close they were.

"No, this will be a secret from everyone."

"How about the skill of seduction? How would you rate that?"

"That's ten out of ten. Perfect! At every moment you knew exactly what I needed. It was very enjoyable to be seduced like that."

Her phone had been ringing. Her sister wanted her to join the party. I'd have rather it was the other way around, of her sister joining our party, but you can't always get what you want. Maya explained she needed to be at Republic Square soon. I still glowed with satisfaction. In the cold light of day I wouldn't score Maya's face above a six but her body was sensationally fuckable, close to a ten. Railing her had felt like mainlining cocaine. It was as if my body was designed for nothing but to ravish her.

"Next time you're in Belgrade, message me" she said as we made our farewells. I had every intention to do so.

Chapter 28
FANTASTIC BELGRADE

Back at my apartment the same evening, the student came over to collect his bags. While we sat outside, my phone buzzed. It was Jelena, asking what I'm doing right now. Hope springs eternal and I wondered, was this to be another of those magical two-notches-one-day experiences? We swapped a few texts and then Jelena threw her big shit test. I'd sent her a ping photo of the local brand cola, called Cockta. By putting my thumb over the last two letters, it said, of course, Cock. Most girls found that funny. Jelena, not so much.

"You're reading my mind. I just wanted to ask you something considering your perverted thoughts. Wouldn't it be pointless meeting up for a drink, tomorrow night, if you want to get laid and I don't?"

Damn, that's a tough one!

"It's tasty cola. There's no perversion in my mind! What are you doing now?"

"Hahaha, oh there is. And that's not an answer to my question. I'm going to take a shower. I have to get up early."

Realising she wasn't serious about meeting, I rolled with it. "Enjoy the shower. See if you can wash all of that inconvenient logic away."

Given our bantering tone and that she'd almost put out quickly on the first date, I thought such playful texting was the smart move. Evidently, I'd underestimated Jelena's seriousness and her reservations. I'd stirred her up in the wrong direction.

"But I just pointed facts. Nothing inconvenient. Totally logic."

"I never try to make anyone, man or woman, obliged to give me anything. I don't see any problem here." It got a bit messy as she misunderstood my English a few times. Finally, it seemed to straighten out.

"So, I don't feel obligated to give you something. Whatever you meant by that."

"I don't want you to feel obligated. That's why I don't see a problem."

"I can't be sure. I don't know you.... Don't forget we met just few days ago."

There was a time when I enjoyed such exchanges and viewed them as a challenge. How do I divine a girl's true intention and burrow deep to neutralise her objections? Increasingly, it became a pain in the arse: just fuck because you want to, or don't because you don't. Why go through this tedious rigmarole? I understood she was future-projecting her own possibly negative post-sex emotions. Most of the girls I chased were of a type to whom casual sex was a daring, shocking act. I didn't blame them for having reservations. Jumping into bed with me would clash with their self image.

Knowing this, I poured in comfort.

"Jelena, I want to meet you for a drink. You don't need to promise anything more than that. Oh, and to laugh at my jokes. Of course."

"I think I laughed last time, as I promised."

"Yes. I felt so cool and manly. More please."

"Ego increasing. Ok. So you answered my question. See, it wasn't that hard."

The crisis had blown over and Jelena agreed to meet the next evening, my last night in Belgrade. Having had her on my bed, worked through her resistance over text message, and having her agree to come out nevertheless, it looked very much on for my second notch. I began counting my chickens.

At 3pm on the day of glory my phone buzzed. Jelena.

"Niiiick! Something came up for tonight. I have to pick up my little brother from his grandma. There's no one else to baby sit him. I'm sooorry."

I was crushed. Last Chance Saloon had called time on my trip.

Or had it? My tears hadn't even begun welling up when my phone buzzed again. I assumed it was Jelena offering more excuses but no. It was a WhatsApp message from Mina. She explained she'd logged onto WiFi but didn't have mobile internet. She also suggested we continue to communicate through SMS.

"No worries. How are you surviving the heat? I'm relying on lots of ice cold lemonade," I replied, using SMS.

"I refuse to leave the house until the sun moves a bit. What are your plans for today? Wanna have a drink tonight some time?"

Those same fireworks, thunderclaps and lightning strikes exploded in my brain and ricocheted around wildly. Thunderbolts and lightning, very very frightening me! This was a massive come-on. After all that double-penetration talk — and Mina knowing it was my last night in town — she was inviting me out for alcohol. Only ten minutes before I'd been ready to curl up into fetal position and sing myself lullabies until flying home.

Nonchalantly, as if I *wasn't* jumping up and down ecstatically like a dog watching his master return home from a holiday, I replied, "Yeah sure. Are you allowed to stay out late?"

"Well, I don't plan to stay out late, cause I have to go to work tomorrow early in the morning."

We agreed to meet at half six, in the usual spot under the horse statue in Republic Square.

Mina arrived ten minutes late, dressed nice in vest and short-shorts but not looking especially sexual. I didn't how to calibrate her: was this the massive come-on I'd assumed, or just an innocent drink before sending me on my way? We walked off to the moustache bar.

It went well. She didn't reciprocate my pawing at her but nor did she swat my hands away or put me in my place. She participated fully in the conversation. So I put this down to the same issue as with Maya: she fancied me, wanted sex, but was unwilling to act due to having a boyfriend. For a man, seeing this kind of indecision can be maddening. For a woman, she gets free attention while dithering, so it's win-win for her. Mina was to tell me later that she'd deliberately held back her compliance to amuse herself with how hard I'd try, and to see if I'd get desperate. Evidently I passed that test.

When first walking into Blaznavac, I'd gotten some good luck. One of the many odd furniture features is an old horse-drawn carriage mounted on blocks in the beer garden that they've turned it into a snug little couple's bench. It was free, so we climbed aboard and sat next to each other. I imagine it was the closest I'd get to how Casanova dated his women.

I did all my routine date escalation: prodding her thighs, checking her calf muscles with my hands, playing with her hair and so on. She let it happen. We drank two beers each, a good sign. Whatever her game was, it was, so far, in alignment with my own. Time for a location change.

Mina struck me as being in full control of her faculties. She had none of Jelena's starry-eyed glee nor Maya's smouldering horniness. I thus

Girl Junkie

judged it too early to take her home. There was a basement bar close to my apartment called Das Boot that was fashioned after a submarine interior. I hadn't yet tried it, now taking the risk of an unknown bar simply because its location was so favourable, being almost next door to my apartment.

Das Boot was empty. The doorway opened into a staircase down to the basement which was split into three linked rooms. We could sit completely isolated in the back room while I drank whiskey and Mina sipped beer. As interesting as our conversation was, it was an ordeal because I was so focused on having to get laid here and now with no further delays.

By nine o'clock I upped the ante further, telling wild sex stories from my chequered past. If this isn't your first volume of my memoir, you'll already know some of them. The squalor and comedic timing made Mina laugh. I wrapped the stories in a blanket of male camaraderie, of friends travelling as a Rat Pack. My purpose was to skew my self-presentation heavily towards 'adventure sex guy' knowing that Mina wasn't sizing me up as a replacement for her boyfriend.

Finally I reached across the table, grabbed her chin, and kissed her.

She pretended to resist but I saw the pink flush on her face and spark in her eyes. For the first time since we'd met I began counting my long-suffering chickens.

"Come here, next to me," I commanded and Mina stood up and squeezed past the table to join me on the sofa. I pulled her towards me to check how floppy she felt. She was halfway towards what I wanted. A girl keen to fuck will usually collapse against you and sigh. Mina nuzzled against me briefly but her skeleton continued to hold human form, suggesting she wasn't decided in my favour just yet.

"I'm amazed how openly we can talk," she said.

More whiskey and beer flowed. I was reassured by her continued alcohol consumption and physical presence, but reminded that she had work the next day. Was she running down the clock until escaping on her last bus home? By eleven o'clock the date still felt precarious. I had to pull the trigger, no matter what. I'd tried the smooth route but couldn't yet see the finish line. The only remaining option was the Big Move. To just go for it.

"Drink up and I'll show you my apartment. It's next door and has a beautiful courtyard where you can see the night sky."

"Okay but only for a minute. I won't stay."

She walked in with me and out into the courtyard for a smoke. Each time I sidled up close to kiss her, she flitted away. Her face was twisted in consternation, clearly weighing up what to do. The boyfriend was evidently a huge obstacle.

Finally, she decided against me.

"I want to get some cigarettes and go home. Will you walk with me?"

"Sure."

The short walk to the kiosks by Studenski Park was painful. A sinking feeling in my gut seemed to suck energy from my legs. The lay was rapidly slipping through my fingers. I tried hard to maintain my unaffected calm demeanour but inside I cursed my luck. Both chances to get laid tonight — Jelena and Mina — had fizzled out.

Time to gamble again.

Standard PUA advice when attempting to influence a girl is, "don't change her mind, change her mood." Well, I'd changed Mina's mood but her mind was still cock-blocking me. I decided to logic her into bed. I pushed the adventure sex frame harder, providing her all manner of rationalisations.

Her response snuffed out that flame. "Meeting you has made me realise I love my boyfriend," she said.

That's a tough one. How to respond?

"That's good, that it's helped clear your mind. You've found the guy you want and you can get married, have children, and have a good life. The thing is, your body is obviously crying out for one last adventure. It's like trying to hold your breath underwater — you can use training and mental discipline to stay under longer, but biology forces you to come up for air eventually. You will fuck at least one more guy, your body demands it, the question is just who and when. You have unfinished business."

As the words left my mouth, free-form and unrehearsed, I congratulated myself. *Nick, you magnificent bastard! This is seduction gold.* Mina was listening intently.

"The way I see it, you've got a choice. You can wait a while until you can no longer control your urges, and you fuck a local Serbian guy. Probably he'll try to make you into his girlfriend and when you say no, he might keep calling you, or post onto your Facebook wall, or just make trouble for you so people find out. Alternatively, there's me. I'm leaving the country tomorrow. I'm English, I don't speak Serbian, and I have zero interest in making you my girlfriend. I'm looking for a simple, exciting adventure. Nothing more."

Girl Junkie

Mina had bought her cigarettes and walked alongside me as I steered her back to my apartment. The whole time she puffed silently on her cigarette, her arms folded. We turned into my street and that spurred her to action.

"You're obviously saying that because you want to fuck me," she retorted.

"Of course I want to fuck you. I'm just saying you can do it without any effect on the rest of your situation here."

"I don't know. It's not easy for me," she replied and by now I'd inserted my door key into the lock and we had entered my apartment. Logistics trump everything.

There was nothing more I could do. I'd pushed all my chips into the pot. Kissing her, touching her up, dirty talking and so on would just make her feel pressured. More logic would cross the thin line from persuasion into browbeating. I'd learned Mina was a smart girl with a strong rebellious streak.

I'd have to be patient while she made up her own mind.

She walked into the courtyard and puffed on a second cigarette, staring at the night sky and saying nothing. I hung back, sitting on a chair by the door. It felt like waiting for the results of an HIV test. I was drunk and horny. Mina was standing with her sleek long legs shining beautifully under the mixed street — and moonlight. Hot pants pulled her ass pertly into shape. I so desperately wanted to fuck her. In the circumstances, it meant far more than mere sex. It was a validation of my tenacity to never give up when there was still some skirt out there somewhere waiting to be plucked.

Mina casually stubbed out her cigarette, grinding it into the rough concrete floor. She turned and walked slowly towards me, passed inside to the bedroom and sat on the bed. I rose, and followed her in. She lay back, stretched out on the duvet. She stared at the ceiling, perplexed.

Obviously she *wanted* sex, in the sense raw sexual desire throwing her into illicit union with me. However, the thought of cheating on her boyfriend bothered her. I lay next to her but took care not to touch. Napoleon once said, "never interrupt your enemy when they are making a mistake." I wasn't about to interrupt Mina as she convinced herself to fuck me. My vibe projected a light carefree attitude I didn't at all feel.

Mina looked over at me, then at the ceiling, then at me.

"Okay. I'll do it," she blurted out suddenly without preamble, "but no anal."

I mentally fist-pumped. I kissed her and said, "let's relieve you of all these unnecessary clothes"

After such dramatic build-up it was always going to be great sex. Mina looked excellent naked, being gym-toned and lean. She went wild like it really was her last adventure on earth. I smashed her from pillar to post and enjoyed every moment of it. I tried anal anyway, but she refused. Finally, after an hour of strenuous rutting I was all-in and close to heart failure.

We showered separately and dressed then I walked her up to Republic Square to catch her last bus home. Just before boarding I told her, "I'm not going to hassle you, but we can stay in touch and if you'd like to see me again, just let me know."

She gave me a big kiss as if I'd done her a big favour in seducing her, then skipped onto the bus like a happy schoolgirl. As it pulled away she leaned round to wave out the back window. I waved back and walked home extremely relieved, once more ruminating on how something as tiny as noticing one girl's earrings can trigger a chain of events that turn a Euro Jaunt from "frustrating" to "awesome."

Extreme volatility remained my default way of experiencing life.

With Street Attraction

Vesna pops around

Chapter 29
RUMINATION

My flight home took me back through Prague and I stayed a week in transit. Very quickly, I realised my mistake. My feet dragged, my head bowed, and I shuffled through the streets like a washed-up hobo. My sudden crash in enthusiasm shouldn't have surprised me, given my year to date had been a never-ending cycle of mania then depression. Still, surprise me it did. Whatever emotion I felt at a particular time seemed to be the only emotion I'd ever felt and ever would.

I was losing all sense of perspective.

For years — decades even — I'd prided myself on my stable far-thinking mindset. I planned everything in advance. I made plans and stuck to them. It's how I'd achieved all my success in life. Now I was a shambling wreck jonesing for another hit on the daygame crack pipe.

My room in Prague was shitsville. Prices had sky-rocketed for the peak summer season. The endless money-hose that was *Daygame Mastery* hadn't yet interrupted its flow of gold coins into my bank account. While I was hardly rich, my income still comfortably covered expenses with a pleasing surplus to tuck away and replenish my war chest. There was no danger I'd need to get a real job anytime soon. I didn't just act like a hobo. I lived like one. My room was a tiny affair, long and thin. It was on the second floor above a pub in the Old Town, the ceiling slanting heavily on the side facing the beer garden situated in the interior courtyard. My bed was a battered uncomfortable mattress and at night drinking sounds wafted up on the air currents, disturbing my sleep. It cost me £20 a night for the dubious privilege.

Girl Junkie

My daygame wasn't without success, though I managed only a few sets per day. The hottest girl was yet another Tania Russof-a-like who I accosted outside the *Paul's* French patisserie on the main Na Prikope shopping street. She was called Tania, too. A slim black-haired Russian girl with angular cheekbones and cat-like eyes. The set had gone well and she followed me into the patisserie for an idate. That went an hour then she followed me to Batalion bar and ordered wine.

So far, so good, I thought.

"What do you study?" I asked. She gave a general answer, including the word gymnasium. I'd learned such answers meant she hadn't yet begun university and was likely aged seventeen or eighteen. She confirmed the latter. I logged the exchange for future reference: to check if a girl is underage, you don't need to actually ask directly. If she's specialising in a single subject, that means university and thus eighteen or older. Anything general suggests high school.

Tania artfully evaded my escalation and by the time we exchanged numbers and said goodbye I was pretty sure she'd had a look at me, had her fun diversion, and decided not to see me again. That turned out to be a depressingly accurate inference. We never met again.

I had another stunningly hot Russian on a coffee idate in the same Paul's and she turned out to be literally underage, at fifteen years old. You'd never tell by looking at her but I didn't plan to use that line of defence at trial. So, I kept the conversation light and didn't ask for her number. That was equally depressingly, though for the opposite reason: I was sure she fancied me.

The closest I came to getting laid was a blonde Czech girl who was in her first year at university, studying fashion. She wasn't especially hot but had bumps in all the right places and seemed initially very keen. We idated in Batalion and made out, then she came home with me the same evening. After a roll around on the bed she thought better of it and left. We exchanged messages and two days later she met me for a drink at the beer garden under my apartment window.

That's on, I figured.

It wasn't. She bored me to tears on the date, prattling on about God knows what. I realised she'd been equally boring the previous meeting but I'd been so blinded by my desire for a same day lay that I hadn't noticed. The first date I'd made all the conversational running and also focused on a steady physical escalation. Now that momentum had died, I sat back on my slatted wooden chair and let her talk.

It bored me, something I struggled to hide.

I didn't even fancy her much. Definitely worth a poke, but not if I needed suffer another few hours more of her interminable prattle. I tried circumventing it by pulling her upstairs but she refused. I let her go and deleted her number.

The same evening I gutter-gamed outside Palladium mall and bounced another girl back to my seedy dive. She kissed but didn't stay long. I remember very little about it. Even looking at my notes from the time, she's only recorded as a single line: Czech, 20, LMR. I can't visualise her face. If not for that single line logging the bounce-back, there'd be no historical recognition of her contribution towards the London Daygame Model's continued theoretical progression.

I wasn't completely without satisfying female company. Ivanna was as keen as ever to meet up so we had coffee one time, and ate out at an Italian restaurant another. She was busy but still more than happy to be kissed and mauled. Just as every previous time, she was incapable of sex. Knowing how grotty my room was, I made a strategic decision not to invite her back. Banging her was already a low probability as each previous time she'd mentally locked up when I pushed my dick against her lady parts — even after agreeing verbally we should 'try' to have sex. Too many times pulling without success can leave an impression on a girl's subconscious (and perhaps mine too). So, I did a gentle push by chatting, pawing in pubs, but not trying to bang her. With the dramatic tension sidestepped, I enjoyed hanging out with her.

Another time I was walking through the Old Town when I heard the patter of fast-moving feet catch up behind me. A little blonde minx leapt in front of me, smiling. It was Oksana, the bubble-assed Ukrainian I'd closed the previous November and then banged again in March.

"Nick! You are here!"

"Yes. Smart girl. I thought you were in your village." Oksana's family had moved from Ukraine to a small Czech city when she was young, about an hour by train from Prague. The reason I hadn't seen her since March was she'd quit her job at the shoe shop and returned to live with her parents.

"I still live there. I'm just visiting."

I tried to get her up to my shitsville room, out of habit rather than interest, but she claimed to be busy. I wasn't especially fussed. The raging desire to smite hot girls with my righteous meat-sword that I'd felt in Belgrade had long deserted me. She said goodbye and wiggled her arse off towards Na Prikope. I watched that fantastic bubble-butt undulate from side to side but felt nothing in my blood. Not a stir.

I just wanted to go home.

Before that happened, I felt as a matter of player professionalism I should at least organise my next trip abroad. Surely the skirt-chasing urge would resurface after a few days back in Newcastle. I'd need somewhere to go, and someone to go with.

Eddie and I were keen to try Kiev. We'd both heard good things about it on the daygame grapevine but neither of us had visited. Steve had waxed lyrically about a leggy blonde he'd once met there. In spring, after finishing work in Marbella, he'd gone with Jonathan. They spent a few weeks in Kiev and Odessa getting drunk, hitting on girls, and — if I knew Jonathan — a ton of time in strip clubs.

"Nick, you should visit us in Kiev, mate!" he'd messaged me one spring evening. "You'd love it here. Slim birds in high heels everywhere."

I'd been busy with other plans, so declined. Nonetheless, Kiev was on my to-do list. There was also my Turkish friend Kenan who was keen to join me there. He was even willing to pay for a day's coaching to lure me there. I had mixed feeling about that. On the one hand I'd be pleased to take a few hundred quid to impart my wisdom. On the other, Kenan and I knew each other reasonably well now so I didn't want a friend to pay to hang out with me. I wasn't sure how much Turkish customs and hospitality drove his generosity. I didn't want to take advantage.

We WhatsApp messaged while I was in Prague.

"Hey big bro!" he said, his pet name for me. "Can I visit you in Kiev?" That was a polite invitation, rather than a request.

"Sure boss, I look forward to seeing you."

"Give me you bank details, I'll wire you the money."

"Wait. Are we hanging out or am I coaching? If it's coaching, I'll take your money but I have to work for it, formally. If you just wanna drink beer and chase skirt, that's free."

We agreed a compromise, that Kenan would pay me for one day of coaching even though he'd spend the weekend there. At round the same time, Eddie confirmed he was in for a week, immediately following Kenan's departure. So, I booked ten days to straddle both of my friends' stays.

I wasn't due until the 21st of August, three weeks after touching down in Newcastle airport. My body was telling me to ease off and spend some time at home. The travel and adventure had wound my nerves tight, making me distracted and incapable of focus. I'd find it impossible to sit still and even reading a paperback novel had become an ordeal requiring extreme willpower.

At times I seemed to sleepwalk. I'd be sitting in a cafe staring into space and suddenly zone out. I'd come back to my senses to see five minutes had passed and my phone was somehow in my hand. The Twitter app would be open and there'd be an inflammatory anti-Islamic or anti-immigration tweet that I'd just written. Now, I'd also tweet such sentiments when fully lucid too, so don't take this as an attempt to evade responsibility for my writing: I still stand by those sentiments now, as I write. My nation was under attack by hostile third-worlders and my culture facing an existential crisis. Indeed it still is, but 2015 was the peak of globalism and progressivism and thus the nadir of nationalism and sanity. Things are far better now.

Anyway, my point is not that this period of my life felt like End Times. Sure, the African migrant invasion, the transexual acceptance movement, the pedophile acceptance agit-prop, and the climate change hoax were all legitimate worries. They ate into my hope for the future. Europe appeared to be committing suicide and thus deep down I felt that settling down and raising a family would be an awful mistake. This apparently bleak future, of the lights of Western civilisation being both smashed and turned out, seemed to justify my increasingly aimless hedonistic lifestyle.

The world is fucked, so might as well shag hot lasses.

I already knew this at a conscious level. For years I'd discussed the political climate with Jimmy and Steve. What I didn't yet understand was its effect on my brain chemistry. My devotion to hedonism was rewiring my brain. It felt like my brainwaves were being retuned to ever shorter frequencies, making me jumpy and irritable. My life was resembling a hunt for dopamine spikes.

I'd become a girl junkie.

This is why in unguarded moments my smartphone would sneak into my hands and my fingers would type Tweets. My attention span had been wrecked by the high-excitement of chasing girls. I was wired to seek quick fixes and few things are as addictive as Twitter. That I had almost ten thousand followers and plenty of engagement made it even more compelling.

I needed to be home to relax. Slow down the pace of life. Keep myself away from the lure of girls. I booked a week in Warsaw from the middle of

August, giving me a full fortnight staying with my parents first. I planned to spend that time finishing the editing and marketing of *Black Book*.

My parents greeted me enthusiastically. My mum plied me with undrinkable instant coffee and a selection of chocolate bars. On my first evening back I ordered a massive beef fried rice delivery from a local Chinese restaurant and stuffed my face until I needed to loosen my belt. Looking down I was unnerved by my rotund protruding belly. For years I'd been slim, a combination of daygame walks and fitness training in the Château RSG gym room. Over the past year I'd let myself go a bit. Less fitness training and more sloppy diet. I stepped onto the scales and was shocked to see I'd gained six pounds in a month. It was supposed to be the other way around — gain weight in Newcastle and burn it off on the road. I sucked my belly in until it was flatter. *Maybe it's just posture*, I reassured myself. Not getting fat, really. I'm getting older and my muscles are maturing.

The next day I took the bus into Newcastle city centre and bought a new Playstation 4 and a copy of *Bloodborne*. My PC was a good one, so there'd been no reason to drop down in graphical fidelity to buy a console. However, in March my favourite developer — Japanese firm *From Software* — had released a Playstation exclusive title and spiritual successor to my beloved *Dark Souls* games. All summer I'd resisted the urge to purchase a console just to play one game. The slew of 10/10 reviews had shaken my resolve. Finally, my resistance crumbled and I shelled out the cash.

It had been years since I'd felt so much excitement over video games. The four months of self-denial had built up expectations such that simply carrying the big Playstation 4 box home on the bus felt like I'd raided Santa's Grotto. For years I'd simply bought whatever I wanted, without need to wait or to save up. Fortunately, I had modest material desires so nothing strained my finances. *Bloodborne* was different. I'd waited over a year for it, since finally completing its predecessor *Dark Souls 2*. The game was everything the reviews had promised and I played it obsessively for three days straight.

It never once occurred to me to think about shagging birds.

A three-day video games binge may sound trivial but it caused me to ruminate at length. Perhaps my attention span wasn't destroyed after all. I could play *Bloodborne* for ten hours straight, pausing only as long as it took to rush to the bathroom for a piss. When I really wanted something, I could still focus intently. Maybe my malaise had another cause.

My daygame had certainly changed.

This year has been all about experimentation, I thought. I'd grown tired of the *Daygame Overkill* model because, though it had brought me great success shifting to that style, I was growing bored of it. That had been the same thing over and over again, following The Model. I grew bored easily. There had to be another step forwards, I just didn't know what it was. In such cases I trust my subconscious to point the way and let my logical forebrain figure out the details later. My subconscious was telling me this: take shorter trips abroad; pull much faster; sexualise stronger; abandon the model.

So when the Euro-jaunt season had rolled around in mid-March 2015 with my trip to Prague with Tom, that's what I'd done. It had since been a slapdash affair with epic highs and incompetent lows. For the first time ever I'd suffered more near-misses than lays (about a 2:1 ratio). The average age of girl I was banging was twenty-one, slightly lower than previous years. Equally gratifying, the quality had crept very slightly upwards and my average meet-to-sex time was now down to two hours.

High risk, high reward.

It made things very volatile but the dopamine spikes were frequent and exciting.

For years I'd been looking to squeeze as much value out of the model as possible. I'm a born optimizer. Simply shifting my risk/reward meter further towards the extreme marked 'adventure' wasn't enough. I wanted to get *better*. I wanted to bring the uncontrollable under my control. So I'd kept plugging away tenaciously, stoically absorbing the near-miss pain, and continued to look for patterns.

I was fumbling around in the fog again. The daygame cycle of learning was familiar to me having completed it several times. There'd been the initial phase from around 2010-11 in trying to figure out a viable model of daygame, back when street game wasn't anywhere near as comprehensively theorised as night game was. We'd plied our trade on the streets of London: Jimmy, Fernando, Johnny, Mick and I. Then I'd compared notes with Tom and his wing Antony, and we'd all been influenced by pioneers such as Yad, Andy Yosha, and Americans like Gunwitch. That cycle of learning ended with the publication of *Daygame Nitro* in May 2011, my first book. The second cycle ended in February 2014 with the publication of *Daygame Mastery*. I'd recently completed the third cycle with *Daygame Overkill*.

So, now I was six months into my fourth cycle of learning. As with the early stages of other cycles, I was groping blindly. I could sense a new model taking shape but true understanding was a long way off — years off, probably. For now, I could only try my best to listen to my subconscious, to deconstruct my behaviour, and to try to find wisdom from other sources. These ruminations would continue throughout August and I'd write notes that would later become a blog post.

My theoretical musing was mostly along the following lines.

First, I was going into each approach or date like a scientist scanning data sets in order to tick off a checklist. This was a departure from earlier years, where I was more like a chef following a recipe. *Daygame Mastery* was written as a detailed linear model of "first do this, then do that". It worked, as my own experience proved. The problem is it put a player's focus on *himself* and what *he* is doing. That can make a man blind to his environment and the feedback contained within it. Lately, I'd become all about *the girl* and what she was *ready* for. It is a subtle but powerful mental shift towards better calibration. I liked the analogy of a boxer throwing his punches according to the opportunities his opponent offered rather than according to his favourite combinations he'd practised on the heavy bag.

The real skill of daygame comes in setting the girl up for your preferred moves. You'd don't passively wait on opportunities — you manufacture them. In boxing that's called drawing. In set, my mind was increasingly focused upon ticking off her indicators so I knew the time to move things forwards. If I ticked them off in five minutes, I'd pull the trigger in five minutes. Other times it may take three or more dates. The girl's reactions would set the pace.

Secondly, I'd learned from my finance background to consider Key Performance Indicators. What signals tell you where she's really at? What is the signal versus the confusing noise? The old style of Game was grounded in *Mystery Method* and the three phases of Attraction, Comfort, and Seduction. Nothing I'd experienced in the past six years negated this core pillar of Game theory. However, there were ways to be more precise and more certain when you'd done enough of one phase and needed more of another. I'd noticed I'd do something to provoke a response (for example the poking and prodding I did on dates) and then analyse a girl based on three KPIs that let me know if she was a strong lead for adventure sex. These indicators were: electric eye-flash some time during the first five minutes, acceptance of my attempts to close the distance between us, and a strong reply to my first text message. These three KPIs combined gave me a very good idea of how likely some bedroom fooling around would be, and thus where to deploy my energies and how fast to move a girl.

A third pillar of my newly-emerging stylistic change was to understand my instinctive feel for a girl. Every advanced daygamer has a finely-tuned spider sense. It crackles at key moments and lets you pick out a girl on a crowded street from fifty metres away. It sends a thrill through your body during the street stop. It screams "pull the trigger now!" The theoretical challenge was to deconstruct that gut feel into elements that can be identified, understood, taught, and — hopefully — optimised. My ruminations led me to believe I'd gotten part-way there. Key signs were: an ovulating walk, subtle pre-approach IOIs, early eye sparkle, giddiness and sway, and unsolicited touch.

These were the signs a girl was immediately sexually receptive, what we'd long since termed Yes Girls. We theorised the strong magnetic effect was created because the man's and woman's DNA codes have pinged each other and agreed to have sex before your forebrains got the memo. An enterprising daygamer should train himself to unburden his DNA and let it roam, hunting down his best sets subconsciously. Let the spider-sense direct him.

My fourth observation came from a frequently occurring situation on idates and first dates with highly enthusiastic girls. They would act in an extremely giddy and girlish manner, like an airhead. They'd say things like "I don't know why I'm following you home" or "my brain has stopped working". After sex (or, sadly, sometimes just before it) the girl would snap out of her trance and wonder how she'd gotten herself into such a position, like a sleepwalker waking up. My best guess was that her hindbrain had so overwhelmingly decided to fuck that it impeached her forebrain and switched it off. It was similar to mesmerists and hypnotists getting high levels of compliance from audience volunteers. You couldn't force it onto an unwilling participant but the effect was nonetheless very real. I'd seen it dozens of times and gotten laid because of it. I'd come to call it 'brain fry', like her mind was a motherboard being short-circuited.

Girls often verbalised their brain fry, sometimes incredulous at the feelings overtaking them. A girl may say, in giddy disbelief, "I can't believe I'm doing this but I can't stop." I'd triggered brain fry most often on a strong first kiss with added light neck biting and hair pulling. Something deep stirred in the girl. Brain fry became especially powerful when coupled with the momentum of a sexualised idate and the strong momentum of rapid escalation.

It wasn't all positive, mind. The high risk side of the equation was that brain fry could frighten a girl and trigger an emergency shut-down response. Her forebrain makes one last-gasp attempt to avoid being fucked. When those shutters slam down, like I'd recently experienced with Jelena in Belgrade, there is no way to beat last minute resistance. Often, the girl is gone forever.

I felt that I was onto something. Eventually, I'd emerge with a new daygame model. My personality is INTJ by the Myers-Briggs classification. That means ideas usually simmer in a morass of impenetrable slop before suddenly appearing before me as fully-formed theories in a moment of gestalt understanding. I wasn't there yet, but I felt it coming on.

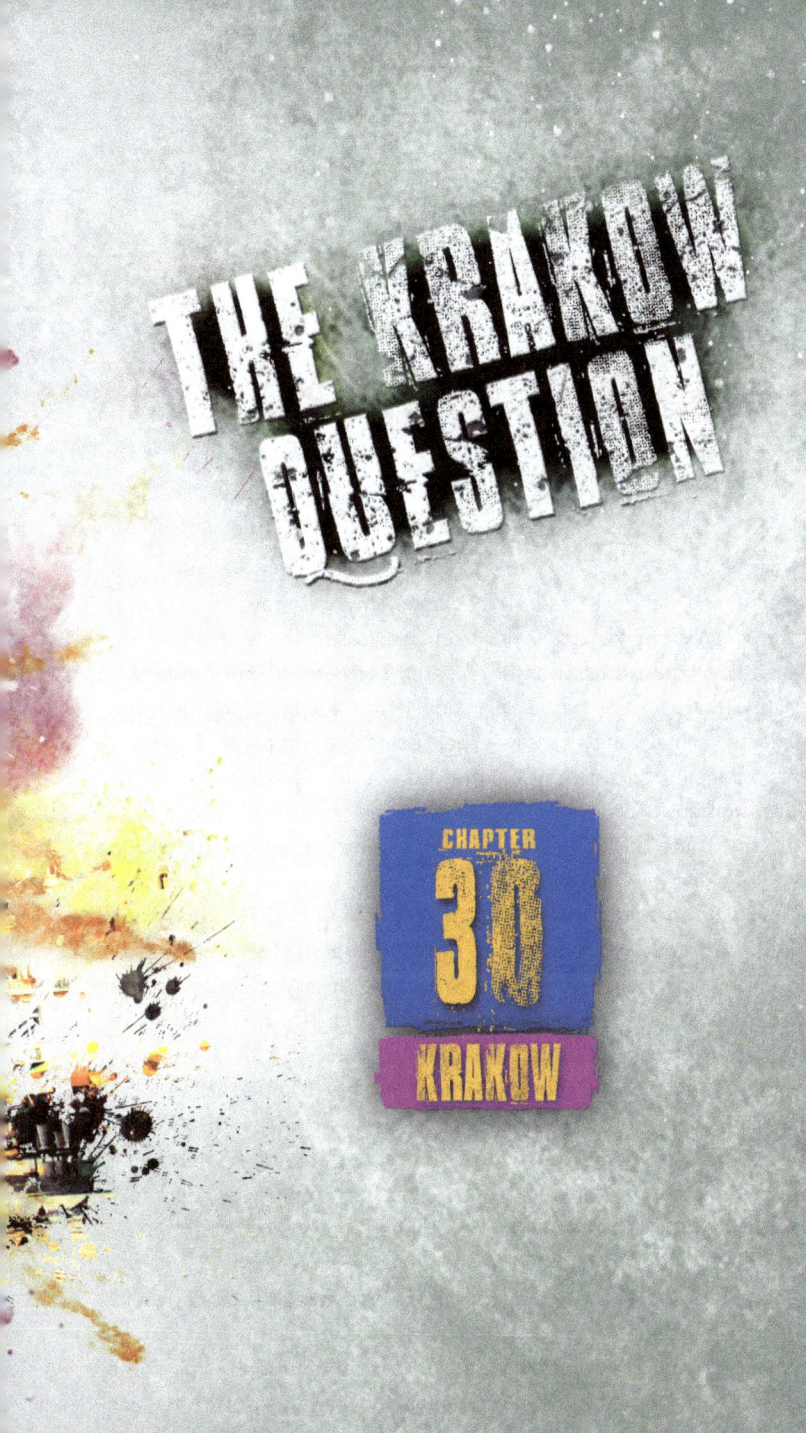

Chapter 30
THE KRAKOW QUESTION

The budget airline Jet2 was rapidly becoming my gateway to adventure. They offered only two direct flights from Newcastle to destinations that would interest a daygamer: Krakow and Prague. In both cases flights were twice a week, designed for bachelor parties planning long-weekend drinking binges. I'd like to take this opportunity to say I look down on groups of degenerate English men descending on a sleepy Central European city to drink beer and harass the local women.

I'd like to say that. But, didn't Jesus say something amount removing a beam from your own eye before criticising others?

Flight prices veered wildly from a pittance to a king's ransom depending upon how far in advance I booked, and whether the weekend in question fell on an English bank holiday. Rarely can I make up my mind more than a week or two in advance, stubbornly clinging to my hard-own freedom. I still flushed with pleasure to think I could go wherever the hell I liked, whenever the hell I wanted. All those endless days of drudgery trapped in an office cubicle, years ago, had left a mark. Like a galley slave finally throwing off the yoke will always resent any metal constricting his neck, I resented having my life planned out. I was prepared to pay a cash premium for the simple pleasure of not being committed to anything, ever.

My flight touched down in Krakow on August 14th, a Friday. The plan was to have a few drinks with Ash then see if Olga was still up for jollies. I'd already settled on taking the train to Warsaw the following Monday and on to Kiev on the Friday. The tight schedule didn't give me much opportunity to work the streets but any longer in one place and I'd have gotten bored.

Girl Junkie

My Krakow apartment was beautiful, if twee, ancient terraced house. A ground floor window looked onto a long thin leafy garden. It was a few streets out from the north of the Old Town, certainly close enough to walk to should I get a bounceback. A small white-painted wooden table was set up to take advantage of the view. My bed was on a small mezzanine level with a stepladder leading up. I liked it.

Ash came out straight after work. We sat eating burgers in a speciality Bobby Burger bar opposite the large Galleria Mall. Poland has a fascination with burger bars so a dozen rival franchises compete, making for a high standard of cheeseburger. Ash filled me in with his usual humble-bragging of meeting local Polish girls then showed me his modern apartment above the Bobby Burger. He'd feathered his nest quite nicely, with a corporate job at the nearby business park and a city centre flat directly overlooking one of the best daygame spots in the world.

"Let's have a walkabout, see what sets are out," I suggested.

"Aye, man," agreed Ash. Aye man, repeated in laconic agreement to most reasonable suggestions, represented maybe fifty percent of his total conversational repertoire with me.

Summer had assaulted Poland hard, such that it could be uncomfortable being in direct sunlight for more than a half hour. Well, for me with my white Northern English skin. Ash is ethnically Indian so I'm surprised he didn't need a hat and gloves. We crossed the busy road that runs from the airport down past Galleria and alongside the Old Town. On the mall side is a nice broad pavement that has good footfall. We'd only just got to the main mall entrance when a perfect set appeared. She was a tall curvy blonde walking self-contentedly at half speed. Her hips shucked side-to-side provocatively and her big round bosom stretched out her turquoise t-shirt. I guessed her to be Polish and in her early twenties. Before I'd had a chance to second guess my own mood, I was standing in front of her saying hello.

"I like.... Right. I'll tell you what I like," I began. The girl batted her eyelids and settled into a comfortable pose with her hips pushed out slightly. "I like this."

I pointed to her blonde hair pulled back into a high pony tail, displaying the smooth contours of her neck.

"And I like this."

Now I pointed to her style, expansively, with both hands making a loose hour-glass shape several inches from her actual hour-glass figure. She smiled. She hadn't said anything but it was going well.

"And don't tell anyone, but I also like these."

I pointed to her breasts, then put my finger to my lips as if to entreaty silence. From there it was a solid sexual hook point. Ash stood off, leaning against the mall windows, and lit up a cigarette. Having done lots of daygame himself, he could recognise hook point and knew I'd gotten lucky.

"I'm Nick."

"I'm Gosia."

"So, Gosia, Gosia, Gosia. What brings Gosia to Galleria mall on such a beautiful sunny day?"

"I just arrived, by train. I'm visiting friends for a hen party tonight."

"You're not from here?"

"No, I'm from-" and she mentioned some name I couldn't pronounce much less remember. Polish is a dumb language made up entirely of the high-value letters on a Scrabble board. Her train ride explained why she wore a rucksack. I was all for that as it pulled her shoulders back and thrust her breasts forwards. They were fantastic breasts. I could see ample cleavage down the low cut t-shirt.

"You're a village girl? Oh my God! This must be so frightening, all of these tall buildings and the iron horses in the streets." I pointed to the cars whizzing past for emphasis. "Look, I was just saying goodbye to my friend over there," I said, loudly and gesturing at Ash so he understood. "I've got a little while. Let's have a coffee."

Gosia agreed and I walked off with her towards the Old Town. Nothing warms the heart of a travelling daygamer like getting a promising SDL opportunity on his very first set of a trip but that's exactly what I was looking at. We walked down the wide pavement and under a pedestrian underpass that gave out onto the ring of grassy park that encircles the Old Town. I figured the main tourist street of Florianska was my best bet but before we reached the top I noticed a perfectly suitable pub with outside patio. I probed logistics.

"When do you meet your friends?"

Gosia checked her watch. It was 6pm, though it felt like midday. The sun and heat had deceived me. "At 7pm."

We sat at the patio and ordered a cold beer each. The street was narrow with a constant stream of pedestrians — students and tourists — walking past. A street artist had set up next to the tables, stacking a display of his canvas art against the brick wall. He sat on a stool waiting for custom. Few times in my life has a beer tasted so good. The sky was bright blue and my skin warmed pleasantly such that the amber nectar refreshed me wonderfully. Gosia seemed happy to be there and I made no secret of ogling her breasts. She was buxom. Very, very buxom. Like a fertility goddess.

The clock was ticking so I probed further, to see if I should conduct the date with a view to meeting her another day, one with more favourable timing.

"When do you return to your little potato village?"

"Sunday morning."

"And what's the plan on Saturday?" That would be the only free day.

"We have a big excursion planned with the girls, outside the city. Then dinner and a party."

"Busy day!" I replied, hiding my disappointment.

"Yes, so busy!"

I checked my watch. It was half past six. Already Gosia's phone was beeping as messages poured in. I suggested a walk and she agreed. We headed north, along a residential street leading to my apartment.

"Where are we going?"

"Let's get a can of beer from a shop. I have a beautiful garden with grass, flowers, and hedgerows. It's very relaxing in summer." No doubt this was all true, but something of a pretext.

"Okay, but I don't have much time."

Krakow is a city of hardcore alcoholics. Almost every street has a corner shop with heavy protective metal gratings over the windows, a cubicle protecting the cashier like in a bank, and then all walls lined with cheap lagers and vodkas. As we approached one at the end of my street I noticed a group of four red-faced alcoholics sitting on the pavement outside with cans of high-strength lager cradled in their hands. We stepped around them, bought a can each from the shop, and went on to my apartment.

Things went swimmingly. Gosia seemed very much at ease. What anxiety she betrayed seemed entirely due to her attempt to juggle dating me with reaching her friends later. She took a phone call, so I motioned her to a seat by the window and opened the two cans.

"My friends," she explained, sitting down. "They ask where I am."

Sean Connery or Carey Grant would've handled the situation different to myself, I think. They'd have made a quip, stretched out their legs laconically, and oozed masculine charm. Gosia would have been overcome by desire and, eyes sparkling, have laced her conversation with innuendo and suggestion before pushing herself up into position to be kissed.

I lacked such finesse.

"I like your breasts," I said. "They are like two puppies fighting in a sack."

"Thank you. I have nice breasts, I think."

"I want to touch them. Come here."

I pulled her over to sit on my lap. To my surprise, she wiggled her arse into a comfortable position on me and stayed there, sipping her can of beer. Emboldened, I reached my hand down the front of her t-shirt and took a handful. Her breasts were firm, full, and everything I'd dared hope for.

"Yes, very nice."

"Thank you."

That was the cue for her to lean down and kiss me. We made out a minute then I pulled her t-shirt up over her head and unhooked her bra. Gosia sat topless, two glorious breasts right in my face. She must've been able to feel my hard-on pressing against her ass.

"These are my favourite two things in Krakow," I said, then sucked on her breasts.

Gosia's phone began ringing. We ignored it a while but it wouldn't stop. She disengaged from me and answered. I played with her breasts and she half-heartedly slapped my hands away, smiling. She hung up and turned to face me.

"I'm already late. I must go."

She stood up and stuffed her breasts back into her bra.

"Tell your friends you got lost. Say your train was late."

"No, they won't believe me."

"Then tell them to fuck off. You're having fun here."

"No, I can't. It's a hen party! The bride is one of my best friends since elementary school."

"Meh! You can be half an hour late. You've got all weekend with them."

Gosia's firm resolution to leave suggested perhaps she hadn't been as overly committed to sex as I'd hoped. If a girl really wants to be fucked, she'll find a way. It wasn't too much to ask her to hang around a half hour longer, so the fact she wouldn't couldn't be entirely due to her friend's exhortations. Still, we'd only met less than an hour earlier. You can only expect so much. I accepted defeat and walked her back to the mall. We exchanged numbers and kissed goodbye. It had been another exercise in extreme volatility.

My body trembled with excitement, a heady cocktail of hormones pulsing through my system. Daygame had offered up another hit on the crack pipe.

That evening I met Olga but she seemed determined to friend-zone me. We made out a little but she wouldn't come back with me, nor let me to her place. She mentioned a boyfriend. "We started dating a month ago," she explained.

The next afternoon I tried a solo daygame session. It began with a coffee idate of a Belarusian girl on Florianska shortly after lunch. She was cute and friendly but our connection didn't feel sexual. She explained she needed to get a train that evening and, an SDL seeming less likely to happen than an Islamic Reformation, I let her go. I did two laps around the arcade in the main square, slipping into a happy relaxed vibe. Two girls chatted with me but neither interaction went anywhere. Then I struck south from the square, down another pleasant tourist path with the hilltop castle visible to my right.

The street was bisected by a road with tram tracks. As I reached it I saw a very pretty young thing approach. She was a tall leggy brunette in very short denim cut-offs and t-shirt. Although I could see probably seventy percent of her skin's total surface area she maintained an air of innocence. I imagined her frolicking around a park with her chums, drinking lemonade and fussing over boys.

I opened.

Ela was seventeen years old, loved horse riding, was a book worm, was on a day trip into Krakow from her village for a music lesson, and was very pleased to meet me. These attributes were all to her credit, but what mattered most to me was her flawless vibrant skin, long slim legs, and flat stomach. She had a pretty face too. After a short chat I suggested coffee. She agreed so I walked her to the same patio as I'd been the previous day with Gosia, and we took the same table.

Years ago — eons ago, to measure how it felt — I'd enjoy idates purely for the experience of masculine-feminine polarity. Sitting across from a pretty girl would energise me, especially if she twittered on girlishly. Many times I'd shared coffee with girls in London, back when I lived there, and even when they declined to kiss or meet again I'd walk away enthused. *This is life! This is what daygame gives a man!* I felt young and relevant again. The company of a pretty feminine woman was like the smell of freshly-cut grass, or the tinkle of a mountain stream at dawn. Gradually that feeling dropped off, from familiarity as much as anything else. Female company was still nice, but it needed to lead to something. Otherwise it was a waste of time and energy.

Time and energy that could be deployed on higher-probability targets.

Something about Ela rekindled the old simple joy of basking in female radiance. She was a smart conscientious girl. Rather too conscientious perhaps, as I began to think she didn't realise I was trying to bang her. Too sweetly innocent. I wasn't sure how to progress. There was another problem compounding my escalation.

Ela was dull.

That's not to say she was lacking energy, charm, or ambition. Rather, she was a seventeen year old village girl whose primary passions — music and horses — held no interest for me. She lacked the kind of sultry sexual energy that welled up in Gosia, so I doubted that ogling Ela's breasts would help advance matters. We had no shared interests and I judged fast sexual escalation to be a bad strategic error.

So, what on earth should we talk about?

Had both of us been in town for weeks, or months, I'd have made a genuine effort to get to know her. But she'd already told me she was getting a train home in a few hours.

"Do you come into Krakow often?"

"No, just once every couple of weeks to see my music teacher. How about you?"

"I'm going to Warsaw the day after tomorrow, then Kiev."

My enthusiasm drained away like blood into desert sand. The long game was logistically shut off, the short game unlikely, and Ela hadn't yet given me any clear signal she fancied me. PUA theory offers some advice: talk about what *you* are interested in. The rationale is that too many men are deferential towards women, or too thirsty for sex, and will thus pander to whatever the woman wants to discuss. As a player overcomes that hurdle he can fall into a second trap, of choosing topics conducive to seduction (in theory) but in which he has so little interest that his vibe is sapped. So, what is gained through the content of the conversation is lost through it's sapped energy.

Without any better idea, and already having subconsciously given up the ghost, I talked about the topic most on my mind.

Jews.

Girl Junkie

It seemed appropriate. Auschwitz was the local concentration camp, just a short bus ride from the Old Town. If I sucked in a deep breath I'd likely ingest at least some particles of an incinerated Jew from the atmosphere.

Well, if the Holocaust had actually happened, of course.

And that there was my lead-in to the day's topic of conversation with Ela.

"Have you been to the tourist sites in Krakow?" she asked.

"Not really no. I've looked around the Old Town, of course. It's beautiful. I love medieval Europe, back when architecture promoted the Christian virtues of love, hope, and faith. When beauty was something to celebrate. I've been to the castle," though I neglected to mention the context, involving fingering Olga in a dark alcove, "and I saw the fire breathing dragon statue but I haven't done any excursions."

"Will you go?"

"I'd like to see Auschwitz. My friend Eddie was there and said seeing the gas showers and the ovens made him decide the Holocaust was a myth. He said it wasn't big enough to process the number of victims that the media claims. He said the ovens weren't even big enough for a city centre pizza takeaway on Thursday night."

"Oh, I see."

"As far as I can tell, there were two Holocausts. There was the real one, which actually happened. That was when the Wehrmacht pushed into Eastern Europe with Operation Barbarossa in 1941. In the occupied areas behind the expanding front, the SS and police militias were sent into villages. They rounded up Jews, walked them out into the forest, made them dig a trench, then shot them all. That was real. There's plenty of evidence and it makes sense, given Nazi priorities. Very efficient. Done and dusted in one afternoon, on-site."

"I see. And the second?"

"That's the fake one that didn't happen: the concentration camps. There's no way the most efficient and deadly race in the world, Germans, would commit genocide by rounding Jews up in one city, sending them by train to another, then keep them alive for several years before exterminating them in, of all things, gas showers. That's nonsense. Not surprisingly, there's not much evidence those camps were anything more than holding camps and the deaths primarily from illness and over-work. It's certainly a horrible way to treat people, but it's not a Final Solution."

I knew this topic wasn't conducive to seduction but it was what interested me so, damn it, that's what I was going to talk about! Ela was fascinated as I suppose Polish school kids from villages near Krakow hear a different history. I hadn't yet decided if I believed the position I was outlining, but I enjoyed exploring it. The one thing I knew for sure was that official history was a lie. Every single time — without fail — that I'd investigated a topic sufficient to become an expert, I'd found the official or mainstream view was knowingly fraudulent.

Now I applied that same heuristic to any topic: whatever the truth may be, the one thing we can be sure of is that the official story isn't it. The moon landings? Roswell and Area 51? Who started World War 2? The assassination of John F. Kennedy? There were all kinds of "conspiracy theories" that I hadn't researched but it was interesting to begin with that radical foundational assumption. It was reasonable. The whole of history is a conspiracy. Every time a political party banded together to win an election, it was a conspiracy. Every time a military junta overthrew that democratically-elected party, it was a conspiracy. If such claims strain credulity I urge you to perform a simple internet search for "list of Byzantine usurpers." In the ten centuries of the Byzantine Empire there were no less than twenty-six emperors who rose to the throne due to their own initiative through revolt or coup d'etat. There were a further forty-eight unsuccessful attempts at usurpation.

Seventy-four in total.

Conspiracies. Every single one of them.

It's thus more intellectually accurate to call "conspiracy theories" by the name "conspiracy queries."

I'd researched the Jewish Question and it is an unarguable fact that Jews are heavily over-represented in media, academia, finance, and government. In cities like New York or London their over-representation is of comical proportions, like a science fiction movie about a secret invasion by shape-shifters. That's not to say it is necessarily nefarious infiltration but I was coming to believe the historical record showed that's just what it really is. The media and academia was full of pronouncements about the "end of Whiteness" and the need to open up the European nations to mass third-world immigration. We were constantly exhorted that globalism was a moral good, and inevitable. Pride in your own culture — if you're white — is evil and racist.

I'd noticed that whenever I looked into who was writing these articles, introducing the laws, or funding the think tanks it was always Jews.

Every. Damn. Time.

I'd thus become hostile to the Jewish infiltration and manipulation of my homeland, and of Jewish attempts to destroy my culture and people. Of course I didn't blame every single Jew for this, any more than I'd blame every German who wore an army uniform in WWII for the Nazi's depredations. However, the trend was clear. I'd come to believe the only problem with the Nazi's Final Solution was that it wasn't sufficiently final.

I'd tweet things like that. It brought me plenty of heat.

Seventeen year old Ela sat on the receiving end of a thirty-minute lecture about the nefarious Jewish plot to subvert the West. She sipped a second cappuccino and paid rapt attention. It's likely she either didn't understand, didn't care, or didn't agree with my polemic. But, being a girl, she was fascinated by the sudden conviction with which I delivered the lecture. I saw her eyes sparkle in sexual attraction.

Perhaps I'd broken new ground in PUA story-telling.

My central proposition was this: that the Nazi Final Solution, if it really happened, was little more than an over-reaction to thirty years of Jewish provocation. Beginning in 1916, when Germany had already won the First World War, the British War Cabinet met with representatives of international Zionism based in New York to broker a deal: the Jews would exert their influence to bring the USA into the war if Britain would support a Palestinian homeland for Jews. That turned the war against Germany and prolonged it a further two years, at a cost of millions of white European Christian deaths. Jewish industrialists then swooped into defeated Germany and bought up all of it's depressed industries. They destroyed the currency with fiat banking and usury, and blackballed ethnic Germans from professions in their own lands. The crazy excesses of the Weimar Era were little different to the Roaring Twenties in the USA or the degeneration of 2000s NYC and Los Angeles. It was caused by rich nepotist Jews corrupting white women with drugs, booze, parties, and sex.

The Jewish Bolsheviks attacked and seized control of Russia, conducting a reign of terror against Russians and then immediately set about seeding world revolution. Lenin, Trotsky and Stalin sent agents to foment insurrection and carry out numerous terrorist attacks on German soil. They starved the peasants of Ukraine in the Holomodor, murdering ten million white Christians.

Somehow, the Nazis gained power in 1933. Popular sentiment was in favour of reining-in Jewish depredations. It began by reasonable and not especially violent means. For example, the ancient Jewish practice of hiding their identities and affiliation by taking on names imitating their host people was thwarted by requiring the wearing of identifying patches. This struck me as completely fair. When a close-nit high-trust group infiltrates your country under disguise you should assume nefarious intent and treat them with suspicion. Especially when that nefarious intent has been realised on every single previous infiltration.

So, international Jewry declared war on Germany on March 23, 1933. Google it, you can find the announcement on the front pages of all the major newspapers. It began as an anti-German boycott and soon wiped twenty percent off the GDP of a country already in deep depression. Note this was a full eight years *before* Operation Barbarossa and the Nazi's mass murder of Eastern Jews.

In 1941, Germany was faced with an existential battle. For twenty five years they'd had international Jews from the West declaring economic and diplomatic war, crushing the economy and turning the tide of a major war against them. Internally, Jews had ravaged their currency and economy, corrupted their women, and stolen their jobs. In the East, Jews had seized control of their great Russian rival and built a totalitarian war machine that had already murdered nearly twenty million white Christians and was fomenting a similar revolution within German borders.

And after all that, the world was at war again.

"Considering these circumstances, I think the Nazis were quite entitled to consider themselves victims of Jewish persecution," I finished with a flourish. "The Holocaust was a mild over-reaction."

I stress that I didn't present this polemic as a carefully-researched position. I frequently included qualifiers: I'm not quite sure but it seems; this point is something I read in a blog post and haven't corroborated; this goes against the consensus of historians.... and so on. To this day I'm not sure how fair the position is. However, it fascinated me that it was so easy to make a reasonable prima facie case that the 'greatest horror in the history of, like, everything ever' was actually something that had been a long time coming. That was another heuristic I'd tweeted to many reader's horror: in most of history's genocides, the victims had it coming.

"I need to buy a train ticket now," said Ela. "Will you come to the station with me?"

I walked her to the station in Galleria mall and waved her onto a train. We didn't see each other again. Whether Ela was put off by logistics, my age, lack of interest, or my lengthy monomania on the Jewish Question was never confirmed.

My train to Warsaw left on Monday morning.

Down the memory hole for you inconvenient truth

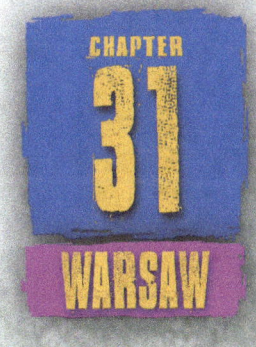

CHAPTER 31
WARSAW

Chapter 31
WARSAW WARRIOR

I looked down at my feet as I stood in the shower. Hot water splashed my head and snaked down my body in rivulets. My stomach sagged, the paunch suggesting I'd drunk too many beers and sugary milkshakes over the summer. Sucking it in, I could better see the muscles of my thighs. They too didn't look right. After years of kickboxing and bodyweight exercise I'd developed strong lean legs. There was a time I'd perform five hundred deep-knee bends in only eleven minutes, without stopping. When I'd kick a heavy-bag the resulting thwack sounded like a shotgun blast, reverberating from wall to wall in the gym.

Sadly, those days were over.

My thighs were smooth and fleshy. They looked okay in jeans, just as my torso gave the illusion of a healthy v-shape when wearing my black leather biker jacket. Not the soft nappa leather jacket I'd worn in 2014, but the stiff cow leather successor I'd bought for colder weather. It was odd. I didn't feel any older. In my heart and mind I was still a young man.

"A man is only as old as the woman he feels," quipped Groucho Marx. I didn't consider it a joke. Wise old Groucho had hit upon an eternal truth. The last woman I'd felt was twenty-three year old Olga, and before that twenty-four year old Gosia. The reason I showered was because nineteen year old Lala was coming over for a rattling.

There was a disconnect. Objectively, I was a forty year old man and my body creaked and groaned with advancing age. My morning stretch sounded like a firing squad, a series of rapid cracks as my skeleton protested against the thought of another day on earth. I'd come to put on my socks and shoes from a different seated posture because I could no longer lean over and do it as carelessly as before. I simply wasn't flexible enough these days.

Despite nature telling me I should put on a pair of slippers, light a pipe, and watch *Top Gear* on television, my spirit rebelled. My self-image hadn't aged a day since my first daygame set in 2009. I was still an adventurer, a bold buccaneer of the streets. A procession of lithe young ladies warmed my bed and, to judge by recent results, would continue to do so as long as I summoned the willpower to chase them down.

So, my body and soul were diverging. I was disassociated.

The shower water blasted out relentlessly from the sleek chrome fitting overhead. My new apartment in Warsaw was slightly south of the centre, at the edge of a bar district. It was on the fourth floor of a new building, with a small smoker's balcony overlooking a tiny park. My bedroom was huge. There was also a small lounge with a sofa, and the bathroom was modern with a separate glass-encased walk-in shower. I liked it. Waking up in a clean modern apartment makes the whole day feel better.

I turned the shower handle clockwise, increasing the heat a little until the water stung my skin. I watched the tiny rivers flood down to my feet and coalesce on the beige plastic waterproof flooring. There it formed a tiny whirlpool, the gentle flow swirling in ever-decreasing circles.

Ever-decreasing circles.

That struck me as an apt metaphor for my year. My first trip in April had been several weeks. This trip was less than four days. Any longer in one town bored me.

Disappointingly, Lala was on her period and couldn't have sex. Somehow, I'd expected it.

Next morning, my first full day in town, I woke up feeling chipper and lively. The moody self-reflection of the prior evening was washed away. It was sunny, I was in a good mood, and my new friend Tomas had agreed to a walkabout. Before cracking on with the daygame we sat outside a popular restaurant called Aioli. They served tremendous beef steaks.

I was enjoying my daygame again. There were the usual short dismissals and pleasant chats to nowhere but it didn't take long to get some action. Tomas was fond of a large bowl-like courtyard between the Stalin tower and the main shopping street. Three separate sources of potentially chaseable skirt converged at this one area: the Metro station exit, the park path, and the pedestrian underpass. It was also a meeting point for locals.

The only negative point was it attracted lunatic protestors and buskers. There was a mentally-ill homeless troll who banged metal pots with sticks in what he probably thought was drumming. Other times a troupe of ugly tattooed emo kids juggled fire. On Sundays and religious holidays a Catholic anti-abortion group held up large placards showing photos of late-term abortions. The latter particularly offended me even though I shared the protestors' opinion. In my view, the public space should be treated with an element of restraint and circumspection. Showing photos of murdered babies struck me as rude, like shitting on the floor. Or getting your dick out in a pub.

It was when walking through the nearby underpass that Tomas bumped into a friend, another local daygamer. We stopped in the middle of the commuter flow and I was introduced. Hordes of fast-moving commuters walked past us, parting like water encountering rocks. It was that a slim and pretty blonde walked by. I sensed rather than saw her eyes flick towards me. Maybe I just imagined it.

Either way, it was all I needed. My spider-sense told me she'd like me so I opened.

Magda wasn't the most gifted girl facially. Her eyes and mouth were nice, her lips full and parting nicely. But, had I been tasked to paint her a flattering portrait for display in the National Gallery, I'd have made her nose less pointy and her skin less blemished. Her make-up was heavy, thrown on like the USSR still subsidized its use. She wore tight black leather trousers like Catwoman, and a flimsy white t-shirt.

We chatted a couple of minutes, struggling to understand each other with her faltering English. It was long enough to establish Magda was twenty years old, lived in a nearby small town, and had come in to go shopping. She obviously liked me.

"Let's get coffee now," I said. "There is a Starbucks at the top of those stairs."

"Okay."

After the heat of the unsheltered streets, the blast of air conditioning inside Starbucks was a blessing. We stood in line while I bought our coffees, then sat on stools by the window. Magda seemed entirely suggestible, almost entranced. We shared a little of ourselves but once more the demon of rapid escalation seemed to possess. Just five minutes in, I began sexualising her.

"Tell me a secret about you. Something naughty."

"Hmmmm. I like bad boys. My boyfriend is in prison."

Naturally, my ears perked up at that. Such information can redirect one's view of the optimal seductive path. I pulled her closer until our legs were touching. Simple proximity does wonders for upping sexual tension. We shared a few stories, with me telling her about a girl I'd banged. Her eyes widened and she softly bit her lip.

I looked at my watch. A total of half an hour had elapsed since my underpass opener. Half my filter coffee remained in the cardboard cup. What should I do for the next drink? Beer?

Why even wait for the next drink?

"I have an idea. My apartment is a minute's walk away. Lets take these coffees out. We can sit on the balcony and enjoy the view."

"I shouldn't."

"Do you think I'm a bad boy?"

"Yes."

"Are you nervous?"

"Yes."

"Great. Let's go."

I suspect if I'd waited for an overt verbal agreement from Magda I'd have not gotten one. However, by standing up and walking out, she trotted along beside me. We walked back down into the underpass complex but took a southerly exit and headed down a busy road until the right turn into my street. Unconsciously, I was holding my breath. I didn't quite believe she'd follow me back so easily.

We walked upstairs and into the bedroom. My laptop was plugged in at the wall and rested on a writing table in the corner. A swivel chair stood next to it. A large double bed took up most of the floor space but there was a clear area of polished wood floor by the sliding glass door leading to the balcony.

We put our coffee cups down on the desk and I sat down in the swivel chair. I pulled Magda to sit on my thigh, my arm around her waist, while I opened YouTube and found a music playlist. Then I kissed her. Getting to this position so quickly and with so little resistance was a fantastic sign, so it was no surprise when Magda almost tore my face off in her passion.

Not wanting to squander the momentum, I stood up and pulled her into me. She kicked off her heels and reached up onto tip-toe to kiss me. My hands explored her breasts and ass and I tugged down her trousers. She stepped out of them, now wearing just her t-shirt and panties. Her arse and legs were fantastic. Whatever sport she did, I hope other Polish girls will join her team.

```
         Well, why not judge
            for yourself?
```

We were no longer talking. Communication was purely physical.

I picked her up and dropped her onto the bed then lay on top. She let me strip her naked until I was looking down at a lean, curvy, twenty year old. I pulled off my shirt then began fingering her.

"Wait. No. I don't know."

Magda seemed confused and anxious.

"What is it?"

"I'm a virgin."

Dress me in spandex and call me Captain Surprised. Magda's leather pants, criminal boyfriend, and willingness to be spirited into my apartment in under thirty minutes had all indicated she was a sexually uninhibited girl. Same day lays tend to be smooth, when viewed in hindsight, and this had all the signs of one.

"Really?"

"Yes. I'm sorry."

"Don't worry. It's not a problem. I know what I'm doing."

I reached into my wallet for a condom. Magda drew her hands up to her chest, crossing them at the wrist as if to protect herself from a gust of cold air.

"No. I can't have sex."

"Do you want to have sex?"

"Yes, I do. But I can't."

We spent the next ten minutes alternating between kissing and talking. Magda stuck to her guns. She wouldn't even put her hand on my dick. When I tried to put it there she shook in fear.

"Have you ever touched a dick?"

"No."

I wondered what kind of criminal her boyfriend was. Criminally timid. Clearly he wouldn't make an effective rapist or flasher if he'd dated Magda and still not had his dick out. Perhaps I should've satisfied my curiosity by asking how far she'd gone with him. To look at the naked trembling wreck on my bed, her body pulsing from uncontrolled passion as much as from anxiety, I suspected I'd gotten further in half an hour than any man in the prior twenty years.

Finally, I had to let her go. We exchanged Facebook details and kissed goodbye. We chatted on Messenger that evening, when she was out with friends. She returned to her village the next morning and though we kept up a chat and she sent me some of her amateur modelling photos, we never did meet again. There were two times when our paths almost crossed and she seemed keen to date should they do so, but the logistics kept us apart until the momentum completely stalled.

Perhaps her boyfriend had been paroled.

I went back out to join Tomas who was now in Terasy shopping mall. It felt like I'd been away for hours but, checking my watch, literally less than one hour had passed since my saying to him, "I'm opening this one" to him asking "how was it?" when I reached Terasy.

Tomas did some sets and I did mine. Later, we stood at the western edge of the big grassy park at the foot of the Stalin tower. The spot offered excellent sight lines of pedestrian traffic coming from the fishbowl area by the Metro. In the other direction, the pedestrian crossing outside Terasy mall deposited girls in front of us as they entered the park. I stood there with Tomas as he chatted to another daygame friend. He seemed to know everyone in Warsaw.

I scanned the park, levering my 20/20 vision to get first dibs on any good sets.

A buxom brunette approached. She wasn't as slim as I normally prefer, but her hips and breasts were full, giving pleasant proportions. She was built like a Russian peasant, I thought, which wasn't far from the mark as she was Ukrainian. Her trajectory would bring her right past our little trio, I noticed, as she seemed headed for the mall. Once she was ten metres away, and thus noticed us, I stepped out of the group, held my arms expansively to each side, and hollered in cheerful manner.

"Girl with brown hair. Stop! I want to talk to you."

My vibe was great. Adding that to the ballsy confidence of my opener and she was already smiling as she covered the last dozen steps to come to a halt in front of me. I don't remember what else I said. She was called Daria, from Kiev, and working in an office. She didn't tell me her age but I'd guess it to be around twenty-two. Her skin was smooth, clear, and unwrinkled even at the eyes when she smiled.

"Where are you going?"

"I go shopping, at the mall," she said, pointing her finger over my shoulder.

"Let me correct your English. Repeat after me. I was planning to shop at the mall, but now I met a handsome Englishman and I will join him for coffee."

She didn't repeat it, but she did laugh and allow me to lead her away to Chmeilna and my favourite Caffe Nero. Our second drink was a beer at Pictures Bar next door and then she came back to my apartment. Once more I sat on the swivel chair with a girl on my knee. Daria enjoyed the kissing and breast-groping but she wouldn't let me stretch her on the bed nor unclothe her. After half an hour of fruitless effort, I realised she wouldn't buckle so I took her number and suggested she finish her shopping.

Daria too engaged me in texting and went so far as to agree a time and place for a date the next evening before cancelling with two hour's notice. I didn't see her again. I messaged Tomas.

"Mate, you're my lucky charm. We should wing together more often."

Two near-misses in one day, one of them very near indeed, had drained me. When you're riding the rapids of successful seduction, your body responds. There's a dump of adrenalin, of seratonin, of oxytocin, and of dopamine. Probably some other things too. It's precisely this cocktail that makes daygame so addictive, and why I'd become such a junkie. Like all highs, it's exhausting and there's a comedown. Mine hit hard. I was too tired to move, too buzzed to sleep, and my eyes too unfocused to read.

At a loss over how to prevent boredom while in my diminished state, I searched YouTube for some medieval tavern music and collapsed onto my bed, staring at the ceiling and letting the events of the day unspool in my mind's eye. I'd now spent considerable effort in the company of six girls since landing in Krakow. I'd kissed five, had four in my bedroom, and failed to shag all of them. As of yet, I didn't know how I felt about it. Does a crack-head ruminate on the significance of his score, or does he just enjoy the buzz?

At some point I fell asleep dreaming of tankards, wenches, and bubonic plague.

There was a time when a run of near misses would crush my spirit. *So close!* I'd whimper and then endlessly replay the interactions in my mind, seeking the source of my error or to identify missed opportunities. It's a dangerous game because while it's wise to optimise technique and eliminate errors, it is self-defeating to assume everything is within your control. The only people who believe you can bang every girl — so long as you just deploy the correct sequence of techniques — are people who never bang any girls.

Most of the time, the girl is a No.

There's a pertinent philosophical question on how near a near miss really is. Like other philosophical questions, it won't be solved in my lifetime. I pushed it to one side. I slept well and woke up with renewed vigour. Rather than sap my will, the recent run-ins with recalcitrant fillies had fired me up. Nothing could keep me off the streets.

There was sex out there. I intended to get mine.

My next shot at sex crept up on me by surprise. Well, perhaps it's more accurate to say it bumped into me. Definitely a surprise, anyway.

It happened on the main shopping street, Marszalkowska, around rush hour. I'd found that Novy Swiat and Terasy mall were quite reliable during the mid-afternoon lull because students and shoppers respectively had reasons to be there. The main appeal of Marszalwhatssit lay in the metro stations at the top and bottom of it, which encouraged a steady flow of commuters during busy times. It was also good to gutter game due to the three separate bar districts at its north and south ends, and eastern flank. Gutter game is best when street lights or shop window lights illuminate the pavement and thus diffuse the atmosphere from "very rapey" to the optimal "slightly rapey". Marszablahblahski was excellent in this regard too. So, at around 6pm I found myself wandering aimlessly towards the large C&A clothing store, waiting for dusk to come. My eyes were glassy and unfocused. It was the twentieth time I'd paced the length of street that afternoon. The world was a blur around me.

The TK Maxx building has a pedestrian route through to Chmielna, a wide paved area on both sides of a small entrance leading to an escalator headed upstairs. It was this corner I approached, my head pointed to the right, carelessly looking across the road at the Stalin tower rather than in the direction I was walking. Just as I reached the corner a sudden flash of movement to my left caught my eye. My head snapped around and I almost collided with a girl stepping out in front of me, her having rounded the blind corner from Chmielna.

We both stopped in time, not quite making contact.

"Oh!" I said.

"Oh!" she repeated.

She was pretty. Tall, for a girl, or perhaps that was an illusion created by her high heels. The length of those plus her blonde hair had me immediately assuming she was Ukrainian. Her face was pleasantly peasant-wide, matching her very wide hips. If Godzilla needed a human female to sire Godzookie, she'd make the short list due to her strength of hips alone. Her hair was cut slightly above the shoulders and her dress looked businesslike. This girl must've just finished work.

"You nearly killed me. I could've died in Poland, a thousand miles from home," I said. "What would my parents say about that?"

I didn't expect an answer, and this blonde wasn't able to speak. She was tongue-tied. But I liked her, and her instinctive reaction was to smile. So, I continued.

"You look nice. I like your hair. I'm Nick."

She realised I'd been joking and was actually hitting on her. That made her smile again and self-consciously flick her hair. "I'm Alisa."

"You're Ukrainian aren't you?"

"Yes, I am. How did you know?"

"High heels," I said, pointing. "Only Ukrainian girls are crazy enough to wear them so high."

We had a short chat and then, confirming she only intended to window-shop before heading home from work, I diverted her towards Caffe Nero on Chmeilna. It was still warm and sunny, so we sat outside at a table. Conversation was easy. Alisa told me she worked in an office doing an okay-but-don't-really-care clerical role. She liked Poland and hoped to get permanent residency. That described every Ukrainian and Belarusian I'd ever met in Poland, bar the short-term tourists.

Ten minutes in, I was complacent. Alisa exuded the lucky-to-be-here vibe.

I gazed out onto Chmielna, people-watching during a lull in the conversation. From my left, I noticed two men approach, their likely trajectory taking them directly past our table. One looked vaguely familiar, with short dark hair and a heavy beard on a face that looked to be approaching thirty. His eyes were morose and as the men drew closer I could hear them talking in English. The second man was small and thin, the type you pick up and throw out the window should you find yourself behind him in a queue.

It would appear I was more than vaguely familiar to them. As they walked past the bearded one glanced surreptitiously sideways at me and a few seconds later I caught a snippet of conversation on the breeze, "yeah, it's him."

That allowed me to place him. It was a guy doing an anti-daygame daygame channel on YouTube. A commentor on my blog had linked a video of his a few weeks earlier. The video was a rambling monologue about how Game doesn't really work, you just need to be yourself and flow with the go. Or something. I don't recall. It had sounded like bullshit to me and the world is too full of bad daygame channels for me to keep up.

Still, I was pleased. Alisa was hot and sitting next to me with a big smile on her face. If I'd been caught idating a hatchet-faced rotter I'm pretty sure that night's YouTube would've announced it to the world, probably with a long-range smartphone video attached as evidence. On very rare occasions I've consented to invite mediocre birds onto dates, but usually only very late at night when I'm half-cut and trying one last gutter game set before bedtime. I never worried about getting "exposed" as a fake, or for banging dross, because my public image was not based on lies. Any keen daygamer curious about my quality and ability needed only step onto the main daygaming street while I was in town. He'd soon see me in set, or on a date. Failing that, so many men had seen me in action that word-of-mouth made it easy to verify my bona-fides.

I took Alisa to *Pictures Bar* for a drink and she made some noises about having to work the next morning. Ignoring that, I kissed her then walked her back to my apartment. She seemed almost grateful to be invited in. We sat on the sofa watching YouTube and drinking from beer cans I'd bought in anticipation of further bouncebacks.

Sex looked on.

I upped the ante and undressed my new Ukrainian import. In less time than it takes to firebomb a mosque I had her stripped to her panties. Then, finally and disappointingly, her LMR kicked in.

"I can't."

I was getting very tired of hearing those two words from girls. Perhaps frustration showed on my face, though Alisa can't have known I wasn't so much frustrated at her but at the accumulation of similar blockades thrown up by six successive girls.

Alisa would later get lucky

"I'm sorry. I want to have sex, but I just can't. It's too quick."

Looking inward, interrogating my gut-feel, I was surprised at how little her rejection impacted me. Sure, I was disappointed. However, had I booted up my Give-a-shit-o-meter to register my score, the needle would've have moved out of the safe green area. Had I finally become inured to near miss anguish? That was progress.

Alisa put her clothes back on, stayed a little while longer, then went off to get a good night's sleep. I too slept well, the dawning realisation that neither Krakow or Warsaw wanted me to get laid not dampening my spirits at all.

Next stop Kiev

A bridge in Kiev park

Chapter 32
MASQUERADE

Thursday 20th was my last night in Poland before heading to Kiev. Kenan had been in touch to confirm he was indeed arriving on schedule. He was heir-apparent to a large business combine in Turkey and his parents were grooming him to take over its management. Such responsibility often frustrated him when last-minute business troubles forced him to cancel holidays. He'd already cancelled one with me the year before at late notice, and cancelled a residential coaching week with Steve that had netted my friend a clean £4,000 for doing absolutely nothing.

Having never been to Kiev, I didn't much fancy going alone, twiddling my thumbs until Eddie rolled up. Kenan's confirmation settled my nerves. I headed out onto Warsaw's streets on Thursday lunchtime feeling good, eagerly anticipating the next trip. *No point daygaming today*, I resolved. *It would need to be an SDL and those haven't been coming through.* That was a prescient prediction, as fate had decreed I would not get laid beneath the Warsaw sun.

My brain was tightly wound again, the radio dialled to the shortest frequency possible. Attempting to unwind, I took a long relaxing walk along Novy Swiat to a large park past the university. I scoffed another strawberry and vanilla ice cream, briefly wondering if the remaining year's daygame might walk off my increasing body fat. There was a delightful Caffe Nero on a corner by the park so I sat inside with a coffee, taking great satisfaction in small pleasures: the smell of freshly-roasted beans, the tan leather of the sofa, a light breeze through open windows. I hadn't yet lost my strong association of pleasure in cafes that I'd developed in Tokyo fifteen years earlier. An emotional connection had been forged: nice cafes equals happiness. In London, I'd transferred the object of the connection from Starbucks, to Costa, to Caffe Nero.

Irrational, I know. But should you be lucky enough to find an irrational source of happiness that you can tap into at will, and doesn't harm you, well, you'd be stupid not to indulge now and then.

My brief reverie on The Good Life was broken up by a beggar entering the cafe. He was the least-convincing beggar I'd ever seen. He lacked the usual whiskey-reddened nose, broken capillaries, piss-sodden clothes, and the plastic carrier-bag full of god-knows-what. This beggar was a middle-aged man in clean, well-laundered, new clothes. His hair had clearly been washed and brushed that very morning. If he wasn't going from table to table holding out his hand asking for money, you could have assumed he was a school teacher waiting for a colleague, to discuss the curriculum or something.

That offended me. He was a chancer.

Worse, he was aggressively thrusting his palm at people. When they didn't give money, he harangued them. It was all spoken in Polish, and thus probably gibberish anyway, but I didn't need to understand the words to get the point. My peaceful cafe reverie was wrecked. The other patrons, mostly small old women or mousey shy university girls, looked very uncomfortable.

He came up to me, disturbing my tranquillity. That was unforgivable.

"Zla xyye walowhd whoop whoop skolbierski," he said, or at least something that sounded just like it. His eyes held thinly-disguised aggression, the type I often see on the homeless trolls in Prague, who sit on benches stinking to high heaven. It's the same look the gypsy beggars of Belgrade give, coming to invade your meal at a patio cafe and looking at you like *you* are the cunt.

He thrust his palm aggressively, staring me down. I held his gaze.

"Get fucked, you worthless piece of shit," I said.

His reply would've won a Scrabble game in one turn, had it been placed over a Triple Word Score.

"I said get fucked, you parasitical loser."

It's rare that I'll insult someone in their own country. I'm the guest, so I'd better behave myself: that's my rule. I'd been known to tweet that non-whites were not English and therefore shouldn't be allowed to vote, and that foreign-born residents running for political office should be executed as spies. So, if I was to throw my weight around insulting the Polish and telling them how to live in Poland, I'd be a hypocrite wouldn't I?

I don't mind being called racist, sexist, homophobic, Islamophobic, or even genocidal. But I draw the line at being accused of hypocrisy in my public manners.

This cunt had gotten my goat, so I let him have it. He turned away in disgust. There were only two staff, both tiny little women, and they asked him to leave. His invective was turned on them, giving quite a show of his being a victim, of suffering persecution, while resolutely refusing to move, or buy anything, or stop harassing the paying customers. The Polish have a maxim: the Jew cries out in pain as he strikes you. He seemed of that mindset.

Perhaps my run of near misses had stealthily increased my growing resentment after all. I was furious. He deserved a kicking but I wasn't quite that angry. Instead I stood up and pushed him.

"Give me an excuse, you vermin. Give me an excuse to knock you the fuck out."

Technically this wasn't bullying. He was about my age and at least 40lbs heavier. It wouldn't surprise me if his clothes cost more money and had been washed more recently than my own. His beady eyes stared at me and I tried my best to project furious murderous rage through my own expression. I visualised him being Jewish, rifling the bank accounts of my countrymen. Then I visualised him as Pakistani, leading a gang of rapists out grooming white girls in Midlands cities while police and councillors turned a blind eye.

He got the message and shuffled off, muttering darkly. The two female baristas thanked me profusely, more than I'd expected and it seemed genuine. A minute later they brought me a New York cheesecake on the house, my favourite. It's as close as I've ever felt to being a hero.

Time passed. It was my last evening in town and already dark. *Am I ever going to get laid in this town?* I wondered. I'd made a half-arsed effort at doing a few sets but the sense of futility and run of near-misses sapped me of drive. Aioli served up another delicious surf'n'turf beef steak which I washed it down with a glass of beer. The warmth spread out from my stomach and I glowed in a sudden satisfaction: Kiev tomorrow! Once more the heady drama of stepping into the unknown. Deep dark Ukraine. Hadn't there been a war there recently? I recalled something about George Soros and Hillary Clinton conspiring with the Federal Reserve Bank to overthrow the democratically-elected government and all Ukraine's gold being mysteriously shipped out of the country. Unlike with Colonel Gaddaffi, Hillary hadn't put a death sentence on the Ukrainian president's head so he was spared the Arab's fate of being dragged from a sewer, sodomised with a bayonet, and then executed with a pistol shot. "We came, we saw, he died," laughed Hillary in a famously chilling video interview.

Jesus, how fucked is the West? Obama now, an absolute fraud of a Manchurian Candidate, and then Jeb Bush manoeuvring to throw the next presidential election over to the psychopathic murderer Hillary. I put it out of my mind. Such darkness will sour a daygamer's vibe. Half the reason I was travelling around Europe chasing skirt was precisely *because* the West was so fucked. I wanted to bang the hot white girls before the invading Muslims raped them.

Anyway, all of Ukraine's fighting was down in the Crimea. I'd be in the north of the country.

It was getting on to 10pm. Mindful of the next afternoon's flight, I finished my second beer, paid the bill, and took a long farewell to Warsaw daygame by walking along Marzalwhogivesafuck towards my apartment. As expected interior display lighting streamed out of the shop windows to illuminate the now thinly-populated pavement. There weren't any sets, something I was faintly relieved about.

I ducked down into the underpass and came back to street level on the south side. I passed an off-licence and bank branch. Two more corners until my street. I noticed a blonde girl coming up behind me, walking quickly. As she passed between me and the office block's windows, I threw a cursory sideways glance to check her out.

Medium height. Blonde hair to shoulder length tied in a pony tail. Nondescript blue denim jacket, grey skirt, and a canvas bag slung over her shoulder. She was alright. Looked young and possessed of decent curves, but I'd not have remarked her if not for three things.

First, she wore shiny shoes. They looked like Vans deck shoes but covered in glitter that caught and reflected the street lights. Second, my spider-sense tingled for unknown reasons. I felt she was horny. Lastly, she glanced quickly at me as she passed. It was a slyOI.

We entered bullet-time.

How can I describe this to a man who has never daygamed? It felt like a scene from the first *Matrix* movie, where the world slows down but your mind runs at normal speed, your senses heightened. My blood bubbled. The sun could've risen and set at the end of another day in the time it took for the next ten seconds to elapse. I started slightly at her glance, as if she'd thrown a stone at me. She was already turning away to face forwards but had caught my reaction in her peripheral vision and glanced back at me briefly a second time. We held momentary eye contract.

Pretty girl. Youthful and cherub-like. I quickly rated her as a six: curvy, fresh, fuckable but objectively unremarkable. I hesitated and she kept walking.

Then, she looked at me a third time. What more did I need to inspire action, a Supreme Court ruling?

"Right! I have to tell you. I like your shoes."

Go easy on me. It was the best opener I could think of while shocked out of my late-night homeward-bound daze. We were approaching the street corner turning in to my apartment. My mind had been focused entirely upon the hot shower I intended to stand under upon return.

The blonde smiled, thanked me, and we made light conversation while walking the next ten metres to the crossing on my corner. Sexual tension was electric.

"Look, I was on my way home. Right there." I pointed at my balcony, then at a pub directly opposite my building. "Let's get a drink there.

"Okay."

It seemed awfully easy. We'd been speaking for less then twenty seconds. The bar, which I'd only ever walked past and never been inside, was a tiny traditional type with a small counter in the corner with two beer taps and rows of liquor bottles on the shelf behind. A haggard old women with dyed red hair busied herself piling chairs upside down on the tables.

"We're closed," she said. Damn.

"There is a liquor store around the corner," said the blonde. "We can buy something there and I'll get cigarettes."

"Okay. You can smoke on my balcony."

She took me back onto the main road and to the next crossing. She got her smokes and I bought four cans of local beer. As simply as that, we retraced our steps and she came up into my lounge. Out of curiosity, I checked my watch. Ten minutes had elapsed. Even by my recent standards of impatience, this was a fast bounce-back. We sat on the sofa, cracked open the cans, and watched to YouTube. Our conversation had taken a turn towards adventure topics. Perhaps I had a hand in steering it there.

"What's the craziest thing you ever did?" I asked.

"One time last year I went to a music festival with three guys I didn't even know. I was hitch-hiking. Didn't even have a ticket to get in. Their car pulled over and the guys looked cool. I sat in the back smoking dope with them and we went to the festival."

"I'm surprised you weren't raped."

"I guess, yes. It was a risk."

"Would you have liked it, getting raped?"

"Maybe. I didn't sleep with them."

"That's entirely your call. A girl needs some adventure in her life."

"Can I smoke outside?"

I walked her through the bedroom to the balcony and she sparked up, sucked in a long drag, and blew smoke in a single unbroken stream. She cocked a hip and folded her free hand under her elbow.

"Nice view. I like this apartment," she said, looking far across the rooftops. "I live close by. It's a good area."

A gentle night breeze fluttered leaves on the trees in the small park below. Our vibe relaxed. We knew the seductive subtext but hadn't broached the issue of kissing and sex directly. The blonde girl — we still hadn't exchanged names — was throbbing slightly, whether from anticipation or anxiety I couldn't tell. Sensing it sympathetically, my own knees trembled slightly. My body knew sex was for the taking.

She stubbed out her cigarette and walked back into the lounge.

"I have an idea," I said. "Let's play a questions game. Two rules. First, you can ask absolutely anything, without taboo." She nodded, keen. "Second. You cannot tell the truth. Every answer must be a convincing lie."

That was a new twist. It only occurred to me because I still hadn't asked her name. For the next ten minutes we lied our asses off with ever-increasing chutzpah.

"When was the last time you had sex?" I asked.

"Five minutes before we met, with a homeless man in the underpass. He smelled awful. How about you?"

"Including prostitutes?"

"Yes."

"Last night. Her body is still in kitchen freezer, cut into parts."

She cackled, showing a wicked smile. This girl had a dark sense of humour. I'd have never guessed from looking. Her skin was unblemished and free of both tattoos and piercings.

"How old are you?"

"Eighteen." My eyes opened wide. I'd guessed as much. "Wait! I'm supposed to lie," she corrected. "I'm twenty five. I never went to collage and I've spent ten years working on the railways, driving trains."

The oddness of the situation fascinated me. Not only was it a fast late-night bounce-back of a pretty young lady, but that intrinsically memorable situation was further spiced up by our ludicrous roleplay of deliberately trying *not* to get to know each other. After suffering dozens of formulaic dates going through the motions, it was liberating to dispense with routine.

I pulled her in and we kissed. Then I lowered her back to the sofa and stripped her naked. As I stood up to pull down my jeans she offered half-hearted resistance.

"I don't know. This is very fast."

"Thirty minutes, according to my watch. Live a little."

Then I slipped my dick in raw-dog and banged her for a couple of minutes. It wasn't at all comfortable on the sofa so we adjourned to my chambers. Things became fun very quickly. She knelt down and sucked me off a while, then I banged her doggy style on the floor. Seeing how easily she'd accommodated to fast sex I decided to up the ante.

I turned out the bedroom lights, opened the sliding exterior door, and made her kneel naked on the balcony, overlooking the park. Residents in any of over a hundred overlooking windows could see us, should they open their curtains. Despite the lack of backlight illumination, pedestrians looking up from street level would get an eyeful too.

At almost eleven pm, there was nobody afoot.

I slammed her hard, making her moan, all the while feeling the gentle cold breeze on my bare skin raise goosebumps. After ten minutes I brought her back in and pushed her onto the bed. I rolled a condom on, which seemed rather belated.

"What are you doing?"

"Be quiet. I'm going to do you in the ass."

"Aah."

I rolled her over and she scooted up into position resting on her elbows and knees, poking her delightful rear end my way. It was quite difficult trying to squeeze in.

"Slowly! It hurts!"

"Have you done anal before?"

"No!"

Result.

It took a minute's perseverance before I was able to employ forward-backward motion. She bit her lip and pressed her eyes tightly closed, gripping the duvet hard. The poor girl was in pain.

"Are you okay?"

"Yes. More."

Another minute of gently intruding in her back-passage and she became fully relaxed. I slammed her as hard as possible. Gradually, her posture gave way under my assault until she was lying flat on her stomach. I curled her legs up and rolled her onto her side, in fetal position. Then, pushing a finger into her pussy, I continued banging her ass.

"Harder!" she gasped.

I wasn't sure it was physically possible to meet her demand. I was already plowing with enough pounds-per-square-inch that I worried the tensile strength of her rectum may not withstand it. I slipped a second finger into her pussy and tried to finger her roughly at the same time as banging her backside. It was a delicate operation, like patting your head and rubbing your stomach at the same time.

"More fingers!" she demanded. I obliged, making a mental note that this little blonde hamster had taken to anal faster than any girl in recorded history. It was delightful.

Twenty minutes of carnal carnage ensued before I walked her to the shower, banged her under the spray, then put her on her knees to suck me off and cum on her face. Very happy with myself, but utterly spent, I retraced my steps to the bedroom and flopped onto the mattress.

Recovering, we each showered separately and dressed.

"You're welcome to stay over," I offered. "My flight isn't until lunch time."

"No. My parents are expecting me home. I'd have to make excuses." She picked up her bag and slung it over her shoulder, then drained the last of her open can of beer. "Thank you, I had a great evening."

"Me too. So, what is your name?"

"I won't tell you. It's better that everything is secret."

She was right. We'd shared arguably the most memorable night of my whole life. The raw wanton unlikelihood of it thrilled me. It was as ridiculous as that *Private Triple X 10* scene that had motivated me in Belgrade, but with a different blonde tart getting done in the arse without a so much as a by-your-leave. Except, of course, my experience was a legitimate pick-up rather than a staged porno scene.

Chapter 33
EASTERN FRONT

My first impression of Kiev was negative. Online sites warned me to be wary of airport taxi drivers so I'd organised a twenty-euro transfer with my new landlord. A shifty-eyed Slav was waiting in the arrivals lobby holding a sheet of paper with my name mis-spelled on it. I followed him outside for what felt like a mile to the far end of the car park and his broken-down old jalopy. He didn't speak English so the twenty-minute ride to Kiev's city centre was experienced entirely to a background score of Ukrainian pop music.

I looked out the window, trying to get a feel for the country.

Most of the cars looked older than my dad, and I've never seen so many Lada hatchbacks outside of an old Cold War movie. Occasionally, a brand new black sedan whizzed past, no doubt containing a chauffeur, a hooker, and a gangster. For a long time, the motorway was lined with just trees and large advertising billboards. Then we passed clutches of small houses and, soon, endless rows of tall Soviet-era apartment blocks. It was bleak, like Minsk but dirtier.

Traffic snarled and it took a while to get across the long bridge spanning the Dnieper. I hadn't seen a river so wide before. No wonder the Russians hadn't bothered invading Kiev in the recent war. So long as they could beat NATO to the Dnieper there was no way a battalion of tanks could cross that river. It gave me newfound respect for Napoleon and Hitler, that they'd gotten past the East bank. A large golden statue of a woman raising a sword and shield above her head looked out over the river from a hill. Lots of ancient artillery pieces and tanks were on display, in some kind of army museum. It looked nice. It was the first indication that Kiev wasn't a rat-infested shit-pit.

My mood improved further as we continued into the Old Town towards the famous Khreshchatyk boulevard. The Soviet-era architectural eyesores gave way to Tsarist-era buildings with all the pomp, complexity, and beauty that it entails. It was dirtier than Prague but felt more like a capital city than did Belgrade's Knez Mihailova. The traffic was part of that. Every street was rammed. I don't like busy streets.

My driver pulled in just before a roundabout at the bottom of Khreshchatyk, opposite a sleek shopping mall called Gulliver. I took my rucksack off the back street expecting the driver to follow me to the door. He didn't. He remained in his seat and leaned over the passenger side to hold an up-stretched palm out the window.

I hadn't a sow in local money.

I took my cash card out and indicated to him the empty wallet. With a disgusted grumble, he laboured out of the car and, shaking his head, took me down into an underpass filled with small shopping boutiques. He continued to grumble as I used an ATM by the stairs and handed him his money.

He rifled through it, seemingly unhappy not to have Euro notes. Then he grunted and walked off. I followed, still thinking he was to take me to the door but he slid heavily into the driving seat, turned the ignition key, and roared off. I stood bemused at the side of the road with no idea where my apartment was.

Thankfully, a man rushed out of a nearby small archway that lead to a courtyard behind two buildings.

"Nicholas?" he asked. Some keys jangled in his hand. Thank fuck for that.

My apartment was shit but I didn't care. It was up some exterior stairs, along a corridor, and up a winding concrete staircase. Wallpaper hung loose on the walls, every tile seemed cracked, and it stunk worse than an Indian restaurant. I dropped off my bag and lay flat on the bed.

Nothing could faze me. I'd banged an eighteen year old girl in the arse the night before. Even a second disaster at nearby Chernobyl wouldn't sour my mood.

"Shit! My bank card!"

I checked my wallet and turned out my rucksack. Nothing! I'd left my card in the ATM machine, in arguably the worst country to do so, as Ukraine is rife with identity theft. Evidently something could faze me. I rushed outside, noting ironically that there was an actual Indian restaurant two doors down in a basement, its air conditioning outlet pushing the sweet smell of curry out of a pipe mere feet from my front door.

I reached the ATM. My card had either been stolen, or swallowed by the machine as a precautionary measure. I returned to my apartment, logged onto WiFi, and Skype-called my bank to get the card stopped. Ttwenty euros of local currency remained from the sheaf I'd withdrawn to pay off the driver. I messaged Kenan. He confirmed his arrival the next morning. I explained my banking mishap. "No worries, big bro. I'll give you some cash." he reassured.

At least the weather was good

It was still mid-afternoon but a cloudy overcast day. I took a walk along Khreshachyk, following the advice Lars had given me on where to find the daygame. A mobile phone store on the west side sold me a local SIM card. Then I continued up the street, evaluating it for quality and quantity of footfall. I wasn't at all impressed. Fast traffic tore down a straight road, four lanes in each direction. The roar was ear-splitting and very distracting compared to the relaxed pedestrian areas of Chimielna in Warsaw. Fumes clogged the air and a light drizzle bleakened matters further.

I think I've made a big mistake, I wondered aloud. Whatever pretty girls lived in Kiev, they certainly weren't walking down my side of the street. I crossed the road using an underpass mid-way up and was gratified to find the east side of the street considerably more daygameable. It boasted two wide pavements, one at road level and the other elevated and lined with shops. Both pavements looked convenient for daygame, especially the latter which was offset quite far from the distracting traffic.

There was a Zara store. In front was a row of park benches and small grass squares with a tree in each. Even in the dull greys of an unseasonably bleak day it looked nice. I walked into Zara. There was a pretty girl wandering around in tight black leather trousers and high heels. She had big lips, big lashes, and quite probably big tits but I couldn't see because of her fluffy grey jacket. She looked like an Ewok caught in a tumble dryer.

I opened.

She was polite but not receptive to my moves and edged away after a minute. Nonetheless, I was pleased. That simple act had ripped the shrink-wrapping off my new city. I'd begun to daygame Kiev.

I followed up with two more sets outside and then it began to rain heavier. I rushed back to my apartment, which meant walking past that huge roundabout, on the centre of which was a massive old building housing an indoor meat and vegetable market. The traffic did my head in and I was in a foul mood by the time I reached my room. Except for five minutes in and around Zara, everything had felt seedy.

I booted up my laptop. John was online.

"How's Kiev?" he asked.

"Shit, by the looks of it."

"Tom said it's amazing."

"He says everywhere is amazing."

I spent all evening playing the Ukrainian-made shooting game *STALKER: Shadow Of Chernobyl*. It had been on my hard drive for six months without my having yet loaded it up. It's a game of nuclear accidents, mutated wildlife, and treasure-hunting bandits, all based around the nearby city of Pripyat. Somehow, it felt appropriate to my mood.

Kenan arrived shortly after lunch the next day, a Saturday. Much to my surprise, Kiev felt like a radically different city. It's incredible how much bright sunshine and a public holiday can up the foot traffic and with it, the vibe. It was apparent that the east side of Khreshchatyk was the place to be, with its wide pavement, brand-name shops, and the main exit of a Metro station into a large square that functioned as a meet-up location. The whole street catered for tourists as well as locals.

I'd gotten an apartment on the shit end of the street with the busy roundabout, grotty buildings, and the nightclub district called Arena City for the pay-for-play crowd of mostly Turks. The opposite end, past Maidan square and fountains also trended towards "high-end" bars where Turks meet local escorts. However, between those two centres of filth was a very long stretch of prime daygame real estate which I was now beginning to appreciate.

Speaking of Turks.

"Kenan, mate. Doesn't it feel weird being around all these sex pests from your country?"

"My family roots go back to Greece, bro. These sweaty brown men are from Anatolia and the East. Turkey is really two countries, European and Asian, split on either side of Istanbul."

"Constantinople," I corrected.

He laughed and tapped a cigarette out of his packet. Kenan always dressed extremely well and wore a thin herringbone tailored jacket over jeans that looked more expensive than my laptop. His jet black hair and moustache contrasted against his white skin. He did indeed look more European than Near East.

"What shall we do, big bro? Some daygame?"

I agreed and we walked up towards Maidan. A troupe of male street dancers was breakdancing and posturing on a sheet of linoleum in front of the McDonald's on the main square. I'll grant breakdancing is hardly an Olympic sport but these lads had the strength and agility of gymnasts — which they probably were at school a few years earlier. A large enthusiastic crowd gathered around. Slightly further up the road, but not yet out of the main square, some hawk-faced men had set up a free-standing chin-up bar that local lads were taking turns to dead hang from. A sign promised them a cash prize should they survive two minutes. That looked very easy to me, assuming the carnies weren't allowed to bash your ribs in during the countdown, but every last lad failed.

"The bar they hold is loose. It turns in the socket," advised Kenan, confidentially. "That makes it extremely difficult."

There was also a fairground style punchbag with flashing lights that claimed to measure your knockout power. It was extremely popular among the young men, who took run-ups of a length to shame Brazilian free-kick maestro Roberto Carlos. They then hurled their entire bodies into the bag, it seemed, the follow-through almost tipping the heavy machine over. I thought if their army over-committed so recklessly on the battlefield it was no wonder the Russians had handed their heads to them the year before.

It was a lovely atmosphere. Even in my sixth year of euro-jaunting I still felt trepidation before settling in a new city. Perhaps it was from watching the torture porn *Hostel* movies as a teenager, or the Gothic vampire movies before that. I still couldn't shake the feeling that central and eastern Europe abounded with vampires, werewolves, and rabies-enraged villagers. It took five or six good street approaches to shake off the mystique.

You couldn't ask for a better fishing spot

Kiev is blessed with a surfeit of good takeaway coffee kiosks, two on each side of the breakdancers. Kenan and I bought a cup each and continued up towards Maidan. We began opening. It took a while to build a head of steam but the girls seemed very receptive to my Turkish chum. We'd agreed to get the coaching out the way early, so I hung back watching him in action. I'd bought a cheap phone and SIM card so that, with the hands-free set connected, it functioned like a wireless microphone but allowed two-way communication and didn't look so bloody obvious.

I gave him feedback after each set, though he was so well-practiced at daygame he didn't need it. He already had a reputation in the Istanbul community as the top daygamer. Good luck came his way at a grassy square just before the large Maidan amphitheatre. A pair of pretty MILFs were sitting on a ledge and Kenan opened them with cocky swagger. His target, a buxom woman with straight black hair, really took to him and after a ten minute chat he rejoined me, the proud owner of a solid-looking number. The day continued in this vein until tea-time.

We ate in a Belgian cafe-restaurant called *Le Cafe*, with a raised wooden patio garden built onto the pavement, slightly back from the main thoroughfare. I didn't realise it then, but it would become my favourite fishing spot in the whole country. Kenan and I ate, chatting about life.

"You should come to Turkey in summer. My family have a hotel at the beach. I'll give you the best rooms and we can hit the beaches and the nightclubs together. The Turkish girls will like you, bro."

It was most kind, but I couldn't imagine what I'd do on a Turkish beach or in a club. Beach game was well out of my comfort zone, being a pasty-white Englishman with a rapidly-expanding paunch. In the club, I'd be more likely to get bummed by some toilet puffs than pull a hottie.

"What's daygame like in Istanbul? I've only ever visited with girls. I never tried it."

"It's good, man. Not like Kiev. So many girls have boyfriends or don't want to talk to strange men. Erdogan has changed the tone," he said, referring to the Islamist dictator who was attempting to undo the secularism imposed by Kemal Ataturk after World War I. Islam wasn't just threatening my country. It was fucking up the daygame in Kenan's too.

Once the sun set, Turk sex tourists came out in force. It was strange to see how organised they were, co-ordinating as though everything was agreed ahead of time on a sex pest internet forum. Our cafe faced a short stretch of maybe one hundred metres, passing the Zara, lined with park benches. Grotty, chubby local women sat in pairs chatting or staring into space. At first I assumed it was local custom to sit enjoying the evening ambience, much like Serbs in Belgrade all walk slowly to Kalemegdan park on pleasant Sunday evenings. I was mistaken.

The Turks roamed in groups of three. It seemed regulation that one wear a battered black leather jacket and one of his friends have slicked-back greasy hair. They paced up and down the short stretch south of the Metro (never to the north) eyeing the seated girls furtively and then, often fifteen minutes later, go over and sit with them. Again, it took me a while to cotton

Girl Junkie

on. At first I thought they were enterprising Lotharios trying their hands at a clumsy daygame.

What decided me against that hypothesis was the patient tolerance the girls showed such clumsy approaches. The Turks were so creepy and pandering that a normal girl would've likely given an eye roll, a hand wave, or a bitch-face blowout. But no, these girls wore expressions like staff in a mobile phone store dealing with an indecisive customer. A couple of time the girls stood up, linked arms with the Turk, and walked off stony-faced.

Hookers, of course.

You can always tell. There's never any vibe, nor the ebb-and-flow of a natural conversation.

I noticed a pretty girl in our cafe seated a table over and one down from our own. She was young, perhaps twenty-one, and slim. A seven. She hunched over a small beer, crying. Her shoulders heaved and she sniffled quietly. The poor girl looked like she'd been opened by Deepak Wayne.

I inclined my head towards her, subtly. "Have you seen that?" I asked Kenan.

"Are you going to open her?"

That thought hadn't previously crossed my mind. Now it did. *No, she's having a crisis*, I thought. Still, I did fancy her, what I could see when he face un-scrunched between sobs. Opening became a moot point because she suddenly got up and left, rushing out of the bar.

Kenan looked at me, and me at him. He shrugged, as if to say, *well are you going to?*

I didn't.

He raced off and stopped her twenty metres from the entrance. She gave him immediate rapt attention. Then he stepped in close to her, as we'd been working on in the day's coaching, and squeezed her shoulders. They talked five minutes then he said goodbye to her and returned to me without having taken her number.

"Looked solid. Boyfriend?"

"No, bro. She really liked me. She asked what I'm doing this evening."

"Wait, what? It was massively on. Why are you talking to me when you could've been on an idate?"

"Bro, I'm in Kiev to visit you."

"Get right back out there! Get her number! It's a sacrilege, spitting in the eye of the daygame gods to walk out on a set that good. She's a pretty girl."

Kenan shrugged, both entertained and bemused, then raced off. Ten minutes later he came back and sat opposite me, laughing. "Okay, big bro. I got the number. She wants to meet me later tonight."

We had another drink and I returned to player *STALKER* while Kenan prepared for his date. The next morning we met up for lunch under a blazing Sunday sun.

A new apartment right over the Metro

"How'd it go?"

"Okay, I think. We had a drink and then she came back to my hotel. I didn't want her to come in, but she insisted. Then we made out and she was naked, but no sex."

"LMR?"

"No, I said I didn't want to. I didn't have a condom."

Fortunately my beer hadn't arrived, or I'd have spluttered it all down the front of my shirt. Who on earth turns down sex with an extremely keen and pretty girl who is throwing herself at you? A same day lay opportunity, at that!

"What?"

"My mother works with doctors. She told me many times to never sleep with Ukrainian girls without a condom. HIV is a massive problem in this country. Everyone in Turkey knows this."

"Well, its probably you cunts bringing it into the Ukraine. That girl obviously wasn't a sex worker. And why not go down to the hotel bar and ask for a condom? Did she ask for money?"

He shrugged his shoulders. "She never asked. It's not a big deal."

"You are the only Turk I've ever met who would turn down sex with a white woman."

"Bro, you laugh but you would not believe how thirsty men are in my country, especially the village Muslim men. There was a story on the television news recently. A man climbed the fence in a zoo and tried to fuck an alligator."

"That can't possibly be true."

Kenan was leaning back, smoking a cigar now. "You don't know my country, bro."

That evening he had a date with the MILF from the fountain. He took her for one drink then fucked her in his hotel. Another hour after that he came around to my apartment. I'd invited him to do a *Womanizers Bible* podcast talking about our coaching and his own learning experiences. His flight home was in the middle of the night. He had a call from his secretary and needed to cut the trip a day short to deal with some business problem.

It had been a fun visit. I did a little solo daygame and the next morning, a Tuesday, checked into a beautiful big apartment in the best possible location for a fast-moving Kiev daygamer. We were at Khreshchatyk 17, directly facing the McDonald's on the main square, and the three bars tucked behind it. Everything we could need from meet to sex was inside a thirty metre radius of our front door, including the flow of pretty young women.

Eddie arrived. That made it the third country I'd met him in this year.

Chapter 34
HOG WILD

I was astonished by how misleading my first impression of Kiev had been, that bleak rainy first evening. For Eddie and I, roving cavaliers of daygame hijinks, things went fantastically well. It felt like watching the three reels of a slot machine line up on a jackpot. The weather held, the streets were busy, and we found more girls walking around than we could possibly open.

"Is this it? Is this pussy paradise?" I joked. Players always dream of the mythical land where hot girls can't wait to jump into your bed.

"It's a step up from London, that's for sure."

Interviewing Eddie for my channel

We were soon camped out at the Belgian patio bar during the peak early-afternoon heat, and walking around Khreshchatyk, Maidan, and a small university district around the corner at Shevchenko park when the sun cooled. With Eddie having been so helpful as to interview me for his *Street*

Girl Junkie

Attraction channel, I returned the favour and we shot a video interview for my *Womanizers Bible* podcast.

We were living the dream. Hot weather, hot girls, and hot action. Well, neither of us were getting hot action just yet, but the early returns were promising.

My first serious action came with a late-evening set near the McDonald's. A curvy blonde in hot pants and vest walked past and every fibre of my being vibrated. She told me her name was Zlata and I needed to use Google Translate on my smartphone to make myself understood. She liked me. I liked her long legs, wide hips, big tits, very long thick hair, and Slavic face. We walked up to Maidan which had gotten busy due to some kind of public performance. The elevated levels of the amphitheatre were all thronged with relaxing locals taking in the ambience.

A road curved up into a hill, with long patches of grass such that small groups picnicked on them. We found our own patch and, being unable to converse, I began escalating. Zlata seemed wrapped up in the moment and keen to kiss. There was only so much I could do without getting indecent in front of families eating sandwiches and drinking lemonade on the grass nearby. It was already late, having gutter gamed Zlata, so after an hour she explained she needed to go home and work early the next day.

A date with Zlata

That next day she came out for an evening date. We met outside the same McDonald's and this time Eddie was ready with his video camera to shoot a short "proof" clip to splice into one of my YouTube montages. Zlata had unwittingly helped out by putting a lot of skin on show and she looked great. We had a short walk then I sat her down in the beer garden of a pub next to our apartment building. She was clearly keen so after just the one drink I took her up to my apartment.

"Extracting. Keep clear," I had texted Eddie, so the apartment was empty on arrival.

We sat on a leather sofa in the large lounge. I went through the usual motions of putting on YouTube music and pouring wine. Then we began fooling around.

Her t-shirt came off.

Then her bra.

Then her shoes.

It really did look like I'd be knobbing a sexy nineteen year old Ukrainian blonde. Sadly, once I fiddled with the button of her denim shorts her heels dug in and I wasn't getting any. It wasn't all bad. I got to put her big tits in my mouth. Making out with hot teenagers never really gets old, I've found.

After an hour of limited jollies, I saw Zlata back to the Metro station, noting I still had a week to arrange what might well be the Big Date. Eddie was posted up at the main square, alert for sets. He number-closed a slim artsy girl with dyed orange hair and I got most of it on camera for his own montages.

Our sets were going well. So much better than I'd anticipated.

Perhaps we'd encountered unusually favourable streets, due to the season and buzz of local activity around us. Perhaps we'd bottled lightning with our own vibe. Whatever it was, I'd identified that Eddie's presence as a wing was a fantastic influence on me, as it had been in Riga. It felt like a return to the *Rock Solid Game* days with Jimmy, Mick, and Fernando: daygaming with a man of equal experience who wasn't a daygame obsessive. Sure, I'd winged a lot with Tom and John the last two years but their energy was different. Tom and I had been around the same level of technical ability and constantly in competition to outdo each other. We were both obsessives. That rivalry pushed us to ever-greater efforts and, thus, ever-greater results. John too was a good wing but I was clearly in the position of mentor and needing to babysit him at times.

Jimmy, Mick, and Fernando had been both solid friends in the normal-person sense of the word, and also patient, savvy players. That's how it felt walking the Kiev streets with Eddie. The raw edge of competition wasn't there. It was just two friends comfortably passing time and taking turns to chase skirt. Now that my love for the game was volatile, I preferred that. The

Girl Junkie

balls-to-the-wall always-on attitude I'd maintained for years was increasingly draining. If you could describe my earlier experiences as similar to a car with the motor always running, I was now more like the Rocket Ranger, either gliding effortlessly through the air, or else blasting the afterburners on his jet-pack and racing high.

On, or off. No middle ground.

We were as happy as pigs in shit

My next near miss came with a large-chested seventeen year old called Justine. She was small of stature, bless her, and reminded me of a squirrel. I'd opened her outside Zara mid-afternoon and taken her for a quick coffee at *Le Cafe*. She lived in a nearby city but explained she was frequently in Kiev and often stayed with her grandmother there. I took a number, let her go and not until our text messaging did it start to feel on.

We met for a drink early the next evening. By now Eddie and I had figured out a simple path of logistics: meet outside McDonald's, bounce to the patio bar of the pub around the corner, then inside another pub called Porter's Bar in the same square, then finally to the apartment. Every stage of the date occurred within a space no larger than a basketball court.

"Kiev was made for daygame," I'd commented. "It's like the urban planners knew what we wanted."

Justine was shy and reserved at first, as may be expected from a teenage small-town girl meeting a foreign man over twice her age. She soon loosened up, chatting confidently. Something inside seemed to fire and I sensed she was ripe for the taking. I leaned over and kissed her half an hour in. She reciprocated with enthusiasm. We finished two drinks and she came up to my apartment, after first making suitable protests about having never done "this", not being "that kind" of girl, and having never met "a foreign man" before.

For all that, she was clearly thrilled — midway between excitement and anxiety.

Beast mode was active. Something about her tight curvy body drove me insane. Personally, I blame her pheromones. Her breasts pushed out from under her thin wool sweater so invitingly. More invitingly than ought to be possible considering its modest cut. Clearly I was getting carried away with myself and my perceptions were distorted.

I was seeing what I wanted to see.

"Come on then," she said, seductively. She stretched out her finger and beckoned me, then slowly placed her fingertip on the tip of her breast. She bit her lip and pouted, then firmly grasped both breasts and pushed them together as though discovering them for the first time.

Wait. No.

None of that happened. It was entirely in my imagination. I was fantasising about what I'd do to her if only she'd let me. In the real world, Justine was perched nervously on the edge of the sofa with a gap of two feet between us. She held the glass of wine I'd poured but didn't drink. I think she was talking. About an art project or something. I wasn't listening.

Her full breasts pulsed and jiggled with every breath. I estimated them at well over a handful each. One time she stretched a little, pulling her shoulder blades together, and both breasts positively leapt forwards.

"Come here," I said. She came, shuffling towards me. "Closer."

She shuffled more, sitting right up against me.

"Put your glass down." She put.

Then we got at it. It was frenzied kissing, her pent-up anxiety releasing in a flood of passion. She moaned and grabbed the back of my head, pulling me in. I stood up, hooked my hands under her thighs, and whipped her legs up off the floor. Taking the hint, she wrapped them around the small of my back and hung on. I walked — well, more like waddled — into the bedroom with this little squirrel thing attached to my front.

I sat on the edge of the bed, Justine's weight dropping so she sat in my lap. That let me finally get a good grip on her breasts. It was certainly a pleasant feeling. They were as firm as hoped, with the slight give that God designed in order to optimize their jiggle. I pulled her sweater over her head and unhooked the bra.

Once more, I had large teenage Ukrainian breasts in my face. I hoped it was the beginning of a trend.

Trends in the stock market are erratic, where even a rising market will suffer some daily plunges. So it was with my recent streak of good luck. Justine broke away.

"No. I can't go further."

"We are going just great."

"No. I'm not comfortable."

She stood up and walked to the window, looking out over the bustling hordes on Khreshchatyk five floors below. Then she returned and we kissed some more. Finally, she put her bra and sweater back on and said she needed to go back to her grandmother. Eschewing the elevator, we took the stairs down. They were wide, stone steps, the edges no longer sharp after a hundred years of use but instead drooping like melted chocolate. At each floor's landing, I pushed Justine up against a wall and we made out. By the time we reached the first floor I was fingering her through her jeans.

She gasped and clung tight. Thinking perhaps the tide had turned my way I tried to put her in the elevator to go back upstairs.

"No. I really must go," she said. I kissed her goodbye outside the McDonald's.

Eddie was nowhere to be found. I sent him a message and he replied he was on a date with the orange-haired girl, a student at nearby Shevchenko university. My mood soared like Icarus astride the Apollo 69 rocket. I worked solo gutter game until I'd taken a few more numbers.

My phone buzzed, from Eddie.

"+1. She's gone. Coast is clear."

"I'm outside."

"Two minutes."

Eddie came out and I patted him on the back in congratulations and we debriefed each other on our respective dates. Then we got back into the daygame. I had a run of five fast blow-outs which soured me. It was dark now and the street had taken on a seedier evening feel, the natural transition towards a gutter-game vibe. Being mid-week, the Turks were all back in Istanbul but I was surprised to see local men hitting on girls.

They weren't daygamers, or at least not in the sense I understood it. It appeared Kiev had its own tradition of skirt-chasing.

`Not impressed with the night clubs`

"There's a couple," said Eddie, pointing out two men who'd just walked over to a pair of MILFs at an ice cream stand. The shorter man appeared to be the leader, at my estimation well into his fifties. He had lush chief-executive hair, very obviously dyed black, and a colourfully flamboyant shirt open at the collar. His friend was ten years younger and much taller. His fashion was more typically Slavic, as though he was on the way to the grocery store and had thrown on the nearest clothes — in this case a zipped wind-breaker, loose jogging trousers, and white sneakers.

"The little guy looks like Joe Pesci in *Goodfellas*," I commented. He really did. "Do you think they are paying, like the Turks?"

"We can find out. Let's stalk them a while."

We followed Pesci and his friend up and down Khreshchatyk for twenty minutes. There was no doubt about it: they were local men trying to seduce local girls. For free. We could see them scanning the crowd, sizing up opportunities, and amending their trajectories to intercept oncoming girls. Their conversations had the awkward jumpiness of real-life opening, then would settle down if hook point was achieved. It was quite impressive, really. Pesci was not a high-SMV man. He was grinding it out.

Girl Junkie

I didn't like it, though. At least not that first time. In later days I'd see him out grinding, often solo or with different wings. He became as familiar a fixture as the coffee kiosks and the street dancers. Before long I felt a little sad if I didn't see him. But that all came later. The first time I didn't like him at all. I never like *any* daygamer the first time I see them.

"Cunt," I said to Eddie. "Just as the Turks go home, the locals come out."

This happened in the midst of my five blowouts. Little Pesci swanning around getting the occasional hook-point while Mighty Krauser got blown out. Obviously it couldn't be allowed to stand.

"Fuck this. I'm angry. It's time to rage open."

It felt like tapping in the nuclear codes and pressing the big red button labelled Armageddon. It was my last throw of the dice. Time to make the whole world burn! Funnily, using the temporary heat of rage (well, indignation, to be more accurate) often gave me strong hook points. The girls wouldn't sense the anger and it was all a bit tongue-in-cheek anyway. All it really did was make the initial few seconds of my approach more belligerent that usual.

Outside the McDonald's, I saw a likely target. Mousey brown hair, mousey features, and good curves. This girl was only a high six but it was dark and I'd recently had my boner pushed up against a hot teenager's pussy, frustrated by two layers of denim between them. I was horny. Eddie had gotten his. I wanted mine.

"You! Stop!" That was rapidly becoming my best opening line. Eddie had the camera rolling.

The girl stopped. I laid my full-power mesmer beam onto her and began all kinds of touching. I shook her shoulders, tossed her hair, held her hands. Everything I could think of that wasn't outright sexual harassment. She stood spellbound.

Tatiana, as I found her name was, came on a very short instant date walking around the square and up to Maidan. I walked her to my front door but she wobbled at the threshold and refused to come in. She gave me her number and left. By then I'd stolen a few kisses. I returned to Eddie and nothing more of interest happened that evening.

Chapter 35
SHOUT IT OUT

It would seem Kiev wasn't finished throwing hot seventeen year olds into my path. The very next day Eddie and I sat in the Belgian restaurant again, on wooden benches across a table. I was facing the street, Eddie no doubt surrendering the best view to me because he'd already gotten laid and didn't share my hunger. I noticed a slim girl walking our direction. She was very slim indeed, like a ballerina. Her hair was dyed dark red with a fringe and the sides cut to not far below her ears. An image immediately sprang to mind: the character Faith from the futuristic parkour video game *Mirror's Edge*.

She was awfully hot.

"I might do this one," I said aloud. "I dunno. She's small. Might be underage."

Eddie swivelled in his seat, looking over his shoulder. "That one? In the white t-shirt and jeans?"

"Yes. Looks like the singer from Republica?"

"Who?"

"Baby I'm ready to go. From the rooftops, shout it out!"

"Ah yes."

I'd talked myself into being ready to go, but decided that rather than shout it out from our elevated position I should descend the two steps to pavement level. I got up and timed my so I could wave her down just as she walked past the patio entrance. She stopped and stared wide-eyed with a mischievous, excited smile.

This girl was very happy that I'd stopped her, and I'd not even spoken. Had she been looking for trouble?

"Right, I'll do this in English because I can't speak Ukrainian. You look nice. I like your hair-cut especially. With the red, and the fringe, you look like the singer of Republica. Do you know Republica?"

She had no idea was I was talking about. I felt like I was talking to my dog, because she looked at me with thrilled incomprehension, as if to say, "I don't know what you're talking about but I'm sure it's awesome."

Seeing this, I pulled out my phone and booted up Google Translate. We passed it back and forth a few times. I explained I thought she was pretty and she told me I was cool because I was from England. None of that mattered. It was obvious she fancied me. There were only two pertinent mysteries: did she fancy me enough to fuck, and was it legally advisable to find out? Both questions could be best answered by inviting her into the very same cafe I'd just left.

An idate with a rebel

"Let's drink coffee," I said, gesturing as though raising a mug to my mouth then pointing to the nearest table. She nodded. We stepped up onto the wood decking. I figured she might have noticed I was with Eddie, so I thought it best to bring that fact into the open.

"Eddie. I'm just gonna have a quick coffee with this lass. I'll join you in a minute."

"No worries."

Once the girl, who introduced herself as Elita, began perusing the menu I saw Eddie bring out his camera and place it as covertly as possible on the table. He was sat a table back and across a short pathway so it was unlikely Elita would fully turn around and thus bust him.

An awkward twenty-minute idate commenced, conducted entirely through gesture and Google Translate. She told me she was seventeen years old, from Kiev, and liked dancing. I noticed a stud through her tongue, which fitted what little I knew of her character. She was a little rebel, making her early steps outside of mainstream respectability. Well, she'd found the right man for that. Perhaps more than she'd care to handle.

The raw physical attraction between us was obvious, not least by our mutual willingness to endure a painfully inefficient form of communication and our lack of any common ground. I was excited because she was so damn pretty. Her body fat was extremely low but her skin still flushed with glowing health and I'd already noted a pert, firm ass. By the end of our coffee, we'd reached the point where prolonging the date would only risk deflating the vibe, becoming tiresome.

I took her number. She promised to start a Facebook account so as to chat with me. She was as good as her word. That evening I received a friend's request from her. I wasn't quite ready for what was on her new profile.

Her profile user information said she'd been a member since August 29th, today. She had one Facebook friend: me. So far, so predictable. Slavic girls all use VK Kontact rather than Mark Zuckerberg's CIA-funded psy-ops site. She'd posted just three photos of herself, all from a school dance performance taken from a distance where I couldn't even be sure which girl was her. Nothing there surprised me.

Her cover photo was of two Nazi soldiers manning an MG-42 machine gun during World War 2. She'd chosen the surname of a famous Nazi war criminal as her Facebook surname. It certainly didn't sound Ukrainian or Russian. What was she up to? It would seem Elita was quite the rebel. This boded well, in terms of the likelihood of her letting a foreign man twenty-three years her senior rattle her little lithe body.

We chatted a little that evening and agreed a mid-afternoon date the next day. That was to be Eddie's last night in town and he had a first date lined up an hour before mine. We agreed to take turns shooting date footage, with me taking the camera first.

I was sat at *Le Cafe* with my late lunch when Eddie came in with his date and took the table opposite, as planned. We ignored each other, acting natural, making me feel like a character in a private eye story staking out a suspect's house. His girl was a slim brunette with an overall impression of crustiness, like she'd smoke dope or dabbled in ayahuasca. Genetically, she

Girl Junkie

was pretty. Give her a good shower and a £300 gift voucher for Mango and she'd look good on your arm.

I set my phone camera rolling, then left it on as I ate.

Twenty minutes in, she went inside to use the bathroom. Eddie turned to face me, careful not to get up in case she came back unexpectedly.

"She's well up for it," he said. "But I'm not overly enthusiastic. A bit skanky."

"I've got another half-hour before Elita. So if you pull the trigger before then, I'll capture it all on video."

We resumed our feigned ignorance of each other and the girl soon returned. By then I was onto my desert of cheesecake and beer. I didn't worry about the calories. It's scientifically proven that you can't gain weight while daygaming.

"She's talking about having had threesomes now," Eddie texted me, his phone under the table. "Gross."

"From here, it looks like she's gagging for it," I replied. Her body language had been excellent and she was constantly leaning over the table towards Eddie, pawing his forearm, and agreeing enthusiastically to everything he said. Three o'clock came and I needed to go for my date. I paid the check and left.

"I late," messaged Elita. I hung around by McDonald's. It was the hottest day yet so my eyes popped out of my head at all the female skin on display. My phone buzzed again. Eddie was calling.

"Didn't do it. She was gagging but she's gross. I might catch something. Where are you?"

"McDonald's."

"Right. I'm just coming out the apartment now with the camera. I'll find a spot and record you."

"Remember she's already seen you once. Don't get too close."

Ten minutes later Elita showed up. She flashed a beaming smile, then stood on tip-toe to give me a welcome hug. She stepped back a moment and I checked her out. White t-shirt, light blue jeans, sneakers, and.... wait... what did that say on her t-shirt?

White Girl, around a Celtic cross.

I was already extremely excited because I was dating a lithe seventeen year old girl with an beautiful face and lively vivacious manner. Now I realised I could add "white nationalist" to the list of her adorable quirks. If I was really lucky, and her Facebook suggested I was, she'd be a neo-Nazi.

God, I hoped that were true!

We walked off to the little courtyard with the three pubs. I picked the middle establishment and walked down a flight of brick steps into a large open-plan restaurant. We found a table in a corner and ordered coffee.

As expected the date was slow-going and awkward. We passed the telephone between us to exchange messages. I stuck to simple positive statements and Elita mostly limited herself to enthusiastic agreement. Nobody would ever suffer such boredom if not to get laid. Our second drink was beer. When the waitress came over with the glasses, Elita asked something. It was for the WiFi password.

Now that she was online, she used her own smartphone.

The first time she passed it over with a Google Translate message, I noticed her screen had an electronic watermark in the bottom right-hand corner. It was a reproduction of the SS badge. Brilliant! I was growing rapidly fonder of this rebellious little fruitcake.

Note the Nazi logo
in the bottom right

"What do you like about me?" I typed.

She put a finger to her lips and stared at me thoughtfully. Then she looked me up and down with what she probably intended to be salaciousness, but looked to my more mature eyes like a child eyeing a teddy bear in Hamley's toy store. She put her head down and typed, deleted, typed, deleted, and finally proudly handed over her phone, smiling.

"I like that you are English and I like your beautiful blue eyes."

That was awfully sweet. How could anyone dislike a Nazi like that?

The date presented numerous technical challenges, principally due to the absence of speech but also my own inhibitions from how young she looked. In normal circumstances I'd have suggested *Porter's* next door, a dark atmospheric pub, and used a heady mixture of alcohol, flirting, and prodding until the kiss was waiting to be claimed. That simply wasn't possible in the bright restaurant, surrounded by families. We patiently passed the phones back and forth, with long periods of silence, and of looking at the screens. We were reliant upon the translator and thus risked undetected translation errors that might lead to a social faux pas.

Vibe protection was crucial. It was extremely hard to maintain a carefree flirtation with such long pauses. So, sitting in a pub was out, for now. We'd need to go for a walk: fill the dead space with motion.

"Let's go walk in the park, past Maidan," I suggested. She nodded. We went out.

We walked together up Khreshatyk, through a public park including a dramatic communist archway flanked with heroic statues of the proletariat. The park ended at a viewing platform overlooking a small forest and the winding river far below. I made trite comments on this and that, just to fill the space. Elita nodded.

She's only seventeen, I reminded myself. *Who knows if she'll freak out from this awkwardness. She'll have never been on a date so silent.*

"Don't worry about speaking," I wrote. "We have a nice energy. I'm comfortable like this. The communication barrier isn't a problem."

She nodded. I was fine with silence and nodding if it all led to my bedroom.

We took stone steps up to a higher level of the park. A long strip of land banded the top of the hill upon which this part of town was built. We passed an open-air stage, a footbridge across a chasm upon which lovers had attached hundreds of padlocks, no doubt to symbolise eternal love. None of this really sunk in. My mind was entirely consumed with figuring out the best way to escalate Elita.

Should I go for the kiss? It felt premature. Not correctly set up.

I needed to make some kind of move. The sexual intensity was low, not much above the friend-zone. My biggest worry was the male-female polarity would crash entirely and, despite her keenness, Elita's instincts would write me off. *Do something!* I commanded myself.

We crossed the bridge and then I reached over and took Elita's hand in mine. She looked up, processing my statement of interest. Deciding it was a good thing, she smiled. I squeezed her hand and she returned the pressure. Great! The frame was established. Both of us visibly relaxed. I checked my watch and realised it was past six pm. Time hadn't flown, it had crawled. And yet, here I was. We'd almost reached the end of the park, far from Khreshachyk, when a firework went off with a loud crack far behind us. I turned to see if a show was starting — it seemed early because the sky hadn't darkened much. There were too many trees to see much, so I shrugged and we continued walking.

Elita typed something into her phone then held it in front of my face. She wanted to show me the Holomodor museum, not far from our present position. I agreed and we walked out the park and along a beautiful street lined with pre-Bolshevik buildings. There was a restaurant so I took Elita inside and we had a light dinner.

By the time we reached the Holomodor museum dusk had settled and the sky darkened quickly. We walked along official guide paths and saw Russian orthodox altars (or at least that's how they looked to me) and big displays with photos and accompanying text explaining local history. We reached the end of the park and it was now fully dark. There were no street lights and the paths wound through copses of trees. There were only a few other visitors.

Elita typed another message explaining there was another park she wanted to show me.

This time I needed to use the torch function on my phone just to see the path ahead. It seemed odd to find such an unkempt park in the centre of a capital city. I'm sure it would be beautiful in daytime as it consisted of small rolling hillocks with a rich covering of oak trees. Gravel footpaths wound through it all, branching off in different directions. Now and again we met wider tarmac, no doubt for the use of the park ranger or other staff.

We were soon deep inside the park. No one else was around. It felt like descending into a pit. Several times Elita seemed confused, stopping and looking around. Was she lost?

Another thought came to me. I remembered a story Tom had told me about Moscow. He'd met a seventeen year old girl in a shopping mall and swapped numbers. She'd insisted on meeting him a dozen Metro stations outside the centre, in a suburban residential zone.

"I left the Metro and waited outside at street level, like we agreed," he'd explained. "She was ten minutes late and had a funny vibe, standing too far away when she said hello. Suddenly, some thug rushed up behind and punched me in the cheek. The girl shouted something at me and left with the thug. He was young too, so I think it was her boyfriend."

"Why on earth would she lure you out into the suburbs just so her boyfriend could punch you? If she didn't want to meet, she could've simply not replied to your texts."

Tom has been punched more times than any other daygamer. Doubtlessly, he was withholding key details of the story. "Dunno, mate. Bitches be crazy."

Fairly or not, that story now came to my mind. Elita was leading me into the dark depths of a deserted park in the middle of a strange city. *Is Elita underage?* I wondered. She'd told me she was seventeen but what did I really know? If she was fifteen I'd be in big trouble, and not just with police. How well did I really know her?

Another, darker theory formed. More dangerous because it fitted all the puzzle pieces neatly into place. What did I know about Elita? She was a neo-Nazi. She was underage (possibly). She evidently never had an interest in learning English. Thus it was highly probably that she was a Ukrainian nationalist and fiercely loyal to her country. Quite likely she resented foreign sex tourists entering her lands and preying on the looser women. Perhaps her boyfriend, a neo-Nazi skinhead football hooligan, had strongly expressed these ideas to her. Likely as not, they'd hatched a simple plan: lure the seedy foreigner to a secluded location so a gang of hooligans can kick the shit out of him.

Him, in this case, being me.

Oh dear! I'd let my horniness lead me into trouble.

Elita still looked around, finger to her lips in that cute manner of hers. She reached sudden decision, grabbed my hand, and led me further downhill. We were on a tarmac road. It curved strongly to the right but trees obscured the view around the corner. I could hear a car engine idling and two voices talking behind the obscured curve.

It would appear the moment of truth had arrived.

My heart beat fast. I felt my pulse thump in my temples. Elita too looked anxious.

We reached the corner. My eyes furiously scanned the treeline, my imagination seeing an entire firm of hooligans hidden in the undergrowth.

I saw the vehicle. It was a small utility van, like those used by tradesmen running their own plumbing or electrician businesses. Beside it, a man was leaning against the driver's side door, talking through the open window to a man behind the wheel. Both looked middle-aged and had full heads of hair.

So, not within the neo-Nazi skinhead demographic.

A minute later the taller man turned away and went inside a small nearby cabin. The van drove off. Elita and I were alone. I'd had quite a scare. You never feel bolder than after surviving a near-death experience, even if said experience occurred entirely within your own fevered imagination. I pulled Elita in and we had our first kiss. She seemed very pleased with it. I certainly was.

"Let's go somewhere else," I wrote. She agreed, suggesting the military museum not far from our current location. The same one I'd seen high on the hill upon my arrival from the airport.

We walked out hand-in-hand, stopping to kiss. I briefly considered trying to shag her there and then amongst the trees. Nobody was about. A daygamer is always thinking of such things. There didn't appear to be any suitable stretches of grass and I reasoned it was a bit much. Too close to what a rapist would do.

"I just took her into a dark secluded park and shagged her, your honour," wouldn't go down well in court.

We walked more streets, the atmosphere serene and ghostly in the absence of people. We walked past closed-up offices, long high walls outside government buildings, and tourist attractions shuttered for the evening. Once we arrived at our destination, we saw far more people. The museum was free and open air. It had the feeling of a regular park, with joggers, dog walkers, and couples.

I felt great. Elita did too, when I put my arm around her shoulders. You're as only as young as the girl you feel.

We wandered around, checking out exhibits of artillery, field guns, tanks, and other pieces I didn't recognise. We took a path below the surface to an underpass lined with friezes depicting wartime scenes, then out the other side to the foot of the big statue. There were low-slung rectangles of stone and marble which appeared to be intended as benches. I sat down on one and pulled Elita into my lap.

She weighed nothing, like a kitten.

Sometimes we kissed. Sometimes we stared into space, holding hands.

"I never thought I would kiss an Englishman," she wrote.

"I never have kissed an Englishman," I replied.

It was approaching ten o'clock. Elita explained she'd need to go home to her parents. The date had gone as well as I could've hoped, considering the potential obstacles and my inability to ascertain what Elita had originally intended. I reminded her the following day was my last in Kiev. We agreed to meet in the afternoon. We took a taxi. Elita organised it to get the local price. In the minute it took me to pay off the driver at Khreshachyk, I'd probably earned more money online than the taxi cost. Which isn't saying much about my riches, by the way.

"How was the date?" asked Eddie, back at our apartment.

"I'm in love." I then filled him in, placing great emphasis on Elita's political leanings. I'm not sure who was acting more like a lovestruck teenager, Elita or myself.

Sure, she was very pretty but my interest was something more than that. Perhaps it was her age. There's something magical about it. Sixteen is too young. Off limits. Eighteen is fully adult. In the grey area of seveteen you get all the thrill of transgressing mainstream morality without actually doing so. That thrill of doing something I considered morally acceptable that was nonetheless looked down upon by polite society appealed to me. Like murdering an African immigrant.

It did make me pause for thought. *Why* was it so thrilling?

Everyone likes to feel young, and few things produce that magical feeling so vividly as banging a young woman. However, banging a twenty-year old does it too. Why had I gotten hung up on the seventeen year old factor? Now I thought about it, one statistic I'd been doggedly tracking was the steadily declining average age of the girls I dated. I viewed it as a victory.

But why?

There was the obvious reason, that younger women are in their sexual prime and in far greater demand than older women. Many older gents have told me the boilerplate feminist nonsense that "women enter their sexual peak in their thirties". This is patent nonsense, a polite fiction for men unable to do better than busted old shrikes.

This isn't a subjective personal assessment, but an easily-proven objective fact. Economists talk of 'revealed preferences'. Don't ask people what they want, because they either don't know or will lie to you. Instead, watch what they spend money on when given multiple options. That's how you find out what they really want. In the world of female sexual market value, men's value judgements can be seen clearly by examining the successful women in industries in which men pay money to access female sexuality.

Strippers.

Escorts.

Porno.

Photo posters and calendars.

When men spend their own money on female sexuality they always choose girls at or around twenty years of age. It's why escorts of that age are so much more expensive than the busted old ones. Everyone knows this, so it amazes me how many men will weasel around the obvious truth. Women too know it well. You don't see the cosmetics industry marketing itself to twenty-year old women with promises to make them look fifteen years older, as it would if the myth of "women enter their sexual peak in their thirties" were true.

This also matched my own vast experience of seduction. Single women over thirty are really easy to fuck. The only challenge is finding one worth fucking. Once you do, it is almost game over. Every five years off you knock off a girl's age she becomes twice as hard to seduce.

Such ruminations did not, however, explain my fascination with Elita. She was no hotter than Lala in Warsaw and only a point hotter than Valda in Riga. I'd been pleased to get nineteen-year old Lala, of course, but far more excited with Valda primarily because she was one year younger. That extra year may has well have been a millennia, for how good it felt.

Something was off. Irrational.

Had I ruminated further, I'd have realised my personality had subtly shifted over the past year of skirt-chasing. I'd already achieved my goals in the Player's Journey and felt comfortable with my new identity. I didn't experience the slightest whiff of cringe when I described myself as a player. I'd arrived. I'd shifted towards hedonism, using daygame as a crack-pipe where previously it had been a tool to reach my life goals. Now daygame was simply a hobby. When a man focuses on his hobby to the exclusion of his wider life goals, he can begin creating substitute goals within that hobby: faster lays, new sexual acts, and.... younger women.

Rapid bounce-backs. Anal sex. Teenage birds.

Perhaps that's what Elita represented to me. To me, she was like an enthusiast discovering a fine old wine, or a lost painting from a Master. She was the exemplification of daygame success. Younger. Hotter. Tighter. She ticked all the boxes and thus could be held up as an example of my continued progress. By this crooked value system, what could be better than a slim, petite, beautiful, Ukrainian seventeen year old?

The only way I could make Elita better would be by dressing her in an SS uniform. These musings occupied me over lunch on the last day.

"What time are you meeting her?" asked Eddie.

"Three."

At three, Elita messaged me. "I late. I message again."

Four o'clock came and went. Five o'clock approached. Dread bubbled away in my gut, that premonition that a lead is dropping off the hook. I couldn't blame her. It had been a big ask. I felt nervous and pessimistic, like on Election Night and seeing Labour take an early lead in the exit polls.

My phone buzzed.

"I here," she wrote.

My groan of relief was audible across Siberia. Perhaps some wild timber-wolves howled in reply. Eddie had his camera to hand. I spotted Elita standing by the coffee kiosks and walked over, with Eddie standing back to record the meeting. She threw her arms around me and gave a kiss. Great. It was very much on.

We bought cans of beer at the off-licence on the ground floor of my building and went straight up. Our lounge had a balcony overlooking the busy street, the view from which had fascinated Justine and Zlata. It would be a shame not to take advantage of it now in such nice weather. We sat on wicker chairs, drinking. Elita looked happy. She trembled in anticipation.

I'd initially planned to finish the first drink patiently and only then smoothly escalate. Now that I had Elita in my clutches, I couldn't wait. The beast roared.

I pulled her to me and she sat comfortably in my lap. She kissed and I felt her up. It was going swimmingly. Mindful of the electric light streaming out from the lounge, I stood up, told Elita to wait, and switched it off. No longer were we illuminated for the pedestrians below to gawp at. I pulled her sweater up. Reflexively, she crossed her arms protectively over her chest.

"My breasts are not big," she typed into her phone.

"You have a ballerina body. It's sexy," I replied.

Thus calmed, she let me pull off her top and bra and I mauled her in the open air. She'd clearly long since decided to fuck, so I carried her into the lounge, lay her on the sofa, and relieved her of her remaining clothes. Then I banged her.

A great view from my balcony

How many times have I banged a girl on a sofa purely to maintain the momentum of an escalation before retiring to a bedroom? I reflected on this trend as Elita and I did exactly that. As I threw her down on the bed she sprang back up to sitting position, fire dancing in her eyes. She was loving it.

Me too, darlin'.

Elita seemed to be inexperienced in sex, but not at all virginal. My guess is she'd had at least one real boyfriend in high school. It was a delight to look down at her naked body as I held her by the ankles and rattled her. She stared up at me with satisfaction, as if *she'd* won a prize. How little she knew about my own sense of gratification! I'd have banged her for hours but she needed a break after fifteen minutes to regain her breath. Not surprisingly really. I was twice her weight and retained lots of 'mat strength' from my BJJ days. We lay flat on our backs staring at the ceiling.

After five minutes, I pushed her head dickwards and she sucked me off.

Girl Junkie

My dick looked gargantuan-sized in Elita's tiny hands. She appeared more sure of herself bobbing her head up and down in my crotch than she had underneath me. So perhaps her experience of blowjobs outweighed her experience of sex. Then I banged her some more, put her on her knees by the window, and came in her mouth.

She swallowed, bless her.

"I need to come back and pack my bag. Flight is soon," messaged Eddie.

"Ten minutes," I replied.

I showered, then Elita followed. We dressed and stepped out into the fifth-floor lobby just as Eddie was coming out of the elevator. He said hello to Elita and she giggled and looked down sheepishly. I took her to the Metro and kissed her goodbye. Then Eddie and I shared a farewell drink. It had been a good trip for both of us.

That evening I had another small surprise. Ray, my wing in Prague the previous Autumn, had messaged to say he'd been in Minsk the past few weeks. "I'm on my way to Kiev now," he confided.

"Fucking hell, that's fortuitous. I'm there right now."

"How long?"

"Flying back to Warsaw tomorrow, late afternoon."

"I'll be there late tonight."

We had a coffee the next morning and caught up on our recent travels. The world felt smaller.

Chapter 36
MOPPING UP

Considering I didn't especially like Warsaw nor had much ultimate success there, I seemed to keep passing through it more than I ought to. Warsaw made logistical sense due to its close connection to Kiev, and also to Krakow, through which I'd fly home. Logistics aside, I had another good reason.

Alisa, the Ukrainian office girl who'd been naked on my sofa two weeks earlier, had maintained steady WhatsApp chat while I was in her home country. She'd apologised for not putting out ("I wanted sex but I just couldn't. It was too soon"), sent me some naked photos, and made it abundantly clear she was itching for the chance to jump my bones. I intended to give her that chance.

I booked two nights in Warsaw, just enough to close Alisa then take the train to Krakow en route to Newcastle. My apartment was on the ground floor of a low ugly concrete building directly facing Chmielna. It was modern, with brand new furnishings. The shower was a beautiful glass-encased walk-in with powerful water spray. The bedroom boasted a four-poster bed in a modern style, as I'd imagine Ikea would do it.

Private, new, clean. Just what I like.

Alisa met me outside TK Maxx after work on the second day, the 2nd of September, a Wednesday. We kissed in greeting then walked along the full length of Chmeilna to Novy Swiat. Directly across the road is a hidden courtyard with over a dozen bars, accessible by an archway between a newspaper store and an off-licence. Tomas had recommended it, saying it was popular with university students and eminently nightgameable. I duly checked it out and agreed. It was also an excellent date location.

"What shall I wear?" Alisa had asked that morning.

"Heels and short skirt. I don't want any trouble getting my dick into you." She'd followed my orders. "Do you like it?" she asked, twirling.

Knowing the notch was a sure thing relieved me of the usual pressures. I needn't concern myself with momentum, windows of opportunity, making the move, diffusing resistance and so on. I could take my time and enjoy the date. I resolved to conduct it such that Alisa would feel a rising sense of anticipation. I wanted to reward her for playing it so straight.

Walking in to the courtyard we were faced with two single-storey blocks that each contained several bars, and a through-pass between them leading to yet more bars. I turned left, walking Alisa to a simple bar with the street-facing wall completely removed. The metal shutters were rolled up, exposing the whole bar to the sunshine. There was a long, high shelf and similarly high stools lined up. We bought beer and sat there, looking out onto a patch of grass, a few trees, and the paved courtyard.

Alisa stared at me with adoring eyes, grinning. I hadn't even begun running game.

"You look nice," I said.

"Thank you. You too are very handsome."

"I like your legs."

"Thank you."

"And your ass."

"Thank you."

"I want to bite it."

It wasn't all sex talk. Alisa asked about my Kiev trip and I made allusions to sexual hi-jinks delivered with faux modesty, correctly judging that Alisa was turned on rather than repelled by my womanizer persona. She said her time at work had been okay and her nights out with friends equally okay. We talked more on routine subjects. It was obvious she was waiting to be fucked. Knowing this, I didn't hurry. Instead, I heated her up to increase her eagerness.

"I'm going to put my dick in your mouth. Not here, obviously. I'm not an animal."

"That sounds nice."

"I'm going to pull my dick out of your mouth and then stick it in your big beautiful ass."

"I've never done anal sex."

"You will."

"What if I don't want to?" She was smiling. It was a challenge.

"I'll hold you down and force it in."

This was coming on rather strong, but I felt secure in my calibration. Having already had her naked on my sofa, sending me dirty photos, and openly agreeing to sex, it didn't feel like a gamble. Still, I did risk overdoing it. A rule in Game is 'don't sell past yes'. I'd gotten my yes ten days ago and yet continued selling.

It was no longer about *getting* the sex. It was about making the sex great again. Donald Trump had recently announced his candidacy for President of the United States. That struck me as a joke but my favourite blogger Roissy was singing his praises. I liked Trump's slogan of *Make America Great Again* and resolved to use bastardisations of it on dates.

We finished our first beer. I let silence hang, as Alisa wondered if I'd buy another round.

Keep the heels on

"You don't want another drink, do you?"

"Not really."

"You want me to take you home and fuck you, don't you?"

"Yes."

The five minute walk to my apartment was a victory lap. If I'd had a bottle of champagne I'd have shaken it, popped the cork, and sprayed forth all over the gathering evening crowd. That they weren't gathering for my benefit seemed besides the point.

"Walk ahead of me. I want to see the ass I'm going to fuck."

Alisa smiled and strode out ahead, giving a subtle wiggle. Then she paused for me to catch up. I tapped the buttons on the keypads to get into my apartment and showed Alisa to the bedroom. I kicked off my shoes and she reached down to do likewise.

"No. Keep the heels on."

There was a children's play area directly outside my bedroom window, which faced an interior courtyard. At this time of night it was deserted, thankfully. I pulled the shutters half-down, so we wouldn't be overlooked by other residents. Then I moved towards Alisa who was standing by the bed, waiting.

We kissed. I escalated.

I saw no reason to underdress her. I turned her around and told her to bend forwards and put her hands on the bed. She did. I told her to push her ass back towards me, and she complied. Then I stuck my dick in and banged her from behind. Sex was good, us both having been looking forward to it for nearly two weeks. Then we went at in in missionary position. Alisa wasn't one for screaming or clawing. Rather, she was entirely submissive and stared at me with a satisfied smile.

"Turn over. I'm putting my dick in your ass."

She turned. "Be gentle. It's my first time."

"Don't worry. We'll go very slowly at first," I said, rolling on a condom.

It took five minutes to get it all the way in, much of that with Alisa biting her lower lip and whimpering. I felt her relax and finally I could begin in earnest. She turned her face to look at me over her shoulder, her face wracked with a curious combination of pain and pleasure. Before long I was able to give her a solid pounding, then I came in her mouth.

Alisa lay in bed unable to move while I showered. Ten minutes later she still hadn't moved. Her eyes were fixed on the ceiling, vacantly. I was tempted to check for a pulse and jump the border.

"Are you okay?"

She turned her head lazily and smiled. "Yes. Very okay."

"Did you like it in the ass?"

"It was.... unforgettable," she beamed.

"Good. I'll do it again next time."

The next morning I caught an early train to Krakow. I stayed a single night in a beautifully furnished rustic apartment overlooking the square. I tried to get Olga over but she explained she had a boyfriend now and couldn't see me. Exhausted, I read a paperback and retired to bed early. I flew home the next morning.

September was to be a disappointing month, notwithstanding boning a very hot teenager as we discussed earlier. I spent a week back home consumed by my usual activities of playing video games and being shouted at by my mother. Times like those, I didn't quite feel like an international man of mystery, nor a renaissance man and beacon of light to a new generation of masculine men. It did give me a chance to catch up on some of the manosphere blogs I'd been avoiding for months.

I didn't enjoy what I read. My loyalties had split.

On the one hand, I owed a great debt to the Seduction Community. It was to the pioneers of Game that I owed my skills and the sex life that had been enabled by them. Sure, I'd done all the work to get good, but I hadn't been forced into random trial and error experimentation. From the beginning I'd leveraged the accumulated wisdom of *The Mystery Method*, *The Blueprint Decoded*, and the support community of pick-up forums. They'd shown me the way, and then experienced players such as Jimmy and Steve had helped me along at a personal level. My red pill emancipation relied upon trails blazed by men such as Roissy, Rollo and Roosh. I'm not an ungrateful sort, and I don't forget people who help me. So, I felt the need to give back to the Community, such as my frequent blogging and podcasting.

However, the Community increasingly disgusted me.

This disgust said as much about me as it did the Community itself. Psychoanalysts talk about the ego-defence tactic of *projection*: the subject will imbue others with negative traits of his own, in order to externalise them and relieve the anxiety caused by them. Pick-up is a hard narrow path and we all fall prey to numerous psychological sleights of hand, fooling ourselves we are something greater than we really are. Perhaps it's a deep human need to feel special. Travelling the world seducing skirt provides ample fuel to power the engine of delusion. Every conquest is an invitation to puff out your chest and strut the stage — as I just did in the previous chapter.

It's quite a challenge to keep your feet planted on terra firma, look in the mirror, and see yourself as you really are. It helps if you have experienced, strong-minded men around you to call you on your bullshit. The harsh feedback of the street gives a feminine reflection of your abilities but you need the masculine view too. Now that I had a popular blog, a best-selling book, and a growing army of followers there was a real danger I'd come to believe my own press clippings. What I really needed were friends unimpressed by my preening, who wouldn't shy away from calling me a potato head or bald Geordie bastard. I missed it.

The Community had grown since I'd been involved in its early stages. Mostly, this was a good thing. Despite my online spats with Roosh, I greatly respected the care he devoted towards curating his websites and the behemoth RooshV forum. I'd read Rollo's blog in fascination that he still gave a shit about exploring theoretical limits of sexual dynamics, and advising a seemingly never-ending stream of deluded men who presented him with the same problems over and over again. The other great blogger, Roissy, had moved away from pick-up and become increasingly politicised, pushing a white nationalism that alienated half of the pick-up crowd. I happened to agree with him. Readers didn't seem to grasp the concept of the Overton Window: that there is a narrow band of expressible opinion outside of which everyone is branded an 'extremist' and attacked by the mob. That window shifts over time and we were living in an era where it had reached its Leftmost limit and was slowly turning back towards sanity.

The central fact of successful propaganda is: you don't know you've be propagandised until long after the fact. It's like one of Nassim Nicholas Taleb's famous parables explaining *black swans*: the turkey being fattened for Christmas can't even conceive of his impending neck-wringing because the only world he knows is of being fed every day by the farmer. It's no surprise the turkey doesn't fear his murderer because he couldn't imagine that murder was approaching. So it is with the Overton Window. It's quite literally *fundamental to the concept* that to say something genuinely transgressive you must be outside the window, and therefore the mob will hate you for it.

Roissy lived outside the Overton Window. I thought him incredibly brave to do so.

Any coward can speak his mind when his opinions match prevailing ideology. There's no courage in that. It's a man's commitment to speak the truth as he sees it — knowing full well that it'll bring the ire of the howling mob — that marks him as courageous. George Orwell is frequently credited with the quote, "during times of universal deceit, telling the truth becomes a revolutionary act." Repeat that quote, and every single member of the mob will nod their heads in agreement. But, try actually *telling* them the truth and they'll howl for your blood.

At various times, Roissy, Rollo, and Roosh had all been subject to such mob attacks for criticising the prevailing anti-male ideology of culture, politics, and law. Roissy had recently struck out into new territory: nationalism. He had divided the manosphere. I was fully supportive of Roissy. He was making what struck me as an obvious point: we men weren't merely getting cucked by feminism. White men are also getting cucked by globalism and multiculturalism. In what world is it acceptable for an entire race to be under constant attack in their own homelands, denied all the rights freely granted to other races?

It's okay to be white.

America was founded for the posterity of the settlers — that was literally written into the Constitution. The Founding Fathers very clearly saw themselves as English, and that America was founded for the future descendants of England. It wasn't until the influx of Jews and Irish in the early 1900s that the original ideology behind the Constitution came under attack by what would later become progressivism. It was here that the great 'melting pot' myth was concocted, and even etched onto the Statue of Liberty. Foreigners had begun their grand project of stealing America from Americans.

This attack was enshrined in a new ideology of Civic Nationalism: the idea that America is a 'proposition nation', that anyone who subscribes to the ideals of the Constitution is therefore American, no matter their *actual* nationality. Civic Nationalism stands in contradiction to the most important point of the Constitution, written in the preamble: that the Constitution exists to protect the rights of the Founding Fathers' *posterity*. Their blood. Their nation.

Civic Nationalism was a fraud from the beginning. A mere toe in the door for the anti-white creed of Globalism. It is the official ideology of the cuckold, imposed upon him by his would-be conquerors.

I couldn't yet outline the evil of Globalism in these terms, but Roissy knew it and was fearless in putting his reputation and audience on the line to rail against the "Globohomo Alliance." It took him a while, toying with and then discarding different formulations, such as the original term of "The Cathedral" to describe what we now call "The Narrative." Reading it, I knew he'd scored a bullseye. The West was being over-run by an evil alliance of psychopathic anti-white globalists and most of the victim populations were completely in the thrall of Fake News propaganda.

The Seduction Community didn't like Roissy's change of direction. They were still heavily propagandised and still choking on the intersexual red pill. The racial red pill was one pill too many for them. Not only that, but I'd come to realise the Community was at least 50% about brown and black men chasing white women. It was verboten to mention, but I'd seen it. In London, the large Saturday Sarge weekly meet-up was three-quarters Indian. Anything racial on the RooshV forum was howled down, as I'd personally experienced.

The ethnic diversity of the Community and its de-facto promotion of miscegenation put me in a bind. I felt absolutely zero loyalty towards the enemy tribes invading my homelands and shagging our women. Helping such invaders is tantamount to treason. I hold no animosity towards brown and black men per se. So long as they stay in their own countries, that is. Should the globalist attack be repelled and Europe be once more in the control of Europeans, I was sure my passions would subside and I'd no longer fantasise about firebombing mosques or gunning down border jumpers. But until then, we were at war. It was an undeclared war and not only was my side not even fighting, but most of it was welcoming the invaders and virtue-signalled their "anti-racism."

I sided with Roissy. My blog readers didn't like that. Fuck them. I have no time for traitors.

Thus I felt estranged from the Community of which I'd been a part. I despised all the mewling lard-asses moaning that hot women wouldn't have sex with them. I despised the pay-for-play "lifestyle gamers" who tried to hide their whoremongering behind a veneer of Game. I despised the talking shop of theory from men lacking the basic masculine drive to cold approach.

I suppose you could say I despised a lot. Some of that was projection, and I didn't know how much. So, I'd been mostly avoiding the blogs and trying to have as little to do with the Community as possible. As far as I was concerned, my perfect customer was someone who bought all of my products and then never talked to me. This revulsion was a class apart from my previous temporary sabbaticals away from daygame. Previous revulsions were brought on by sheer fatigue, usually at the end of a hard year chasing skirt. This time was different. I was revolting against an ideology I'd shared and a group I'd identified with.

Naturally, my Twitter became unusually active. It was an easy way to vent my frustration and to throw out half-formed ideas I hadn't yet fully worked through.

On the 11th, I flew to Prague again to spend three nights before flying on to Belgrade. My room was a shitbox up near the museum at the top of Wencelas street. Usually, I rented a full apartment but this time I had only a private room. Ivanna came over two nights and we rolled around in bed but both times encountered the usual issue: she wanted sex but locked up as soon as my dick was out. I'd grown resigned to this so it didn't bother me. I enjoyed her company and never tired of pawing at her buxom body.

I did only a handful of sets in Prague, not really seeing the point of rousing myself for such a short trip. One approach went very well. The girl was called Dominika and she was a performing musician and keen rock climber. She was slim and toned with a kooky vibe that I first thought beatnik but she later explained that she was a practising Buddhist. The street approach was short, on the first day, and the next evening we went for a date.

Predictably, I took her to Batalion. We had a drink upstairs, then another in the basement.

It went smoothly and Dominika was entirely poised throughout. That disconcerted me a little. Not because I doubted myself or my chances, but rather because I simply couldn't get a read on her. I knew she liked me and would be comfortable with sex, but I didn't know why, when, or how. We made out plenty and I found her engaging company. I liked her a lot.

"We won't have sex tonight," she said, after the second drink. Rather than fashion a PUA-type reply, I figured directness would work best.

"Why is that?"

"I like you but it's the first date and I haven't made up my mind."

"Okay, let me know when you do."

We had another drink, kissed more, and said goodbye at Mustek station. I'd thoroughly enjoyed it. Ivanna came over afterwards so I still got to roll around the bed with my face buried in a pair of ample breasts.

My stay in Belgrade was scheduled for ten days but the moment I stepped off the plane I knew daygame was beyond me. Perhaps I'd manage to force out a couple of sets, but getting them done would be as difficult as deporting an ISIS terrorist from a Labour district. The landlord at my favourite Studentski Park apartment gave me a nice cash deal and I resolved to spend my time eating at Hot Spot Cafe across the road and then banging whichever regulars would have me.

Vesna, Milena, Marijana, Sofija, and Maya all obliged, although the latter was on her period so I had to satisfy myself with fumbling around with her massive tits. I did less than a half-dozen approaches, one of which was a bounce-back of a scroaty little girl who warned me her boyfriend, a name gangster, was in prison. Having her man banged up must've left her frustrated because she came ever so close to letting me rattle her before deciding better of it.

It wasn't a memorable trip. Aside from my regulars, there was a single highlight. I'd maintained a text chat with Petra, a tall brunette I'd had a kiss-free date with in July. She was a dead-ringer for Milena, and thus matched my archetype of a perfect woman. I'd come to think of her as a replacement, in an odd sort of way. Milena was possibly my all-time favourite girl that I'd met in my entire life. It was hard to say exactly, as I fondly remembered half a dozen girls who had each possessed a wonderful combination of attractive characteristics. But, in terms of raw beauty, Milena was my favourite. She had the sultry Sofia Loren type face, long black hair, and the tall curvy "greyhound" figure I loved. The only problem was Milena had put on weight in the three years since we'd met, in addition to getting a little older. Petra looked just like her but was three years younger and (now) eight kilos lighter.

Petra came out for a second date, meeting me at Republic Square. Her suspicions of me hadn't dissolved any which, frankly, I considered a good thing. If she could see through my bullshit it made me respect her more. We walked down into Dorcel and the Das Boot pub, sitting in the same seats I'd shared with Mina on my previous trip. The date went great. Petra was smart, spoke good English, and had precisely the thoughtful and reserved introvert manner that gets me thinking of rings and wedding dresses. She rebuffed my first few kiss attempts but finally succumbed.

I tried taking her home but she wasn't having it.

Nonetheless, if heaven sent down an angel to observe my sleeping face that night, he would've seen a broad smile of satisfaction. I truly felt caught between two life paths. On the one hand was the freebooting adventuring casual sexing swathe I attempted to cut across Central Europe. On the other, a growing sense that perhaps I'd banged enough women and I should be filtering for the right lady with whom to build something serious. I wasn't yet ready for monogamy and considered the West in terminal decline, but my subconscious had begun to show flashes of interest in that settled life.

I returned to Prague on the 25th feeling over-sexed, on account of my Belgrade regulars. That too sapped me of motivation to approach. Fortunately, I didn't need to. Dominika had agreed to a second date.

We met outside New Yorker and walked towards the river. Earlier in the year, Tom had recommended a bar called *Al Capone*, tucked in a back street a five minute walk from Na Prikope. So far, I'd considered its logistics unfavourable and steered my dates elsewhere. This time, I felt more secure in having a second date with a girl I'd already kissed, and my apartment was in that direction too, up a steep hill almost directly south from Al Capone.

Dominika was dressed up, with a slimline leather biker jacket, black tights, and black t-shirt. On another girl, I'd have expected to see associated tattoos, piercings, and sexually transmitted diseases. With Dominika, it was simply her unassuming preference in ladies fashion. She took her health and wellness seriously. We kissed lightly and struck off to the bar.

It was everything Tom had advertised it as. A small front room greeted us on entrance, lit both inside by electricity and outside from the sun through large windows. We carried on up a small stair into a back room that was considerably more sleazy and intimate. By that I mean perfect for a date.

The room was barely big enough to house a pool table and still leave sufficient clearance for the cues, but fortunately there was no such table. Slatted wooden benches lined each wall and small tables were evenly distributed, with associated chairs. We took one of the corners, sitting at the angle on benches. I figured that would make my projected kissing and prodding easier. There were a few other couples having quiet drinks. I loved the atmosphere. It was the perfect balance of comfort and sleaze, just like Chapeau Rouge and Batalion. Strained though my relationship was with Tom, I felt I ought to tip my hat to him. He always did have a nose for good date venues.

The date was a straight line towards sex, the only concern being to move at the correct speed. Then another concern popped up. Ivanna messaged me.

"Nicholas. What are you doing?"

I threw Dominika an excuse for me to go to the bar, so I could reply, ten minutes later.

"I'm with friends. You?"

"I'm free. Shall I come over?"

There are precious few times in a man's life when he dissuades a buxom Serbian teenager from inviting herself to his apartment at night. This was one of them.

"I'm a bit busy. We are drinking. I'm getting smashed."

"That's okay. I want to see you."

"I'll be steaming drunk. Smelly breath, farting, rude. You won't like me."

"You are so funny. So, I can come?"

"I'll try to rape you. Beware!"

"That's okay. What time?"

Suddenly I didn't want to dissuade her. Ivanna was still a virgin and there remained a slim chance for me to correct that particular karmic imbalance of hers. Frantically, I future-projected likely scenarios with Dominika, depending on how she received the soon-to-begin escalation. I still didn't have enough information to construct a reliable timeline. It was better than even odds I'd bang the rock-climbing Czech, but as to precisely *when*? No idea. And what if she wanted to stay overnight?

"Okay, let's meet. I'll message you in an hour. I need to arrange with my friends," I told Ivanna.

I returned from the bar carrying two beers. We chatted, kissed, and talked airily about things that didn't matter. A change came over Dominika's demeanour, the perceptible signs of a window of opportunity being opened. It was expressed through her giggles, flashing looks, and occasional pawing at my forearm when emphasising a point. Such signals didn't escape my attention. I felt a sudden closeness, like the world around us blurring and fading away.

"I like these," I said, squeezing her thighs. "Very strong and limber. I imagine you're flexible."

"You imagine, do you?"

"I can't tell you what I'm imagining right now. It would scandalize you."

"Try me."

"You asked for it. I have a very clear image in my mind, right now, right here." I tapped a finger against my forehead, where my mind's eye might be presumed to reside. "It involves you naked, underneath me. You nipples are hard and your stomach tight from tension. Your hair is loose." I saw her gasp slightly under the impact of the sexualisation. "Can you guess where, in this mental image, my dick is?"

"I think I know."
"Let's go."
"Okay."

We walked up the steep bank in comfortable silence. Dominika had known before leaving her apartment that we'd be banging, so the date was no more than a final rubber stamp. My apartment was on the third floor of an old Gothic building overlooking a crossroads. At this time of night, around 9pm, the streets were almost deserted. We took the elevator up and went through the usual formalities to set the mood. Dominika sat on my bed with a smile on her face. She was looking forward to this.

I made excuses to visit the bathroom and checked my phone. Ivanna had left a string of messages. They were far from insistent — she was far too placid to hassle me — but the intimation was clear: she was killing time until I let her visit.

"I'll be free at 11pm," I said, texting her my address.
"Okay."

Seduction is easy when a girl is already committed to sex. Dominika and I kissed and I patiently escalated. I took my dick out and she sucked me off, then I stripped her naked and commenced the evening's rattling. Dominika's body was everything I'd hoped it would be. She wasn't especially gifted in any department but everything was present, accounted for, and immaculately conserved. Her breasts wouldn't draw stares in a bar but were ample for the hand and pleasantly firm. Her ass was similarly well-shaped for my hands and her tight stomach and limber legs gave everything a sense of proportion that would please an anatomist.

Would it surprise you if I said I enjoyed fucking her?

That's perhaps the greatest boon of cold approach: you only ever open girls you're sufficiently attracted to for them to leap out at you from the crowd. A daygamer isn't limited to whatever frumps are in his office, or the slags on Tinder. Thus when you do finally nail one — and my oh my, does it feel like you *earned* it — she's obviously a bird you're keen to bang.

QED.

Dominika gave it a good go. She was indeed limber, so I could wrap her up in contortions that might've injured a lesser girl. Her rock-climber's ass withstood a fantastic pounding, though she repelled all my attempts to slip discreetly into her brown-eye.

Remembering the experience in Warsaw with the unnamed blonde, I took Dominika out to the balcony and had her cling to the railing while I drilled her from behind. I couldn't help checking my watch. It was half-past ten. As eye-poppingly sexy as it was to look at Dominika's firm figure bouncing around in front of me, my eyes couldn't help but scan the streets. Several times I thought I saw Ivanna approach the crossroads, but they were false alarms.

Why was I doing this? There was no need to take such risks, either of cutting the scheduling so fine, or of brazenly displaying Dominika naked on my balcony with Ivanna due at any moment. Clearly, I was thrill-seeking. I brought Dominika back into the bedroom so that she could suck me off and swallow my cum.

We showered.

"I should go," she said. I didn't enquire as to her reasoning.

"Okay. Let's talk tomorrow."

I kissed her goodbye at the street door and took the elevator back upstairs. My phone was ringing. It was Ivanna.

"I think I'm here."

"Wait. I'll go to my balcony and look outside."

I did so. Dominika was walking down the hill to my left, the nearest spoke from the crossroad. At the opposite side, on a corner, I could see Ivanna. She was only a small speck in the distance but her big hair, wide hips, and colourful tights were a giveaway.

"Wave your hand," I said. She waved. "Right, I see you. Walk straight ahead across the crossroad. I'll see you at the other side in two minutes."

I should've been relieved at the narrowness of my escape. Instead, I was disappointed it hadn't been even narrower. I'd have preferred if Dominika had met Ivanna at the door and I'd needed to bluff my way out of it.

Ivanna gave me a kiss and followed me upstairs.

It was after eleven and I was feeling the pace from a long evening. Ivanna stripped naked and cuddled up next to me in bed. I wondered if the room smelled of sex. I'd left the balcony window wide open and pre-emptively scanned for floor for tell-tale evidence of another lady's presence. Still, I'm a man, and men can't spot such things like a woman will. I'd been mindful to bang Dominika over rather than under the duvet, rightly assuming Ivanna would spend the night and fearing she'd detect wet patches on the sheets.

My mind was all over the place. I was ecstatic about notching Dominika because every moment of the experience had been great, and I liked her a lot. I was also excited at the prospect of getting two notches in under an hour. Ivanna was amorous and keen to lose her virginity. Already, she rubbed up against me, though she remained too shy to grab my dick without my ordering it.

"Did you have a good night?"

"Yes, I was out with university friends," she said. "I'm a little drunk."

"And a little horny, it seems."

"Yes," she replied, then convulsed in laughter like she'd said the rudest thing in the world. That was something I liked about her. She was exceptionally traditional and demure.

We made out and she showed uncharacteristic pro-activity in wrapping herself around me.

"Hang on. I'm supposed to be raping you, not the other way around!"

She giggled again and straddled me. She re-adjusted herself so that her pussy was rubbing against my dick, like dry humping but without the interfering clothes. I put my hands on her hips and let her take the initiative. Slowly at first, she began grinding back and forwards along the length of my dick. Her hands pressed down onto my chest for balance, pushing her breasts into an ample cleavage. Her nipples hardened as she increased the pace.

"Oh, this is nice," she moaned, continuing a back-and-forwards rocking motion.

I slapped her ass a few times. Grabbed her breasts. It seemed wise to let her continue as far as she could take it. The times I'd taken the initiative she couldn't relax sufficiently for sex to be physically possible. More grinding and moaning ensued. It wasn't at all unpleasant. She throbbed a little and I wondered if she'd come. I lifted my hips a little and, as she raised her butt up a little to match, I took hold of my dick to point it upwards to glory.

She tried to sit down onto it, but it wouldn't go in.

"Try again," I said.

She reached behind her, took hold of my dick, and tried to jam it into her pussy. It was only now that I realised she wasn't at all wet. Hard nipples yes, but no tell-tale wetness dripping onto me.

"It won't go in," she said, frustration on her face. "I want to have sex."

"Believe me, I do too." That was an understatement. We'd spent almost a year trying to fit my dick inside her and every time she was jammed up, tight and dry.

"Try grinding again."

She did, but it didn't help. We spent another fifteen minutes trying variations under my initiative. Each attempt ended the same way: after surmounting the physical difficulty of locating and opening her vagina (her body wasn't responding, so it was locked down), the moment I pressed my dick into her she recoiled in pain. It was tough just getting a finger in there.

"I'm sorry," she said. "I really do want to sleep with you."

We did sleep together, but in the lesser sense of the term. I wasn't so disappointed, because I'd expected it, and I had Dominika to thank for relieving my blue balls.

I flew home on the 28th.

Eddie, Tom and I had floated ideas for a year-end seminar in London and we'd recently reached agreement. The potential for a needless spat between coaches, earlier in the year, had been completely defused. I'd travelled to Riga and Belgrade with Eddie, and Tom had just completed a week in Almati, Kazakhstan with him. Win-win indeed.

"We need a name for the seminar," Tom said to me.

"I like the idea of pushing the outsiders angle. We are showing up in foreign cities and secretly stealing the women. It reminds me of the biker gangs in the TV show *Sons Of Anarchy*. It's like we are outlaws. A small tribe of them."

"I like it."

"How about that, then? Shall I knock a logo up?"

And thus *Outlaw Daygame* was born. It was to be a one-day speaking event in Covent Garden. Eddie had already found a venue. The three of us would speak, along with Richard. The name encapsulated how I felt: an outlaw. I was unmoored from regular society. I was a wandering player. An outcast.

All I was good for was shagging women.

Or, in Ivanna's case, not shagging them.

Chapter 37
CHISINAU

"**B**ig bro! When are we having the next holiday?"

"I don't want to think about it. I only just got back to Newcastle. I'm knackered. Can't take any more game."

By that I mean the chasing girls variant of game. With the psychopathic murderer simulator variant called *video* games I was, by contrast, having a whale of a time. At that moment I was lying on my bed, atop a faux-fur duvet cover, with my usual monster feet slippers. A large 48" television was wall-mounted at the foot of the bed and on it ran *Mad Max*, a post-apocalyptic open world game based on the reboot of the famous movie franchise of the same name. I was pleasantly occupied in scoping out a dilapidated old shack, rummaging around the bins for discarded dog food, and for brackish water with which to slake my thirst. In that sense, it was little different to my first night in Kiev a month earlier.

"We should go to Moldova. Beckster says it's a hidden goldmine for hot girls," Kenan persisted.

"If Beckster told me it was sunny outside I'd take my umbrella."

"Come on, man. You were just saying in Kiev how you needed new locations to keep your interest in daygame."

"Okay, you're convincing me. What have you got in mind?"

"I can take a long weekend off work, from the 8th." That was less than a week away.

I told Kenan I'd scope out flights and accommodation then give him a firm answer. Prices were favourable and I was heartened that Moldova was on the Ukrainian border and an easy hop to Kiev, which I'd grown to like. Little Elita messaged me every day on Facebook, and Justine too seemed keen. Moldova is the poorest country in Europe but even if it was absolute shitsville, it was halfway to the promised land of nubile, willing teenagers that is Kiev.

"Right I'm in."

That's how I came to be stepping off the plane in Chisinau International Aeroport, a modern airy building that seemed far too nice for the country it served. Riding the bus downtown disabused me of any notion that Moldova was a rising economy. It was like a gypsy favela without the gypsies. On the plus side, everything was dirt cheap. I quartered in a beautiful old apartment one street behind what was evidently the town centre. I wasn't sure at first that it was the centre, because it wasn't much busier than Gateshead High Street, but I spotted a McDonald's next to two side-by-side parks. There were big government offices and a small cathedral in one park, and a monument to Stephen The Great in another.

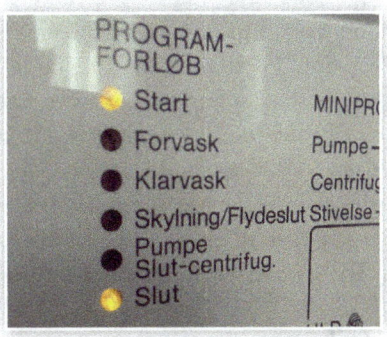

At least the washing machine bode well

I figured if a dude named Stephen is the greatest in your country's history, you've probably got a shit country.

Still, could've been worse. It could've been Rio.

My apartment was furnished like an ambassador's reception, missing only the trays of Ferrero Rocher chocolates. Thick sliding doors opened onto the lounge, which had two brown chesterfield sofas, a bookcase full of crusty old tomes, and a writing desk of the type a dictator uses to sign death warrants. I wanted to recline in the swivel chair, put my feet up, and light a fat cigar.

"I'm here, bro," messaged Kenan. He always stayed in five star hotels. His wasn't far away.

Both of us had arrived early so we went walkabout, scoping out the daygame potential. It didn't strike me very favourably.

"Are you sure this is the main street?" I asked. "It feels like one of the connecting streets between the good streets in Kiev. The kind that you hurry through to get to where the good stuff is."

"I checked forums and asked around. This is the centre."

Daygamers visualise streets in terms of footfall and flow, much like how an urban planner might. Imagine one of those city-planning video games such as *Sim City*. The menus offer options to redraw the screen according to key attributes. For example, click the "power" icon and all the buildings and people are whited out and different colour overlays identify which buildings and zones have adequate or insufficient electricity. That's how we daygamers view the streets. All we see are sources of hot-girl inflow, choke points, fields of view, and fishing spots on key junctions.

In the case of Chisinau the hub was clearly the McDonald's, due to both its prime location and it being the hip place for our target demographic to hang out. Further down the same street were a small number of stores but within a hundred metres they petered out into the occasional clutch of mobile phone accessory stores, old-women shoe shops, and many, many gambling joints. It was a far cry from the Zara, H&M, and Mango of Warsaw's main shopping street. At the other side of McDonald's the road turned downhill to a few kebab takeaways and a small ratty mall. The two parks looked like they'd have potential in sunny weather.

"This looks a bit shit," I said.

"Let's try, all the same."

The girls looked exactly as you'd expect based on viewing Moldova on a map: a cross between Romanian and Ukrainian. It's a pleasant mix because I like the dark colouring and sultry aspect of Romanians and also the legginess of Slavs. Sadly, though the type suited me the general quality did not. Most girls looked like the Macedonian hookers who mill around Burger King in Prague at night. They had that ratty steal-your-smartphone-while-you-shower look about them.

Kenan and I each got a few phone numbers and the girls seemed quite thrilled to speak to us, the few who understood English, though in every case their eyes darted around nervously as if expecting us to be setting them up for a kidnapping and life of sex slavery in Albania.

Girl Junkie

Our new town vibe wore off quickly. There simply weren't enough sets to maintain momentum.

Some of the birds were hot

"Let's eat, bro."

"Where?"

"I don't know."

That's when we found out Chisinau doesn't have any nice restaurants. We'd spied a couple of shopping malls further out but they were so far away as to seem impractical for daygame. Additionally, we hadn't found any Metro or bus stops nearby. The malls had big car parks half-full with battered old bangers tied together with duct tape and glue. If any girls were inside the mall, they'd have been driven there, which didn't bode well for them being either single or up for it.

"There's a cigar and whiskey club by my hotel. Let's go there," said Kenan.

There was a brass plate of the club name by the door and a doorman in livery. He gave us the once-over before admittance, only stepping to one side once he realised we were tourists. A high-class hotel and restaurant occupied most of the building but by going through a door to our left we entered the large single-room of our destination. It was the expected mix of leather sofas, smoking chairs, tuxedo-wearing bar staff, and American sports playing silently on the televisions mounted above the book cases.

Good enough. We felt sophisticated. It was an oasis of cleanliness in a desert of scroats.

Sophisticated

We smoked cigars, drank whiskey, and chatted. At midnight, we each went our separate ways to ruminate upon the skirt-chasing potential of Chisinau.

Overnight, I heard a storm breaking. Thunder disrupted my sleep and heavy rains battered the windows. Waking the next day, I pulled the curtains aside in trepidation. It was still raining. Kenan was waiting for me inside McDonald's, which was almost empty at lunch time. The collar of his expensive wool coat was still pulled up and his chin dug in. He wore half of Moldova's gross domestic product on his person.

"Wet!"

"Yes. Fucked."

There were breaks in the rain in which we valiantly tried to work the streets. It was miserable work but we rustled up a few more phone numbers. I had an excellent set with a beautifully sultry girl dressed to the nines in brand name fashion. She was on her way into a nail salon. We swapped numbers.

The sun came out late afternoon and we were able to enjoy a walk around the park and carry out a reconnaissance further out of town, in the vain hope we'd simply settled in the wrong area. That effort was disappointing. There was no doubt about it. We were in the centre and Chisinau really was that shit.

"We can go nightclubbing. It's Saturday and I checked the internet. I found the name of the best club. I'll get a table," offered my Turkish friend.

"My night game is shit. I'll join you, of course, but don't expect me to be much use."

"No problems big bro. It's my treat."

That evening we visited a tiny bar district on the far side of the park, only ten minutes walk from the McDonald's. It had a few long open-air bars with transparent vinyl "windows" rolled down to the floor to keep the heat in and rain out. Tucked into the corner of this horseshoe-shaped complex was the entry to a basement nightclub.

Kenan signed us in and a lady took us to a small round table by the stage. It was a small club, such that I wondered if we hadn't made a mistake and the main room must be elsewhere. At that moment, technicians were setting up amplifiers and instruments for an impending live performance. We were on the left side of a narrow dance floor and half a dozen similar VIP tables lined each side, and then at the opposite end, behind us, was a raised standing area with the bar.

The club was half full, which translated into about fifty people. It was a youngish crowd. Of the VIP patrons, Kenan and I were the only two who didn't look like gangsters.

"I'm not sure we should be cold approaching in here," I said. "The only hot girls are milling around with the tough guys. I wouldn't want to get on the wrong side of them."

"Don't worry about it," he replied, patting my shoulder confidentially. "I know how to work a club. You'll see."

He did try, getting into a few sets that were tolerably receptive. However, he was only beginning to build momentum when the live band came on and drowned out all hope of talking. I became sullen and miserable because we couldn't talk at all. I felt like I was trapped in the 1980s Soviet Union, after all the hot girls had been shipped off to a Siberian gulag.

I felt guilty, being such miserable company when Kenan had splashed a considerable amount of cash setting us up as VIPs.

"Sorry mate. I'm just not in a good mood. I don't mean to put a downer on the evening. I feel terrible. Completely exhausted."

"That's okay. We'll hang out. I've ordered a bottle of Johnnie Walker, it's on me. Have fun and we'll do daygame tomorrow."

As if things hadn't started badly enough, they got worse on Sunday. It was pouring with rain again. Kenan and I bought umbrellas and stood outside McDonald's — the one place with any foot traffic at all — and tried our best to open sets. Our feet were wet through and a cold wind whipped my face. Kenan's phone rang and he paced apprehensively for ten minutes while I looked out at an empty pavement. Heavy drops of rain hammered off the ground like fifty calibre bullets. He hung up, looking dejected.

"That was my father. I need to fly home tonight. Sorry, bro."

Positively overflowing with gash

Kenan had been scheduled for two more days. This kind of upset happened frequently and I understood it was the nature of his business responsibilities.

"I must have a good set. I'll stay here till I get one."

We spent two hours daygaming during the storm. It was madness, really. My limbs shivered, my teeth chattered, and my toes squelched in my socks each time I took a step. Finally, Kenan took his leave so as to pack and catch his flight.

I stayed out another hour, by myself. I must've looked a sorry state.

On the positive side, the hot rich girl had agreed to a date that evening. I returned home to shower, have a lie down, and change into dry clothes. We met at the McDonald's and she showed me to a nice rock'n'roll basement bar nearby. It was quiet but a few patrons laughed and drank, giving it some life.

Our conversation was difficult and I was forced to resort to Google Translate. She obviously liked me but was far from gagging for it. An hour in she artfully refused my kiss, and then again an hour after that. It was getting late and she took her taxi home. I went back to my ambassador's lounge and collapsed on the sofa. My shivering was now uncontrollable and my head ached. Finally, it dawned on me that I'd become ill. I'd overdone it obsessively pounding the streets in the rain and now I'd caught the 'flu. What a miserable evening! I must endure three more nights in town before flying to Kiev.

It was awful.

All alone in a shithole city, laid up with 'flu, and a storm raging outside.

I wished I was in Kiev but as it was I was barely capable of getting to my own bathroom unaided. My few leads were lukewarm, but even had my phone been blowing up with interest that may have been worse as I was physically unable to date. The same logic applied to the streets: was it unlucky that the streets were undaygameable in the rain, or lucky because had they been rammed with hot-pants clad slags, I'd have gone out of my mind being chained to the apartment?

Shitsville.

Facing no other option, I lay on the sofa, watched YouTube, and felt sorry for myself.

My fever broke on the last night and I felt considerably refreshed. I'd have been foolhardy to run outside for gutter-game but at least I'd stopped sweating and sneezing. My eyes could focus. It was during this rebound that the girl I'd dated began messaging.

It was 10pm and she was horny.

First she sent a speculative "hi." I replied. She transitioned towards lots of smiley faces and kisses. Having nothing to lose, I suggested a date.

"No, I'm busy. It's too cold."

I didn't reply. Why bother? She'd given me a firm no.

Half an hour later she tapped me up again, sending a photo of her sitting on the bed in her dressing gown, her calves exposed provocatively.

"Nice. More," I replied.

I got more. Over the next fifteen minutes she took photos in increasingly racy poses and her dressing gown was replaced first by a negligible negligée and finally her original birthday suit. Her face was obscured by her hair or cropped out of frame. Her tits and ass, however, were not.

It seemed clear this girl was teasing me, but who knows how these gypsy half-breeds really think. I invited her over. She was a solid eight, after all.

"Come here. Get a taxi."

"Why do I come?"

"So I can kiss you."

"And?"

"And touch you."

That earned me more smiley faces and another ass photo. She seemed to be warming herself up and for ten minutes of frenetic texting she appeared to be on the verge of jumping into a cab. Then she danced away from the subject, suggesting it was all just a coquettish game. I wasn't too fussed. Of course I'd have loved to bang her, but in such debilitated state, I'd have likely done myself an injury.

The next morning I woke up feeling close to full health. In relative terms, bouncing off such a sustained low point, I felt fantastic, as if I'd snorted ten lines of coke off a stripper's ass. I felt ready for Kiev. In fact, more than ready. I was going to tear the town apart.

Girl Junkie

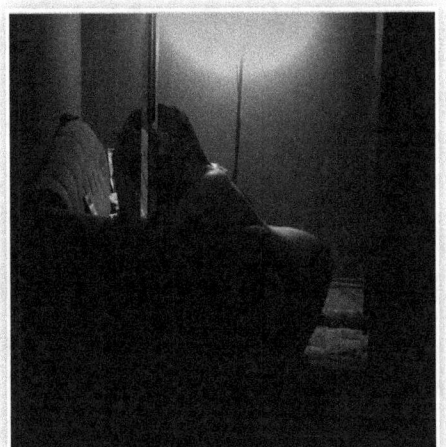

Chapter 38
VAMPISH

I had three weeks booked in Kiev and was bloody well going to take advantage of it. You could've dug a moat around Khreshchatyk, filled it with alligators, and smeared me with pork dripping but *fuck you all* I'd still swim across to get at those high-heeled slags. Do you remember the famous Queen song about cocaine, *Don't Stop Me Now*, where Freddie tells us he's a rocket ship on the way to Mars, on collision course, out of control?

Yeah that one.

Fuck Freddie the faggot and his flaming fireworks to afar. Nick bastard Krauser was going supersonic, pour me a gin and tonic, I feel positively demonic. Kiev was gonna get raped, along with all the girls in it.

The Krauser Train had arrived. Choo! Choo!

Ray and Adrian had also flown in so we got cracking, often walking around as a trio. The weather turned rather blustery but there was no lack of street talent. Something had caused my vibe to explode, probably the snap-back from several days bed-ridden in Chisinau, coupled with my positive expectations of Kiev, and the eager anticipation of rattling little Elita some more.

The week that followed was unquestionably the best street game I've ever done.

Imagine you've just endured a few years working in the smog-ridden conditions of early-twentieth century London (and these pea-soupers continued well after the war too). Every morning upon waking you toss your alarm clock across the room, rise up to sit on the edge of your bed and begin coughing up phlegm. You shuffle across the linoleum floor into the shower

Girl Junkie

and let the hot water take some of the edge off your early start. A glass of orange juice and a freshly-brewed coffee temporarily clear your persistent headache and you dress for work.

Closing the heavy wooden front door you step onto the street and breath in the damp air. Is it mist or smog that softens those distant buildings? It's time to trudge to the Underground station and jostle through the crowd onto a rickety carriage, swapping bacteria with the other passengers. By lunchtime you scurry out because today you've got an appointment with your physician and the boss has let you take an afternoon's leave. Sitting in the waiting room you see crying babies softly bounced on their mother's knees, and an old couple patiently staring at the various information leaflets pinned onto the noticeboard by Reception. The nurse calls you in and after fifteen minute's tapping your chest, taking your blood pressure and shining a light into your ears and mouth, the physician offers his professional advice.

"You've got a developing case of Chodular Fever. It's not far gone but I imagine you've already had trouble sleeping, frequent bouts of irritability, and unexplained periods of low mental function" he says.

Yes, you recognise the symptoms. You thought this was just a normal part of ageing in the modern world. The physician pulls his notepad across and begins scribbling in illegible script.

"I'm going to recommend you take a Euro Jaunt," he says, handing you a prescription.

This is how my mind wandered on the streets of Kiev.

It was a blustery day so Ray, Adrian and I had our jackets zipped up and woolly hats firmly set on our heads. As we walked through a park in front of Shevchenko university a thought occurred to me: *this is so pleasant.* So much so that I could imagine a doctor recommending Kiev daygame as a convalescence holiday, as alluded to above. We stopped at one of the many specialist coffee carts and ordered cappuccinos. While I made small talk with the young barista, Ray told me he'd recently been to New York. I let my eyes wander to the long rows of tall trees covered in yellow autumn leaves. Adrian was at another coffee cart a few metres away chatting to a young university student he'd just stopped.

We took our coffees and walked back through the park to a small square where retired old men in flat caps played chess on specially-installed tables, their dozens of quiet conversations melding together into a gentle buzz.

It was nice to see the elderly getting out of their apartments and socialising around a shared passion — I mean the men, not Adrian and I.

It was almost 3pm. I was able to pick a girl out of the rush streaming from the nearby Metro station to the university, hurrying to lectures. I don't remember if I got her number. I checked my pedometer and we'd already logged 8km walking and it would reach 15km by the end of the evening by which time the three of us were sitting in a quaint restaurant styled like a 1960s Parisian cafe, working our way through bowls of the local borsch soup.

We raised a toast to The Good Life.

The sheer joy of daygaming reminded me of the advice physicians would give back in the late-19th century onwards to city dwellers who were getting run down by city life. Britain had a whole network of spa towns, often in the mountains or by the seaside, where you could book in for a fortnight and let the worries of life fall from your shoulders. Fresh sea air, sunshine, walking, resting, sleeping, and of course sipping coffee with friends as you watch the world go by. Perhaps even meet a few like-minded souls.

My mind turned over, making further leaps of logic.

I thought back to the hit Nintendo DS game in Japan, *Brain Training*. The (pseudo)-scientific rationale trumpeted in the game's marketing was that solving the video game's puzzles would keep your brain ticking over and maintain cognitive function longer into old age. Thus, the games activities were all chopped down into short exercises that could be rattled off on the train to work or on short coffee breaks. The popular London equivalent of *Brain Training* was to take a sudoku or logic problems workbook with you on your commute.

Daygame is convalescence and brain-training combined.

What did my typical Euro Jaunt involve? How did it relate to convalescence?

The first thing is to get out of Dodge and roll up in a new foreign town full of its own local quirks and charms. Chisinau had disappointed but Kiev most certainly had not. Almost unfailingly, Euro Old Towns have fresher air than London and a slower pace of life. There is none of the crush that the average working Londoner endures each and every weekday. Once I've set my bags down and settled into a daily pattern it goes thus:

Wake up whenever I damn well please, after my body has declared itself fully rested. I suffer none of the persistent sleep deprivation that is the baseline state for a city worker. Open my front door and I'm immediately in the mix without any kind of commute. I walk where I want under my own steam without contending with ticket machines, virus-bearing commuters, immigrant jihadis, or delayed trains. Roll up at my favourite cafe a few hundred metres away and work my way through a (very) late breakfast of orange juice, coffee and pasta. At some point my friends arrive and our morning routines converge.

Once we feel like it, we take a walk. Chat, enjoy the atmosphere of the streets, and pick off girls as and when we feel like it.

Daygame makes the taste of freedom almost *tangible*, like every breath of air and every step forwards contains a piece of it. Daygame had become so pleasant for me. By the end of the day Ray, Adrian and I had been in the open air for hours, walked many kilometres, and done an extended cardio routine without even noticing. Often my feet ached and it wouldn't be until I checked my pedometer that I'd realise I'd completed another urban hike. This is the kind of patient low-intensity exercise that city slickers will drive into the countryside once a month to obtain. My legs felt supple and strong. My posture was good because the whole time I was keenly aware of it, seeking to project myself positively to girls. It's the opposite of being chained to a cubicle in an artificially-lit office with the nearest window ten metres away.

That explains the convalescence effect of daygame, but how about the brain training?

Imagine doing twenty engaging and fascinating crossword puzzles over a few hours. That's how your brain is working when doing twenty sets with girls you are trying to poke. You're trying to calibrate her reactions, engage your creative juices, and logically work through a model. Then, in the time between sets, you can comfortably flip into a meditative state of mindfulness.

Twenty times over a few hours.

A fun — but disciplined — session of daygame leaves you mentally drained like a hard gym workout can. When you raise the glass of your first beer to toast your friends, you've earned it. Your brain wants rest. I sometimes return from a Euro Jaunt feeling like a boxer the day before a big fight. My body and mind are dialled-in and respond with lightning speed. Gone is any trace of slothfulness, inertia or lack of focus.

A man's mindset regarding daygame sets the frame for his experience of it.

It's a common joke among the physically fit that carrying your shopping home is "training". Walking up the stairs because the escalator is broken is "training". We laugh because it's true, if facile. The lifestyle of convenience is a fool's errand. A man must engage his body and his mind on a daily basis to remain alert and alive. We grow by pushing against resistance. Daygame is not about lying on the sofa right-swiping Tinder. It's not about pouring toxins down your throat in a noisy smoky bar full of braying jackasses. It's not about outlasting the other chodes at 5am in a nightclub.

Getting harder to hide the fat belly

Once you've overcome the anxiety of it, daygame is an intrinsically healthy activity. Just as small children don't realise that running around playing tag is training their lungs, muscles, coordination, and alertness, it's easy for us daygamers to forget that no matter what the day returns us in terms of phone numbers or dates, it always gives us convalescence and brain training.

It was with this bubbling positivity that I worked the streets of Kiev with Ray and Adrian. Something had clicked. The planets were in alignment. I was a rocket ship out of control. There was no stopping me. The blustery weather should've killed it at birth, like a New York City abortion doctor.

For a start, it was cold and rainy. The streets lacked that lets-just-hang-out-because-it's-fun-to-be-here vibe for the hot girls and the men who chase them. Most of the time we encountered girls hurrying to be somewhere, trying to keep their street time to a minimum. Gone were the summer days of girls sitting around on kerbs eating ice cream, gazing absently into space. It also meant that being on the streets took a little out of us because it was so cold.

You'd think that would translate into a shitty daygame trip, but no.

It was weird.

For some reason I'd accidentally sprayed on Pussy Catnip and my experience was like the fantasy promises of a men's deodorant advertisement. For the first five days in Kiev I was constantly checked out by girls. Any given day I'd get at least *thirty* of them, some of which were head-turning tongue-hanging-out mong looks from younger-hotter-tighter girls. Pretty much every set I opened hooked strongly and my phone rapidly filled up with girl's contact details. I thought to myself, "Jesus fucking Christ, I'm going to smash this town!"

Adrian and Ray were getting agitated being around this vortex of outlandish results. They were doing well themselves, judged by normal standards. However, it was like the biggest two bodybuilders in the gym showing up for a Mr Olympia competition and finding The Incredible Hulk waiting backstage. I was a black hole, sucking in all the vibe and all the attention. Ray found it especially funny, often laughing out loud at some of the reactions girls gave me.

I began counting my chickens, future-projecting all the notches I'd be getting when my numbers progressed into dates.

Alas, it was not to be. I was to get a lesson in the iron self-discipline of Ukrainian girls in sticking to their boyfriend script. Had Warsaw/Krakow metrics applied, I think I'd have gotten laid every single night of my trip. In actuality, I didn't get a sniff throughout the first week. Not even a bounce-back. Worse, Elita wasn't replying to my messages at all.

I was half-way to Pussy Paradise, which is the same as being nowhere near.

It was like being served a cup of tea without the milk and sugar. What's the point of that? Many thoughts flashed through my mind during the first week of the trip. Once the initial disbelief at my great reactions died down, I thought: *this is what it's like to be Steve Jabba, where literally half the girls in a town get wet just looking at you.* I could pick and choose my approaches according to who I liked best and who gave me the strongest come-on. There was no need for the hard discipline of cold approach when I could be so cavalier with girls' interest. *Why can't it always be like this?* I bemoaned. *It's so easy and so much fun.*

My brain worked overtime to figure out if there was a way to bottle my pre — and early-set magic. By the second week, when the flaking epidemic hit, I wondered if there was in fact any magic to bottle, or if it had all been fools gold. Girls' reactions were so extreme and so consistently positive that there was definitely *something* different going on.

What was driving it?

I'd gotten back into the gym and gained around eight pounds of muscle in 2015, but put on a fair bit of fat too. Whereas during the first Kiev trip in August with Eddie I had to wear t-shirts and shorts due to the heat, in October I could layer up with a leather jacket. So, I gained all the advantage of my increased size without any of the disadvantages of looking a bit thick around the middle. A girl's initial once-over to clock my body shape was now more favourable.

My fashion was back to my proven *Daygame Overkill* style: leather bike jacket, open shirt, t-shirt, accessories, jeans, leather boots, hat. It stood out against the local men. I literally didn't see anyone who dressed remotely like me. It's harder to differentiate yourself in summer clothes.

My vibe positively glowed. From the very first day I was in a great mood and the constant stream of good reactions and IOIs snowballed it. I felt extremely attractive, like walking into a nightclub knowing you're the best-looking man there. My cold approach game had been honed through five years of being sexually invisible in London right up until the moment I got in front of a girl and opened my mouth. It was nice to play the game on easy mode like a good-looking guy and my vibe responded, creating a virtuous spiral.

Both my face and body language were open and pure. I was congruent and disarming. Walking around feeling great, letting it radiate outwards, I felt like I'd been carefully cleaning and polishing the lens on my 'movie projector' for years and now it was time to spool the reels and see an image projected with perfect fidelity. I continued to follow the principles of my game, but I frequently abandoned the prescriptive model, following my trend for the year. I'd open girls by shouting at them from ten metres away: "Hey you! Miserable looking girl with the black coat. Stop!" (that was a catwalk model I instant dated, but she flaked). I'd open by pointing and not saying a word. Nothing mattered because I was in full flow and riffing off all the lessons I'd internalised.

Yet for all this, despite the unbelievable strength of my initial reactions, things dropped off sharply when it came to getting laid. I suffered a terrible flake epidemic. Why was that? Almost every girl replied to my feeler text but very few came out on dates. Frustratingly, many would keep up a fun flirty exchange, send me photos and then, when I sent the date invitation and they finally had to get off the fence, they literally didn't even reply. A few girls messaged me things like "I'm on Khreshatyk street now, let's meet!" and then when I replied "Ok, outside McDonalds in 15 minutes?" they ghosted me for several days.

Why on earth would they do that? It was maddening.

I was in Bizarro World where nothing meant the same as it would mean in any other city. Black was white, up was down, war was peace, and diversity was strength. At the end of the first week I changed apartment from a perfectly-located pad overlooking McDonald's to a ground floor place one street behind. It was still logistically great.

My first stroke of good luck came the same day I moved apartment. Adrian was off on a date. He'd had a more subdued opening week than myself, but his leads had been far stickier. He'd already rattled one girl. Ray and I were staking out the square outside the Metro, watching the street-dancers, Turk sex pests, and the girls. Joe Pesci was back, grinding it out. It felt almost good to see him, like he was the inverse to my Turk Nemesis in Prague.

A tall girl with thick tresses of raven hair flitted past me. That hair went all the way to her ass. The ass was tightly confined within dark red trousers. She had nice legs and high heels, but my mind was already made up at the hair and ass. I opened.

Her only response was to open her eyes wide, like I'd already put my dick in her ass.

"I'm Nick. You are pretty."

More of the eyes. Her lips parted now.

"I like this," I said, lifting up some of her hair. It felt reassuringly heavy in my hand.

Her eye went wider still. She was enjoying it. Finally she stammered some words in broken English and we had a parody of a conversation. I took her number and she went on inside the Metro station. Having gotten so used to flakes, I walked back to Ray dispirited despite the flush of feminine energy that had set my heart racing.

"How did it go?"

"Brilliant. She'll flake."

Katerina did not flake, thank God. We had a date the next evening.

She started out amenable, following me into a bar by the Metro and nodding and smiling at all the appropriate moments. Her facial expression is best described as *heated*. The poor girl was boiling in her love juices. If the Ukrainian army were to weaponise those juices they may develop an incendiary bomb to rival white phosphorus. We went next door into Porter's and kissed. It was only then that she became arsey.

"I don't like."

"Don't like what?"

"Don't like you."

"Okay."

Katerina turned petulant but it seemed to me an expression of her own conflicting emotions rather than a commentary on anything I was doing. Presumably it was the age-old conflict between her forebrain telling her to be a good girl, and her hindbrain trying to find an excuse to get fucked.

I gave her that excuse.

After the second drink I walked her back to my apartment. We didn't say a word. She followed me in, put her handbag on the table in the lounge, and sat on the sofa. Needless to say, I was very excited. Not just because she was very hot, but also because seven days of dashed hope had begun to wear on me. Finally I had a chance to cash in my chips.

I'd earned this.

I pulled Katerina to her feet and we kissed. She moaned and her eyes told the story, chapter and verse, illustrated in colour. We walked into my bedroom and lay down. Clothes flew off and we began fucking. She looked excellent naked. An objective observer would call her a low-eight. She had the head-turning *god-I-want-to-poke-that* quality which elevates an eight over a merely pretty seven. However, I couldn't quite see myself running around the bedroom in post-sex celebration with my shirt over my head Ravanelli-style. I'd be pleased, but not proud. So, not a "solid" eight.

Not that any of this matters. What did matter was her good tits, flat stomach, shapely legs, bubble butt, and outrageously good hair. Not until 2017 would I bang a girl with better hair. Even now I remember how it looked swirling and twisting around her body, the bed seemingly upholstered by the stuff. Anywhere I posted my hands for balance, I felt her hair underneath.

Sex was really good for ten minutes and then it got weird quickly.

Perhaps I'd been overdoing the dominance. I tend to smash girls hard, which they always seem to like. Katerina, not so much. She wasn't playing fair. I hadn't even tried to put it in her ass.

"No," she said.

"No what?" I asked, not knowing to what she referred but if there was a problem I wanted to know.

"No," she said, slapping my hand away from its place on her hip.

"What's wrong?"

She scuttled away, then lay next to me. Her body stretched out, ankles and knees touching, like some Japanese businessmen had paid to eat sushi off her stomach. I still had no idea what the problem was. To my mind, the last minute of sex had been no different than the previous nine. It's not as though I'd suddenly upped the ante.

I asked again and she wouldn't reply, instead staring at the ceiling.

"Okay, suit yourself." I was pissed off now. You don't just jump into bed and then change your mind halfway through. I had rights!

Silence continued for five minutes, or something like that. T-Rex played on my Bluetooth speaker and at least one full song came and went without us sharing a word. Seeing as it was late and I was exhausted, I rolled over to sleep. Katerina seemed of the same mind, but she didn't snuggle up. The T-Rex album ran on to the end and YouTube's autoplay turned to Bowie.

Katerina sat up suddenly. She stood and began scooping her clothes from the floor. It was dark but I could just about see. The overhead light had been switched off from before we'd had sex, but the glow of street lights came through the windows and from the Laptop screen. Still, it was pretty dark.

"Where my panties?" she said, forcefully.

"Over there," I pointed, remembering where I'd thrown them, at the moment of victory. A moment that now felt like weeks ago.

"Where my panties?" she repeated.

"There. Right there."

"Where my panties?"

"Right fucking there!"

Katerina stood, clutching her trousers and blouse to her naked breast. Her eyes blazed like white hot orbs. Perhaps I'd mistaken that look for passion on the street when really it represented bat-shit insanity?

"I don't see."

"Turn on the light."

"Where?"

"There," I pointed to the light switch mere inches from her right shoulder.

"Where my panties?"

"They'll be shoved up your fucking arse if you don't shut your yap, you crazy slag."

"What you say?"

"I said, the light is there. Next to you."

"Where my panties?"

Katerina had gotten stuck in a loop. There was no rational reason why she couldn't see her panties on the floor where I'd pointed, nor the light switch next to her. Whatever emotion was driving her, I'd ceased to care. There'd been nothing wrong with my seduction. She'd played along the whole way and offered almost no last minute resistance.

"Where my panties?"

I don't exaggerate in my written account here. She said those same words at least twenty times, like a broken record. Finally, I couldn't take it any more. I jumped out of bed, turned on the light, snatched up her panties, and thrust them into her hands.

"Here they are. Now get the fuck out!"

She sniffed in contempt, walked next door, and dressed in the lounge. Then I heard her high heels clip-clop across the floor and the door slam.

Good fucking riddance.

Shevchenko park

I turn to writing music

Moldovans have
the right idea

Chapter 39
CLOSING THE SHOW

The Katerina story gave Ray and Adrian a grand old laugh at lunch the next day, at my expense. I already had something new to think about, something far more pleasant then the Katerina shenanigans. I'd lost Belarusian Valeria back in February, in Palermo. That still left me with one hot Belarusian, Ksenia. I'd closed both girls on consecutive days back in June 2013 and dated both ever since. Of the two, I'd been closer to Valeria, twice bringing her to England, but Ksenia had also visited me in Prague and I rather liked her.

Ksenia was getting the overnight bus from Minsk to Kiev and would arrive early the next morning. She was staying for three nights at my new apartment. I was looking forward to it. I dare say that after the high drama and frustration of the holiday's first eight days, it would be a relaxing change of pace to hang out with a dependable girl. The only thing that worried me was Ksenia's poor English. What on earth would we talk about?

Tomorrow arrived and my alarm woke me rudely at seven thirty. Its shrill beep bounced around my skull. My body rebelled, failing to respond to my brain's repeated signals to get up. Months of late rising, combined with recent days of excessive alcohol consumption, made early starts a struggle. I rolled out of bed, literally, then climbed to my feet, pulled on the nearest clothes, and stumbled outside. Wishing to sink back into blissful sleep at the earliest opportunity, I forswore takeaway coffee and tried to keep my eyes half shut.

Ksenia was waiting for me outside McDonald's at 8am, as agreed. Getting up that early for a girl made me feel like a chode, but I did like her and she'd come a long way to see me. She stood sheepishly with her feet together and head down, almost as if bracing herself emotionally for me to no-show, then she brightened up as I approached.

"How was the journey?"

"It's okay."

"Are you tired?"

"Yes."

"Me too."

I hoisted her travel bag over my shoulder and walked her back to my apartment. There was a little small talk but we never did speak to each other much. We went straight to bed, and by that I mean I went back to sleep. Ksenia slid in next to me in her underwear and I put my arm around her while she snuggled up. She seemed happy with that. I wasn't at all stand-offish, merely exhausted.

A two-hour kip refreshed me. I drifted between sleep and wakefulness, Ksenia's lovely body alongside mine, noting she'd trimmed up a little since we'd met the previous summer. Her tits and ass were still ample but now her tiny waist was drawn even tighter. I pawed at her. I'd already decided to raw-dog her for the first time. She seemed surprised, but quite accepting. It was slow, lazy, morning sex. Aside from my desire to bang her, I also wanted to make her feel welcome as I did appreciate her time investment coming here.

"Did anyone give you trouble?" I asked. She'd expressed concern as a Russian speaker coming into Ukraine when a border war was still ongoing.

"No, it is okay I think. People are nice to me."

We whiled away the next few hours in bed dozing and banging. It's something I rarely do. My experience with Valeria in Palermo had chastened me regarding long stays with a single girl, as I usually find the first shag extremely enjoyable and then my interest plummets logo-rhythmically each day. As an experiment to forestall such disappointment, I resolved not to cum the whole weekend Ksenia was with me, in the hope it would help maintain my interest.

That was a partial success.

Day one was great. I truly enjoyed banging her every which way most of the morning and afternoon. Problems arose when we weren't banging. She lacked the English to make interesting conversation and I lacked the spark of enthusiasm to fill the gap. I explained to her I was comfortable with her around and happy with long periods of quiet. She nodded, probably relieved.

She'd never been to Kiev so we had a look around the usual tourist sites. There was the Golden Gate a few streets back from Khreshchatyk, and Shevchenko park, and then up through Maidan and the parks up that way. It was relaxing in a chodey faggot sense. We took photos, ate together, and walked hand-in-hand.

"I remember these days forever," she cooed, which touched me.

Walking with Ksenia

Her second day was more of the same but now I was growing agitated. Ksenia was good as gold and as attractive as ever. My natural introversion reared its head and I came to resent Ksenia's ever-presence. Not helping matters was my feeling that each hour with her was an hour not opening local slags. I owed Ksenia an explanation, so I typed one into my phone translator for her.

"I should explain to you. I become quiet when I'm with someone all day. It is my introversion. I'm happy you are here, and I like your company, but I will appear withdrawn at times. I hope this is okay."

Evidently it was. She suggested she go sightseeing a few hours by herself to relieve me. I concurred and that lifted the pressure. On the final evening I gave her a rogering as dominant as Horatio Nelson's victory over the French and Spanish at Trafalgar. Then finally I came, on her face. The next morning I took her to the train station for her long ride back to Minsk. It had been a pleasant interlude.

Just as I watched her train pull away and wondered precisely when to climb back into the daygame saddle, my phone buzzed. It was little Elita. She'd been ghosting me for over a week, her last message one day before my arrival from Chisinau.

"Nick. I sorry I no message. I in hospital. I better now."
"That's okay. I hope you are well. Let's meet."
"Okay. When?"
"Tonight, 7pm?"
"Okay. McDonald's?"
"Yes."

Elita showed up looking as pretty as ever and in the full bloom of good health. Even if the language barrier hadn't been there, I'd probably not have inquired into the nature of her health problem. Probably it was just 'flu or fever. I don't like to think about girl's health. Their bodies are useless and always breaking down. Best not think about it.

In my time away from Kiev I'd come to hope Elita would become a proper regular — like Ksenia, or Valeria, or Vesna — but it quickly became apparent that was a forlorn hope. I walked her to Porter's bar and we sat in a quiet back room across a wooden table, the only free space in the whole pub. My intention was to have a talkative date, via smartphone, and deepen our connection. What I hadn't counted on was the thick brickwork of the basement blocking all mobile signal and the bar's own WiFi being utterly useless. With our drinks already ordered and no Google Translate there was nothing for it but to hold hands across the table, smile, and make awkward gesture-based conversation. We couldn't even fool around physically because the pub was rammed.

Elita didn't seem to mind but I got her out of there in half an hour. She'd come out to get fucked so I walked her home and did just that. Fun though the sex was, midway through shagging boredom set in. A subconscious switch had flipped. I hadn't intended it, but it happened and I was stuck with the consequences: I didn't particularly care to keep her around. We could barely communicate and once the thrill of banging a new girl wore off, it was just sex.

Meaningless animal rutting.

I let her get on top and ride me while I philosophised upon this unexpected change of attitude.

Elita had no idea what she was doing up there, bouncing up and down like a child on a bouncy castle. Her hands were on her hips, then my chest, then held at her breast. She didn't know where to put them. It was cute, and I realised she probably wasn't the slut I'd suspected. A girl who'd already let her classmates bang her out would presumably know how to take top position. Elita didn't.

To resuscitate my interest in sex, I upped the tempo and wrecked her. I flipped her over and smashed her from behind. She whimpered and cried with pleasure. I flattened her onto the mattress, slapped on a choke-hold, and did her some more. She bleated like an abused dog while I banged her but every time I eased off, she turned to face me and smiled. Then I made her suck me off and came in her mouth.

After our respective showers, she asked to take a selfie with me.

That confirmed my suspicion that I was just an adventure for her, and that we likely wouldn't meet again. During the first trip and much of our messaging she'd adopted the manner of a lovestruck young girl. This time round, she lacked the same dewy eyes and dopey smiles. It was just about sex. Ah well, can't win 'em all. I saw her back to the Metro, kissed, and never saw her again. I pinged her a week later but she didn't reply.

It was time to daygame.

Ray and Adrian were still in town, so I had my wings. Both had been laid now, so our trio had a relaxed air.

As described earlier, I had spent my first week in Kiev in the enviable position of being able to feed entirely on girls who IOI'd me or who otherwise triggered my spider-sense of being susceptible to approach. That was shooting fish in a barrel, at least for the first few minutes of a set. It was daygame made easy because all traces of approach anxiety disappeared and I could rely upon consistently positive reactions. It reminded me that good-looking men have no business talking about approach anxiety. They don't understand how incredibly easy they have it when girls are visibly checking them out all day long.

Every open I did I felt bulletproof from the very first moment.

Playing on easy mode brought with it a downside. After a week of picking only warm targets, I'd lost interest in pure cold approach. Now that I was walking around with Ray and Adrian again, I was struggling to get myself into set without having first received a come-on.

"I'm not gonna approach blind," I said, aloud. "I might as well use this novel situation as an opportunity to practice warm approach game. Finally, I've got enough sets to be able to collect real data and try different things."

When I did contemplate a blind open (i.e. the girl gave no indication whatsoever that she liked me or would be amenable to stopping) I was reminded it requires character strength and I thought, *fuck that, why bother?* I tried warm-approach for a day but felt guilty the whole time. There were girls I fancied who didn't look at me and I let them go simply because I wanted things done the easy way. I was losing my self-discipline.

"You're totally stalled," laughed Ray. "You're a chode again."

"No mate, this is more advanced game. That's why you don't understand it."

"Yep, chode," Adrian agreed with Ray.

A hot well-put together blonde walked past me in the Maidan underground mall. I felt a DNA tug. She hadn't even noticed my existence. There was no spider sense, that she was horny or up for it. She walked briskly up the stairs towards street level and the nearby bus stop. Obviously, she'd just finished work. She was smartly dressed in expensive well-coordinated clothes.

I looked at Ray and sighed.

"Do it!"

I sighed again, looking for any excuse to weasel out.

"Do it!" he urged again.

She was moving fast, already halfway up an escalator. I didn't catch up until street level.

"Um, excuse me. Blonde girl with nice clothes."

"Yes, can I help you?"

She was stone-cold, expressionless and answered everything with clipped polite language.

"Actually, no you can't-" I began, smiling roguishly.

"Then what do you want?"

Not to be deterred I ploughed on and she softened. She told me her name was Nadya and she worked at the Prada store by Khreshchatyk. Two minutes in she brought our chat to an end.

"My bus comes now."

"Okay. Let's have a coffee sometime. Would you like that?"

She liked it at least a little because she gave me her number. Mentally, I filed the set in the draw marked Going Nowhere. Undeterred, I send out my feeler text the next day.

"Hey Ukrainian girl. It was nice to meet you."

"Hey. Sorry I'm busy at work."

Ouch. There were other girls to chase so I rolled off forty-eight hours and tried again.

"I'm enjoying a lazy Sunday afternoon, walking in the park. How about you?"

"I'm working. In what park did you walk?"

"Botanical garden behind the university. How about tomorrow for coffee?"

Surprisingly, Nadya agreed. I'd figured she wasn't much of a texter when she didn't bite on the banter fodder I threw out. Everything had seemed low interest, making me wonder if I was setting myself up to have my time wasted. She then quibbled over the meeting location, so when I found myself waiting for her at the same spot we'd first met, I wasn't especially optimistic. Kiev's flaking epidemic had worn me down.

That's a typical day's stroll

Was I to be drawn into a frame control battle? Or worse, simply entertaining a bored shop girl? The thing is, nobody kicks a dead dog. Girls rarely initiate frame-wars with a man they are uninterested in. I'd invest an hour over coffee to find out where Nadya stood, I resolved. It wasn't as though I was wading knee-deep in pussy.

Nadya turned out to be of the greyhound mentality. A high value girl, mainstream in attitude and fashion, intelligent, strong-willed, and unwilling

Girl Junkie

to surrender the frame without a strong test. I know greyhounds so I knew the battle-plan. Ten minutes into the date I gave up on the squirrel/cat strategies of spiking them silly or turning on the secret society sleaze. Nadya would demand a good look at me and time to make her mind up. That suited me fine.

She was a pleasure to talk to and her English was good. We agreed a nice walk through a park to finish in a cafe she recommended. I enjoyed the sights, turned my style towards talking eruditely on more sophisticated topics, and tried to resist the urge to rapid escalate. With girls of her type, you don't need to kiss on the first date so long as you make a clear move somehow. They judge you as a value proposition rather than a spur-of-the-moment adventure. Everything about Nadya suggested her forebrain was in full control, chaperoning her hindbrain like a Victorian aunt. Her eyes never sparkled, her laughter was dinner-party-like, and when she allowed me to kino-test her fingers and hair she looked at me like a ballroom dancer being led through steps she's already studied.

I felt her warming to me and could almost hear her private 'suitable man' checklist being ticked off. What I didn't know is if the final score would add up to, *yeah I'll fuck him*. She tested me a little, such as wandering off a bit, leaving long silences, asking impertinent direct questions and so on. It didn't feel the slightest bit impolite and I could pass her tests easily. It felt more like a dance than a fight. I was reminded of the famous banjo scene in the 1970s movie *Deliverance* where a city slicker throws out challenging chords and a hill-billy kid smashes them back with interest until a solid banjo jam is going.

Nadya was the slicker, I was the inbred retard.

The heavens opened, rain falling heavily. After an hour of the date, I had to make my excuses to go, setting a limit on my time. We walked through the park to her bus stop. Time to make my move.

"Can you see that lamppost?" I said, pointing. She nodded. "That's where I'll kiss you."

She smiled but deftly eluded my three kiss close attempts. I didn't try too hard. All that mattered was she receive the message. The retarded hill-billy kid had run up and down the scales, now it was up to her.

An intermediate player spends a lot of his time learning how to blow the love-bubble and prevent its bursting. From the moment you stop a girl on the street you must entice her to talk, to enjoy it, and to let you lead her forwards. That's a real skill, if she hasn't already decided to fuck you based upon an initial sizing up — which for us normal men means 95%+ of girls and *all* the hotter ones. If you take her onto an instant date the bubble remains blown ever longer. However, there comes a point where you must either pull her home, or take a number.

I'd experimented all year with pulling hard and fast. I had almost twenty near misses to show for it, in addition to my fourteen notches. I still didn't have the right answer but nobody could accuse me of being unwilling to explore the possibilities. Assuming the more patient approach, like I had done with Nadya, the bubble will burst and she wakes up the next day to her normal life. Her subsequent texting (or lack of it) will clue you in to what she really wants. If she responds well you've got a date coming up and the bubble gets re-blown.

You can only fuck the girl when she's in the bubble. What happens in the bubble does not accurately foreshadow what will happen when it bursts. That's why it is so tempting to just go for it with a bounce-back. It's the re-blowing of the bubble that makes a girl's first message the most important one. How does she respond to your feeler text after the street stop? How does she respond to your ping the day after the date? That's the single best piece of data to gauge her interest.

The medium is the message.

I had my own list of encouraging signals to look for: a fast reply, either by clock-time, or by a busy girl responding soon after her first available break; a long reply asking you questions; smiley faces and stretched-out words (e.g. heeeeyyyy); offering unsolicited information about herself; following your conversational lead.

You can sense when somebody is keen. Being a writer of seduction textbooks, sense is not enough: I have to break it down like I did above. Spend enough time around women and you don't need over-analyse it. So with that in mind, Nadya's response after our date was a good one.

"Hey. I'm relaxing with coffee. How's your day?" I pinged.

"Hey. I'm having dinner. Did you try borsch? It's Ukrainian soup."

I didn't invite her out again until four days later, towards at the end of my trip. There was little strategy to my decision. It was determined more by my enjoying the street game and having other brighter prospects. Nadya rebuffed my invitation and I didn't ask again. She kept the texting momentum alive. When I still didn't ask her out a second time, she began chasing me. I felt the energy shift.

Any time a girl chases you, let her come. Don't snatch the reins and start leading. Finally, Nadya invited me out. Our second date was on the 5th of November. I would certainly remember, remember, the gunpowder, treason, and plot.

She was still hard work.

We began with a drink in a bar by McDonald's. Nadya remained shrewd and self-possessed as though still judging me. She knew what I wanted and had come out to see more of me, so I was free to escalate. There was an Irish bar nearby. It had dark, secluded booths ideal for fooling around privately.

"I don't want to go there" she said. At first I thought she was being arsey, and I showed surprise. "It's too near my work," she explained. "I'd rather not see my colleagues."

That struck me as reasonable. I'd blundered by not realising the issue ahead of time.

"There is a place I like. It is close. Let's go there," she said, snatching the reins yet again.

That place turned out to be a brightly-lit Italian restaurant and Nadya wanted to eat. Sensing bullshit, I lost all interest in her. I couldn't be bothered to talk to her and fought the urge to walk out without even ordering. My patience with go-nowhere dates had been ebbing away all year.

"I will have pizza. Do you eat?" she asked.

"Um. Beer."

It took mental discipline for me to stay on the date. *Give it ten minutes, and if she doesn't wise up, walk out*, I thought. Nadya wasn't being rude, simply non-compliant. I'd become such a stone-cold player that her not moving forwards was tantamount to dating treason.

I'd stopped talking entirely. My gaze wandered.

Nadya couldn't help but notice my change of mood. She looked worried. I barely looked at her, refused a slice of her pizza, didn't order a second beer, and gave short non-committal answers to her questions. It wasn't a ploy. I really had lost interest in her, but couldn't quite decide to leave. Nadya tried hard to rebuild the mood and this display of conscientiousness on her part convinced me she wasn't just messing me around. I softened and felt like talking again.

With the benefit of hindsight, this episode functioned as an effective push.

"I want to go to a proper bar," I declared. Nadya was almost finished her pizza.

"Where would you like?"

"There's a bar near Arena City, in the basement. It's kind of hipster-like, called Divan, but not as bad as that sounds."

"Okay."

Good vibes came rolling back into Nick Town. We sat down in a booth in Divan, Nadya across from me. She became tight-lipped and difficult again, perhaps because she'd smoothed out my earlier impatience and now felt she was in the driver's seat once more. The date had derailed. It felt like a battle.

No more bullshit! I resolved.

Nadya had reached the end of the line. I'd played out all the rope I was willing to give her. Things would have to get overt. Quickly. Slavic girls are extremely good at playing the *will-I-won't-I* grey area to waste your time. To find out where I stood, I needed to make things black and white. It's uncomfortable, but a man's aversion to dating discomfort is what time-wasters rely upon to get away with their bullshit.

"Come here. Sit next to me."

"Why?"

"Because I'd like you to."

"I'm comfortable here."

"I'm not comfortable with you there. Come here."

Reluctantly, Nadlya obliged. As if to express her distaste, she sat with a six-inch gap between us and placed her handbag in it as a shield. I moved her bag out of the way and pulled her in.

"What are you doing?"

"I want you to sit closer."

"Why?"

"So I can touch you."

"I don't want you to touch me."

"Why not?"

She was silent. Things couldn't have been more black and white if I wore a Newcastle United football shirt while riding a zebra through the set of a 1920s movie and singing *Gonna Eat Ma Chicken Till I'm Fried*. Nadya was a strong-minded, very pretty, 26 year old greyhound. Such women are not swept away on a wave of momentum. She remained silent.

There was but one more string to my bow. The Talk.

"I like you and you know what I want," I explained. "Now you have to decide what you want. If you decide you just like me as a friend, that's okay, but I will walk out. I won't be angry, but I don't have female friends and I don't want to be your friend. If you are sexually attracted to me and want to be more than friends, that's great. That's what I want too."

"I just like meeting you, and practising English. We're just friends."

I looked her dead in the eye.

"Think very carefully before you answer. Is that what you really want?"

She clammed up and looked into space, thinking furiously. It was put-up-or-shut-up time and I wasn't about to let her wriggle out of it. Obviously, Nadya *was* sexually attracted to me. This was a frame-control question: whose script were we to read from going forwards, hers or mine? She wanted me to go at her pace and jump through her hoops. I'd just made it clear I'd jumped through quite enough hoops, thank you very much, and now it was time for her to jump through mine.

Would her pride allow it?

Did she like me enough to tear up her script, or at least hastily rewrite it to bring the happy ending forwards?

Five full minutes passed, dragging as painfully as a Katy Perry song. I sipped my beer and watched Cheburashka on the wall-mounted television. That's not embellishment, by the way. Staff had turned the television to a kid's channel.

Finally, Nadya spoke.

"Nick, I do like you as a man."

"Okay, kiss me," I said and pulled her in. She resisted and I went stone cold again.

"Not here," she said. Admittedly, it was a crowded bar.

"I will kiss you tonight" I said.

"Yes, okay. Just not here."

I didn't have the patience to sit through another hour in Divan. It was getting late. I drank up and told Nadya I'd walk her to the bus stop. She was timid and quiet now. Halfway up Khreshchatyk we passed a striking old art deco building with a grandiose staircase leading up to it.

"I'm going to kiss you there," I said.

She followed me.

At the top of the stairs I pulled her in and we kissed. She went floppy for a second and then jumped me. It was like a damn bursting. She was very much into it. I dare say I'm a damn attractive man when I mean to be.

Was it on, right now?

I was alert for any sign that Nadya was ready to be dragged home, but she never let her crotch push into mine, and never quite gave the telltale sighs, squeezes and grinds that signal 'take me home now'. I walked her up to the bus stop, gave a soft kiss goodnight and let her go.

I was satisfied. I'd correctly called a difficult situation and executed the correct play. Girls like to put up defences and reward a man sufficiently determined to smash them into rubble. It's a game and they know full well what's going on. I've had girls resist like hell-cats and then thank me afterwards. Bitches be crazy.

Nadya's defiance reminded of a scene in the novel *The Shadow Of Tyburn Tree* by a favourite writer of mine, Dennis Wheatley. A girl is explaining to the book's hero why she was such a bitch before he ravished her. I'll quote it at length:

'Yet you have found the way to my heart", she sighed contentedly. 'All that you needed to be a perfect lover was the violence of a Russian. You were too soft, too considerate, to woman-like before. You allowed me to bully you unmercifully without complaint, and that is wrong. No woman of my country ever believes that her man truly loves her unless he beats her now and again. Even the Empress Catherine has taken her beatings from the Orlofs' Potemkin and other favourites, and loved them for it all the more. Roje Christovorich, you are now my master and I your slave. Lie down here while I kneel at your feet and you, my lord, shall tell me how best I may pleasure you this night'.

I couldn't quite claim such an overwhelming victory as the novel's protagonist but I'd certainly revved Nadya up. She sent me a few goodnight messages.

"Hey man! You know that you woke me up. I need to sleep! But I don't want. I'll try to count Cheburashkas."

I felt confident I'd fuck her. The question was whether sex would be on this trip or if I'd have to wait until next spring. Ray was drinking in Porter's bar so I joined him at a table in the back room and we debriefed the set. We agreed the big problem was time. My last night in town was almost upon me.

On that last night, Ray and I went back to Divan for an end-of-season send-off drink. It was 9pm and I ordered some traditional dumplings and soup. Nadya was messaging me but not quite committing to coming out on a date. She was with her friends, drinking wine.

"Okay, you're busy. I understand," I wrote, consciously pushing her away.

"Do you want to join came to my company? You are the most welcomed."

"No thanks. I can meet you when you've finished with your friends."

I wrote that mostly because I was genuinely torn between dating Nadya and waiting for my food. She didn't feel like a dead-cert lay. I didn't want to get another runaround when I could be getting steaming drunk with Ray, and I was just plain tired of Kiev and tired of girls generally. As far as I was concerned, 2015 was done. My mind was consumed by thoughts of my faux-fur duvet cover, 48-inch television, and *Fallout 4* and *Metal Gear Solid V*.

A Kiev girl painted me
this as a present

This zero-fucks-given attitude was both a blessing and a curse. On the downside all but my most compliant leads withered and died from want of nurturing, depressing my overall lay count. On the upside, I don't want to be a man who begs for pussy. Strong personal boundaries feel good. As I sat in Divan sipping beer with my mate, it felt fifty-fifty whether Nadya would come out. She'd have to come to me.

"Where are you? My friends will go in another place."

"I'm in Divan."

"And.."

"Come here."

"I don't want in Divan."

"I'm here now. We can go somewhere else next."

She tried to talk me into going to a bar called *Alchemist*. I was getting frustrating, and my food still hadn't been served.

"Are you alone?" I asked.

"Now I'm with my friend. Her name is Veronika. Another one leave us."

"Thanks but I'm not interested in meeting your friends."
"Okay. And your proposed..."
"I would like to meet you, alone, and we can get a drink together."

That did the trick.

"Ok. I'll message you, but I don't want go to Divan," she wrote and then soon after, "5 min and I'll be outside."

As if to emphasise my dilemma, the staff chose this moment to serve my soup and dumplings. I was ravenously hungry. Ray picked up his knife and fork, eyeing my plate eagerly. He had a better idea of what I'd do next than I did myself.

"Fuck it. I'm going to meet her. You can have my scoff."

"Great."

I pulled a few notes out of my wallet to cover my tab.

"Sorry I didn't hang around for the drink. Obviously I have to prioritise the chance of skirt. It's literally my last night of the entire 2015 season. And she is hot."

"Understood, mate. Good luck."

We shook hands and vowed to reconvene the following spring. I walked outside into the cold night air. Divan was inside the loop of a busy roundabout and cars whizzed past. Groups of youngsters stood outside smoking. Across the road was a small art gallery holding an exhibition. I spotted Nadya approaching. I waved and she trotted across the road.

She looked very excitable. When she kissed me I understood why. I could taste the white wine on her lips. Nadya had been getting sloshed with her friends and increasingly horny. Greyhound, my arse! At this moment in time she was simply a horny bird hoping to get poked. A player must always be ready to switch up his game-plan. There's a difference between "not tonight" and "take your chance, big boy".

I know that difference. My spider-sense activated: *Take her home! Pull the trigger!*

"Do you like wine?" I asked, as we turned the first corner and walked in front of a late-opening supermarket. Not late enough, though. It was closed.

"Yes, I'd like wine."

I had a bottle of red at home but it was corked. There was no corkscrew.

The priority was to buy a twist-capped bottle and then walk Nadya home. The only problem was everywhere had closed. The big supermarket was locked up. We walked five minutes up to the McDonalds, and the 24/7 off-license at the ground floor of my old apartment building. That too was closed, temporarily, for next thirty minutes while they cashed up. The only other off licence I knew was outside my new apartment, and had already closed by 10pm.

Fuck.

Decision time.

Do I suggest a drink in a bar and risk losing momentum? Hell no! Nadya's vibe screamed "take me home now." Okay, it was an easy decision.

"I've got a bottle of red in my apartment," I said.

She came in, I put on some music, and she opened the wine by sticking a spoon in the cork and hammering it down into the bottle.

"In Ukraine we learn to be resourceful," she said, proudly.

Great. I let ten minutes of sexual tension build over the first glass of wine and then made my move. It was a smooth, easy escalation without a spot of resistance on Nadya's part. I had her shirt off while we sat on the sofa, then, when she straddled me, I picked her up and carried her to the bedroom.

Smash, bang.

Fantastic sex.

Nadya was a gym junkie, so her body felt tight and firm. She grabbed me with unexpected strength, clawing and biting me. It felt like wrestling John Cena. I smashed her thoroughly, like I would the windows of my refugee neighbour's house. It went on a good while and Nadya's thick red lipstick was smeared over both our faces by the end.

We showered and she fell asleep with her head on my chest.

I'd gotten a last minute save.

"+1" I texted to both Ray and Brian. The latter had been pestering me all day on WhatsApp.

Nadya left early and my flight was at lunchtime. Just like with Dennis Wheatly's above-quoted Russian minx, Nadya was now fully aboard the Krauser Train. She messaged me while I waited in the airport lobby.

"I'll take a shower at the time and I will not smell like you," she wrote, somewhat incomprehensibly.

"It's a sexy smell. Me."

"Yeah. Your smell excite me."

"Yes, that's understandable. I'm at the gate waiting for my flight. Goodbye Kiev!"

"Goodbye England! I found a bruise on my back. I think it's hard mattress and your pushed."

And so my season ended, with a last-gasp winner. I'd stolen virtue from the jaws of defeat.

Chapter 40
OUTLAWS

I found myself on a train to London on December 5th.

Eddie had found a good venue for our *Outlaw Daygame* event in the basement of Covent Garden's Comedy Club, making the event a go. I hired a third-world graphic designer on the Fiverr website to knock up some logo ideas, then Eddie and Maciek took the best and made a proper job of it. Eddie, Tom, and myself all posted event notifications on our platforms and it was of intense curiosity to me just how many daygame enthusiasts were still knocking around in the Big Smoke. Ticket sales went well and we found a hundred takers. London is an expensive place to stay so Eddie was kind enough to put me up in the spare room of his centrally-located apartment.

I like year-end seminars. The high-pressure grind of travelling and shagging can be wound up and then, like an athlete recuperating post-season, I can turn my mind to normal life. *Outlaw Daygame* offered a public stage upon which to collect my thoughts and try to thrust the tip of the PUA theoretical spear further forwards. Tom and I no longer talked and by now he'd entirely scrubbed me from his YouTube channel, as though I'd never existed. At the end of every month I emailed him a summary of sales from our *Beginner Daygame* book, together with a PayPal remittance of his 50% royalty. That was our only communication.

We did briefly discuss the content of our talks, so as not to overlap. Tom wanted to cover escalation, Eddie had been reading about pimp game, and Richard hadn't yet decided. My interest was mostly in further iterations of the Model, as 2015 had seen me testing many new ideas. Now I needed to parse those ideas, break them down, and make it all teachable from slides.

Girl Junkie

My topic was to be how to increase masculine-feminine polarity on the street, taking the audience from pre-open through to the number close and advising technical tricks to add in. Everything was set.

That evening, the day before the event, Eddie and I were hanging out in his lounge, chatting.

I still quite like that branding

"How was Almati, then?" I asked, referring to his recent trip to Kazakhstan with Tom. Just as Eddie and I had used our Riga trip to hang out and see if we got on, so Eddie and Tom had gone to the pan-faced slant-eyed desert country of Tamerlane the Gruesome.

"Rubbish. The trip was fun, but it was awful for women. Almati is in the East, which is the wrong side of the country. It's all Chinese types. The only hot girls were the rare ethnic Russians."

"I noticed you didn't show much in-field or dating on your YouTube videos. Halfway through the week you were both up in the mountains eating goat meat and talking to medicine men. I figured if the street game was productive, you'd have stayed in the city."

"Basically, yeah. Nothing for us to shoot at. We tried."

Eddie told me Tom had experienced a few calamities. First, he had left his mobile phone in the back of a taxi, thus losing all his daygame leads. Then, he'd dropped his expensive camera, breaking it. Lastly, he'd been queuing in a petrol station to buy food when a local man walked in and decked him.

"I don't know any daygamer who has been punched as many times as Tom," I mused.

"It was weird. I was sitting in the taxi. I saw Tom waiting in line, the guy came in — a middle-aged normal kind of dude — and after a few words he punched him."

Eddie pinged me this from Almati

A few weeks later Tom told Eddie that the Kazakh taxi driver had returned his phone, mailing it to his home address in the UK. To call that story unbelievable is an understatement. My guess is Tom faked the loss as an excuse to explain away his lack of dates. It made no sense. Almati was tough and Eddie already knew there was nothing to chase. Why did Tom feel the need to make shit up?

We discussed a few other red flags. "Tom has a fluid concept of truth," I opined.

Later that night we checked through each other's slides and prepared the equipment. I went off to the spare room to lie in bed, watching YouTube. Curious as to how Tom was doing, I browsed to his channel and was blind-sided again, almost a year since his fake in-field fiasco. He'd interviewed NYC-based pick-up charlatan Justin Wayne for his weekly podcast. The video was only one day old. I rushed back into the lounge carrying my laptop.

"Have you seen this, Eddie?"

"What?"

I showed him the podcast and we both groaned. Justin had already been exposed as a scammer a few years earlier, by an oddball called Aaron Sleazy. That time, Justin had created a two-way lifestyle scam that worked as follows: He advertised in an NYC trade classifieds for actresses who wished to audition for a reality show on the MTV channel, Justin posing as the producer. He wasn't. It was entirely fabricated and MTV knew nothing about it. He then advertised on his PUA website for men who wished to be part of a 'lifestyle experiment', living with Justin and "his girls". Of course, the men paid for the privilege, not knowing about the actress audition scam that was use to round up all of these women. Justin was then able to shoot lots of "in field" video of him interacting with them. The girls thought it was an audition, and his PUA audience thought they were pick-ups.

Quite clever, really.

Justin muted the dialogue in his YouTube videos so there wasn't any risk that the girls would say anything dangerous to break the illusion. By framing it to them as a reality TV audition, he could put the girls in situations around his apartment or in public where they knew the camera was there, so to a naïve viewer it appeared Justin had these girls "deep converted", that is, bent to his supreme masculine will.

Aaron Sleazy smelled a rat and went looking for dirt on Justin. He found the original classified ads still online, received emails from some of the duped girls, and one girl even recorded a Skype video chat with Justin where she threatened to sue him for scamming her and then she sent the recording to Aaron. Justin was completely busted. He literally ran away to Puerto Rico, shutting down all his accounts and going underground.

Like all scammers, once the heat blew over he returned to NYC and dreamt up a new scam. The pick-up industry is constantly refreshing with new customers and it has a short institutional memory. A new crop of credulous beginners were out there who wouldn't know about Justin's squalid history. I checked out his channel and noted his latest videos looked suspicious and, some time later, he was busted for hiring actresses again — this time by a *Vice TV* documentary crew. Though Tom didn't know of the latter expose (as it hadn't happened yet) he knew full well about the Aaron Sleazy bust.

To my mind there was no excuse. It was co-promotion with a known scammer.

Eddie and I were furious. Twenty-four hours before we were due on-stage to tie our names together in a public event, Tom had pissed in the pool. He was dragging us into the world of scammers and fraudsters, just like he had twelve months previously when busted for faking one of his own videos. I was especially livid, because he'd spent all year scrubbing his channel of my name so it was doubly ironic that when he did finally re-associated with me, it was to tie me in with a scammer.

I called him.

"Yeah, yeah, I know he's a scammer," Tom admitted. "He doesn't even approach now, he said off-camera. He's always down Florida working some non-approach game. He said NYC is really hard for him and he hasn't got the motivation to grind it out any more."

There wasn't really much for me to say. Tom wasn't the slightest bit ashamed and the milk was already spilled. I filed the incident away and let it drop. Jimmy's words from 2013 came back to haunt me: *Nick, he's a fruit. You'll regret getting pally with him again.*

The next morning I joined Eddie and the *Street Attraction* team in setting up at the event in Covent Garden. The basement room was large and specially designed to have a crowd watching a stand-up performer on stage. There was a bar at the back to get them drunk too. We set out the chairs and Eddie arranged the cameras. The room was low-ceilinged and the walls painted black. We couldn't have asked for a more appropriate venue. It looked like where a gang of outlaws would meet.

The crowd arrived, a pleasingly good attendance who throbbed with energy. Eddie opened the show with his talk on pimp game. Halfway through that, the bartender called his manager on the phone, then came over and asked us to take down the large *Comedy Club* banner hanging behind Eddie's head. They didn't want their business associated with us. To their credit, they didn't give us any other trouble and the event went off without a hitch.

Richard did his talk. I'm not sure what it was about, even though I watched it all. The phrase "gutter game" came up a few times.

A London-based guy who helped *Street Attraction* on boot camps, Genalt, worked the microphone as compère and he gave me a funny rabble-rousing introduction. I took the stage to the accompaniment of 1980s wrestling superstar The Ultimate Warrior's theme tune. My talk is still online on my YouTube channel, should the content interest you.

I enjoyed speaking but it drained me. After an hour we broke for lunch. I noticed Daniel Blake outside having a cigarette break but we didn't talk. It was still some months before an enterprising *Sluthate* sleuth would find

Girl Junkie

smoking gun evidence that Daniel had faked that Krakow same day lay infield video, so while I remained suspicious of him, those suspicions weren't yet confirmed. We had, however, exchanged a few choice words online so I was surprised he'd shown up. In the back of my mind I also wondered if local Muslims would gatecrash the talk. I was still receiving death threats on Twitter for my English nationalist sentiments, and I often had haters from the PUA community show up in my blog comments and on YouTube. Eddie and I had discussed contingency plans if any trouble spilled out, but nothing did happen.

Tom's talk went well

"Hey mate!"

I was standing in a small huddle with three men who'd just introduced themselves as *City Daygame*, a new player's blog based in London. One of the three, Xants, was scrolling through his smartphone showing me naked pictures his Hungarian girlfriend had sent him.

I turned.

"Hang on a second," I said, to the tanned skinhead who'd hailed me. He was wearing a smart suit and a beaming smile.

"So what score do you give her?" asked Xants, keen to see if the hotness of his Hungarian sufficiently bolstered his resume as a player. We'd already spoken online the previous week and I'd told him I'd review his photos and publicly comment on his bona fides to my readership.

I was Pontius PUA.

"Probably an eight," I concluded aloud. "Definitely a very pretty girl and if I'd been the one shagging her I'd be proud of it too."

Then I turned to the suit-clad newcomer.

"Hey Nick, how you doing?"

"I'm alright," I replied, non-committally. Every man and his dog wanted to shake my hand all of a sudden. Then realisation dawned. I knew him.

"Hang on a minute. *Salman?*"

Probably the last time the three
of us would be together

It was the wild-haired ill-calibrated lad I'd taken infield during February's filming of *Black Book*. Now, he looked like a different man. Better style, better vibe, and buzzing with positive energy.

"Fucking hell, weren't you a Paki? What happened?"

"Half-Indian. I've been doing sessions with Colin on my inner game It's really helped. Plus I've got a few nice birds in daygame, so I'm enjoying it more."

There was no denying it, the man had transformed himself. I'd never expected it, though looking back with the clarity of hindsight I remembered Salman had shown exceptional technical discipline in February. You only get that if you're a man who can formulate a plan and execute. I congratulated him on his turnaround and by then the lunch break was coming to a close.

I'd only gotten halfway through my slides so we took an audience poll and decided I'd put in another hour to finish the talk. By the end of it, I could barely speak. My brain was fried. Tom put in a rousing curtain raiser, his manner and energy more upbeat and comical than my own. He even brought a blow-up doll on stage to "demonstrate" escalation gambits.

Girl Junkie

It was funny.

"We'll call the event was a success," I said to Eddie.

I'm hazy on the ensuing evening festivities. The speakers and friends all went to the local *Wagamama* Japanese restaurant for a celebration dinner, and a few hangers-on snuck in too, who we tolerated. Considerable amounts of alcohol followed, across several pubs, though I'd have been drunk even without the beer. It's all a blur but I remember enjoying it tremendously.

London was good.

The very next day I flew from Heathrow to Belgrade for a week's holiday. Balkan winters are freezing cold, predictably, and I had no intention of daygaming. Towards the end of autumn my Belgrade regulars had become unusually responsive and my long-lost rotation of girls had spontaneously reformed itself. It seemed a shame not to take advantage, especially with winter hibernation encroaching upon me. My apartment was in Dorcel, way down the steep bank near Strahinica Bahna. I had two bedrooms and a comfortable lounge. The shower water was strong and hot, and the radiators warm. It was all I needed. For the next five days, I had a procession of girls come over.

Maya, the massive-chested nineteen year old I'd closed that summer, was first. We met in the upstairs of a luxurious cafe, a few doors down from Knez Mihailova, next to my favourite burger bar, Submarine Burger. It was early evening. We sat with coffees, neither of us really sure what to do next.

"I need to go in thirty minutes," she said. "I'm meeting my boyfriend."

"Okay, let's go."

I walked her down to my apartment and sat her on the sofa. There were twenty minutes remaining.

"I don't have much time," she reiterated.

"Take your clothes off."

I stripped her and raw-dogged her on the sofa, then took her next door to the bedroom to finish her off. She didn't have time to shower, pulling on her clothes and rushing out with a quick wave goodbye. Marijana came over the next evening, the tall folk singer I'd closed at the end of 2012 and saw only occasionally since. We met on Knez, had a drink to settle her nerves, then she came back with me.

"I feel strange. We don't talk but every time we meet, we have sex," she mused aloud.

I tried doing her from behind but she rebelled, claiming it made her feel like an animal. Marijana was extremely traditional and quite the primadonna.

She was not one to take it in the ass, either. She'd never given me a blow job and seemed to think even holding my dick was a scandalous display of wanton lust. So long as she lay in missionary, she could relax and give a good account of herself, but that's as far as it usually went.

"Get on top," I said.

"No, I can't. It's slutty."

"Try it. You'll enjoy it."

"I don't know how."

"Just try. You can stop if you don't like it."

She tried, bless her. The sex was okay.

On the third day, Vesna came over. I banged her on the sofa and again in the bedroom. I was able to do her in the ass a second time, having taken her anal virginity in summer.

"I still can't believe I can take it in the ass," she said, in her odd-ball manner. "I never would have imagined it. My boyfriend would go mad if he knew you were doing this to me. I'd never let him do it." Vesna had spent most of the year in a serious relationship with a rich American businessman who lived in the US and flew her in for long trips. "I should tell him about you. I feel guilty and now that I am serious with him, we shouldn't have any secrets."

"I'd keep this one a secret. No man reacts well to finding out his live-in girlfriend is getting sodomised by a travelling cad."

The fourth evening, Sofija came around. We met at the top of Studenski Park and, the vivacious blonde being very petite, I picked her up and carried her in the crook of one arm. She giggled and wrapped her arms around my neck. Sofija always seemed to lose her mind in my presence. I banged her hard in the bedroom and finished her off in the lounge.

As I sat back on the sofa, exhausted, she sat in my lap staring at my face, stroking every inch of it in fascination. Then she slipped to her knees and held my dick, staring at it for several minutes. It was like her new toy. Well, she had been a virgin when I'd closed her the previous summer and I seriously doubted she'd even kissed another man since.

"If you are going to stay down there, suck my cock."

She did. For ten minutes. I had to tell her to stop.

We dressed and prepared to leave. Sofija sat on a kitchen chair waiting for me, her high black felt boots and fur coat already on. I couldn't help but walk over, get my dick out, and make her suck me off again.

I didn't shag the fifth girl, Milena, the Sofia Loren lookalike I'd closed in 2012 and still considered a top-three lifetime girl. We'd continued a regular sexual relationship ever since, but it had dropped off in mid-2015. She'd gotten a boyfriend and thus wouldn't even kiss. That didn't surprise me, as she was from a small Bosnian town and extremely traditional.

More importantly, she'd put on even more weight. I wasn't much interested in making it five-for-five.

A lovely girl, though, so Milena and I had a good long talk and a few beers in Blasnavac before she joined me for a non-sexual nightcap at my apartment. You could make a case that I'd finished the year on a high point — what with four sexy tarts in my bed — but you'd be mistaken. The final evening gave me much to ponder.

While in Blasnavac, Milena said something, a careless comment, that chilled me to the bone. We were sitting indoors, to the right hand side of the entrance, on wooden slat seats at a table. I had beer and she a cocktail. We'd been reminiscing, I sifting my thoughts and feelings of completing yet another year in the game, my seventh.

"You are different to when we first met," she said.

"How so?"

"You were nicer then. You have a cold, hard edge now."

Coming from a random first-date girl I'd have laughed it off, teased, and found a way to leverage it towards further sexual escalation. Milena saying it made all the difference. It wasn't important just because she knew me very well and had an opinion I respected. Rather, Milena's intimate relationship with me spanned several major waypoints in my personal development as a man, and as a player. She knew me from when I was first fumbling around with euro-jaunting and working through my inner game issues. Since then I'd become comfortable in the identity of a nomadic adventure sex player, I'd surpassed one hundred notches, and I'd assumed a popular public position as an expert daygamer.

I was a different person now.

By Milena's assessment, it wasn't clear that it was a positive development. In this respect, she concurred with Valeria, the girl who knew me next-best, and for a similar length of time. The two girls who knew me best, who I'd been closest to, agreed I was now a stone cold player.

That was something to ponder over winter.

Continue your Player's Journey with Nick Krauser's other resources!

The Model

Everything you need to know about street pick-up is packed into these cutting-edge textbooks. Each volume is written to match your own progress in learning the art form. *Daygame Nitro* introduces the basics of street pick-up and inner game in a simple, easy-to-follow guide. *Daygame Mastery* breaks apart the model into minute detail to help you fine-tune your method. *Daygame Infinite* unlocks your potential with extensive vibe and calibration advice.

 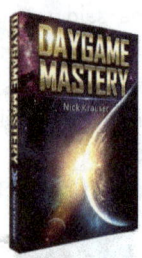 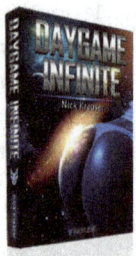

The Journey

Dive deep into the Player's lifestyle with the most detailed and most insightful Game memoir ever written. Four massive volumes take you through every stage from zero to hero as Nick tells you his story. Higher level knowledge seeps out of every page. Live the life!

The Demonstration

It's one thing to understand the theory but another to watch, on video, how to run street game and master dating. *Daygame Overkill* provides a play-by-play breakdown of Nick's infield videos, showing you how to get Adventure Sex. *Black Book* explains the dating model in detail, and *Womanizers Bible* provides high-level theory on the Player's World.

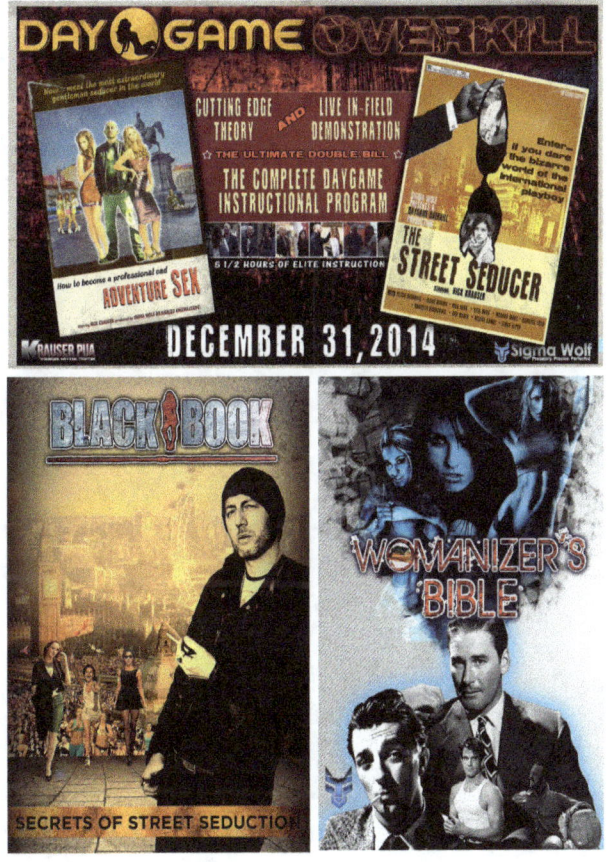

Check out sigmawolf.com and daygameoverkill.com to access these amazing resources.

www.ingramcontent.com/pod-product-compliance
Lightning Source LLC
Chambersburg PA
CBHW071328080526
44587CB00017B/2760